THE PHENOMENON OF THE BOOK THAT HAS TAKEN THE COUNTRY BY STORM:

The book has become one of the biggest publishing successes of the year. More than 230,000 copies of the hardcover book are in print, and Prentice-Hall claims to have received more than 11,500 orders on a single day in November.

THE AMITYVILLE HORROR

"I stared into the mirror in sheer disbelief. 'That's not me! That can't be me!' I screamed. I, Kathleen Lutz, am a young blonde-haired housewife with pale soft skin—but that's not what I saw in my reflection. I had turned into a disgusting-looking 90-year-old hag! My hair was white and scraggly. Ugly creases and crow's feet scarred my face. I drooled all over my shriveled up, dried skin. It was the work of horrible evil spirits that plunged my family and me into chilling terror for 28 days ... that turned our dream house into a hell house."

TURN THE PAGE AND NOW, GO ON WITH THE STORY!

THE AMITYVILLE HORROR

BY JAY ANSON

*This low-priced Bantam Book
has been completely reset in a type face
designed for easy reading, and was printed
from new plates. It contains the complete
text of the original hard-cover edition.*
NOT ONE WORD HAS BEEN OMITTED.

THE AMITYVILLE HORROR

*A Bantam Book / published by arrangement with
Prentice-Hall, Inc.*

PRINTING HISTORY

*Prentice-Hall edition published September 1977
13 printings through March 1978
Bantam edition / August 1978*

2nd printing

3rd printing

ISBN 0-553-04984-4

*Bantam Books are published by Bantam Books, Inc. Its trade-
mark, consisting of the words "Bantam Books" and the por-
trayal of a bantam, is registered in the United States Patent
Office and in other countries. Marca Registrada. Bantam
Books, Inc., 666 Fifth Avenue, New York, New York 10019.*

PRINTED IN THE UNITED STATES OF AMERICA

The names and some identifying details of several individuals mentioned in this book have been changed to protect their privacy.

CONTENTS

PREFACE by Reverend John Nicola

The problem to which this book addresses itself is one which, although it is as old as mankind, needs to be brought to the attention of thoughtful readers today. All civilizations have expressed some sense of insecurity and fear over the spotty but recurring reports of phenomena that leave men feeling victimized by hostile beings with superhuman powers. Human beings in different societies have responded to such challenges in various ways. Words, gestures, and amulets or other objects have been ritually employed in response to demonic attacks; this was as true of the ancient Semitic civilizations like the Babylonians and their feared Udug demons as it is of present Christian rites of exorcism.

In our modern Western world, there are three main

stances which, in various combinations, characterize the multitude of attitudes individuals assume toward reports of siege by mysterious powers. The first, the *scientific*, views the world—and perhaps the universe—as governed by unvarying laws that have been discovered, or at least are discoverable, by scientific investigation. Diametrically opposed to this is a stance that seems to deplore, if not ignore, the findings of science seeing empirical reality as shallow and meaningless; it focuses instead on unseen spiritual realities, and may be characterized as *superstitious*. The third stance contains something of each of the other two. While adhering to science as a method, it broadens the vistas of positive science, incorporating spiritual dimensions of reality through theological and philosophical considerations. This we may call the *religious* stance.

One certainty is that the phenomena reported in this book do happen—and to ordinary people and families who are neither exhibitionists nor attention seekers. Often the response of the positive scientist is to deny the reality of reported data and to refuse even to examine the evidence; here, it appears, we are dealing with a prejudice. On the other hand, those scientists who credit the evidence and apply scientific methodology to attempting an explanation generally restrict the possibilities to science as it is known today, or presume that projected findings of empirical science will one day explain the phenomena. This is one reasonable and integral approach.

Superstitious people seize on psychic phenomena as justification for a sometimes unreasonable approach to life. Interjecting irrational fears and senseless preconceived notions or explanations into situations like the Amityville case Jay Anson describes here simply increases the suffering of those involved. The prejudice thus exhibited is clear.

Needless to say, incorporated in a religiously oriented person's point of view are the data of revelation. Since revelation presumes communication from God, and in turn presumes the existence of God and His interest in human affairs, we can see that here, too, a prejudice is implied—to wit, the prejudice of faith. The balanced person of faith will admire and accept the findings of modern science but conclude that, even projecting future developments, it is myopic to think that nature does not reveal a depth of reality beyond the empirical realm of natural science. As is the case with an open-minded scientist, a sensible believer may also accept an integrated approach to psychic phenomena.

Thus we observe that whatever stance an individual adopts, it will rest on certain prejudices that cannot be proven to the satisfaction of those who choose to adopt a different construction. When psychic phenomena occur in the life of a family, and that family looks for help, its members may be repelled equally by the naïveté of the superstitious, the uncertainty of those who profess belief in the supernatural but seem ashamed and confused at their own beliefs, and by the haughty pride of the positive scientist asserting with certainty things contradictory to one's own experience.

Unfortunately, this complex web of ignorance, bias, and fear causes a great deal of suffering for the unsuspecting family suddenly tossed into an upsetting and frightening situation. It is just such a case to which Jay Anson addresses himself. If the story were fiction, it would easily be dismissed as irrelevant. It is, however, a documentary told by the family and the priest who actually experienced what is reported; and as such, the tale must give us pause for thought. Those of us who have been involved in psychic investigations can verify the fact that the case is not atypical.

Because of the uncertainties connected with the paranormal, I, as a believer in science and in religion, would be remiss not to warn readers against the dangers both of an arrogance that professes a grasp of the unknown and of a bravado that boasts of a control of the transcendent. The wise man knows that he does *not* know— and the prudent man respects what he does not control.

PROLOGUE

On February 5, 1976, the *Ten O'Clock News* on New York's Channel Five announced it was doing a series on people who claimed to have extrasensory powers. The program cut to reporter Steve Bauman investigating an allegedly haunted house in Amityville, Long Island.

Bauman said that on November 13, 1974, a large colonial house at 112 Ocean Avenue had been the scene of a mass murder. Twenty-four-year-old Ronald DeFeo had taken a high-powered rifle and methodically shot to death his parents, two brothers, and two sisters. DeFeo had subsequently been sentenced to life imprisonment.

"Two months ago," the report continued, "the house was sold for $80,000 to a couple named George and Kathleen Lutz." The Lutzes had been aware of the killings, but not being superstitious, they had felt the house would be perfect for themselves and their three children.

They moved in on December 23. Shortly thereafter, Bauman said, they had become aware that the place was inhabited by some psychic force and that they feared for their lives. "They talked of feeling the presence of some energy inside, some unnatural evil that grew stronger each day they remained."

Four weeks after they moved in, the Lutzes abandoned the house, taking only a few changes of clothes. At present, they were staying with friends in an undisclosed location. But before they left, Channel Five stated, their predicament had become known in the area. They had consulted the police and a local priest as well as a psychic research group. "They reportedly told of strange voices seeming to come from within themselves, of a power which actually lifted Mrs. Lutz off her feet toward a closet behind which was a room not noted on any blueprints."

Reporter Steve Bauman had heard of their claims. After doing some background research on the house, he discovered that tragedy had struck nearly every family inhabiting the place, as well as an earlier house built on the same site.

The Channel Five announcer went on to say that William Weber, the attorney representing Ronald DeFeo, had commissioned studies hoping to prove that some force influenced the behavior of anyone living at 112 Ocean Avenue. Weber claimed this force "may be of natural origin," and felt it might be the evidence he needed to win his client a new trial. On camera, Weber said he was "aware that certain houses could be built or constructed in a certain manner so as to create some sort of electrical currents through some rooms, based on the physical structure of the house. Again, the scientists said they 'are investigating that, to rule that out.' And after they rule out all reasonable or scientific explanation, then it's going to be referred over to another group at Duke University, who will delve into the psychic aspects of the case."

The report concluded by saying that the Catholic Church was also involved. Channel Five stated that two emissaries from the Vatican had arrived in Amityville in December, and were reported to have told the Lutzes to leave their home immediately. "Now the Church's Council of Miracles is studying the case, and its report is that indeed 112 Ocean Avenue is possessed of some spirits beyond current human knowledge."

Two weeks after the telecast, George and Kathy Lutz held a press conference in attorney William Weber's office. The DeFeo lawyer had met the couple three weeks before through mutual friends.

George Lutz stated to reporters that he would not spend another night in the house, but he was not planning to sell 112 Ocean Avenue just then. He was also awaiting the results of some scientific tests to be conducted by parapsychologists and other "sensitive" professional researchers of occult phenomena.

At that point in time, the Lutzes cut off all communication with the media, feeling that too much was being overstated and exaggerated. It is only now that their whole story is being told.

1 **December 18, 1975**— George and Kathy Lutz moved into 112 Ocean Avenue on December 18. Twenty-eight days later, they fled in terror.

George Lee Lutz, 28, of Deer Park, Long Island, had a pretty good idea of land and home values. The owner of a land surveying company, William H. Parry, Inc., he proudly let everyone know that the business was a third-generation operation: his grandfather's, his father's, and now his.

Between July and November, he and his wife, Kathleen, 30, had looked at over fifty homes on the Island's South Shore before deciding to investigate Amityville. None in the thirty to fifty thousand dollar range had yet met their requirements—that the house must be on the water and that it must be one to which they could move George's business.

In the course of their search, George called the Conklin Realty Office in Massapequa Park and spoke to broker Edith Evans. She said that she had a new house that she wanted to show them, and that she could take them through the place between three and three-thirty. George made the appointment and the broker—an attractive, warm woman—took them there at three in the afternoon.

She was very pleasant and patient with the young couple. "I'm not sure if this is what you're looking for," she told George and Kathy, "but I wanted to show you how the 'other half' of Amityville lives."

The house at 112 Ocean Avenue is a big, rambling, three-story affair, with dark shingles and white trim. The lot on which it stands is 50 by 237, the fifty feet facing the front, so that as you look at the house from across the street, the entrance door is down the right side. With the property comes thirty feet of wooden bulkhead that stands against the Amityville River.

On a lamppost at the end of the paved driveway, is a small sign bearing the name given the house by a previous owner. It reads "High Hopes."

An enclosed porch with wet bar looks out at a preferred, older residential community of other big homes. Evergreens grow around the narrow grounds, partly blocking off the neighbors on either side, but their drawn shades can be seen easily enough. When he looked around, George thought that was peculiar. He noticed the neighbors' shades were all drawn on the sides that faced his house, but not in front or in the direction of the houses on the other side.

The house had been on the market for almost a year. It was not in the paper, but was fully described in Edith Evans' agency listing:

EXCLUSIVE AMITYVILLE AREA—6 bedroom Dutch Colonial, spacious living room, formal dining room, enclosed porch, 3-1/2 baths, finished basement, 2-car garage, heated swimming pool and large boathouse. Asking $80,000

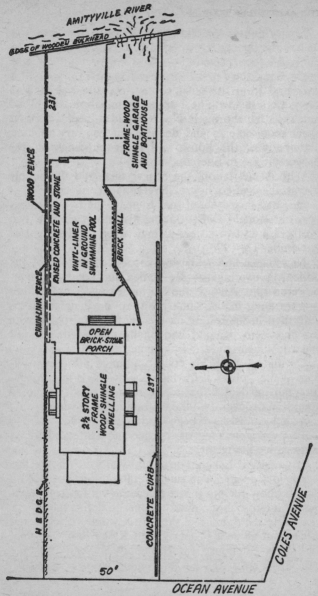

Diagram of the Property, Based on a 1975 Survey

Eighty thousand dollars! For a house described like that in the listing, it would have to be falling apart, or the typist could have left out a "1" before the "8." One might think she'd want to show a suspect bargain after dark and from the outside only, but she was glad to show them inside. The Lutzes' examination was pleasant, swift but thorough. Not only did it meet with their exact requirements and desires, but contrary to their anticipations, the house and other buildings on the property were in fine condition.

Without hesitation, the broker then told the couple it was the DeFeo house. Everyone in the country, it seems, had heard about that tragedy, the twenty-three-year-old Ronald DeFeo killing his father, mother, two brothers, and two sisters in their sleep on the night of November 13, 1974.

Newspaper and television accounts had told of the police discovering the six bodies all shot by a high-powered rifle. All—as the Lutzes learned months later —were lying in the same position: on their stomachs with their heads resting on their arms. Confronted with this massacre, Ronald had finally confessed: "It just started; it went so fast, I just couldn't stop."

During his trial, his court-appointed attorney, William Weber, pleaded for his insanity. "For months before the incident," the young man testified, "I heard voices. Whenever I looked around, there was no one there, so it must have been God talking to me." Ronald DeFeo was convicted of murder and sentenced to six consecutive life terms.

"I wonder if I should have told you which house this was *before* or *after* you saw it," the broker mused. "I'd like to know for my future reference with clients looking for a house in the ninety-thousand dollar range."

Clearly she didn't feel the Lutzes would be interested in such an affluent property. But Kathy took one final look about the house, smiled happily and said, "It's the best we've seen. It's got everything we ever wanted."

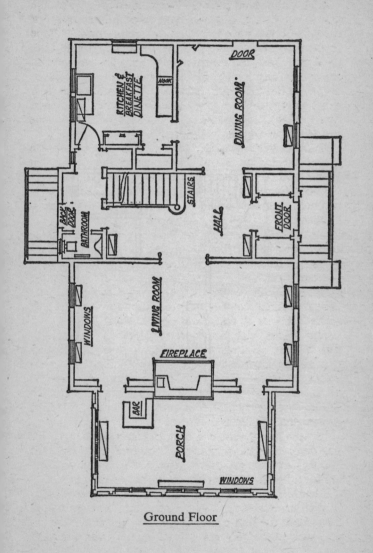

Ground Floor

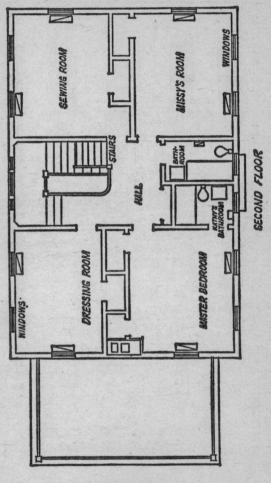

Second Floor

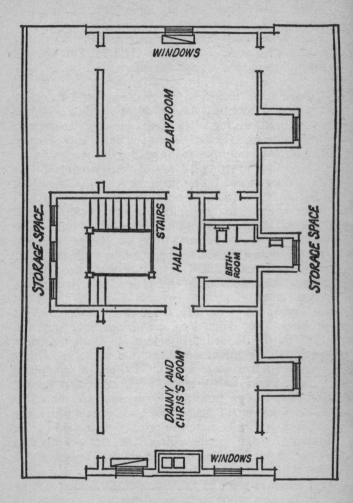

Third Floor/Attic

Obviously she had never hoped to live in such a fine house. But George vowed to himself that if there was a way, this was the place he wanted his wife to have. The tragic history of 112 Ocean Avenue didn't matter to George, Kathy, or their three children. This was still the home they had always wanted.

During the remainder of November and the early weeks of December, the Lutzes spent their evenings laying out plans for minor modifications to be made in the new house. George's surveying experience enabled him to rough out suitable layouts for the changes.

He and Kathy decided one of the bedrooms on the third floor would be for their two boys, Christopher aged seven, and Daniel, nine. The other upstairs bedroom they gave to their children as a playroom. Melissa, "Missy," the five-year-old girl, would sleep on the second floor, across the hall from the master bedroom. There would also be a sewing room and a big dressing room for George and Kathy on the same floor. Chris, Danny, and Missy were well pleased with their room assignments.

Downstairs, on the main floor, the Lutzes had a slight problem. They didn't own any dining room furniture. They finally decided that before the closing, George would tell the broker they'd like to purchase the dining room set left in storage by the DeFeos, along with a girl's bedroom set for Missy, a TV chair and Ronald DeFeo's bedroom furniture. These things and other furnishings left in the house, like the DeFeo's bed, were not included in the purchase price. George paid out an additional $400 for these items. He also got for free seven air-conditioners, two washers, two dryers, and a new refrigerator and a freezer.

There was a lot to be accomplished before moving day. In addition to the physical move of all their belongings, there were complicated legal questions, relative to the transfer of the title, that required sifting and sorting out. The title to the house and property was recorded in the names of Ronald DeFeo's parents. It seemed Ronald, as the sole survivor, was entitled to inherit his parents' estate, regardless of the fact that he had been convicted of murdering them. None of the assets in the estate could be disposed of before being legally settled in Probate Court. It was a difficult legal maze that the executors had to travel, and more time was still needed to provide the proper legal administration of any transactions related to the house or property.

The Lutzes were advised that provisions could be devised to protect the legal interests of all concerned if the sale of the house was consummated; but to arrive at the proper procedure to accomplish this could take weeks or longer. Eventually it was resolved that, for the closing, $40,000 was to be put in escrow for the mortgage until a legal deed could be completed and executed.

The closing date was set for the morning George and Kathy planned to move from Deer Park. They had arranged to close on the sale of their old house the day before. Confident that everything could be worked out, and probably influenced by their anxiety to get settled in their new home, the couple decided to try and get everything done on the same day.

Packing was to be mainly Kathy's job. To keep the children out of her hair and away from George, she assigned them minor projects. They would gather their own toys and arrange their clothing for packing. When the chores were completed, they were to start cleaning their rooms to make their old house presentable for the scrutiny of new owners.

George planned to close his office in Syosset and move it into the new house to save on the rent money. He had included this item in his original estimate of how he and Kathy could afford an $80,000 house. Now he figured that the basement, a well-finished layout, might be the best place. Moving his equipment and furnishings would be time consuming enough, and if the basement was to be the location of the new office, some carpentry would be needed.

The 45 by 22 foot boathouse, out behind the house and garage, was not there just to be ostentatious and an unused decoration for the Lutzes. George owned a twenty-five-foot cabin cruiser and a fifteen-foot speed-boat. The facilities at his new house would again save him a lot of money he normally had been paying to a marina. The task of getting his vessels to Amityville with a trailer became an obsession with him, despite the priorities that he and Kathy were constantly discovering.

There was work to be done at 112 Ocean Avenue, both inside and outside. Although he wasn't sure where the time was going to come from, George planned to attend to some of the landscaping and the garden to prevent frost damage, maybe put framed burlap around the shrubs, put in bulbs and after that, spread some lime on the lawn.

Handy with his tools and equipment, George made good progress on many interior projects. Now and then, pressed for time, he got his hopeful projects confused with his musts. He soon dropped everything to clean the chimney, then the fireplace. After all, Christmas was coming up.

It was quite cold on the actual moving day. The family had packed the night before and slept on the floor. George was up early and singlehandedly piled the first full load into the biggest U-haul trailer he could rent, finishing in barely enough time to clean up and get to the closing with Kathy.

At the legal ritual, the attorneys used up more than their usually allotted heretos, whereases and parties of, and dealt each other long sheets of typewritten paper. The Lutzes' lawyer explained that because of the impediments on the house, they did not have a clear title to the property, though they'd have the best that could be fashioned for their mortgage. But remarkably, the closing was all over a few minutes past noon. As they rushed from the office, their lawyers assured them they would have no problem and eventually would get proper ownership papers.

At one o'clock, George rolled into the driveway of 112 Ocean Avenue, with the trailer crowded with their belongings, and the DeFeos' refrigerator, washer, dryer and freezer that had been in storage. Kathy followed with the children in the family van with their motorcycle in the back. Five of George's friends, young men in their twenties and husky enough to help move bulky items, were waiting. Furniture, boxes, crates, barrels, bags, toys, bikes, motorcycles, and clothing were taken from the truck onto the patio at the rear of the house and into the garage.

Then George walked to the front door, fumbling in his pockets as he went, searching for the key to the door. Irritated, he returned to the truck and thoroughly searched it before admitting to his assistants that he didn't have it. The broker was the only one with the key, and she had taken it with her as she left the closing. George called her, and she went back to her office to fetch it.

When the side door was finally open, the three children leaped from the van, made right for their respective toys and began a parade of unprofessional movers in and out of the house. Kathy designated the destination of each parcel.

It took time to maneuver furniture up the fairly narrow stairwell leading to the second and third floors. And by the time Father Mancuso arrived to bless the house, it was well after one-thirty P.M.

2 **December 18**— Father Frank Mancuso is not only a cleric. In addition to properly attending to his priestly duties, he handles clients in family counselling for his diocese.

That morning, Father Mancuso had woken up feeling uneasy. Something was bothering him. He couldn't put his finger on it, because he really didn't have any particular worries. In his own words, looking back, he can only explain it as a "bad feeling."

All that morning, the priest moved around his apartment in the Long Island rectory in a daze. Today is Thursday, he thought to himself. I've got a lunch date in Lindenhurst, then I must go and bless the Lutzes' new home and be at my mother's for dinner.

Father Mancuso had met George Lee Lutz two years

earlier. Even though George was a Methodist, he had helped Kathy and George in the days before they were married. The three children were Kathy's from a previous marriage, and as a priest to Catholic children, Father Mancuso felt a personal need to look after their interests.

The young couple had often asked the friendly cleric with the neatly-trimmed beard to come for lunch or dinner at their home in Deer Park. Somehow that anticipated meeting had never come off. Now, George had a very special reason to invite him anew: Would he come to Amityville to bless their new house? Father Mancuso said he'd be there on December 18.

On the same day he agreed to come to George's house, he also made a date to lunch with four old friends in Lindenhurst, Long Island. His very first parish had been there. Now he was very well regarded in the diocese, with his own quarters at the rectory in Long Island. Understandably he was always busy and held to a hectic schedule, so he could not be blamed for trying to kill two birds with one stone, since Lindenhurst and Amityville were but a few miles apart.

The cleric could not shake the "bad feeling" that persisted even through the pleasant luncheon with his four old acquaintances. However, he kept stalling his leaving for Amityville, pushing ahead the time to go. His friends asked him where he was off to.

"To Amityville."

"Where in Amityville?"

"It's a young couple in their thirties, with three children. They live on . . ." Father Mancuso referred to a slip of paper. "112 Ocean Avenue."

"That's the DeFeo house," one of his friends said.

"No. Their name is Lutz. George and Kathleen Lutz."

"Don't you remember the DeFeos, Frank?" asked one of the men at the table. "Last year? The son killed his whole family. His father, mother, and four brothers and sisters. Terrible, terrible thing. It was a big story in all the papers."

The priest tried to think back. He seldom read the news when he picked up a paper, only looking for items of special interest. "No, I really don't seem to recall it."

Of the four men at the table, three were priests and they somehow didn't like the idea. The consensus was that he shouldn't go.

"I must. I promised them I'd come."

As Father Mancuso drove the few miles to Amityville, he felt apprehensive. It wasn't the fact that he would be visiting the DeFeo house, he was sure, but something else. . . .

It was past one-thirty when he arrived. The Lutzes' driveway was so cluttered that he had to park his old tan Ford on the streets. It was an enormous house, he noted. Good for Kathy and the children that her husband had been able to provide such a fine home!

The priest removed his clerical articles from the car, put on his stole, took the holy water, and entered the house to begin his ritual of blessing. When he flicked the first holy water and uttered the words that accompany the gesture, Father Mancuso heard a masculine voice say with terrible clarity: *"Get out!"*

He looked up in shock and whirled about. His eyes widened in astonishment. The command had come from directly behind him, but he was alone in the room. Who or whatever had spoken, was nowhere to be seen!

When he finished his ritual of blessing, the priest didn't mention the incident to the Lutzes. They thanked him for his kindness, asked him to stay for supper, such as it would be the first night. He politely refused, explaining that he planned to have dinner with his mother at her house in Nassau. She would be waiting for him; it was getting late, and he still had a bit of a drive.

Kathy really wanted to thank Father Mancuso for his contribution to the occasion. George asked if he would

19

accept a gift of money or a bottle of Canadian Club, but he quickly refused, stating he couldn't accept gratuities from a friend.

Once in his car, Father Mancuso rolled down his window. Repeated thanks and well-wishes were exchanged, but as he spoke to the couple, his expression turned serious. "By the way, George. I had lunch with some friends over in Lindenhurst before coming here. They told me that this was the DeFeo home. Did you know that?"

"Oh, sure. I think that's why it's such a bargain. It was on the market for a long time. But that doesn't bother us at all. It's got the best of everything."

"Wasn't that a tragedy, Father?" said Kathy. "That poor family. Imagine, all six murdered in their sleep."

The priest nodded. Then with repeated goodbyes from the three children, the family watched as he drove off to Queens.

It was nearly four when George had completed the first unloading at 112 Ocean Avenue. He drove the U-Haul back to Deer Park and into his old driveway. As he opened the door to his garage, Harry, his dog, leaped out and would have made a getaway if he hadn't been snared by his head. The fast and sturdy half-malamute, half-Labrador retriever had been left behind to guard the rest of the family's belongings. Now George took him into the truck with him.

As Father Mancuso rode toward his mother's, he tried to rationalize what had happened to him in the Lutzes' house. Who or what would say such a thing to him. After all his experiences in counselling, now and again in his sessions he encountered clients who reported hearing voices—a symptom of psychosis. But Father Mancuso was convinced of his own stability.

His mother greeted him at her door, then frowned.

"What's the matter with you, Frank? Don't you feel well?"

The priest shook his head. "No, not too terribly."

"Go in the bathroom and look at your face."

Looking at his reflection in the mirror, he saw two large, black circles under his eyes that were so dark he thought they must be smears of dirt. He tried to wash them off with soap and water, but it didn't help.

Back in Amityville, George took Harry to the dog compound next to the garage and chained him with a 20-foot steel lead. Now that it was after six, George was almost exhausted and decided to leave the rest of his possessions in the truck even though it was costing him fifty dollars a day to rent the vehicle. He worked inside, placing most of the livingroom furniture in their approximate positions.

Father Mancuso left his mother's home after eight, heading back to the Rectory. On the Van Wyck Expressway in Queens, he found his car was literally being forced onto the right shoulder. He looked around quickly. There was no other vehicle within fifty feet of of him!

Shortly after driving back onto the highway and continuing on his way, the hood suddenly flew open, smashing back against the windshield. One of the welded hinges tore loose. The right door flew open! Frantically Father Mancuso tried to brake the car. Then it stalled by itself.

Shaken, he finally got to a telephone and reached another priest who lived near the Expressway. Fortunately the other cleric was able to drive Father Mancuso to a garage where he hired a tow truck to bring in the disabled car. Back on the Expressway, the mechanic could not get the Ford to start. Father Mancuso decided to leave the vehicle at the garage and have his friend drive him on to the Sacred Heart Rectory.

Coming to almost the very end of his strength, George decided to complete the day's labor with something more pleasurable for himself. He'd rig his stereo up with the hi-fi equipment that the DeFeos had built into the living room. Then he and Kathy would have music to add to the joy of their first night in their new home.

He'd barely begun the job, when Harry began an awful howling outside. Danny came rushing into the house, yelling that Harry was in trouble. George ran out to the back fence to find the poor animal strangling. He had tried to jump over the fence and was now choking on his chain, which had looped across the top bar. George freed Harry, shortened the lead so the dog couldn't try that again, and returned to installing the stereo.

An hour after he was back in his quarters, Father Mancuso's telephone rang. It was the priest who had helped him out earlier. "Do you know what happened to me after I dropped you off?"

Father Mancuso was almost afraid to ask . . .

"The windshield wipers, they began to fly back and forth like crazy! I couldn't stop them! I never turned them on, Frank! What the hell is going on?"

By eleven o'clock that night, the Lutzes were ready to settle down for their first night in their new home. It had gotten colder outside, down to almost 6 degrees above zero. George burned some now-empty cardboard cartons in the fireplace, making a merry blaze. It was the eighteenth of December, 1975, the first of their twenty-eight days.

3 December 19 to 21 — George sat up in bed,
wide awake. He had heard a knock on his front door.

He looked around in the darkness. For a moment, he didn't know where he was, but then it came to him. He was in the master bedroom of his new home. Kathy was there, beside him, hunched down under the warm covers.

The knock came again. "Jesus, who's that?" he muttered.

George reached for his wristwatch on the night table. It was 3:15 in the morning! Again a loud rapping. Only this time, it didn't sound as if it was coming from downstairs, more from somewhere off to his left.

George got out of bed, padded across the cold, uncarpeted floor of the hallway and into the sewing room that faced the Amityville River in the back. He looked

23

out the window into the darkness. He heard another knock. George strained his eyes to see. "Where the hell's Harry?"

From somewhere over his head came a sharp crack. Instinctively he ducked, then looked up at the ceiling. He heard a low squeak. The boys, Danny and Chris, were on the floor above him. One of them must have pushed a toy off his bed in his sleep.

Barefooted and wearing only his pajama pants, George was shivering now. He looked back out the window. There! Something *was* moving, down by the boathouse. He quickly lifted the window, and the freezing air hit him full blast. "Hey! Who's out there?" Then Harry barked and moved. George, his eyes adjusting to the darkness, saw the dog spring to his feet. The shadow was close to Harry.

"Harry! Go get him!" Another rap sounded from the direction of the boathouse, and Harry spun around at the noise. He began running back and forth in his compound, barking furiously now, the lead holding him back.

George slammed the window shut and ran back to his bedroom. Kathy had awoken. "What's the matter?" She turned on the lamp on her night table as George fumbled into his pants. "George?" Kathy saw his bearded face look up.

"It's all right, honey. I just want to take a look around out back. Harry's onto something near the boathouse. Probably a cat. I'd better quiet him down before he wakes the whole neighborhood." He slid into his loafers and was heading for his old navy blue Marine parka lying on a chair. "I'll be right up. Go back to sleep."

Kathy turned off the light. "Okay. Put your jacket on." The next morning, she wouldn't remember having awakened at all.

When George came out the kitchen door, Harry was still barking at the moving shadow. There was a length of two-by-four lumber lying against the swimming pool fence. George grabbed it and ran toward the boathouse. Then he saw the shadow move. His grip tightened on the heavy stick. Another loud rap.

"Damn!" George saw it was the door to the boathouse, open and swinging in the wind. "I thought I'd locked that before!"

Harry barked again.

"Oh, shut up, Harry! Knock it off!"

A half hour later, George was back in bed, still wide awake. As an ex-Marine, not too many years out of the service, he was fairly accustomed to emergency wake-up calls. It was taking him time to turn off his inner alarm system.

Waiting for sleep to return, he considered what he had gotten himself into—a second marriage with three children, a new house with a big mortgage. The taxes in Amityville were three times higher than in Deer Park. Did he really need that new speedboat? How the hell was he going to pay for all of this? The construction business was lousy on Long Island because of the tight mortgage money, and it didn't look like it would get better until the banks loosened up. If they aren't building houses and buying property, who the hell needs a land surveyor?

Kathy shifted in her sleep, so that her arm fell across George's neck. Her face burrowed deep into his chest. He sniffed her hair. She certainly smelled clean, he thought; he liked that. And she kept her children the same way, spotless. *Her* kids? George's now. Whatever the trouble, she and the children were worth it.

George looked up at the ceiling. Danny was a good boy, into everything. He could handle almost anything you gave him to do. They were getting closer, now. Danny was now beginning to call his stepfather "Dad;" no more "George." In a way he was glad he never got to meet Kathy's ex-husband; this way he felt Danny was all his. Kathy said that Chris looked just like his father, had the same ways about him, the same dark, curly hair and eyes. George would reprimand the boy for something, and Chris's face would fall and he'd look up at him with those soulful eyes. The kid sure knew how to use them.

He liked the way both boys looked after little Missy. She was a little terror, but smart for a five year old. He'd never had any trouble with her from the first day he met Kathy. She was Daddy's girl, all right. Listens to Kathy and me. In fact, they all do. They're three nice kids I've got.

It was after six before George finally fell into a deep sleep. Kathy woke up a few minutes later.

She looked around this strange room, trying to put her thoughts together. She was in the bedroom of her beautiful new home. Her husband was next to her and her three children were in their own bedrooms. Wasn't that marvelous! God had been good to them.

Kathy tried to slip easily from under George's arm. The poor man worked so hard yesterday, she thought, and today he's got more ahead of him. Let him sleep. She couldn't; she had too much to do in the kitchen and she had better get started before the kids got up.

Downstairs, she looked around at her new kitchen. It was still dark outside. She turned on the light. Boxes of her dishes, glasses, and pots were piled up all over the floor and sink. Chairs were still sitting on top of the dinette table. But, she smiled to herself, the kitchen was going to be a happy room for her family. It might be just the place for her Transcendental Meditation, which George had been practicing for two years; Kathy, one. He had been into TM ever since the breakup of his first marriage, when he had been attending sessions of group therapy; out of that grew his interest in meditation. He had introduced Kathy to the subject, but now, with all the work of moving in, he had completely ignored his established pattern of going off by himself into a room and meditating for a few minutes each day.

Kathy washed out her electric percolator, filled it,

plugged it in, and lit her first cigarette of the day. Drinking coffee, Kathy sat at the table with a pad and pencil, making notes for herself on the jobs to be done around the house. Today was the nineteenth, a Friday. The kids would not go to their new school until after the Christmas holidays. Christmas! There was so much still to do. . . .

Kathy sensed someone was staring at her. Startled, she looked up and over her shoulder. Her little daughter was standing in the doorway. "Missy! You scared me half to death. What's the matter. What are you doing up so early?"

The little girl's eyes were half-closed. Her blonde hair hung across her face. She looked around, as if not understanding where she was. "I wanna go home, Mama."

"You *are* home, Missy. This is our new home. C'mere."

Missy shambled over to Kathy and climbed up on her mother's lap. The two ladies of the house sat there in their pleasant kitchen, Kathy rocking her daughter back to sleep.

George came down after nine. By that time, the boys had already finished their breakfast and were outside, playing with Harry, investigating everything. Missy was asleep again in her room.

Kathy looked at her husband whose big frame filled the doorway. She saw he hadn't shaved below his jawbone and that his dark blonde hair and beard were still uncombed. That meant he hadn't showered. "What's the matter? Aren't you going to work?"

George sat down wearily at the table. "Nope. I still have to unload the truck and get it back out to Deer Park. We blew an extra fifty bucks by keeping it overnight." He looked around, yawning, and shivered. "It's cold in here. Don't you have the heat on?"

The boys ran past the kitchen door, yelling at Harry. George looked up. "What's the matter with those two? Can't you keep them quiet, Kathy?"

She turned from the sink. "Well, don't bark at me! *You're* their father, you know! You do it!"

George slapped his open palm down on the table. The sharp sound made Kathy jump. "Right!" he shouted.

George opened the kitchen door and leaned out. Danny, Chris, and Harry, whooping it up, ran by again. "Okay! The three of you! Knock it off!" Without waiting for their reaction, he slammed the door and stormed out of the kitchen.

Kathy was speechless. This was the first time he had really lost his temper with the children. And for so little! He hadn't been in a bad mood the day before.

George unloaded the U-Haul by himself, then drove it back to Deer Park, with his motorcycle in the rear so that he could get back to Amityville. He never did shave or shower and did nothing the rest of the day but gripe about the lack of heat in the house and the noise the children were making in their playroom up on the third floor.

He had been a bear all day, and by eleven o'clock that night, when it was time to go to bed, Kathy was ready to crown him. She was exhausted from putting things away and trying to keep the kids away from George. She'd start cleaning the bathrooms in the morning, she figured, but that was it for tonight. *She* was going to bed.

George stayed down in the living room, feeding log after log into the roaring fireplace. Even though the thermostat read 75 degrees, he couldn't seem to get warm. He must have checked the oil burner in the basement a dozen times during the day and evening.

At twelve, George finally dragged himself up to the bedroom and fell asleep immediately. At 3:15 in the morning, he was wide awake again, sitting up in bed.

There was something on his mind. The boathouse. Did he lock the door? He couldn't remember. He had to go out and check. It was closed and locked up.

Over the next two days, the Lutz family began to go through a collective personality change. As George said, "It was not a big thing, just little bits and pieces, here and there." He didn't shave or shower, something he did religiously. Normally George devoted as much time to his business as he could; two years before, he had had a second office in Shirley to handle contractors farther out on the South Shore. But now he simply called Syosset and gave gruff orders to his men, demanding they finish some surveying jobs over the weekend because he needed the money. As for arranging to move his office to his new basement setup, he never gave it another thought.

Instead, George constantly complained the house was like a refrigerator and he had to warm it up. Stuffing more and more logs in the fireplace occupied almost his every moment, except for the times he would go out to the boathouse, stare into space, then go back to the house. Even now, he can't say what he was looking for when he went there; he just knew that somehow he was drawn to the place.

It was practically a compulsion. The third night in the house, he again awoke at 3:15 A.M., worried about what might be going on out there.

The children bothered him too. Ever since the move, they seemed to have become brats, misbehaved monsters who wouldn't listen, unruly children who must be severely punished.

When it came to the children, Kathy fell into the same mood. She was tense from her strained relationship with George and from the efforts of trying to put her house in shape before Christmas. On their fourth night in the house, she exploded and together with her husband, beat Danny, Chris, and Missy with a strap and a large, heavy wooden spoon.

The children had accidentally cracked a pane of glass in the playroom's half-moon window.

4 **December 22** — Early Monday morning, it was bitter cold in Amityville. The town is right on the Atlantic side of Long Island and the sea wind blew in like a nor'easter. The thermometer hovered at 8 degrees and media weathermen were forecasting a white Christmas.

Inside 112 Ocean Avenue, Danny, Chris, and Missy Lutz were up in the playroom, slightly subdued from the whipping the night before. George had still not gone to his office and was sitting in the living room, adding more logs to a blazing fire. Kathy was writing at her dinette table in the kitchen nook.

As she worked over a list of things to buy for Christmas, her concentration wandered. She was upset about having hit the children, particularly about the way George and she had gone about it. There were many

31

gifts the Lutz family still hadn't bought, and Kathy knew she had to go out and get them, but since they had moved in, she never had any desire to leave the house. She had just written down her Aunt Theresa's name when Kathy froze, pencil in midair.

Something had come up from behind and embraced her. Then it took her hand and gave it a pat. The touch was reassuring, and had an inner strength to it. Kathy was startled, but not frightened; it was like the touch of a mother giving comfort to her daughter. Kathy had the impression of a woman's soft hand resting on her own!

"Mommy! Come up here, quick!" It was Chris, calling from the third floor hallway.

Kathy looked up. The spell was broken, the touch was gone. She ran up the stairs to her children. They were in their bathroom, looking into the toilet. Kathy saw the inside of the bowl was absolutely black, as though someone had painted it from the bottom to the edge just below the rim. She pushed the handle, flushing clear water against the sides. The black remained.

Kathy grabbed toilet paper and tried vainly to rub off the discoloration. "I don't believe it! I just scrubbed this yesterday with Clorox!" She turned accusingly to the children. "Did you throw any paint in here?"

"Oh, no Mama!" all three chorused.

Kathy was fit to be tied; the incident in the breakfast nook was forgotten. She looked into the sink and bathtub, but they were still gleaming from her scouring. She turned on the faucets. Nothing but clear running water. Once more, she flushed the toilet, not really expecting the horrible black color to disappear.

She bent down and looked around the base to see if anything was leaking through to the inside of the bowl. Finally she turned to Danny. "Get the Clorox from my bathroom. It's in the little closet under the sink."

Missy started to go. "Missy! You stay here! Let Danny get it." The boy left the bathroom. "And bring the scrub brush, too!" Kathy called after him.

Chris searched his mother's face, his eyes watering. "I didn't do it. Please don't hit me again."

Kathy looked at him, thinking of the terrible night before. "No, baby, it wasn't your fault. Something's happened to the water, I think. Maybe some oil backed up the line. Didn't you notice it before?"

"I had to go. I saw it first!" crowed Missy.

"Uh-huh. Well, let's see what the Clorox does before I call your father and he. . .".

"Mama! Mama!" The cry came from down the hall.

Kathy leaned out the bathroom doorway. "What is it, Danny? I said it's under the sink!"

"No, Mama! I found it! But the black's in your toilet, too! And it stinks in here!"

Kathy's bathroom door was at the far end of her bedroom. Danny was standing outside the bedroom, holding his nose, when Kathy and the other two children came running down.

As soon as Kathy stepped into the bedroom, the odor hit her—a sweetish perfume smell. She stopped, sniffed, and frowned. "What the hell is *that*? That isn't my cologne."

But when she entered her bathroom, she was struck by a completely different odor, an overpowering stench. Kathy gagged and started to cough, but before she ran, caught a glimpse of her toilet bowl. It was totally black inside!

The children scrambled out of her way as she headed down the stairs. "George!"

"What do you want? I'm busy!"

Kathy burst into the living room and ran over to where George was crouched by the fireplace. "You'd better come and look! There's something in our bathroom that smells like a dead rat! And the toilet's all black!" She grabbed his hand and tugged him out of the room.

The other bathroom toilet bowl on the second floor was also black inside, as George discovered, but it had

33

no smell. He sniffed the perfume in his room. "What the hell's that?"

He began to open the windows on the second floor. "First, let's get this smell out of here!" He lifted the windows in his and Kathy's bedroom, then ran across the hall to the other bedrooms. Then he heard Kathy's voice.

"George! Look at this!"

The fourth bedroom on the second floor—now Kathy's sewing room—has two windows. One, which looks out at the boathouse and the Amityville River, was the window George had opened that first night when he had awakened at 3:15. The other faces the neighboring house to the right of 112 Ocean Avenue. On this window, clinging to the inside of the panes, were literally hundreds of buzzing flies!

"Jesus, will you look at that! House flies, *now*?"

"Maybe they're attracted by the smell?" Kathy volunteered.

"Yeah, but not at this time of year. Flies don't live that long, and not in this weather. And why are they only on this window?" George looked around the room, trying to see where the insects had come from. There was a closet in one corner. He opened the door and peered in, looking for cracks; for anything that would make sense.

"If this closet wall was up against the bathroom, they might have lived in the warmth. But this wall's against the outside." George put his hand against the plaster. "It's cold in here. I don't see any way they could have survived."

After shooing his family out into the hall, George shut the door to the sewing room. He opened the other window overlooking the boathouse, then took some newspapers and chased out as many flies as he could. He killed those that remained, then he closed the window. By then, it was freezing on the second floor, but at least the sweet perfume odor was gone. The bathroom stench had also diminished.

This didn't help George in his efforts to warm his house. Though no one else was complaining, he checked the oil heating system in the basement. It was working fine. By four o'clock in the afternoon, the thermostat just off the living room read 80 degrees, but George couldn't feel the heat.

Kathy had scrubbed the toilet bowls again with Clorox, Fantastik, and Lysol. The cleaners helped somewhat, but a good deal of the black remained, stained deep into the porcelain. Worst of all was the toilet in the second bathroom next to the sewing room.

The outdoor temperature had risen to 20 degrees and the children were out of the house, playing with Harry. Kathy warned them to keep away from the boathouse and bulkhead area, saying it was too dangerous for them to play there without someone to watch them.

George had brought in some more logs from the cord stacked in the garage and was sitting in the kitchen with Kathy. They began to argue violently about who should go out to buy the Christmas gifts. "Why can't you at least pick up the perfume for your mother?" asked George.

"I've got to get this place in order," Kathy erupted. "I don't see you doing anything but harping!"

After a few minutes, the squabble petered out. Kathy was about to mention the eerie thing that had happened to her in the nook that morning when the front doorbell rang.

A man, who looked to be anywhere from thirty-five to forty-five because of his receding hairline, was standing there with a hesitant smile on his face and a six-pack of beer in his hands. His features were coarse and his nose was red from the cold. "Everybody wants to come over to welcome you to the neighborhood. You don't mind, do you?"

The fellow wore a three-quarter length wool car coat, corduroy pants, and construction boots. It struck George that he didn't look like a neighbor who would own one of the large homes in the area.

Before they even moved to Amityville, George and Kathy had considered the idea of having an open house, but once in the new house, they had never brought up the subject again. George nodded to the one-man welcoming committee. "No, we don't mind. If they don't mind sitting on cardboard boxes, bring them all."

George took him into the kitchen and introduced Kathy. The man stood there, and repeated his speech to her. Kathy nodded. He continued by telling the Lutzes that he kept his boat at another neighbor's boathouse, several doors down on Ocean Avenue.

The man held on to the six-pack and finally said, "I brought it, I'll take it with me," and left.

George and Kathy never found out his name. They never saw him again.

That night when they went to bed, George made his usual check of all the doors and windows, latching and locking, inside and out. So, when he woke once more at 3:15 in the morning and gave in to the urge to look downstairs, he was stunned to find the two hundred and fifty pound wooden front door wrenched wide open, hanging from one hinge!

5 December 23 — Kathy awoke to the noise of
George wrestling with the wrecked front door. When she
felt the chill in the house, she threw on a robe and ran
downstairs to see her husband trying to force the heavy
wooden slab back into its frame.

"What happened?"

"I don't *know*," George answered, finally forcing the
door closed. "This thing was wide open, hanging on one
hinge. Here, look at this!" He pointed to the brass lock
plate. The doorknob was twisted completely off-center.
The metal facing was bent back as though someone had
tried to pry it open with a tool, but from the *inside*!
"Someone was trying to get *out* of the house, not in!"

"I don't understand what's going on around here,"

37

George muttered, more to himself than Kathy. "I know I locked this before I went upstairs. To open the door from in here, all you had to do was turn the lock."

"Is it the same way outside?" Kathy asked.

"No. There's nothing wrong with the knob or the outside plate. Somebody'd need an awful lot of strength to pull away a door this heavy and tear it off one of the hinges . . .".

"Maybe it was the wind, George," Kathy offered hopefully. "It seems to get pretty strong out there, you know."

"There's no wind in *here*, much less a tornado. Somebody or something had to do this!"

The Lutzes looked at one another. Kathy was the first to react. "The kids!" She turned and ran up the stairs to the second floor and into Missy's bedroom.

A small light in the shape of Yogi Bear was plugged into the wall near the bottom of the little girl's bed. In its feeble glow, Kathy glimpsed the form of Missy lying on her stomach. "Missy?" Kathy whispered, leaning over the bed. Missy whimpered, then turned over onto her back.

Kathy let out a sigh of relief and tucked the covers up under her daughter's chin. The cold air that had come in while the front door was open had made even this room very chilly. She kissed Missy on the forehead and silently slipped out of the room, heading for the third floor.

Danny and Chris were sleeping soundly. Both were on their stomachs. "Later, when I thought about it," Kathy says, "that was the first time I could ever remember the children sleeping in that position—particularly all three on their stomachs at the same time. I even remember I was almost going to say something to George, that it was kind of strange."

In the morning, the cold spell that gripped Amityville was still unbroken. It was cloudy, and the radio kept promising snow for Christmas. In the hallway of the

Lutz home, the thermostat still read a steady 80 degrees, but George was back in the living room, stoking the fire to a roaring blaze. He told Kathy he just couldn't shake the chill from his bones, and he didn't understand why she and the children didn't feel that way too.

The job of replacing the doorknob and lock assembly on the front door was too complex for even a handy individual like George. The local locksmith arrived about twelve, as he'd promised. He made a long, slow survey of the damage inside the house and then gave George a peculiar look, but offered no explanation as to how something like this could have possibly happened.

He finished the job quickly and quietly. Upon leaving, his one comment was that the DeFeos had called him a couple of years before: "They were having trouble with the lock on the boathouse door." He had been called to change the lock assembly because once the door was closed from the inside, it would somehow jam, and whoever was in the boathouse couldn't get out.

George wanted to say more about the boathouse, but when Kathy looked at him, he held back. They didn't want the news spreading around Amityville that again there was something funny going on at 112 Ocean Avenue.

By two in the afternoon, the weather had begun to warm. A slight drizzle was enough to keep the children in the house. George still hadn't gone to work and was in constant transit between the living room and the basement, adding logs and checking on the oil burner. Danny and Chris were up in their third floor playroom, noisily banging their toys around. Kathy was back at her cleaning chores, putting shelf paper in the closets. She had worked her way almost to her own bedroom on the second floor when she looked in Missy's room. The little girl was sitting in her diminutive rocking chair, humming to herself as she stared out the window that looked toward the boathouse.

Kathy was about to speak to her daughter when the phone rang. She picked up the extension in her own bedroom. It was her mother, saying that she would be over the next day—Christmas Eve—and that Kathy's brother Jimmy would bring them a Christmas tree as a housewarming gift.

Kathy said how relieved she was that at least the tree would be taken care of, since she and George had been unable to rouse themselves to do any shopping at all. Then, out of the corner of her eye, Kathy saw Missy leave her room and enter the sewing room. Kathy was only half listening to what her mother was saying; what could Missy possibly want in there, where all the flies had been the day before? She could hear her five-year-old daughter humming, moving about some still-unopened cardboard boxes.

Kathy was about to cut her mother short when she saw Missy come back out of the sewing room. When the child stepped into the hallway and returned to her own bedroom, she stopped her humming. Puzzled by her daughter's behavior, Kathy wound up her conversation with her mother, again thanking her for the tree. She hung up, walked silently toward Missy's room and stood in the doorway.

Missy was back in her rocking chair, staring out the same window and humming again, a tune that didn't sound quite familiar. Kathy was about to speak when Missy stopped humming, and without turning her head, said, "Mama? Do angels talk?"

Kathy stared at her daughter. The little girl had known she was there! But before Kathy could step into the room, she was startled by a loud crash from overhead. The boys were upstairs! Fearful, she raced up the steps to the playroom. Danny and Chris were rolling on the floor, locked in each other's arms, punching and kicking at each other.

"What's going on here?" Kathy screamed. "Danny!

Chris! You stop this right now, you hear!" She tried to pull them apart, but each was still trying to get at the other, their eyes blazing with hate. Chris was crying in his anger. It was the first time, *ever*, that the two brothers had gotten into a fight.

She slapped each boy in the face—hard—and demanded to know what had started this nonsense. "Danny started it," Chris sniffed.

"Liar! Chris, *you* started it," Danny scowled.

"Started *what*? What are you fighting about?" Kathy demanded, her voice rising. There was no answer from either boy. Both suddenly withdrew from their mother. Whatever happened, Kathy sensed it was their affair not hers.

Then her patience snapped. "What is going on around here? First it's Missy with her angels, and now you two idiots trying to kill each other! Well, I've had it! We'll just see what your father has to say about all this. You're both going to get it later, but right now I don't want to hear another peep out of either of you! You hear me? Not another sound!"

Shaking, Kathy returned downstairs to her shelving. *Cool down*, she told herself. As she passed Missy's room again, the little girl was humming the same strange tune to herself. Kathy wanted to go in, but then thought better of it and continued on into her own bedroom. She'd talk to George later when she had a chance to be calmer about the whole affair.

Kathy picked up a roll of shelf paper and opened the door to the walk-in closet. Immediately a sour smell struck her nostrils. "Oh, God! What's that?" She pulled the light chain hanging from the closet ceiling and looked around the small room. It was empty except for one thing. On the very first day the Lutzes had moved in, she had hung a crucifix on the inner wall facing the closet door, just as she had done when they lived in Deer Park. A friend had originally given her the crucifix as a wedding present. Made of silver, it was a beautiful piece about twelve inches long and had been blessed a long time before.

As Kathy looked at it now, her eyes widened in horror. She began to gag at the sour smell, but couldn't retreat from the sight of the crucifix—now hanging upside down!

6 December 24 — It was almost a week since

Father Mancuso had visited 112 Ocean Avenue. The eerie episodes of that day and night were still very much on his mind, but he had discussed them with no one—not with George and Kathy Lutz, not even with his Confessor.

During the night of the twenty-third, he had come down with the flu. The priest had alternated between chills and sweating, and when he finally got up to take his temperature, the thermometer read 103 degrees. He took some aspirin, hoping to break the fever. This was the Christmas season, and with it began a host of clerical duties—a particularly bad time for a priest to be indisposed.

Father Mancuso fell into a troubled sleep. Around

four in the morning of Christmas Eve, he awoke to find his temperature now up to 104 degrees. He called the Pastor to his rooms. His friend decided to get a doctor. While Father Mancuso waited for the physician, he thought again of the Lutz family.

There was something he couldn't quite put his finger on. He kept envisioning a room he believed to be on the second floor of the house. His head swam, but the priest could see it clearly in his mind. It was filled with unopened boxes when he had blessed the home, and he remembered he could see the boathouse from its windows.

Father Mancuso recalls that while ill in bed, he used the word "evil" to himself, but thinks the high fever might have been playing tricks with his imagination. He also remembers he had an urge, bordering on obsession, to call the Lutzes and warn them to stay out of that room at all costs.

At the same time, in Amityville, Kathy Lutz was also thinking about the room on the second floor. Every once in a while, Kathy felt the need for some time to be by herself, and this was to be her own personal room. She had also considered the room, along with the kitchen, for her meditation. That third bedroom on the second floor would also serve as a dressing room and storage place for her and George's growing wardrobes.

Among the cartons in the sewing room were boxes of Christmas ornaments that she had accumulated over the years. It was time to unwrap the balls and lights, get them ready to put on the tree her mother and brother had promised to bring over that evening.

After lunch, Kathy asked Danny and Chris to bring the cartons down to the living room. George was more interested in his fireplace logs and only halfheartedly worked on the Christmas lights, testing the many colored bulbs and disentangling their wires. For the next few hours, Kathy and the children were busy unwrapping tissue paper that enclosed the delicate, bright-colored balls; the little wooden and glass angels, Santas, skaters, ballerinas, reindeer and snowmen that Kathy had added to each year as the children grew up.

Each child had his own favorite ornaments and tenderly placed them on towels Kathy had spread on the floor. Some dated back to Danny's first Christmas. But today, the children were admiring an ornament that George had brought to his new family. It was an heirloom, a unique galaxy of crescents and stars wrought in sterling silver and encased in 24 karat gold. There was a fixture on the back of the 6-inch ornament that let one attach it to a tree. Crafted in Germany more than a century before, it had been given to George by his grandmother, who in turn had received it from her own grandmother.

The doctor had come and gone from the Rectory. He confirmed that Father Mancuso did indeed have the flu and advised the ailing priest to remain in bed for a day or so. The fever was in his system and could remain high for another twenty-four hours.

Father Mancuso chafed at the idea of remaining idle. He had so much work to do. He agreed that upcoming items on his busy calendar could be put off for a week, but some of his clients in counselling could not afford the same kind of postponement. Nevertheless, both the physician and the Pastor insisted that Father Mancuso would only prolong his illness if he insisted upon working or leaving his apartment.

There was one thing he could still do, however, and that was to call George Lutz. The bad feeling he had about that second-floor room remained and it made him as restless as his fever. When he finally made the call, it was five P.M.

Danny answered the telephone and ran to get his father. Kathy was surprised by the call, but not George. Sitting by the fireplace, he had been thinking about the priest all day. George had felt an urge to call Father Mancuso, but couldn't decide just what he wanted to say.

He was sorry to hear of Father Mancuso's flu and asked if there was anything he could do. Assured there was nothing any man could do to relieve the priest's discomfort, George began to speak of what was happening at the house. At first it was a light conversation; George told Father Mancuso about bringing down the ornaments to trim the Christmas tree that Jimmy, his brother-in-law, would be delivering at any moment.

Father Mancuso interrupted George. "I have to talk to you about something that's been on my mind. Do you know the room on your second floor that faces the boathouse—the one where you had all those unopened boxes and cartons?"

"Sure, Father. That's going to be Kathy's sewing and meditation room when I get a chance to fix it up. Hey, you know what we found in there the other day? Flies! Hundreds of houseflies! Can you imagine, in the middle of winter!"

George waited for the priest's reaction. He got it.

"George, I don't want you, or Kathy, or the children to go back into that room. You have to stay out of there!"

"Why, Father? What's up there?"

Before the priest could answer, there was a loud crackling sound on the telephone. Both men pulled back from their earpieces in surprise. George couldn't make out Father Mancuso's next words. All that remained was an irritating static noise. "Hello! Hello! Father? I can't hear you! There must be a bad connection!"

From his end, Father Mancuso was also trying to hear George through the static and only faintly heard the "Hello's." Finally the priest hung up, then dialed the Lutzes' number again. He could hear the phone ringing, but no one picked it up. The priest waited for ten rings before finally giving up. He was very disturbed.

When he could no longer hear Father Mancuso through the crackling, George had also hung up his receiver. He waited for the priest to call back. For several minutes he sat in the kitchen and stared at the silent telephone. Then he dialed Father Mancuso's private number at the Rectory.

There was no answer.

In the living room, Kathy began wrapping the few Christmas gifts she had accumulated before moving to Amityville. She had gone to sales at Sears and to the Green Acres Shopping Center in Valley Stream, picking up bargains in clothing for her children and other items for George and her family. Sadly, Kathy noted that the pile of boxes was rather small and silently berated herself for not leaving the house to go out shopping. There were few toys for Danny, Chris, and Missy, but it was too late to do anything about it.

She had sent the children up to the playroom so she could work alone. She thought about Missy. She had not answered her daughter's question about talking angels—Kathy had put it off by telling Missy she'd ask Daddy about it. But it never came up when she and George went to bed. Why would Missy come up with such an idea? Did it have anything to do with the child's peculiar behavior yesterday in her bedroom? And what was she looking for in the sewing room?

Kathy's concentration was broken when George returned from the phone in the kitchen. He had an odd expression on his face and was avoiding her gaze. Kathy waited for him to tell her about Father Mancuso when the front doorbell rang. She looked around, startled. "It must be my mother! George, they're here already and I haven't even started supper!" She hurried toward the kitchen. "You get the door!"

Kathy's brother, Jimmy Conners, was a big, strapping youth who genuinely liked George. That evening, his face exuded a special warmth and charm. He was to be married on the day after Christmas and had asked George to be his best man. But when mother and son entered the house, Jimmy lugging a sizable Scotch pine, both their faces changed at the sight of George, who hadn't shaved or showered for almost a week. Kathy's mother, Joan, was alarmed. "Where are Kathy and the kids?" she asked George.

"She's making supper, and they're up in the playroom. Why?"

"I just had the feeling something was wrong."

This was the first time his in-laws had visited the house, so George had to show his mother-in-law where the kitchen was located. Then he and Jimmy hefted the tree into the living room. "Boy! That's some fire you've got going there!"

George explained that he just couldn't warm up; hadn't been able to since the day they moved in, and that he had already burned ten logs that day. "Yeah," Jimmy agreed. "It does seem kind of chilly around here. Maybe there's something wrong with your burner or thermostat?"

"No," answered George. "The oil burner's working fine and the thermostat's up to 80 degrees. Come on down to the basement and I'll show you."

In the Rectory, Father Mancuso's doctor had warned him that one's body temperature normally rises after five in the afternoon. Even though he was uncomfortable and his stomach hurt, the priest's mind kept turning to the strange telephone problems the Lutzes were having.

It was now eight o'clock, and his repeated attempts to contact George had been fruitless. Several times he had asked the operator to check to see if the Lutzes' phone was out of order. Each time it rang interminably until a supervisor called him back to report no service problems with the line.

Why hadn't George called him back? Father Mancuso was sure George had heard what he said about the second floor room. Was there now something terribly wrong? Father Mancuso did not trust 112 Ocean Avenue, he could wait no longer. He dialed a number he normally used only for emergencies.

The Christmas tree was up at the Lutzes' home. Danny, Chris, and Missy were helping their Uncle Jimmy trim it, each urging him to hang his *own* ornaments first. George had returned to his own private world by the fireplace. Kathy and her mother were in the kitchen talking. This was her "happy" room, the one place in the new house where she felt secure.

She complained to her mother that George had changed since they moved in. "Ma, he won't take a shower, he won't shave. He doesn't even leave the house to go to the office. All he does is sit by that damned fireplace and complain about the cold. And another thing —every night he keeps going out to check that boathouse."

"What's he looking for?" Mrs. Conners asked.

"Who knows? All he keeps saying is he's got to look around out there—and check on the boat."

"That doesn't sound like George. Have you asked him if there's anything the matter?"

"Oh, sure!" Kathy threw up her hands. "And all he does is throw more wood on the fire! In one week, we've gone through almost a whole cord of wood."

Kathy's mother shivered and pulled her sweater tighter around her body. "Well, you know, it *is* kind of chilly in the house. I've felt it ever since I came in."

Jimmy, standing on a chair in the living room, was about to fix George's ornament to the top of the tree. He too shivered. "Hey, George, you got a door opened someplace? I keep getting a draft on the back of my neck."

George looked up. "No, I don't think so. I locked up everything before." He felt a sudden urge to check the second floor sewing room. "I'll be right back."

49

Kathy and Mrs. Conners passed him as they came in from the kitchen. He didn't say a word to either woman, just ran up the stairs. "What's with him?" Mrs. Conners asked.

Kathy just shrugged. "See what I mean?" She began to arrange the Christmas gifts under the tree. When Danny, Chris, and Missy counted the meager number of prettily wrapped packages on the floor, there was a chorus of disappointed voices behind her.

"What are you crying about?" George was back, standing in the doorway. "Knock it off! You kids are too spoiled anyway!"

Kathy was about to snap back at her husband for yelling at the children in front of her mother and brother when she saw the look on George's face.

"Did you open the window in the sewing room, Kathy?"

"Me? I haven't been up there all day."

George turned to the children near the tree. "Have any of you kids been in that room since you brought down the Christmas boxes?" All three shook their heads. George hadn't moved from his position in the doorway. His eyes returned to Kathy.

"George, what is it?"

"A window is open. And the flies are back."

Crack! Everyone in the room jumped at the loud sound that came from somewhere outside. Again came a sharp knock, and outside, Harry barked. "The boathouse door! It's open again!" George turned to Jimmy. "Don't leave them alone! I'll be right back!" He grabbed his parka from the hall closet and headed for the kitchen door. Kathy began to cry.

"Kathy, what's going on?" Mrs. Conners said, her voice rising.

"Oh, Mama! I don't know!"

A man watched as George came out of a side door and ran toward the back of the house. He knew the door led from the kitchen because he had been at 112 Ocean Avenue before. He sat in a car parked in front of the Lutzes' home and observed George shut the boathouse door.

He glanced at his watch. It was almost eleven o'clock. The man picked up the microphone of a car radio. "Zammataro. This is Gionfriddo. You can call your friend back and tell him the people in 112 Ocean Avenue are home." Sergeant Al Gionfriddo of the Suffolk County Police Department was doing a job this Christmas Eve, just as he had been on the night of the DeFeo family massacre.

7 **December 25** — For the seventh night in a row, George awoke at exactly 3:15. He sat up in bed. In the winter moonlight flooding the bedroom, George saw Kathy quite clearly. She was sleeping on her stomach.

He reached out his hand to touch her head. At that instant, Kathy woke up. As she looked wildly about, George could see the fright in her eyes. "She was shot in the head!" Kathy yelled. "She was shot in the head! I heard the explosions in my head!"

Detective Gionfriddo would have understood what had frightened and awakened Kathy. Filing his report after the initial investigation the night of the DeFeo murders, Gionfriddo had written that Louise, the mother of the family, had been shot in the head while sleeping on her stomach. Everyone else, including her husband who was lying right beside her, had been shot in the back while lying in the same position. This information had been included in the material turned over to the Suffolk County prosecution team, but never released to the news media. In fact, this detail had never come out, even at Ronnie DeFeo's trial.

Now, Kathy Lutz also knew how Louise DeFeo had died that night. She was in the very same bedroom.

George held his shaken wife in his arms until she had calmed down and fallen back to sleep. Then once again, the urge to check out the boathouse came over him, and George quietly slipped from the room.

He was almost upon Harry in his compound, when the dog awoke, springing to his feet. "Shhh, Harry. It's all right. Take it easy, boy."

The dog settled back on his haunches and watched George test the boathouse door. It was closed and locked. Once more he reached down and reassured Harry. "It's all right, boy. Go back to sleep." George turned and started back toward the house.

George circled around the swimming pool fence. The orb of the full moon was like a huge flashlight, lighting his way. He looked up at the house and stopped short. His heart leaped. From Missy's second floor bedroom window, George could see the little girl staring at him, her eyes following his movements. "Oh, God!" he whispered aloud. Directly behind his daughter, frighteningly visible to George, was the face of a pig! He was sure he could see little red eyes glaring at him!

"Missy!" he yelled. The sound of his own voice broke the grip of terror on his heart and body. George ran for the house. He pounded up the stairs to Missy's bedroom and turned on the light.

She was in bed, lying on her stomach. He went to her and bent over. "Missy?" There was no answer. She was fast asleep.

There was a creak behind him. He turned. Beside the window that looked out at the boathouse, Missy's little chair was slowly rocking back and forth!

Six hours later, at 9:30 in the morning, George and Kathy sat in the kitchen, drinking coffee, confused and upset with the events that were taking place in their new home. They had gone over some of the incidents each had witnessed, and now were trying to put together what was real and what they might have imagined. It was too much for them.

It was December 25, 1975, Christmas Day all over America. The promised white Christmas hadn't materialized as yet for Amityville, but it was cold enough to snow at any moment. Inside, their three children were in the living room, playing near the tree with what few toys George and Kathy had managed to accumulate before moving in eight days earlier.

George figured out that in the first week, he had burned over 100 gallons of oil and an entire cord of logs. Someone would have to go and buy more wood and a few groceries such as milk and bread.

He had told Kathy about trying to reach Father Mancuso on the telephone after the priest had warned him about their sewing room. Now Kathy dialed his number herself and got no answer. She reasoned that the priest might not be in his apartment because of the holiday and could be visiting his own family. Then she volunteered to go for the wood and food.

There was no question as to where Father Mancuso was on this Christmas Day. He was in the Long Island rectory, still suffering. It had not disappeared in the twenty-four hours forecast by the doctor, and his fever had not gone below 103 degrees.

The priest roamed his rooms like a caged lion. An energetic worker who loved the long hours he devoted to his calling, Father Mancuso refused to remain in bed. He had a briefcase full of files; those that he had to deal with as a family counsellor, and those of some of his parish clients. In spite of the Pastor's request that he rest, the priest would put in a full day on Christmas. Above all, Father Mancuso could not shake the uneasiness he felt about the Lutzes and their house.

George heard Kathy return from her shopping. He could tell she was backing the van in because of the grinding sound the snow tires made in the driveway. For some strange reason, the noise bothered him and he became annoyed with his wife.

He went out to meet her, took two logs from the van, put them into the fireplace, and then sat down in the living room, refusing to unload any more. Kathy fumed; George's attitude and appearance were getting on her nerves. Somehow she could sense they were heading for a fight, but she held her tongue for the moment. She took the bags of groceries from the van and left the remaining logs stacked inside. If George felt cold enough, Kathy knew, he'd go get them himself.

She and George had cautioned Danny, Chris, and Missy to stay out of the sewing room on the second floor, without giving them any reason. That made the children even more curious about what might lie hidden behind the now closed door.

"It could be more Christmas presents," Chris suggested.

Danny agreed, but Missy said, "I know why we have to keep out. Jodie's in there."

"Jodie? Who's Jodie?" asked Danny.

"He's my friend. He's a pig."

"Oh, you're such a baby, Missy. You're always making up dumb things," sneered Chris.

At six o'clock that evening, Kathy was preparing supper for her family when she heard the sounds of something tiny and delicate striking against the glass of her kitchen window. It was dark outside, but she could see it was snowing. White flakes were tumbling down through the reflection of the kitchen light, and Kathy stared at them as the rising wind whipped the snow against the pane. "Snow at last," she said.

Christmas and snow: it brought a reassuring sense of familiarity to the troubled woman. She recalled her own childhood days. There always seemed to be snow at Christmas time when she was young. Kathy kept looking at the little snowflakes. Outside, the multicolored lights from neighborhood Christmas trees gleamed through the night. Behind her, the radio was playing Christmas carols. She became peaceful in her happy kitchen nook.

After supper, George and Kathy sat silently in the living room. The Christmas tree was all lit up and George's tree-topping ornament made a beautiful addition to the decorations. Reluctantly he had gone out to the van and brought in more of the wood. There now were six logs in front of the blazing fireplace, just enough to last through the night at the rate George was shoveling them in.

Kathy worked on some of the children's clothes—patching the boys' trousers that were forever wearing through the knees, letting down a few of Missy's denim pants. The little girl was growing taller, and already the hems were above the tops of her shoes.

At nine o'clock, Kathy went up to the third floor playroom to get Missy ready for bed. She heard her daughter's voice coming from her bedroom. Missy was talking out loud, obviously speaking to someone else in the room. At first Kathy thought it was one of the boys, but then she heard Missy say: "Isn't the snow beautiful, Jodie?" When Kathy entered, her daughter was sitting in her little rocker by the window, staring at the falling snow outside. Kathy looked around the bedroom. There was no one there.

"Who're you talking to, Missy? An angel?"

Missy looked around at her mother. Then her eyes went back to a corner of the room. "No, Mama, just Jodie."

Kathy turned her head to follow Missy's glance. There was nothing there but some of Missy's toys on the floor. "*Jodie?* Is that one of your new dolls?"

"No. Jodie's a pig. He's my friend. Nobody can see him but me."

Kathy knew that Missy, like other children of her age, often created people and animals to talk to, so she assumed it was the child's imagination at work again. George had not yet told her of the incident in Missy's room the night before.

There was another surprise waiting for Kathy when she got to the top floor a few minutes later. Danny and Chris were already in their own bedroom, changing into their pajamas. Usually both boys fought to stay up past ten. This night, at nine-thirty, they were getting ready without being told. Kathy wondered why.

"What's the matter with you two? How come you're not arguing about going to sleep?"

Her sons shrugged, continuing to undress. "It's warmer in here, Mama," Danny said. "We don't want to play in there anymore."

When Kathy checked *in there*, she was struck by the freezing chill in the playroom. No windows were open, yet the room was ice cold. It certainly wasn't uncomfortable in Danny and Chris' bedroom, nor in the hallway. She felt the radiator. It was hot!

Kathy told George about the cold in the upstairs playroom. Too comfortable by the fireplace to want to move, he said he'd check it out in the morning. At midnight, Kathy and George finally went to bed.

The snow had stopped falling in Amityville, as it had fifteen miles away outside the windows of the Long Island rectory. Father Mancuso turned away from his window. His head hurt. His stomach pained from the flu cramps. The priest was perspiring, and the feeling of suffocating heat made him take off his bathrobe. When he did remove the robe, he began to shiver with a fit of uncontrollable chills.

Father Mancuso couldn't wait to get back into bed. It was cold under the blanket, and he realized he could see his breath in the air. "What the hell's going on?" he muttered to himself. The priest reached out to touch the radiator next to his bed. There was absolutely no heat.

The sick man now felt his body starting to sweat again. Father Mancuso burrowed deep under the blanket, curling up in a tight ball. He closed his eyes and began to pray.

8 December 26

One night—George doesn't remember exactly which—he woke again at 3:15 in the morning. He dressed and went out, and as he was wandering around in the freezing darkness, he wondered what in God's name he was looking for in the boathouse. Harry, their tough half-breed watchdog, didn't even wake up when George stumbled over some loose wire near Harry's compound.

When the Lutzes lived in Deer Park, Harry also had his own doghouse and slept outside in all kinds of weather. Normally he would remain awake, on guard, until two or three in the morning before finally settling down and going to sleep. Any unfamiliar noise would bring Harry to alert attention. Since they had moved to 112 Ocean Avenue, the dog was usually fast asleep whenever George went out to the boathouse. He would awake only when his master called to him.

George vividly remembers the day after Christmas, however, because that was the date set for Jimmy's wedding. It was also the beginning of a severe case of diarrhea he developed after checking out the boathouse. The pain was intense at first, almost as if a knife had pierced his stomach. George became frightened when he felt nausea rising in his throat. As soon as he re-entered the house, he made a dash for the bathroom on the first floor.

It was daylight outside when he settled back into bed. The abdominal cramps were intense, but finally he fell asleep out of sheer exhaustion. Kathy awoke a few moments later and immediately roused him to remind him of the wedding affair that evening. There would be a lot of arrangements to be handled before her brother came to pick them up. She would be busy with her clothes and hair. George groaned in his half-sleep.

Before going down to prepare breakfast for herself and the children, Kathy went up to the third floor to check the playroom. It was still cold inside when she opened the door, but not as icy as the day before. George might not like to move from his fire, but he would just have to in order to check the radiator. It was working all right, but there was no heat in the room. Certainly the children couldn't stay in there any length of time, and Kathy wanted them out of the way until it was time for them to dress for the wedding. She looked out of the window and saw the ground covered with slush from the melted snow. That settled it. The three would remain indoors today. She decided they would have to play in their own bedrooms.

After they were fed, Missy obediently started up to her own bedroom. Kathy warned her that she was not to go into the sewing room; that she was not even to open the door. "That's okay, Mama. Jodie wants to play in my room today."

"That's my good girl," Kathy smiled. "You go and play with your friend."

The boys wanted to play outside, arguing that this was *their* Christmas vacation from school. It was the way they persisted and answered her back that angered Kathy. Danny and Chris never questioned her requests before this, and she was becoming more aware that her two sons had also changed since they had been in the new house.

But Kathy was not yet aware of her own personality changes, her impatience and crankiness.

"That's enough out of both of you!" she yelled at her sons. "I see you're asking for another beating! Now shut your mouths and get up to your room like I said, and stay there until I call you! You hear me? Scat! Upstairs!"

Sullenly, Danny and Chris mounted the stairs to the third floor, passing George on his way down. He didn't acknowledge them. They didn't say good morning to him.

In the dinette, George took one sip of coffee, clutched his stomach, and headed back upstairs to his bathroom. "Don't forget you've got to shave and shower today!" Kathy yelled after him. Considering George's speed in running up the stairs she wasn't sure he had heard her.

Kathy returned to her breakfast nook. She had been making up a shopping list, checking items in the refrigerator and cabinets that had to be replaced. Food was again running low, and she knew she just had to get herself up and out of the house. She couldn't depend on George to do it. The big freezer in the basement, one of the free items they had received from the DeFeo estate, was clean and could be filled with meats and frozen foods. Her cleaning materials were almost exhausted, since she had been scrubbing the toilet bowls day after day. Most of the blackness was gone by now.

Kathy planned to go to an Amityville supermarket the next morning, Saturday. She wrote "orange juice" on her pad. Suddenly she became aware of a presence in the kitchen. In Kathy's current state of mind over the eroding situation of her family, the memory of the first touch on her hand flooded back, and she froze. Slowly, Kathy looked over her shoulder.

She could see the kitchen was empty—but at the same time, she sensed that the presence was closer, almost directly behind her chair! Her nostrils caught a sweetish scent of perfume, and she recognized it as the odor that had permeated her bedroom four days before.

Startled, Kathy could actually feel a body pressing against hers, clasping its arms around her waist. The pressure was light, however, and Kathy realized that as before, it was a woman's touch—almost reassuring. The unseen presence didn't give her a sense of danger—not at first.

Then the sweet smell became heavier. It seemed to swirl in the air, making Kathy dizzy. She started to gag, then tried to pull away from a grip that tightened as she struggled. Kathy thought she heard a whisper, and she recalls something deep within her warning her not to listen.

"No!" she shouted. "Leave me alone!" She struck out at the empty air. The embrace tightened, hesitated. Kathy felt a hand on her shoulder, making the same motions of motherly reassurance she had felt the first time in her kitchen.

Then it was gone! All that remained was the odor of the cheap perfume.

Kathy slumped back into her chair and closed her eyes. She began to cry. A hand touched her shoulder. Kathy jumped. "Oh, God, no! Not again!" She opened her eyes.

Missy was standing there, calmly patting her on the arm. "Don't cry, Mama." Then Missy turned her head to look back at the kitchen doorway.

Kathy looked too. But there was nothing there.

"Jodie says you shouldn't cry," Missy said. "He says everything will be all right soon."

At nine that morning, Father Mancuso had awakened in the Long Island rectory and taken his temperature. The thermometer had still read 103 degrees. But at eleven o'clock, the priest suddenly felt better. The cramps had disappeared from his stomach and his head felt clear for the first time in days. Hurriedly he slipped the thermometer back under his tongue: 98.6 degrees. His fever was gone!

Suddenly Father Mancuso felt hungry. He wanted to eat ravenously, but knew he should ease back into his normal diet. The priest made tea and toast in his kitchenette, his mind ticking off all the things that had been backlogged from his heavy work schedule. He forgot completely about George Lutz.

By the same time, eleven A.M., George Lutz had no thoughts for Father Mancuso, Kathy, or his brother-in-law's wedding. He had just made his tenth trip to the bathroom, his diarrhea unrelieved.

Jimmy's wedding and reception, an expensively catered affair for fifty couples was to be held at the Astoria Manor in Queens. George would have a lot to do at the hall, but right now he couldn't have cared less.

He dragged himself back down the stairs to his chair by the fireplace. Kathy came into the living room to tell him his office in Syosset had telephoned. The men wanted to know when George planned on coming in to work. There were surveying jobs that needed his supervision, and more and more of the building contractors were beginning to complain.

Kathy also wanted to tell him about the second eerie incident in the kitchen, but George waved her off. She knew it would be pointless to try and reach him. Then, from upstairs, she heard the noise of Danny and Chris fighting in their bedroom again, both boys screaming at each other.

She was about to shout up the staircase at them when George bolted past her, mounting the steps two at a time.

Kathy couldn't bring herself to go after her husband. She stood by the bottom of the stairs and listened to George's shouts. In a few minutes there was silence. Then the door to Danny and Chris' bedroom slammed and she heard George's footsteps coming back down. He stopped when he saw Kathy waiting. They looked at each other, but neither spoke. George turned and went back up to the second floor, slamming the door to his and Kathy's bedroom.

George came down a half-hour later. For the first time in nine days, he had shaved and showered. Dressed in clean clothes, he walked into the kitchen where Kathy was sitting with Missy. The little girl was eating lunch. "You get her and the boys ready by five," he said. Then George turned and walked out.

At five-thirty, Jimmy came to pick up his sister and his best man, and the children. They were due at the Astoria Manor by seven. From Amityville to Queens, the Sunrise Highway was the fastest way, and the trip to Astoria normally took an hour at most. The roads were reported to be icy from the recent light snow, however, and it was a Friday night. Traffic would be heavy and slow. Jimmy had played it safe by arriving early at the Lutzes'.

The young bridegroom looked resplendent in his military uniform, his bright face shining with happiness. His sister kissed him excitedly and invited him into the kitchen to wait while George finished dressing.

Jimmy took off his raincoat and then, from his coat pocket, proudly pulled out an envelope packed with fifteen hundred dollars in cash. He had paid out most of the money at the Manor some months before; this was the balance due. He said he had just withdrawn the money from his savings account and it just about wiped him out. Jimmy put the money back into the envelope and returned it to his raincoat pocket, leaving the coat on the kitchen chair beside him.

George came down, neatly clad in a tuxedo. His face was pale from the diarrhea, but he was freshly combed, his dark blonde beard framing his handsome face. The two men went into the living room. George had let the last of his fire burn itself out, and now he poked around the ashes looking for any leftover embers to tamp out.

The children were dressed and ready. Kathy went upstairs to get her coat. When she came down, Jimmy disappeared into the kitchen to get his raincoat. He returned a moment later, hoisting it over his shoulders. "Ready?" George asked.

"Ready as I'll ever be," Jimmy answered, automatically patting his side pocket to check on the envelope of money. His expression froze. He shoved his hand into the pocket, it came out empty! Jimmy searched the other pocket. Again, nothing. He tore off the raincoat, shaking it, then turned out every pocket in his uniform. The money was gone!

Jimmy ran back into the kitchen, Kathy and George following. The three looked all over the room, then began an inch by inch search of the foyer and living room. It was impossible, but Jimmy's fifteen hundred had completely disappeared!

Jimmy became frantic. "George, what am I going to do?"

His brother-in-law put his arm around the distraught Jimmy's shoulder. "Take it easy. The money must be around here somewhere." George moved Jimmy to the door. "Come on, we're running late now. I'll look again when I come back. It's here, don't worry."

Everything just welled up within Kathy and she let go, crying. As George looked at his wife, the lethargy that had gripped him over the past week fell away. He realized how hard he had been on Kathy; for the first time he wasn't thinking only of himself. Then, in spite of the calamity that had just befallen Jimmy, regardless of the weakness he still felt in his loins from the diarrhea, George wanted to make love to Kathy. He hadn't touched her since they had moved into 112 Ocean Avenue. "Come on, honey. Let's go." He gave his wife a pat on her behind. "I'll take care of everything."

George, Kathy and Jimmy got into Jimmy's car; the boys and Missy clambered into the back seat. After closing the door, George stepped out again. "Just a minute. I want to check Harry."

He crossed to the rear of the house. As he walked in the winter's darkness, George called out, "Harry! You keep your eyes open, you hear!"

There was no answering bark. George came up to the wire fence of the compound. "Harry? You there?"

By the reflection of a neighbor's light, he saw that Harry was in his doghouse. George unlatched the gate and entered the compound. "What's the matter, Harry, You sick?"

George bent down. He heard slow canine snoring. It was only six in the evening, and Harry was fast asleep!

9 **December 27** — The Lutzes returned home from the wedding at three A.M. It had been a very long night. It began with the mysterious disappearance of Jimmy's fifteen hundred dollars, and several other incidents during the evening hadn't added any particular joy to George's appreciation of the happy event.

Before the wedding ceremony, George, the other ushers, and the bridegroom had taken Communion in a little church near the Manor. During the ritual, George became violently nauseated. When Father Santini, the Pastor of Our Lady of Martyrs Roman Catholic Church, gave George the chalice of wine to drink, George started to sway dizzily in front of the priest. Jimmy reached out a hand to his brother-in-law, but George brushed it off and dashed toward the men's room at the rear of the church.

After he had thrown up and returned to the hotel, George told Kathy he had actually become queasy the moment he had entered Our Lady of Martyrs.

The reception ran fairly smoothly. There was plenty of the food, drinking, and dancing usually associated with an Irish wedding, and everyone seemed to be having a good time. George had to go to the bathroom only once, when he thought his diarrhea might be returning, but generally he wasn't too uncomfortable. Kathy's brother and his new bride, Carey, were leaving for their honeymoon in Bermuda directly from the Manor and would take a cab to LaGuardia Airport. George would be driving Kathy and the children back to Amityville in Jimmy's car, so he didn't drink too much.

Then came the unpleasant moment of settling up with the hall's catering manager. Jimmy, his new father-in-law, and George told the man of the unexpected loss of all the cash, but promised they would pay him his money out of their wedding gifts. Unfortunately, when the traditional "Congratulations are in order" was spoken, most of the envelopes left on the table in front of the bride and groom contained personal checks. The actual cash amounted to a little more than five hundred dollars.

The manager was upset, but after a few minutes of haggling, agreed to accept two checks from George for five hundred dollars each—one from his personal checking account, and the other drawn on George's surveying company's account in Syosset.

George knew he didn't have the five hundred in his personal checking account, but since the next two days were Saturday and Sunday, he would have time to cover the draft on Monday.

Jimmy's father-in-law quickly conferred with his relatives and scraped up enough cash for his new son-in-law to pay for the honeymoon. Luckily, the plane tickets were already paid for. The wedding party broke up around two, and the Lutzes headed back to 112 Ocean Avenue.

Kathy went up to bed immediately while George checked on the boathouse and the dog's compound. Harry was still asleep, stirring only slightly when George called his name. When he bent to pat the dog, George wondered if Harry was drugged, but then dismissed the thought. No, he was probably just sick. Must have eaten something he found in the yard. George straightened up. He'd have to take Harry to the vet.

The boathouse door was secure, so George returned to the house, locking the front door. As he went to the kitchen, he glanced down at the floor, hoping to spot the missing envelope of money. No luck.

The kitchen door and windows on the first floor were all locked. George climbed the stairs to his bedroom, thinking about his wife and their warm, soft bed. Passing the sewing room, he noticed the door was slightly ajar. He thought of the children. One of them must have opened it before they left the house. He'd ask them the next morning, when they woke up.

Kathy was sleepy, but waiting for him. During the evening she had gotten her husband's vibrations and was eager for his touch. George hadn't touched her since they had moved in. Usually they had made love once a night from the day they were married in July, but from December 18 to December 27, George hadn't made a move in her direction. But now the children were fast asleep, exhausted from their late evening. She watched George undress, and all the misgivings of the past few days melted from her mind.

He slipped under the heavy blanket. "Hey, this is wonderful!" George reached for Kathy's warmth. "Alone at last, as they say."

That night, Kathy had a dream of Louise DeFeo and a man making love in the very same room she was lying in. When she awoke in the morning, the vision remained with her. Somehow Kathy knew that the man was not Louise's husband. It was not until several weeks after she and her family had fled from 112 Ocean Avenue that she learned from an attorney close to the DeFeos that Louise actually did have a lover, an artist who lived with the family for a while. Mr. DeFeo must have known about the affair and informed the lawyer.

In the morning, Kathy took the van to go shopping in Amityville while George drove the children in Jimmy's car to pick up the mail at his office in Syosset. He even gave Harry a ride, telling his employees he would be in on Monday for sure.

They came home to find Kathy putting groceries into the kitchen refrigerator. She had also brought back a load for the basement freezer. Kathy bemoaned the fact that prices were higher in Amityville stores. "I thought they would be," George shrugged. "Amityville is more affluent than Deer Park."

By then it was after one o'clock. Though Kathy wanted to make lunch, she still had to transport the additional frozen foods and meat into her freezer in the basement. George volunteered to put together sandwiches for himself and the children.

While Kathy was in the basement, the front door bell rang. It was her Aunt Theresa. George had met the woman once before at his mother-in-law's, before he and Kathy were married. Theresa had been a nun at one time. Now she had three children, but George never did learn the exact reasons for her departure from her order.

Now the former nun stood in the doorway, a short, thin woman in her early thirties, plainly clad in a worn black wool winter coat and galoshes. Her face was tired but ruddy from the cold. The weather was bright and clear, the temperatures hovering in the low teens. Theresa told George she had taken the bus to Amityville and walked from the station.

George called down to Kathy that her aunt had come to visit. She said she'd be right up, and told George to show Aunt Theresa around her new home.

The children greeted their great-aunt silently. Theresa's grim face forestalled their natural inclination toward friendliness. Danny asked to go outside with Chris. "Okay," George agreed, "but you have to promise to stay within range of the house." Missy ran down the stairs to the basement. George noted how sad Theresa looked when the children didn't respond to her.

As he conducted Theresa around the first floor, pointing out the formal dining room and the huge living room, George became aware of a chill in the house—a clamminess he hadn't noticed until Aunt Theresa came. She agreed that it had seemed rather cold when she entered the house. George looked at the thermostat. It read 75 degrees, but George knew he'd have to kindle the fire again.

They went up to the second floor. Theresa glanced disapprovingly at the smoked mirrors behind George and Kathy's bed. He could read her thoughts—she believed that such a blatant display smacked of vulgarity —and wanted to tell her that the DeFeos had left the mirrors. But he decided to let the subject pass. The woman was still a nun at heart!

Theresa followed George to the other rooms. She admired all the new space they had, but when she and George stood outside the sewing room, Aunt Theresa hesitated. George opened the door for her. She backed up a few feet, her face turning pale.

"I won't go in there," she said, turning her back to him.

Had Theresa seen anything through the open door? George looked into the room. There were no flies, thank God, or Kathy's reputation for housecleaning would have suffered an irreparable blow! But George could feel the room was ice cold. He looked at Theresa. She was still standing implacably, her back to the room. He shut the door and suggested they try the top floor.

When it came time to examine the playroom, the former nun balked again. "No," she said, "that's another bad place. I don't like it."

Just as George and her Aunt came down, Kathy came up from the basement with Missy. The two women hugged each other, and Kathy, guiding her aunt toward the kitchen, said, "George, I'll finish up downstairs later. I want to transfer some of the canned goods into a closet I found down there. We can use it as a pantry." George went to the living room to build up his fire again.

Theresa hadn't been in the house for more than a half hour when she decided it was time to go. Having expected that her aunt would stay for supper, Kathy was disappointed. "George can drive you back," Kathy offered. But the older woman refused. "There's something bad in here, Kathy," she said, looking about. "I must go now."

"But Aunt Theresa, it's so very cold out." The woman shook her head. She stood up, pulled her heavy coat about her and was heading for the front door when Denny and Chris came in with another young boy.

The three children watched Theresa nod to George and kiss Kathy lightly on the cheek. As she strode out the door, Kathy and George looked at each other, at a loss for words at the woman's strange behavior. Finally Kathy noticed her sons and their playmate.

"This is Bobby, Mama," Chris said. "We just met him. He lives up the street."

"Hello, Bobby," Kathy smiled. The little dark-haired boy looked about Danny's age. Hesitantly, Bobby stuck out his right hand. Kathy shook it and introduced George. "This is Mr. Lutz."

George grinned at the boy, shaking his small hand. "Why don't you three all go upstairs and play?"

Bobby paused, his eyes darting about the foyer. "No. That's all right," he said. "I'd rather play down here."

"Here?" asked Kathy. "In the foyer?"

"Yes, m'am."

Kathy looked at George. Her eyes carried the unspoken question: What's wrong with this house that makes everybody so uncomfortable?

For the next half-hour, the three boys played on the foyer floor, with Danny's and Chris' Christmas toys. Bobby never took off his winter jacket. Kathy went back to the basement to finish making the closet into a pantry, and George returned to the living room fireplace. Then Bobby stood up and told Danny and Chris that he wanted to go home. That was the first and last time that the boy from up the street ever set foot in 112 Ocean Avenue.

The basement of the Lutzes' house was 43 by 28 feet. When George first looked it over, he came down the stairs and saw off to the right batten doors that led to the oil burner, hot water heater, and the freezer, washers, and dryers left from the DeFeo estate.

To his left, through another set of doors, was a playroom, 11 by 28 feet, beautifully finished in walnut paneling, with recessed fluorescent lights in a dropped ceiling. Directly in front of him was the area he planned to use as his office.

A small closet opened into the space beneath the stairs, and between the staircase and the right-hand wall, plywood panels formed an additional closet, extending out about seven feet, with shelving that ran from the ceiling to the floor. This walk-in area, George thought, made good use of what would otherwise be wasted space, and its proximity to the kitchen stairs made it a most convenient pantry.

Kathy was working in these closets. When she stacked some large, heavy canned goods against the closet's wall, one of the shelves cracked. One side of the plywood paneling on the rear wall seemed to give a little. She moved the cans aside and pushed against the panel. It moved farther away from the shelving.

The closet was lit by a single bulb, hanging from the ceiling. The bulb's reflection shone through a small slit opening just enough to give Kathy the impression that there was an empty space behind the closet, under the tallest section of the stairs. She went out to the basement and called George to come down.

He looked at the opening and pushed against the paneling. The wall continued to give a little more. "There isn't supposed to be anything back there," he said to Kathy.

George removed the four wooden shelves, then shoved hard against the plywood. It swung all the way open. It was a secret door!

The room was small, about four by five feet. Kathy gasped. From the ceiling to floor, it was painted solid red. "What *is* it, George?"

"I don't know," he answered, feeling the three solid concrete block walls. "It seems to be an extra room, maybe a bomb shelter. Everyone was building them back in the late fifties, but it sure doesn't show up in the house plans the broker gave us."

"Do you think the DeFeos built it?" Kathy asked, holding nervously onto George's arm.

"I don't know that either. I guess so," he said, steering Kathy out of the secret room. "I wonder what it was used for." He pulled the panel closed.

"Do you thing there are any more rooms like that behind the closets?" Kathy asked.

"I don't know, Kathy," George answered. "I'll have to check out each wall."

"Did you notice the funny smell in there?"

"Yeah, I smelled it," George said. "That's how blood smells."

She took a deep breath. "George, I'm worried about this house. A lot's happening that I don't understand." George saw Kathy put her fingers in her mouth, a sign she was scared. Little Missy always did the same thing

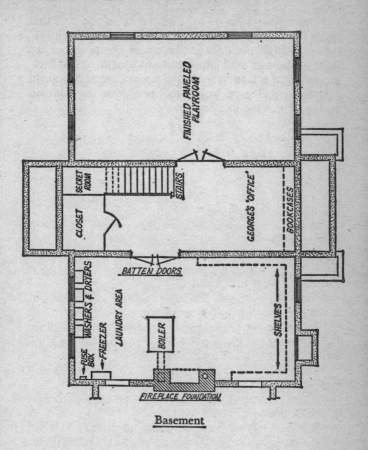

Basement

when she was frightened. George patted his wife on the head.

"Don't worry, baby. I'll find out what the hell that room is all about. But we *can* use it as an extra pantry!" He turned out the light in the closet, shutting out the sight of the rear wall panel, but not obscuring the fleeting vision of a face he glimpsed against the plywood. In a few days, George would realize it was the bearded visage of Ronnie DeFeo!

10 December 28 — On Sunday, Father Frank Mancuso returned to the Long Island rectory after celebrating Mass in the church. It was only several yards from one building to the other, but the priest felt his recent weakness as he walked in the cold air.

In the Rectory's reception room there was a visitor waiting for him—Sergeant Gionfriddo of the Suffolk County Police Department. The two men shook hands, and Father Mancuso led Gionfriddo to his quarters on the second floor. "I'm glad you called me," the priest said, "and I appreciate that you came."

"That's all right, Father. It's my day off this week." The big detective looked over the priest's apartment. The living room was filled with books that overflowed the bookcases onto tables and chairs. He took a stack off the couch and sat down.

Father Mancuso wanted to warm up and he had no liquor in his rooms to offer the policeman, so instead he made some tea. While it brewed, he got right to the point of his request for Gionfriddo's visit.

"As you know," he began, "I'm concerned about the Lutzes. That's why I asked Charlie Guarino to contact somebody in Amityville to check if they were all right." The priest walked into his kitchenette to get some cups and saucers. "Charlie reminded me that they're living in the house where that unfortunate DeFeo family was slain. I'd heard about the case from some friends of mine, but I don't really know how it happened."

"I was on that case, Father," the detective interrupted.

"So Charlie told me when he called back the other night." Father Mancuso brought the tea and sat down across from Gionfriddo. "Anyway, I had a hard time falling asleep last night. I don't know why, but I kept thinking about the DeFeos."

He looked up at Gionfriddo, trying to read the expression on his face. It was difficult, even though Father Mancuso had years of experience in probing people for facts, fancied or real; from his clients in family counselling who came before him. He didn't know whether to reveal what had happened to him on the first day in 112 Ocean Avenue or on the telephone to George.

Gionfriddo quickly read the priest's thoughts and solved the problem. "You think there's something funny going on in that house, Father?"

"I don't know. That's what I wanted to ask you."

The detective put down his cup of tea. "What is it you're looking for? A haunted house? You want me to tell you there's something spooky about the place?"

The priest shook his head. "No, but it'll help me if

you can tell me what happened the night of the murders. I understand the boy said he heard voices."

Gionfriddo looked into a pair of piercing eyes and saw the priest was troubled. He cleared his throat and put on his official voice. "Well, basically, the story is that Ronald DeFeo drugged his family at dinner on November 13, 1974, and then shot them all with a high-powered rifle while they were out cold. At his trial, he did claim a voice told him to do it."

Father Mancuso waited for more details, but Gionfriddo had finished his report. "That's it?" the priest asked.

Gionfriddo nodded. "Like I said, that's it, basically."

"It must have awakened the whole neighborhood?" Father Mancuso continued.

"No. Nobody heard the shots. We found out about it later when Ronnie went into The Witches' Brew and told the bartender. The Witches' Brew is a bar near Ocean Avenue. The kid was stoned out of his head."

Father Mancuso was confused. "You mean he used a high-powered rifle to kill six people, and no one heard all that noise?"

Gionfriddo thinks it was just about then that he began to feel nauseous in the priest's apartment. He felt he had to leave. "That's right. People in houses on both sides of the DeFeos said they never heard a thing that night." Gionfriddo stood up.

"Isn't that rather peculiar?"

"Yeah, I thought so myself," the detective said, slipping on his overcoat. "But you got to remember, Father, it was the middle of winter. A lot of people sleep with their windows shut tight. At 3:15 in the morning, they're dead to the world."

Sergeant Al Gionfriddo knew the priest had more questions, but he didn't care. He had to get out of there. No sooner was he outside the Rectory than he threw up.

By the time he returned to Amityville, Gionfriddo

felt the uneasiness passing. At first he thought of driving past 112 Ocean Avenue, but changed his mind. Instead he headed home, rolling up Amityville Road. He drove past The Witches' Brew on his right.

The Witches' Brew was a hangout for a lot of the kids in town, especially during the season when Amityville was filled with summer-house renters. But now, on a December Sunday afternoon, Amityville Road, the main shopping street in town, was empty. The pro-football playoffs were on television and the regulars were at home, glued to their sets.

As he rode by, Gionfriddo didn't really notice the figure going into The Witches' Brew. The detective was a good fifty feet beyond before he swerved his police car and braked to a stop. He looked back, but the man was gone. The shape of the body, the beard, and the swaggering walk were the same as Ronnie DeFeo's!

Gionfriddo continued to stare at the doorway to the club. "Agh! I'm getting jumpy," he muttered. "Who needs that priest?" The detective turned around, jerked the gear shift into drive and pulled away from the curb, burning rubber like a hot rodder.

Inside The Witches' Brew, George Lutz ordered his first beer. He wondered why the bartender stared at him when he sat down at the bar. The man opened a bottle of Miller's and was pouring it when he stopped. He looked as though he was about to say something to George, but then went ahead pouring the beer.

George looked around him. The Witches' Brew could have been any one of a number of bars George had seen in his travels as a Marine corporal and as a surveyor working the small towns and villages of Long Island: dimly lit, the usual garish juke box, the smell of stale beer and smoke. There was just one other customer in the place, down at the very end of the long mahogany bar, absorbed by watching a television set above the bar mirror as an announcer described the first-half action of the football game.

George sniffed, took a gulp of his beer and looked at himself in the mirror behind the bar. He'd had to get out of the house for a while, be by himself. He couldn't get a handle on what was happening to his family. The little bits and pieces that he would recognize later on were still too isolated for him.

George couldn't understand what was wrong with the children since they moved into the new house. In his eyes, they were wild, unmannered. That had never been the case before, not when they lived in Deer Park.

He thought Missy was acting strangely. Did he really see a pig in her window the other night? And where was Jimmy's money? How could it simply disappear in front of them?

George finished his beer and signaled for another. His eyes returned to his image in the mirror. He recalled now, earlier that week, he'd been sitting like a dummy in front of the fireplace, then standing and staring in the boathouse. Why? And now this business with that red room in the basement. What the hell was that all about? Well, tomorrow he'd begin to dig into the background of his house. The first place to do that would be the Amityville Real Estate Tax Assessment Office, where he could look at the record of improvements that applied to the property at 112 Ocean Avenue.

"Yeah," he muttered to himself, "and I got to get to the bank and cover that check. Can't let that bounce." George drank down the last of his second beer. At first he didn't notice the bartender standing in front of him. Then he looked up and saw the man waiting. George covered his glass with his hand to signal that he didn't want another.

"Excuse me, mister," said the bartender. "You passing through?"

"No," answered George. "I live here in Amityville. We just moved in."

The bartender nodded. "Well, you are a dead ringer for a young feller from around here. For a moment I thought you was him." He rang up George's money. "He's away now. Won't be back for a while." He put the change on the bar. "Maybe never."

George took the money and shrugged. People were always mistaking him for someone else they knew. Maybe it was the beard. A lot of guys wore them these days. "Well, see you around." He headed for the entrance to The Witches' Brew.

The bartender nodded again. "Yeah, drop in again."

George was at the door. "Hey!" asked the bartender. "By the way, where'd you move into?"

George stopped, looked back, and pointed toward the general direction of the west. "Oh, just a couple of streets from here. On Ocean."

The bartender felt George's used beer glass slipping from his hand. When he heard George's final remark, "112 Ocean Avenue," it dropped from his hand and crashed on the floor.

Kathy was waiting for George to come home. She sat in the living room by the Christmas tree, not wanting to be in the kitchen nook by herself for fear of meeting up with that invisible something that reeked of perfume. The children were up in the boys' bedroom, watching television. They had been quiet most of the afternoon, absorbed in an old movie. By the delighted laughter that drifted down to her, Kathy was sure it was Abbott and Costello.

Now she was trying to concentrate on where Jimmy's money could be. Again Kathy and George had gone over every square inch of the kitchen, foyer, living and dining rooms, and closets looking for the envelope. It *couldn't* just have vanished into thin air! No one could have possibly been in the house to take it. Where the devil could it have gone?

Kathy thought about the presence in the kitchen and shuddered. She forced her mind to think of other rooms in the house. The sewing room? The red room in the basement? She began to get out of her chair, then stopped. Kathy was afraid to go down there alone now. Anyway, she thought, sitting back down, she and George hadn't seen anything but the red paint when they were in there.

She looked at her watch. It was almost four o'clock. Where was George? He had been gone over an hour. Then, out of the corner of her right eye, she saw movement.

One of Kathy's first Christmas gifts to George had been a huge, four-foot ceramic lion, crouched, ready to leap upon an unseen victim, and painted in realistic colors. George had thought it a pretty piece and had moved it to the living room, where it now sat on a large table beside his chair near the fireplace.

When Kathy turned and looked fully at the sculpture, she was sure she had seen it move a few inches closer toward her!

After Sergeant Gionfriddo left Father Mancuso's apartment that afternoon, the priest became angry with himself. He hated the way he was handling the Lutz situation and resolved to break his obsession with the whole affair. For the next several hours he dove into issues that were coming up in Court the following week, poring over caseloads that had piled up.

Realizing he had important decisions to make that would affect people's lives, he now cleared his mind of abstractions like Gionfriddo's unsatisfactory explanation of the DeFeo murders and the doubts he had about the Lutzes' safety in that house. As he worked, he slowly became aware that he was regaining his strength. The weakness he had felt in the wintry air was gone. It was now after six, he was hungry, and he reminded himself that he hadn't had anything to eat or drink since that cup of tea with Gionfriddo.

Father Mancuso put down a file, stretched his body, and went into the kitchenette. In the living room, the telephone rang. It was his private number. He picked it up and said "Hello?" There was no answer, only static crackling from the receiver.

The priest felt a chill run through his frame. As he held the telephone in his hand, he began to perspire, recalling his last call with George Lutz.

George was listening to the sharp, snapping pops on his own telephone. It had rung while he was in the kitchen with Kathy and the children.

Finally, after no one answered his repeated hellos, George slammed the receiver back on the hook.

"How do you like that? Some wise guy's on the other end playing games!"

Kathy looked up at her husband. They were eating supper, George had shown up just a few moments before. He told her he had taken a very long walk around the town and he was convinced the street they lived on in Amityville was the nicest.

Kathy thought George looked better for having gotten out of the house. She felt foolish about wanting to mention the lion and forgot the incident now that George was upset again. "What happened?" she asked.

"There was no one on the other end, that's what happened. It was just a lot of static." He started to sit down again at the table.

"You know, it was just like the other time when I tried to talk to Father Mancuso. I wonder if he's trying to reach us?" George went back to the telephone and dialed the priest's private number.

He waited until it had rung ten times. There was no answer. George looked at the electric clock over the kitchen sink. It was exactly seven. He shivered a little. "Don't you think it's getting chilly in here again, Kathy?"

Father Mancuso had just taken his temperature. It was up to 102 degrees. "Oh, no," he moaned, "not that again!" He began to take his pulse, holding a finger on his wrist. The priest started to count when the big hand of his watch was exactly on twelve. He noted it was seven o'clock.

In one minute's time, his heart beat one hundred and twenty times! Normally Father Mancuso's pulse ran about 80 beats per minute. He knew he was going to be sick again.

George left the kitchen for the living room. "I'd better put some more wood into the fireplace," he told Kathy.

She watched her husband shamble out of the kitchen. Kathy began to get that depressed feeling again. Then she heard a loud crash from the living room. It was George!

"Who the hell left this goddamned lion on the floor? It almost killed me!"

11 **December 29 to 30** — The next morning, Monday, George's ankle was stiff. He had taken a nasty tumble over the porcelain lion and fallen heavily against some of the logs by the fireplace. He also had a cut over his right eye, but it hadn't bled much after Kathy put a Band-Aid on it. What disturbed Kathy was the clear imprint of teethmarks on his ankle!

George limped out to his 1974 Ford van and had trouble turning over the cold motor. With temperatures in the low twenties, George knew he could anticipate ignition problems. But finally he got the van going and headed across the Island toward Syosset. His first order of business was to cover the check he had written to the Astoria Manor. That meant drawing funds from the

89

account of William H. Parry, Inc., his land surveying business.

Halfway to Syosset, on the Sunrise Highway, George felt a bump in the back of the van. He pulled over and inspected the rear end. One of the shock absorbers had come loose and fallen off. George was puzzled. This was a mishap that might occur after the shocks were old and worn, if then, but the Ford had gone only 26,000 miles. He drove on again intending to replace the part once he returned to Amityville.

After George drove off that morning, Kathy's mother called to tell her that she had received a card from Jimmy and Carey in Bermuda. "Why don't you bring the children over to my house for a while?" Jimmy's car was still in the driveway, but Kathy didn't feel like leaving home. She said she still had a load of laundry to do, but that she and George might come over New Year's Eve. They had made no plans as yet, and she would ask George when he came back.

Kathy hung up and looked around, feeling at a loss as to what she should do next. The depressed feeling from the day before was still with her, and she was afraid to remain alone in the kitchen or go down to the washing machines in the basement. After the ceramic lion incident, Kathy also hesitated about going into the living room. She finally wound up going upstairs to be near the children. With them, she thought, she wouldn't feel so alone and frightened.

Kathy looked in on Missy in her bedroom and Danny and Chris in theirs before going into her own room and lying down. She had been on the bed, dozing, for about fifteen minutes, when she began to hear noises coming from the sewing room across the hall. It sounded as if someone was opening and closing a window.

Kathy got off the bed and went to the sewing room door. It was still shut. She could see that Missy was in her own bedroom and she could hear the boys running around on the floor above.

She listened. Behind the closed door, the sounds continued. Kathy stared at the door, but did not dare open it. She turned around and went back to her bedroom and got back on the bed, pulling the cover up over her head.

In Syosset, George found a caller waiting for him. The man introduced himself as an inspector from the Internal Revenue Service and explained he was there to examine the company's books and past tax returns. George called his accountant. The IRS agent spoke with him and made an appointment to return on January 7th.

After the agent left, George got on with his priorities: withdrawing five hundred dollars from the William H. Parry, Inc., account and depositing it in his personal checking account; going over the plans that had been completed for several land surveys; deciding how to handle the few assignments that had come into the office since he had been away; and then doing some research into the DeFeo family and the background of 112 Ocean Avenue.

When the men on his staff asked him why he'd been out so long, George told them only that he had been sick. He knew that was untrue, but what other explanation would make any sense? By one o'clock, George had completed his duties in Syosset. He planned to make one more stop before heading back to Amityville.

Long Island's largest daily newspaper, in pages of advertising and circulation, is *Newsday*. George reasoned that if there was any place where he could learn some facts about the DeFeos, *Newsday*'s Garden City office would be the most logical starting point.

He was referred to the microfilm department, where a clerk checked the cross-index files for the dates of the DeFeo murders and Ronnie's trial. George only vaguely recalled the details of the way the son had slaughtered the whole family, but he did remember that the trial had been held in Riverhead, Long Island, sometime in the fall of 1975.

George put the microfilm of the newspaper into the reader and ran it down until he came to November 14, 1974. One of the first items he noticed was a photograph taken of Ronnie DeFeo at the time of his arrest, the morning after the discovery of his family's bodies at 112 Ocean Avenue. The bearded twenty-four-year-old face staring back at him from the picture could have been his own! He was about to read on, when it hit George that this *was* the face he had seen fleetingly on the closet wall in his basement!

The first articles told how Ronnie had run into a bar near his home, calling for help, saying that someone had killed his parents, brothers, and sisters. With two friends, Ronald DeFeo returned to his house where they found Ronald, Sr., 43; Louise, 42; Allison, 13; Dawn, 18; Mark, 11; and John, 9. All were in their beds, all shot in the back.

The story continued that at the time of DeFeo's arrest the following morning, Amityville police said that the motives for the murders were a $200,000 life insurance policy and a strongbox filled with cash hidden in his parents' bedroom closet.

The last item explained that when the prosecution was ready, the trial would be held in the State Supreme Court at Riverhead.

George inserted another microfilm reel, this one containing the day-by-day record of the seven-week trial held from September through November. The record included charges of police brutality in forcing a confession from Ronnie DeFeo, and went on to attorney William Weber's parading psychiatrists to the stand to substantiate his plea of Ronnie's insanity. However, the jury found the youth sane and guilty of murder. Imposing a sentence of six *consecutive* life terms, State Supreme Court Justice Thomas Salk called the killings the "most heinous and abhorrent crimes."

George left the *Newsday* offices, thinking of the Coroner's report that pinpointed the time of the DeFeos' deaths at about 3:15 in the morning. That was the exact moment George had been waking since they'd been in the house! He would have to tell Kathy.

George also wondered if the DeFeos had used the red room in the basement as a secret hideaway for their money. As he drove back to Amityville, George was so absorbed in thought that he never noticed or heard his left tire wobbling.

As he stopped for a red light on Route 110, another car pulled alongside. The driver leaned over and opened his window on the right side. He tooted his horn to catch George's attention, then yelled that George's wheel was coming off!

George got out and examined the wheel. All the bolts were loose. George could feel them turn easily in his fingers. With his windows closed he had dimly heard the racket, but being wrapped up in his thoughts, he just never considered it was coming from his car.

What the devil was going on? First the shock absorber had fallen off, now this. Was someone fooling around with the van? He or Kathy could be killed if the wheel came off while driving at any speed.

George became even angrier and more frustrated when he looked for the jack handle in the rear of the van. It was gone! He'd have to tighten the bolts by hand until he could get to a service station. By then it would be too late to do any further checking on the background of 112 Ocean Avenue.

On Tuesday Father Mancuso could no longer ignore the redness in the palms of his hands, nor the excruciating pain he felt when he touched the sore spots. Even though the doctor had given him antibiotic injections, he had been unable to shake off this second flu attack. His temperature remained high, and every ache and pain in his body seemed intensified and magnified a hundred-fold.

The day before, Monday, Father Mancuso had accepted the redness that developed in his palms as just another manifestation of his illness. When the peculiar coloring and extreme sensitivity remained and it became painful to pick up anything with his hands, Father Mancuso started to become a great deal more concerned.

The next day, the Amityville Historical Society had some interesting information for George, particularly about the very location of his house. It seems the Shinnecock Indians used land on the Amityville River as an enclosure for the sick, mad, and dying. These unfortunates were penned up until they died of exposure. However, the record noted that the Shinnecocks did not use this tract as a consecrated burial mound because they believed it to be infested with demons.

For how many uncounted centuries the Shinnecocks carried on in this manner, no one really knows; but in the late 1600's, white settlers eased the first Americans out of the area, sending them farther out on Long Island. To this day, Shinnecocks still own land, property, and businesses on the eastern tip of the Island.

One of the more notorious settlers who came to the newly-named Amityville in those days was a John Catchum or Ketcham who had been forced out of Salem, Massachusetts, for practicing witchcraft. John set up residence within 500 feet of where George now lived, continuing his alleged devil worship. The account also claimed he was buried somewhere on the northeast corner of the property.

From the Real Estate Tax Assessment Office in town, George learned that the house at 112 Ocean Avenue had been built in 1928 by a Mr. Monaghan. It passed through several families until 1965, when the DeFeos purchased it from the Rileys. But in spite of all he had read in the past two days, George was no closer to a solution of what the mysterious red room was used for or who built it. There was no record of any improvements being made to the house that resembled the addition of a basement room.

It was the night before New Year's Eve. The Lutzes went to bed early. George had checked the sewing room for Kathy, as he had done the night before after returning from *Newsday*. Both evenings the windows had been shut and locked.

Earlier they had discussed what George had discovered about the history of their property and house. "George," Kathy asked nervously, "do you think it's haunted?"

"No way," he replied. "I don't believe in ghosts. Besides, everything that's happened around here must have a logical and scientific explanation to it."

"I'm not so sure. What about the lion?"

"What about it?" he asked.

Kathy looked around the kitchen where they were sitting. "Well, what about what I felt those two times? I told you I *know* somebody touched me, George."

George stood up, stretching. "Oh, come on, honey, I think it's just your imagination." He reached for her hand. "I've had that happen to me too, when I was sure my father had put his hand on my shoulder in the office." He pulled Kathy out of her chair. "I was positive he was standing right beside me. It happens to a lot of people, but it's, it's—I think they call it clairvoyance, or something like that."

The couple had their arms around each other's waists as George turned out the light in the kitchen. They passed the living room on the way to the stairs. Kathy stopped. She could see the crouching lion in the darkness of the room.

"George. I think we should continue with our meditation. Let's do it tomorrow, okay?"

"You think that way we can find a logical explanation for all that's happened?" he asked, drawing her upstairs.

There was no logical or scientific explanation for Father Frank Mancuso as he prepared to go to bed. He had just prayed in his own rooms, searching and hoping for an answer to the question of why his palms were itching so terribly.

12 **December 31** — The year 1976 was just around the corner. The last day of the old year dawned on a heavy snowfall, and to many people that was the signal that a fresh, clean start would usher in the new.

In the Lutz household, there was a completely different mood. George hadn't slept well, even though he had been active enough for the past two days, inside and outside the house. He awoke during the night, looked at his watch and was surprised to find it was 2:30 A.M., not 3:15, as he anticipated.

George awoke again at 4:30 A.M., saw it was beginning to snow, and tried to fall back to sleep under the warm covers. But, tossing and turning, he couldn't find a comfortable position. In her sleep, Kathy was bothered by his restlessness and rolled over against George so that he was pushed to the edge of the bed. Wide awake, he kept having visions of discovering secret caches of money around the house and using them to solve all his financial problems.

George was beginning to choke with the pressures of mounting bills; for the house he had just taken on, and for the office, where he would shortly have a very serious payroll deficit. All the cash that he and Kathy had saved had gone toward the expense of the closing, an old fuel bill, and paying off the boats and motorcycles. And now the latest blow—the investigation of his books and tax returns by the Internal Revenue Service. Small wonder that George dreamed of a simple magical solution to the bind he was in.

He wished he could find Jimmy's money. The fifteen hundred would be a lifesaver. George stared at the falling snow. He had read in the newspaper account that Mr. DeFeo had been extremely well off, with a big bank account and with a very good position working for his wife's father in a big car dealership.

George had examined his bedroom closet and discovered Mr. DeFeo's secret hiding place under the door jamb. The police had found it first at the time of Ronnie's arrest and now it was empty, just a hole in the floor. He kept wondering where else the DeFeos could have stashed away some of their cash.

The boathouse! George sat up in bed. Maybe there was a meaning behind his being drawn there every night. Was some—some *thing* dragging him there? Was the dead man somehow urging him to look in there for his fortune? George was desperate, he knew, even to contemplate such a screwy idea. But why else *would* he be driven to the boathouse, night after night?

At six-thirty, George finally gave up and got out of bed. He knew he would never fall asleep again that morning, so he quietly slipped from the room, went down to the kitchen, and made some coffee.

It was still dark outside at that hour, but he could see the snow was beginning to pile up near the kitchen door. He saw a light on the ground floor of his neighbor. Maybe the owner also had money problems and couldn't sleep, he thought.

George knew he wouldn't go to the office that day. It was New Year's Eve and everybody would be leaving early anyway. He drank his coffee and planned to search the boathouse and basement for some clues. Then George began to feel a chill in the house.

The thermostat automatically dropped the temperature between midnight and six in the morning. But now it was almost seven and the heat didn't seem to be on. George went into the living room and put some kindling and paper into the fireplace. Before the wood blazed up, George noticed that the brick wall was black from all the soot accumulated from his almost constant fires.

A little after eight, Kathy came down with Missy. The little girl had awakened her mother with delighted squeals. "Oh, Mama, look at all the snow! Isn't it beautiful! I want to go outside and play with my sled today!"

Kathy made her daughter breakfast, but couldn't eat anything herself. She had coffee and a cigarette. George didn't want any food and took only another cup of coffee. He had to get it from the kitchen himself because Kathy didn't want to come into the living room. She told George she had a bad headache. Kathy was frightened of the porcelain lion and planned to get rid of it before the day was out. But it was true that she did have a sick headache.

By nine o'clock, George had built the living room fire to a roaring blaze. At ten o'clock, the snow was still falling. Kathy called out to George from the kitchen that a local radio station had predicted the Amityville River would be completely frozen by nightfall.

Reluctantly, George got up from his chair by the fireplace and dressed, put on his boots, and went out to the boathouse. He hadn't had the money to take the cabin cruiser out of the water for the winter. If the river froze, ice would eventually crush the boat, but he had prepared for just this kind of emergency.

George's mother had given him her paint compressor and he had drilled holes in its plastic hose. Now he sank the hose in the water beside the boat and turned on the compressor. It acted as a bubbler system that would keep the water inside the boathouse from freezing.

All that morning, Father Mancuso had been looking at his hands, which had begun to fester the night before. They were now dry, but angry red blisters remained.

His fever also held at a high of 103°. When the Pastor had looked in on him, Father Mancuso had promised to remain in bed for the rest of the day. The priest did not mention what had been happening to his hands. He kept them in the pockets of his bathrobe.

When the Pastor left his rooms, Father Mancuso stared at the ugly manifestation on his skin, and he became angry. All this suffering for just one appearance in an inconsequential house in Amityville? The priest was prepared to give himself in any way that God demanded, but at least, he thought, let it be to help humanity. With all his training, devotion, experience and skill, certainly there had to be some rational explanation he could apply to the enigma. At the moment he couldn't, and that accounted for his rage.

Along with his anger, the pains in his palms increased. He decided to pray for relief. And as Father Mancuso asked for help, his concentration on his misfortune decreased. The numbness in his tightly gripped hands slowly diminished in its pressure. He spread his fingers and stared at the blisters. The priest sighed and knelt to thank God.

Later in the afternoon was the second time Danny and Chris threatened to run away from home. The first had been when they lived in George's house at Deer Park. He had restricted them to their room for a week, because they were lying to him and Kathy about small things. They had revolted against his authority: Both boys refused to obey his orders, threatening to run away if he also forced them to give up television. At that point, George called their bluff, telling Danny and Chris that they could get out if they didn't like the way he ran things at home.

The two youngsters had taken him at his word. They packed all their belongings—toys, clothes, records, and magazines—into bed rolls and dragged the big bundles out the front door. When they were about halfway down the street, desperately trying to move the heavy load, a neighbor spotted them and talked them both into going back. For a while, they stopped their childish fibbing, but now there had come a new eruption.

When she heard them fighting, Kathy had gone up to their room and found the boys on one of the beds. Chris was straddling Danny's chest, ready to clobber his older brother. On the other bed sat Missy, a broad grin on her little face. She was clapping her hands with excitement.

Kathy pulled her sons apart. "What do you think you're doing?" she screamed. "What's the matter with you two? Are you going crazy?"

Missy chimed in, "Danny didn't want to clean up the room like you told him to."

Kathy looked sternly at the boy. "And why not, young man? Do you see what this room looks like?"

The room *was* a mess. Toys were scattered all over the floor, intermingled with discarded clothes. The tubes of an old paint set had been left uncapped, the pigments oozing onto the furniture and rug. Some of their new Christmas toys had already been broken and were discarded in corners of the bedroom. Kathy shook her head. "I don't know what I'm going to do with you. We bought this beautiful house so you'd have your own playroom, and look at what you've done!"

Danny tore himself loose from his mother's grip. "You don't want us to stay in that dumb old playroom!"

"Yeah!" Chris chimed in. "We don't like it around here. There's nobody to play with!"

Kathy and the boys bickered back and forth for another five minutes until Danny threw down the gauntlet and challenged his mother with the threat of running away from home. Kathy, in turn, suggested corporal punishment for their behavior. "And you know who dishes it out around here!"

By dinner time, the Lutz family had settled down. The boys had cooled off, though Kathy could still feel an undercurrent of tension at the table. George had told Kathy he preferred staying home this New Year's Eve rather than facing drunks on the road home from her mother's house. They had made no plans to be with their friends, and it was too cold to go out to a movie.

After they had eaten, Kathy convinced George to move the ceramic lion back up to the sewing room. Again there were some flies clinging to the window pane facing the Amityville River. George angrily swatted them to death before slamming the door shut.

By ten o'clock, Missy had fallen asleep on the living room floor. She had exacted a promise from Kathy to awaken her at midnight in time to blow her party horn. Danny and Chris were still up, playing near the Christmas tree and watching television. George was attending to his fire. Kathy sat across from him, trying to lose her depression by looking at an old movie with the boys.

As the night wore on, Father Mancuso's hands had been acting up again. Now the blisters were worse, breaking out on the backs of his hands. He couldn't put up with the thought of spending the entire night in pain and fright. When his doctor looked in on him, he suddenly shoved his palms out and said, "Look!"

Gently the physician examined the blisters. "Frank, I'm not a dermatologist," he said. "This could be anything from an allergy to an attack of anxiety. Has something been bothering you that badly?"

Father Mancuso turned sadly away from the doctor, his eyes staring out the window at the snow. "I think so. Something. . .". The priest brought his gaze back to the doctor ". . . or somebody."

The doctor assured the priest that he'd have some relief by the morning. Then he left for a New Year's Eve party.

On television, Guy Lombardo saluted the New Year from the Waldorf-Astoria Hotel. The Lutzes watched the ball fall from the Allied Chemical Building in Times Square, but did not share the countdown with announcer Ben Grauer while he tolled off the last ten seconds of 1975.

Danny and Chris had gone up to their room about a half hour earlier, their eyes red from too much television and the smoke from George's fire. Kathy had put Missy into her bed and then come back downstairs to her chair across from George.

It was now exactly one minute after twelve. She stared into the fireplace, hypnotized by the dancing flames. Something was materializing in those flames—a white outline against the blackened bricks—becoming clearer, more distinct.

Kathy tried to open her mouth to say something to her husband. She couldn't. She couldn't even tear her eyes away from the demon with horns and a white peaked hood on its head. It was getting larger, looming toward her. She saw that half of its face was blown away, as if hit with a shotgun blast at close range. Kathy screamed.

George looked up. "What's the matter?" he said.

All Kathy could do was to point into the fireplace. George followed her gaze and he saw it too—a white figure that had burned itself into the soot against the rear bricks of the fireplace.

13 **January 1, 1976** — George and Kathy finally went to bed at one in the morning. They had been sleeping for what later seemed to them no more than five minutes when they were awakened by a howling wind roaring through their bedroom.

The blankets on the bed had been virtually torn from their bodies, leaving George and Kathy shivering. All the windows in the room were wide open, and the bedroom door, caught by the drafts, was swinging back and forth.

George leaped from the bed and ran to close the windows. Kathy gathered the blankets off the floor and threw them back onto the bed. Both were breathless from their sudden awakening, and even though the door to their room had slammed shut, they could still hear the wind blowing out in the second floor hallway.

George wrenched open the door and was hit by another cold blast. Flipping on the light switch in the hall, he was startled to see the doors to the sewing room and dressing room wide open, the gale rushing freely through the open windows. Only the door to Missy's bedroom remained shut.

He ran into the dressing room first, fighting against the gale that hit him, and managed to force the windows down. Then he went to the sewing room and, with the cold now bringing tears to his eyes, closed one window. But George could not budge the open window that faced the Amityville River. He banged furiously on its frame with his fists. Finally it gave and slid to a close.

He stood there, trying to catch his breath, shaking in his pajamas. The wind was no longer blowing through the house, but he could hear it gusting violently outside. The chill remained. George took one more look around the room before he remembered Kathy. "Honey?" he called out. "You all right?"

When Kathy followed her husband out into the hallway, she too had seen the open doors, and that Missy's door remained shut. Her heart thumping, Kathy had run to her daughter's room and burst through the doorway. She turned on the light.

The room was warm, almost hot. The windows were shut and locked, and the little girl was fast asleep in her bed.

There was something moving in the room. Then she saw it was Missy's chair beside the window, slowly rocking back and forth. Then she head George's voice. "Honey? You all right?"

George came into the bedroom. The heat struck him; it was like stepping in front of a fire. George took it all in at once—the little girl safely asleep, his wife standing at the side of Missy's bed, the incredulous look of fright on Kathy's face, and the small chair teetering back and forth.

He took one step toward the rocking chair and it immediately ceased its movements. George stopped in his tracks, stood absolutely still, and motioned to Kathy. "Take her downstairs! Hurry!"

Kathy didn't question George. She lifted the little girl off the bed, blankets and all, and hurried from the room. George came out right behind them and slammed the door, not even bothering to turn off the light.

Kathy went carefully down the steps toward the first floor. It was ice cold in the hallway. George ran up the staircase to the top floor where Danny and Chris were sleeping.

When he came back down from the third floor a few minutes later, he saw Kathy sitting in the dark living room. She held Missy in her arms, the little girl still fast asleep on her lap. He turned on the light in the room, the chandelier casting shadows into the corners.

Kathy turned from the fireplace to look up at George questioningly. "They're all right," he nodded. "They're both sleeping. It's cold up there, but they're okay." Kathy let out her breath. He saw its vapor hang in the cold air.

George hurriedly started a fire. His fingers were numb and he suddenly realized that he was barefoot and hadn't thrown anything on over his pajamas. George finally got a small blaze going with newspaper, then fanned the flame with his hand until some of the old kindling caught fire.

Crouched in front of the fireplace, he could hear the winds howling outside. Then he turned and looked at Kathy over his shoulder. "What time is it?"

That was the only thing he could think of to say, George Lutz recalls. He remembers the look on Kathy's face when he asked the question. She stared at him for a moment, then replied, "I think it's about . . .". But before Kathy could finish, she burst into tears, her whole body shaking uncontrollably. She rocked Missy back and forth in her arms, sobbing. "Oh, George, I'm frightened to death!"

George stood up and walked over to his wife and daughter. He crouched down in front of the chair and put his arms around both. "Don't cry, honey," he whispered, "I'm here. Nobody's going to hurt you or the baby."

The three remained in that position for some time. Slowly the fire burned brighter and the room began to warm up. It seemed to George that the winds were diminishing outside. Then he heard the oil burner click on in the basement and he knew it was exactly six o'clock in the morning on New Year's Day.

By nine A.M., the temperature in 112 Ocean Avenue had risen to the thermostat-controlled 75 degrees. The icy chill in the house had dissipated. George had made an inspection tour of each window, from the first floor to the third. There was no visible evidence that anyone had tampered with the locks on the windows of the second floor, and George remained completely baffled as to how such a bizarre event could have taken place.

Looking back at the episode, he claims that at that time, he and Kathy couldn't think of any reason for the windows behaving the way they did except for a freak of nature—that the hurricane-strength winds had somehow forced the windows up. But he can't answer why it happened only to the second floor windows and not to any others in the house.

Suddenly George felt an urge to go to his office. It was a holiday, no one would be in, but he felt compelled to check on his company's operations.

William H. Parry, Inc., had four crews of engineers and surveyors in the field. The company had created the plans and blueprints for the largest building complex to date in New York City, and for the Glen Oaks Towers in Glen Oaks, Long Island, and was also responsible for planning a forty-block urban renewal project in Jamaica, Queens. In addition, there were several small surveys for title companies. The coordination for setting up each day's work was quite intricate, and for the past few weeks, George had been leaving that assignment to one of the draftsmen—an experienced employee who had worked for his father and grandfather.

Over the past year, after he had taken full control of the company from his mother, George's main concern had been with collecting from the city and construction companies that used his services. The company's payroll and expenses were much larger than they had been when George's father was alive. There was also the matter of paying off six cars and new field equipment. George realized he had been slacking off; it was time to resume his share of the responsibilities.

At ten in the morning, Father Mancuso was also awake. He hadn't slept much and had gotten up several times during the night to soak his blistered hands in Burow's Solution as the doctor had recommended. The priest had been out of bed since seven, even though he was enervated by flu and did feel better when he was lying down.

The medication had relieved some of the discomfort and itching in his palms, but the prescription for his flu had no effect on his high fever. In an effort to concentrate on other things besides his mysterious affliction, Father Mancuso tried reading some of his subscription magazines, searching for articles to divert his attention from his problem. In the succeeding three hours he read through over a dozen new and old periodicals. Then he noticed a slight discoloration on the last magazine he had held.

The priest turned over his hands. The palms were smearing. The blisters looked as if they were about to burst.

By noontime George was in Syosset, working with his adding machine. He had discovered that the money that was coming in didn't balance with what was going out. The accounts payable column was becoming too one-sided lately, and he knew he would have to cut back on his field crews and office personnel.

George hated the idea of depriving men of their livelihood, particularly when he knew they'd have a hard time finding other jobs in the suffering construction industry. But it had to be done, and he wondered where to begin. George didn't dwell too long on the subject, however, because he had other pressing problems. Before the banking week was up the next day—Friday—he would again have to transfer funds from one company bank account to another to cover checks that had been issued to suppliers.

Deeply involved in these manipulations, George didn't notice the passing time. For the first moments since December 18, George Lutz was not thinking about himself or 112 Ocean Avenue.

But his wife was thinking—thinking very hard about the house. Kathy hadn't told George in so many words, but she was becoming convinced that some of the events in the past two weeks had been the work of outside forces. She was sure he would think her conclusions silly, and she had been too embarrassed to tell George of her encounter with the ceramic lion.

She now feels that she had become aware that the little bits and pieces were adding up even before George had. She was frightened and wanted to talk to someone. She thought of her mother, but quickly dismissed the idea. Joan Conners was very religious and would insist that Kathy immediately talk to her old parish priest.

Kathy wasn't quite ready to enter into a world of ghosts and demons; she wanted the discussion to remain on a more general level at first. In her heart, however, she knew perfectly well where the subject would eventually lead.

She went into the kitchen and dialed the phone number of the one person who would understand what she was looking for—Father Mancuso.

She heard the connection go through and the first ring on the other end. As Kathy waited for the second ring, she suddenly became aware that the kitchen was pervaded by a sweet odor of perfume. Her flesh crawled as she waited for the familiar touch on her body.

Father Mancuso's number rang again, but Kathy never heard it. She had hung up the telephone and run from the room.

In the Rectory, Father Mancuso had been bathing his hands in the solution and found that the bleeding in his palms had stopped. The priest had a towel in his hands when the telephone rang in his living room. He picked up his telephone after the second ring.

When he said, "Hello?" the line was disconnected. He looked at the instrument. "Well! What was that all about?" Then Father Mancuso thought of George Lutz and shook his head. "Oh, no! I'm not going through that business again!" He put down the receiver and went back into the bathroom.

The priest looked at his blisters. Disgusting, he thought. Then he looked up at his face in the mirror. "When will this end?" he said to his reflection. His illness certainly showed. The circles under his eyes were darker and there was an unhealthy pallor to his skin. Father Mancuso gingerly felt his beard. It needed a trimming, but the hand would never be steady enough to hold a pair of scissors.

Father Mancuso says that staring at his reflection in the mirror suddenly made him think of the subject of demonology. The priest was aware of the scope of the field and the various occult phenomena its study embraces. He had never liked the subject, not even when he was taking the course in his student days at the seminary, and he had never tried to become too knowledgeable.

Father Mancuso knows of other priests who have concentrated on demonology, but he's never met an exorcist. Every priest is empowered to perform the Rites of Exorcism, but the Catholic Church prefers that this dangerous ceremony be restricted to those clerics who have become specialists in dealing with obsession and possession.

Father Mancuso had kept looking into his own eyes in the bathroom mirror, but found no answers to his dilemma. He felt it was time he confided in his friend, the Pastor of the Long Island rectory.

The morning snowfall had made traveling on the roads hazardous. As the day wore on, it got colder, and cars began to get caught in drifts and skid on icy spots all over Long Island. But the snow had stopped falling while George was driving back to Amityville from his office, and he made it home all right.

The driveway of 112 Ocean Avenue was heavy with fresh snow. George saw he would have to clear a path to the garage before moving the van into the driveway. I'll do it tomorrow, he thought, and left the vehicle parked on the street, which had been recently plowed by the city's snow trucks.

He noted that Danny and Chris had been out playing in the snow. Their sleds were parked up against the steps leading to the kitchen door. As he stepped inside, he saw that they had left a trail of melting snowy footprints through the kitchen and up the staircase. Kathy must be upstairs, he thought. If she'd seen the slush they'd tracked into her clean house, there would have been hell to pay.

George found his wife in their bedroom, lying on the bed, reading to Missy from one of the little girl's new Christmas story books. Missy was gleefully clapping her hands. "Hi gang!" he said.

His wife and daughter looked up. "Daddy!" they chorused together, leaping off the bed and encircling George with delight.

For the first time in what seemed ages to Kathy, the Lutz family had a happy supper together. Unknown to her, Danny and Chris, forewarned by George, had sneaked back down to the kitchen and wiped away all traces of their snowy entry. They sat at the table, their faces still ruddy from hours spent romping in the cold air, and wolfed down the hamburgers and french fries their mother had prepared especially for them.

Missy kept the family in smiles with her aimless chatter and the way she kept sneaking fries off the boys' plates when they weren't looking. When caught, Missy would turn her face toward her accuser and flash a mouthful of teeth, minus one, to disarm him.

Kathy felt more secure with George home. Her fears had momentarily calmed and she gave no further thought to the latest whiff of perfume earlier that afternoon. Maybe I'm getting paranoid about the whole thing, she thought to herself. She looked about the table. The warm atmosphere certainly didn't portend a visit from any more ghosts.

As for George, he had let his depressing business operations retreat to the furthest recesses of his mind. It was as though he had entered a little cocoon at 112 Ocean Avenue. This was the way he wanted life to be all the time in his new house. Whatever the world outside had to offer, the Lutzes would tough it out together from their home. He and Kathy shared a steak. Then, lighting a cigarette, George wandered off to the living room with the boys.

George had brought Harry into the house to feed him and then let him remain to rough it up with his two sons in front of the fireplace. The Lutzes had eaten early, and so it was only a little after eight when Danny and Chris began to nod.

While the boys marched upstairs to bed, followed by

Missy and Kathy, George took Harry out to the dog-house. Wading through the snow that had piled up between the kitchen door and the compound, he tied Harry to the strong lead line. Harry crawled into his doghouse, turned around several times until he found his right spot, and then settled down with a little sigh. While George stood there, the dog's eyes closed and he fell asleep.

"That does it," said George. "I'm taking you to the vet on Saturday."

After putting Missy to sleep, Kathy returned to the living room. George made his usual tour of the house, now double-checking every window and door. He had already inspected the garage and boathouse doors when he took Harry outside.

"Let's see what happens tonight," he told Kathy when he came back down. "It's not blowing at all out there."

By ten P.M., both George and Kathy were feeling drowsy. His blazing fire was running out, but the heat was affecting their eyes. She waited until George had poked out the last embers and had poured water over some still-smoldering pieces of wood. Then Kathy turned off the chandelier and looked around to take her husband's hand in the darkness. She screamed.

Kathy was looking past George's shoulder at the living room windows. Staring back at her were a pair of unblinking red eyes!

At his wife's scream, George whirled around. He also saw the little beady eyes staring directly into his. He jumped for the light switch, and the eyes disappeared in the shining reflection in the glass pane.

"Hey!" George shouted. He burst through the front door into the snow outside.

The windows of the living room faced the front of the house. It didn't take George more than a second or two to get there. But there was nothing at the windows.

"Kathy!" he shouted. "Get my flashlight!" George strained his eyes to see toward the back of the house in the direction of Amityville River.

Kathy came out of the house with his light and his parka. Standing beneath the window where they had seen the eyes, they searched the fresh, unbroken snow. Then the yellow beam of the flashlight picked up a line of footprints, extending clear around the corner of the house.

No man or woman had made those tracks. The prints had been left by cloven hooves—like those of an enormous pig.

14 **January 2** — When George came out of the house in the morning, the cloven-hoofed tracks were still visible in the frozen snow. The animal's footprints led right past Harry's compound and ended at the entrance to the garage. George was speechless when he saw that the door to the garage was almost torn off its metal frame.

George himself had closed and locked the heavy overhead door. To wrench it away from its frame would not only have created a great racket, but would require a strength far beyond that of any human being.

George stood in the snow, staring at the tracks and wrecked door. His mind raced back to the morning when he had found his front door torn open and to the night he had seen the pig standing behind Missy at her window. He remembers saying out loud, "What the hell is going on around here?" as he squeezed past the twisted door into the garage.

He turned on the light and looked about. The garage was still packed with his motorcycle, the children's bicycles, an electric lawn mower that had been left by the DeFeos, the old gas-powered machine he had brought from Deer Park; garden furniture, tools, equipment, and cans of paint and oil. The concrete floor of the garage was covered with a light dusting of snow that had drifted through the partly opened door. Obviously it had been off its frame for several hours.

"Is there anybody in here?" George shouted. Only the sound of a rising wind outside the garage answered him.

By the time George drove off to his office, he was more angry than frightened. If he had any terror of the unknown, it had been dismissed by the thought of what it was going to cost him to repair the damaged door. He didn't know if the insurance company would pay him for something like this, and he just didn't need two to three hundred dollars of extra expense.

George doesn't recall how he ever maneuvered the Ford van over the dangerous snow- and ice-covered roads to Syosset. His frustration at being unable to comprehend his bad luck blocked out any concern for his own safety. At the office, he quickly occupied himself with his immediate problems and for the next several hours was able to put aside any thoughts about 112 Ocean Avenue.

Before he'd left home, George had told Kathy about the garage door and the tracks in the snow. She had tried calling her mother, but there was no answer. Then Kathy remembered that Joan always shopped on Friday mornings rather than buck the Saturday crowds at the supermarket. She went upstairs to her bedroom, intending to change the linen in all the rooms and vacuum the rugs. Kathy's mind raced with the details of thoroughly cleaning her house for the first time. If she didn't occupy herself completely until George returned, she knew she'd fall to pieces.

She had just finished putting fresh cases on her pillows and was plumping them up when she was embraced from behind. She froze, then instinctively called out, "Danny?"

The grip around her waist tightened. It was stronger than the familiar woman's touch she had experienced in the kitchen. Kathy sensed that a man was holding her, increasing the pressure as she struggled. "Let me go, please!" she whimpered.

The pressure eased suddenly, then the hands released her waist. She felt them move up to her shoulders. Slowly her body was being turned around to face the unseen presence.

In her terror, Kathy became aware of the overwhelming stench of the same cheap perfume. Then another pair of hands gripped her wrists. Kathy says she sensed a struggle going on over possession of her body, that somehow she had been trapped between two powerful forces. Escape was impossible and she felt she was going to die. The pressure on her body became overwhelming and Kathy passed out.

When she came to, she was lying half off the bed with her head almost touching the floor. Danny had come into the room in answer to her call. Kathy knew the presences were gone. She couldn't have been out more than a moment.

"Call Daddy at his office, Danny! Hurry!"

Danny returned in a few minutes. "The man on the telephone says Daddy just left Syosset. He thinks he's coming back here."

George did not come back to the house until early afternoon. When he reached Amityville, he drove up Merrick Road toward his street and stopped off at The Witches' Brew for a beer.

The neighborhood bar was warm and empty. The juke box and television set were silent, and the only sounds in the place were those of the bartender washing glasses. When George entered, the man looked up and recognized him from the other day. "Hey, man! Good to see you again!"

George nodded in return and stood up at the bar. "A Miller's," he ordered.

George watched while the bartender filled a glass. He was a roly-poly young guy, somewhere in his late twenties, with a stomach that suggested he liked to sample the beer he sold. George took a long sip, half-emptying the tall stein before putting it down on the dark wood bar. "Tell me something," George belched. "Did you know the DeFeos?"

The young man had resumed his glass-washing. He nodded. "Yeah, I knew them. Why?"

"I'm living in their house now and . . .".

"I know," the bartender interrupted. George lifted his eyebrows in surprise. "The first time you came in here you said you just moved into 112 Ocean. That's the DeFeos'."

George finished off his beer. "They ever come in here?"

The bartender put down a clean glass and wiped his hands on a towel. "Only Ronnie did. Sometimes he brought in his sister Dawn. A cute kid." He picked up George's empty glass. "You know, you look a lot like Ronnie. The beard and all. I think you're older than he is, though."

"Did he ever talk about their house?"

The bartender put a new beer in front of George. "The house?"

"Yeah, you know, like did he ever say there was anything funny going on there? Stuff like that." George took a sip.

"You think there's something bad about the joint? I mean, now after the murders?"

"No, no." George raised a hand. "I was just asking whether he ever said anything before the, er—that night."

The bartender looked around the bar as if to confirm that there was no one else around. "Ronnie never said anything like that to me, personally." He leaned closer to George. "But I'll tell you something. I was there once. They threw a big party and Ronnie's old man hired me to take care of the bar."

George had finished half of his second beer. "What did you think of the place?"

The bartender spread his fat arms wide. "Big. A real big joint. I didn't see too much of it, though; I was down in the basement. A lotta booze and beer flowed that night. It was their anniversary." He looked around the bar again. "Did you know you got a secret room down there?"

George pretended ignorance. "No! Where?"

"Uh-hunh," the bartender said. "You take a look behind those closets and you'll find something that'll really shake you."

George leaned over the bar. "What was it?"

"A room, a little room. I found it that night I was down in the basement. There's this plywood closet built up beside the stairs. I'm using it to ice beer in, see? When I bumped a keg against one end of the closet, it seems the whole wall is loose. You know, like a secret panel, something out of an old movie."

"What about the room?" George prodded.

The bartender nodded. "Yeah, well, when I bumped the plywood, it came open, and I could see this dark space behind it. The light bulb wasn't working, so I lit a match. And sure enough, there's this weird little room, all painted red."

"You're putting me on," George protested.

The bartender put his right hand over his heart. "God's honest truth, man, so help me. You'll see."

George finished his second beer. "I'll certainly have to look for that." He put a dollar on the bar. "That's for the beers." He put down another. "That's for yourself."

"Hey, thanks, man!" The bartender looked up at George. "You want to know something really flakey about that little room? I used to have nightmares about it."

"Nightmares? Like what?"

"Oh, sometimes I'd dream that people—I don't know who they were—were killing dogs and pigs in there and using their blood for some kind of ceremony."

"Dogs and *pigs*?"

"Yeah." The bartender waved his hand in disgust. "I guess the place—the red paint and all—really got to me."

When George got home, he and Kathy both had stories to tell each other. She described the frightening event in their bedroom, and he related what the bartender at The Witches' Brew had told him about the red room in the basement. The Lutzes finally realized that there was something going on that was beyond their control. "Please call Father Mancuso," Kathy begged. "Ask him to come back."

Father Mancuso's superiors had been concerned with his health and had dropped by to look in on him. Father Mancuso told them that he felt much better that morning. They also decided to spend some time together to review the priest's workload. Most of the backlog was quickly cleared up and put in a superior's briefcase. A secretary would do the typing. Father Mancuso saw the clerics to the building's entrance and then walked back to his apartment. The phone was ringing.

He was still wearing the soft white cotton surgical gloves he had found in a drawer. The priest had explained to the Bishop that he had put them on his hands to protect them from cold, but his real motive was to hide the ugly rawness of his blisters. The priest's telephone rang five times before he picked it up. "Hello? This is Father Mancuso."

The voice on the other end came through loud and clear. "Father. This is George!"

The priest couldn't believe his ears. It was as if George was standing right in the room with him. He was so surprised that he blurted, "George?"

"George Lutz. Kathy's husband!"

"Oh! Hi! How are you?"

George held the receiver away from his ear and looked at Kathy standing next to him in the kitchen. "What's with him?" he whispered to her. "He sounds like he doesn't remember me."

Father Mancuso knew who George was, all right, but he was still stunned to hear from him on an open line without any interference at all. "I'm sorry, George, I didn't mean to be rude. I just wasn't ready for your call this way after all the trouble I've had reaching you."

"Yeah," answered George. "I know what you mean."

Father Mancuso waited for George to continue, but there was only silence. "George? You still there?"

"Yes, Father," said George. "I'm here and Kathy's right beside me." He looked at his wife. "We want you to come back and bless the house."

Father Mancuso thought of what had befallen him the first time he had blessed the Lutzes' home. He looked at his white gloved hands.

"Father, can you come right away?"

The priest hesitated. He didn't want to go back there, but he couldn't tell George that in so many words. "Well, George," he finally answered, "I don't know if I can right now. I have the flu again, you see, and the doctor doesn't want me running around in this cold weather—."

"Well," George interrupted. "When *can* you come?"

Father Mancuso began to look for a way out. "Why do you want me to bless the house again? You don't do that just at the drop of a hat, you know."

George was desperate. "Look, we owe you a dinner. You come, and Kathy will cook you the best steak you've ever had. Then you can stay overnight . . .".

"Oh, I couldn't do that, George . . .".

"Well, we'll make you drunk enough to stay!"

Father Mancuso couldn't believe what he just heard. You just don't say such things to a priest. "Listen here, young man, you—."

"Father, we're in a lot of trouble. We need your help."

The priest's anger evaporated. "What's the matter?" he said.

"There are things happening around this house we don't understand. We've seen a lot of . . .". The telephone line began to crackle on both ends.

"What'd you say, George. I didn't hear you."

There would be no more conversation between the two men. There was no longer anything to be heard on the line but static and a loud whirring sound. Both men knew it was no use and hung up their telephones.

George turned to Kathy and looked around the room. "It's started again. It's killed the phone."

By the time Father Mancuso put down the receiver, his hands were burning again. "God forgive me," he said aloud, "but George is going to have to get help from someone else. There's no way I'm going back to that house!"

15 January 2 to 3 — Disappointed that they couldn't convince Father Mancuso to return to their house, George and Kathy discussed other ways of getting help. Both had agreed that now that they had already moved in, it would be unseemly to ask the local parish priest in Amityville to bless the house. Besides, he had been the confessor to the DeFeos, and George recalled from the newspaper accounts that he was an elderly man who pooh-poohed the thought of "voices" in the house telling Ronnie what to do. He wasn't much of a believer in occult phenomena.

At one point, George talked of vandalism. Possibly someone was trying to frighten them out of the house, using violent acts of destruction to hurry their departure? Kathy had her own opinions. When she had said *something* had touched her, had George thought it was just her imagination? He didn't. Could he explain the horrible figure burned into the brick wall of the fireplace? He couldn't. Had they really seen a pig's tracks in the snow? They had. Would he agree that there was a powerful force in the house that could hurt the family? He did. What were they going to do? When they went to bed at night, George told her he had decided to go to the Amityville Police Department the next day.

During the night of January 2, George again had the urge to check out the boathouse and found Harry fast asleep in his doghouse. The next morning, he drove Harry to the animal hospital in Deer Park that he had been using and had them check the dog over thoroughly. It had cost him $35 to discover that Harry was sound and didn't appear to be drugged or poisoned. The vet suggested that the animal's lassitude might possibly have developed from a change in his diet.

On the morning of January 2, Father Mancuso again blessed the Lutzes' home. He didn't perform the ceremony in Amityville, but at the church and the Long Island rectory. In the church the priest held a votive Mass—a mass that does not correspond with one prescribed for the day, but is said for a special intention, at the choice of the celebrant.

Father Mancuso had removed his gloves. He knelt at the altar and opened his missal. He began: "I am the Savior of all people, says the Lord. Whatever the troubles, I will answer their cry and I will always be their Lord."

The priest crossed himself and read aloud the opening chapter of the Mass: "God our Father, our strength in adversity, our health in weakness, our comfort in sorrow, be merciful to your people."

Father Mancuso lifted his eyes to the figure on the cross. "As you have given us the punishment we deserve, give us also new life and hope as we rest in your kindness. We ask this through Christ our Lord."

He closed his missal, but kept his eyes on Jesus. "Lord, look kindly on the Lutzes in their sufferings, and by the death of your Son, endured for us, turn away from them your anger and the punishment their sins deserve. We ask this through Christ, our Lord. Amen."

After the votive Mass, Father Mancuso returned to his apartment to find a stupefying odor of human excrement pervading his rooms!

He gagged but managed to throw open all the windows. The freezing air rushed in, providing momentary relief, but then the stench overpowered even the cold wind. Father Mancuso ran to his bathroom to see if somehow the toilet had backed up. But no, there was nothing amiss—not until you tried to breathe!

The priest knew there was a cesspool under the front lawn of the rectory and dry wells behind the parking lot. He enlisted the aid of the maintenance man and together they found that no animals had been trapped in the wells and that the cesspool was in good working order. There had been no apparent leaks in the plumbing.

Father Mancuso feared that the horrible odor might begin to pervade the entire rectory. Other priests might be driven from their rooms to the school building across the yard. The Pastor would be extremely upset over the incident. Finally, Father Mancuso decided to burn incense to dispel the noxious stench.

Up to that point, Father Mancuso had not attributed the source of the smell to his own apartment. But after lighting the incense in his rooms and returning to the school building with the others, the priest realized that his apartment had been the first struck—evidently while he had been celebrating the special Mass for the Lutzes. He then made the terrifying connection—a disembodied voice in 112 Ocean Avenue had told him to "Get out." Whoever that voice belong to, it had reached clear across to the Rectory to give him the same messages.

There was another connection Father Mancuso had been trying to make. He realized it when he stood by the windows in the lobby and looked across to his apartment in the Rectory, remembering one of the lessons he learned in demonology—the odor of human excrement was always associated with the appearance of the Devil!

In the afternoon, Detective Sergeant Lou Zammataro of the Amityville Police Department went along with George, saw the wrecked garage door and the animal tracks still visible in the frozen snow, and then went into the house. He was introduced to Kathy and the children. She repeated her story of the ghost-like touchings and took the sergeant into the living room to show him the image burned into the fireplace wall.

Even after George and Kathy showed him the red room in the basement, they sensed Zammataro's skepticism. He had listened to George's version of the evil use of the hideaway, nodded when George mentioned Ronnie DeFeo as the builder of the secret room, then asked the Lutzes whether they had any concrete facts to base their fears on. "I can't work on what you believe you've seen or heard. Maybe you ought to get a priest in here," he suggested. "It sounds more like his kind of job than a cop's."

Sergeant Lou Zammataro left the Lutz house and got into his car. He knew he hadn't helped the young couple at all. But there was really nothing he could do for them, except maybe have a cruiser stop by once in a while. There had been no use in frightening them anymore, he had told himself as he drove off. Why make things worse by mentioning that he had felt strong vibrations, "a creepy feeling" the moment he once again walked into 112 Ocean Avenue?

When the sun went down, there still wasn't very much relief from the stench at the Long Island rectory. The heavy smoke released by the burning incense had gotten into the eyes and lungs of everyone who had entered Father Mancuso's rooms. His visitors were no longer able to tell whether they were nauseous from the smoke or from the original smell.

Father Mancuso had left his windows wide open in the hope that the cold air would eventually drive the odor from his rooms. But that effort backfired; the inrushing wind had only blocked the smoke and smell from getting out. The priest had wanted to tell the others that he knew what had happened and why, but he kept his own counsel, praying for a quick deliverance from this latest humiliation.

Immediately after Sergeant Zammataro had left, George noticed the compressor in the boathouse had stopped. There was no reason for the machine's stopping—unless it had overloaded the circuits and blown a fuse. That meant he would have to go down to the basement in the main house and examine the fuse box.

George knew the box was in the area of the storage closets and took a fresh box of fuses down with him. In the cellar he quickly discovered the blown fuse and replaced it. He heard the compressor start up again, making a loud racket as it began to churn, but waited to see if another overload would occur. After a few moments, he was satisfied and started to go back upstairs.

When he was halfway up the cellar steps, George became aware of the smell. It wasn't fuel oil.

He had his flashlight with him, but the lights in the basement were still on. From his position on the stairs, George had been able to see almost the entire cellar. He sniffed and then sensed the foul odor was coming from the area near the northeast corner—by the plywood storage closets that shielded the secret room.

George went back down the stairs and warily approached the storage closets. As he stood before the shelving that hid the small room, the odor became stronger. Holding his nose, George forced open the paneling and shone his flashlight around the red painted walls.

The stench of human excrement was heavy in the confined space. It formed a choking fog. Nauseated, George's stomach began to heave. He had just time enough to pull the panel back into place and shut out the mist before he vomited, fouling his clothes and the floor.

Father Mancuso and the Pastor of the Long Island rectory had been friends for several years, ever since the priest had taken an apartment in the rectory. Even with Father Mancuso's heavy workload and busy schedule within the diocese, their friendship had ripened and the two priests had become close companions. There was a twenty year difference in their ages, Father Mancuso being forty-two, but there was no generation gap.

On the night of January 3, all that changed. Depressed with the unrelenting, disgusting odor that permeated his apartment, Father Mancuso turned on the Pastor and their comradeship was irrevocably destroyed.

It started in the Pastor's office, where Father Mancuso had gone to pick up some reports that had been typed for him. He was about to return to his own rooms when the Pastor walked in with three other priests. Father Mancuso had just finished dinner—such as it was, since he had been unable to rid himself of the odor that clung to his clothes. He glanced across the room to the Pastor who was standing beside a desk. "I don't know why the stink is in my rooms only," he barked. "Why am I the only one chosen for this high honor?"

The Pastor was stunned. He couldn't believe what he had just heard. Why, he thought, the man's completely irrational over the incident. "I'm sorry," the Pastor said gently in reply, "but I really can't give you a logical explanation."

Father Mancuso waved his hand at the Pastor in dismissal. The other priests had looks of amazement on their faces. Father Mancuso had never spoken like this, particularly about his close friend. Now his face became red with rage. "How come you're so nice to me, eh?"

What had gotten into the man? The Pastor looked at the other priests, who were avoiding his glance, embarrassed at being included in the outbreak. Then the Pastor spoke up. "I think this business with the smell is getting the better of you, my friend. It would be better if we talked at another time and in another place." He rose to leave the room.

His determined calm deflated Father Mancuso. He retreated, but continued to glare at the Pastor. There was a look in his eyes that came from someone or something within the priest's body. This emotion had momentarily taken possession of Father Mancuso, just as something had taken possession of, and befouled, his apartment in the rectory.

George had finally managed to clean himself up after the disastrous trip to the basement. He and Kathy were sitting in the kitchen over coffee. It was after eleven P.M. and both were tired from the tension of the ever-increasing incidents. Only the kitchen seemed relatively safe; and they were reluctant to go up to bed.

"Listen," George said, "It's getting chilly in here. Let's at least go into the living room where it's warmer." He got up from his chair, but Kathy remained seated.

"What are we going to do?" she asked. "Things are getting worse. I'm really scared something can happen to the kids." Kathy looked up at her husband. "God knows what's going to happen next around here."

"Look," he answered. "Just keep the kids out of the cellar until I set up a fan down there. Then I'm going to brick up the door to that room so it never bothers us again." He took Kathy's arm and pulled her up from the chair. "I also want to talk to Eric at my office. He says his girl friend's got a lot of experience investigating haunted houses . . ."

"Haunted houses?" Kathy interrupted. "Do you think this house is haunted? By what?" She followed him toward the living room, then stopped in the hallway. "I just had a thought, George. Do you think our TM had anything to do with all this?"

George shook his head. "Nah. Nothing at all. But what I do know is that we've got to get help somewhere. It might as well be . . ."

As they entered the living room, Kathy's scream cut

off the rest of George's words. He looked to where she was pointing. The ceramic lion that George had carried up to the sewing room was on the table next to Kathy's chair, its jaws bared at George and Kathy!

16 **January 4 to 5** — George grabbed the lion off the living room table and threw it into a garbage can outside the house. It took him quite a while to calm Kathy down because he couldn't possibly explain how the porcelain piece had managed to come back down from the sewing room. She insisted that something in the house had done it and didn't want to spend another minute in 112 Ocean Avenue.

George had confided to Kathy that he too felt uneasy about the lion's sudden reappearance. But he couldn't agree on running away without taking a chance at fighting back.

"How can you fight what you can't see?" Kathy asked. "This—this thing can do anything it wants."

 135

"No honey," George said. "There's no way you can convince me a lot of this isn't just our imagination. I just don't believe in spooks! No way, no how, no time!" Finally he talked Kathy into going up to bed with a promise that if he couldn't get help by the next day, they would get out of the house for a while.

They both were completely drained. Kathy fell asleep out of sheer exhaustion. George dozed off, waking every once in a while to listen groggily for any unnatural noises in the house. He says that he has no idea how long he had lain there before he heard the marching music downstairs!

His head was keeping time to the drumbeats before he realized he was listening to music. Glancing at Kathy to see if she had been awakened, he heard her breathe deeply. She was fast asleep.

George ran out of the room into the hall and heard the stomp of marching feet get louder. There must be at least fifty musicians parading around on the first floor, he thought. But the moment he hit the bottom step and turned on the hall light, the sounds ceased.

George froze on the staircase, his eyes and head swiveling frantically to catch any sign of movement. There was absolutely no one there. It was as though he had walked into an echo chamber. After the cacophony of sound, the sudden silence sent chills up his back.

Then George heard heavy breathing and thought someone was right behind him. He spun about. No one was there, and he then realized he was listening to Kathy from all the way upstairs.

Fear of her being alone in the bedroom galvanized George. He raced back up the steps two at a time and into his room, turning on the light. There, floating two feet above the bed, was Kathy. She was slowly drifting away from him toward the windows!

"Kathy!" George yelled, jumping up on the bed to grab his wife. She was as stiff as a board in his hands, but her drifting stopped. George felt a resistance to his pull, then a sudden release of pressure, and he and Kathy fell heavily off the bed onto the floor. The fall awakened her.

When she saw where she was, Kathy was incoherent for a moment. "Where am I?" she cried. "What's happened?"

George started to help her up. She could hardly stand. "It's nothing," he reassured her. "You were having a dream and fell out of bed. That's all."

Kathy was still too dazed to question George any further. She said, "Oh!" meekly got back into bed, and immediately fell back into a deep sleep.

George turned out the light in the room but did not return to his wife's side. He sat on a chair beside the windows, watching Kathy and looking out at the lightening sky of early morning.

Father Mancuso was also watching the new day break —from his mother's house in Nassau, where he had gone shortly after the altercation with his Pastor. Not that he was afraid of a continued outburst, but it had been impossible to sleep in his stench-filled, incense-smoked apartment. Also, he now truly believed that he was the target of the demonic phenomenon and thought that the odor would go if he left the Rectory for a while.

At first Father Mancuso had misgivings about being in his mother's home because he didn't want to involve her in his problem. But then he had begun to feel feverish and decided that if he was to be sick again, he'd rather be under her care.

He hadn't had much sleep and awakened a few minutes before dawn. He felt his palms itching and looked at his hands to examine both sides. He considered talking to his mother, but he didn't want to upset her further; she was already deeply concerned about his illness.

The skies were laced with long streaks of white clouds. He noted they were low and moving fast. With the cold spell still holding in the low teens, that could mean more snow. Father Mancuso turned away from the window and looked at the clock on the night stand. It was only 7:00 A.M.

I'd like to call George Lutz, he thought, to find out if the Mass caused any similar reaction at his house. But no, seven might be too early. Father Mancuso decided to wait a while and got back into bed.

It was nice and warm under the covers. Sleepily he heard his mother stirring in the kitchen and suddenly he was ten years old, waiting for her to call him to get up for school. The recent pains, aches, and humiliations fled from his mind and body. Father Mancuso was sleeping safely in his old bed in his mother's house.

By ten in the morning, Kathy was still in a deep sleep. George had become worried about her condition after the past night's terrifying experience. He couldn't wait any longer. He had to call Father Mancuso again.

Danny and Chris had told their father that they heard on their radio that the Amityville schools were closed because of a heating problem. They were somewhat disappointed, because it would have been their first day at their new school after the Christmas holidays and a chance to meet some new friends.

George thought he was lucky not to have to drive the boys to school. It was clear across town, and he hadn't really wanted to leave Kathy and Missy alone in the house. He fed the children their breakfast and sent them up to play in their bedroom. Then he looked in on Kathy.

Her face was pale, drawn, with deep lines around her mouth. He didn't want to waken her and went back down to the kitchen. When he saw that it was 11:00 A.M., George decided to call the priest.

When he dialed Father Mancuso's private number, there was no answer. George called the Rectory itself and was informed that Father Mancuso was visiting his mother. No, they couldn't give out her number, but would give Father Mancuso the message that George had called.

George sat in the kitchen the rest of the morning, waiting for the return call. He thought he had been a fool to mouth off about "not believing in spooks." Kathy was right—how the hell *can* you fight something that can lift you clear off the bed like a stick of wood? George Lutz, ex-Marine, admitted he was scared.

Kathy came downstairs just as the telephone rang. It was George's office, calling to ask when he was coming in. The Internal Revenue agent was due back and they did not know how George wanted to handle the situation. George squirmed. Finally he told his bookkeeper to call their accountant and postpone the appointment until the following week. As for his coming in, he said Kathy didn't feel well and they were waiting for the doctor.

Kathy sat next to George at the kitchen table and looked strangely at her husband. She mouthed the word "doctor?" to him. George shook his head at her and ended the call by telling his office he'd get back to them later.

"Boy!" he said to Kathy, "are they ever getting fed up with me! I'll just have to go in tomorrow."

Kathy yawned at George and shrugged her shoulders in an effort to ease the stiffness in her body. "God," she said, "look at the time. Why'd you let me sleep so long? Have the kids eaten? Are the boys in school?"

George started counting on his fingers. "First," he answered, "you haven't slept so good in weeks, so I left you alone." He held up two fingers. "Yes, they ate breakfast." Three fingers: "There was no school today. I sent them upstairs to play with Missy."

Good, he thought to himself, Kathy hadn't remembered anything about what happened last night. And I'm not going to tell her. "I've been trying to get hold of Father Mancuso again," George continued. "They say he's at his mother's, but he'll call me as soon as they hear from him."

Father Mancuso's mother didn't disturb his needed rest until almost three in the afternoon. He knew his fever had dropped because he no longer had a light-headed feeling. The priest was doubly pleased when he finally checked in with the Rectory. The priest who answered the phone said that the incense had driven out the horrible smells and that Father could return to his rooms. "Father, also George Lutz called you."

Oh yes, he reminded himself, I meant to call him, but it completely slipped my mind. Father Mancuso said he'd return by evening. He then called George.

The phone was picked up on the first ring. "George? This is Father Mancuso."

"Father, am I glad you called. We must talk to you right away. Can you please come over here now?"

"But I've already blessed your house again," Father Mancuso answered. "I said a votive Mass for you at the church the other day. And by the way, did any . . .".

"It's not to bless the house," George interrupted. "It's more than that now." For the next several minutes George recounted what had happened at 112 Ocean Avenue since he had moved in. He sent Kathy upstairs under the pretext of getting him her cigarettes, and then told the priest about her levitating. "That's why we need you, Father," George concluded. "I'm scared of what's going to happen to Kathy and the kids!"

All through George's recitation, Father Mancuso had feared a debilitating attack. Now he was ashamed to realize that he'd been avoiding the inevitable. Come on, man, he thought to himself, you're a priest. If I don't want to wear the collar and accept its responsibilities—why, by God, I'm not worthy!

Father Mancuso took a deep breath. "All right, George. I'll try and get there to . . ."

George didn't hear what Father Mancuso said next. Suddenly there were several loud moans on the line and then a crackling that almost shattered his eardrum. "Father! I can't hear you!" A continued moaning was the only answer George got.

On the other end, Father Mancuso felt as if he had been physically slapped in the face. He put down the telephone, put his hand to his cheek, and began to cry. "I'm afraid to go back there!" He looked at his sore palms and then buried his face within them. "Oh, God! Help me! Help me!"

George knew it was useless to wait for Father Mancuso to call back. Even if he did, they would have been prevented from talking to one another about the house. But George had one hope. He was sure he had heard the priest say he'd come, but he didn't know when. He'd just have to sit there and wait.

Father Mancuso returned to the Rectory after eight in the evening. Now it was almost ten o'clock, and the priest sat and stared at the telephone. The smell of excrement had gone from his quarters as he'd been told, but the acrid sting of incense still hung in the air. That he could tolerate. What he couldn't stand was his inability to go to the Lutzes. Even the thought of the children being in danger from the demonic behavior couldn't overcome his fear of what might await him at 112 Ocean Avenue.

Finally Father Mancuso decided he would call the Chancellor's office in the diocese. He picked up the telephone, but thought he would go see them in the morning instead. He then prepared to go to bed. He had had enough sleep that morning at his mother's, but he was exhausted again. Before putting on his pajamas, he went into the bathroom to remove the white gloves. The Burow's Solution had helped soothe the affliction and he wanted to soak his palms once more that night.

When he peeled off the gloves, he was stunned. He turned his hands over and examined the palms. There were no more ugly splotches or open sores. There was no sign of bleeding. The blisters were gone!

Kathy had never really come to herself all that day and night. She sat by the fireplace in the living room. George fed the children and eventually sent them off to bed. The boys didn't complain that it was too early because they knew they'd have to get up for school. Evidently the heating problem had been solved, because the local Amityville radio station had announced that the schools would be open the next morning.

George had even helped Missy take her bath. He read his daughter a story before she let him turn off her light. The last words Missy said before he closed her door were: "Good night Daddy. Good night Jodie."

When he saw it was almost eleven, George realized that Father Mancuso wasn't coming that night. Kathy had been drooping in her chair for the past hour, her eyes closing with the warmth of the fire. Finally, she announced to George she was going up to bed.

George looked at his wife. Not once had she mentioned getting away from the house. It was as though none of the frightening incidents had ever occurred and it was just natural for her to want to go to sleep. They went up to their bedroom together.

Kathy mumbled that she was too sleepy to take a bath and would do it in the morning. She was asleep as soon as her head hit the pillow. George sat on the edge of the bed for a while watching Kathy breathe deeply. Then he went out to check on Harry. The dog was asleep again, his food untouched.

George was about to reach down and shake the animal when he heard the marching band strike up in his house. He ran back in through the kitchen. The drums and horns were blasting away in the living room. George heard the stomping of many feet as he tore through the hallway.

The lights were still on, but he could see there was no one in the room. The very instant he could see into the living room, the music had cut off. George looked about wildly. "You sonofbitches, where are you?" he screamed.

George took in great gulps of air. Then he realized there was something strange about the living room. Every piece of furniture had been moved. The rug had been rolled back. Chairs, couch, and tables had been pushed against the walls as if to make room for a lot of dancers—or a marching band!

17 **January 6** — "Your story is very interesting, Frank, but if I didn't know your background as a pro, I'd honestly think you were a little nuts to believe in it." Chancellor Ryan got up from behind his desk and went to the new coffee machine across the room. Father Mancuso shook his head at Father Ryan's offer. Ryan then poured one black cup for Father Nuncio—the other Chancellor—and one for himself.

The Chancellor sat back down at his desk, sipped some of the coffee, then looked at his notes. "In your capacity as a psychotherapist, how many times have people come to you with stories like this? Hundreds, I'll bet."

Chancellor Ryan was an extremely tall man, even while sitting. He was six feet five, with a shock of white hair crowning a ruddy Irish face. The priest was well known in the diocese for his open manner in speaking to the other clerics, be they young parish priests or the Bishop himself.

Chancellor Nuncio, on the other hand, was the exact opposite; short, stumpy, black-haired, young at forty-two, while Father Ryan was well in his sixties, and with a seriousness to his approach that perfectly complemented the other Chancellor's softer touch.

The two had listened to Father Mancuso's recounting of the episodes that George Lutz had said happened at 112 Ocean Avenue, and to his own humiliating experiences, including the latest one that had just occurred at the Rectory. They were impressed with Father Mancuso's fears that the phenomena had a demonic taint to them.

Chancellor Ryan looked up from the pad on his desk and spoke to the troubled priest. "Before we offer any suggestions on how you should handle this as a participant and as a priest, Frank, I think you should know the ground rules." Father Ryan nodded to Father Nuncio.

The other priest put down his coffee. "You seem to think that there's something demonic going on in the Lutzes' house, that the place is possessed somehow. Well, let me reassure you that first of all, *places* and *things* are never possessed. Only people." Father Nuncio stopped, reached into his jacket and withdrew several short cigars. He offered them around, but the two priests declined. He lit up, puffing and talking at the same time. "The traditional viewpoint of the Church sees the devil in a number of ways: He tries through *temptation*, by which he is seen to prod men toward sin in the psychological battles with which I'm sure you're familiar."

"Oh, yes," Father Mancuso nodded. "As Father Ryan mentioned, I've seen and heard many who've come to me as a psychotherapist and as a parish priest."

Chancellor Ryan picked up the thread. "Then there are the so-called extraordinary activities of the devil in the world. Usually these are material things around a person that are affected; that might be what you're up against. We call it *infestation*. It breaks down into different categories which we'll explain in a minute."

"*Obsession*," Father Nuncio put in, "is the next step, in which the person is affected either internally or externally. And finally there is *possession*, by which the person temporarily loses control of his faculties and the devil acts in and through him."

When Father Mancuso had come to the Chancellors' office to keep his appointment, he had been somewhat embarrassed as to how to approach his problem. But he relaxed as the two priests had shown keen interest. Now with their spelling out the guidelines he must take in this kind of situation, Father Mancuso raised his hopes for deliverance from this evil.

"In investigating cases of possible diabolical interference," Chancellor Ryan went on, "we must consider the following: One, fraud and deception. Two, natural scientific causes. Three, parapsychological causes. Four, diabolical influences. And five, miracles.

"In this case, fraud and trickery don't seem plausible. George and Kathleen Lutz seem to be normal, balanced individuals. We think you are too. The possibilities therefore are reduced to psychological, parapsychological, or diabolical influences."

"We'll exclude the miraculous," Father Nuncio broke in, "because the Divine would not involve itself in the trivial and foolish."

"True," said Father Ryan. "Therefore the explanation would seem to include hallucination and autosuggestion—you know, like the invisible touches Kathy experienced—and when George thought he heard that marching band. But let's take the parapsychological line."

"Parapsychologists like Dr. Rhine, who works at Duke University in Durham, North Carolina, define four main operations in the science. The first three come under the general heading of ESP—extrasensory perception. They are mental telepathy, clairvoyance, and precognition, which could explain George's visions and 'picking up' information that seems to coincide with known facts about the DeFeos. The fourth parapsychological area is psychokinesis, where objects move by themselves. That would be the case with the Lutzes' ceramic lion—if it *did* move," he added.

Father Nuncio got up to refill his cup. "All of what we've said, Frank, is part of the suggestion we have for the Lutzes. Have them contact some investigative organization like Dr. Rhine's to come in and look at the house. They'll do extensive testing and I'm sure they can come to some conclusion short of diabolical influence."

"But what about me?" asked Father Mancuso. "What do *I* do?"

Chancellor Ryan cleared his throat and looked kindly at the priest. "You are not to return to that house. You can call the Lutzes and tell them what we suggested. But under no circumstances are you ever to go there again."

"I thought you said I shouldn't consider a belief in such matters as this," Father Mancuso protested.

"Yes, I did," said Father Ryan. "But you've got yourself so worked up over this affair that at the moment the best thing you can do is dissociate yourself from the Lutzes and 112 Ocean Avenue."

After breakfast, Kathy dropped the boys off at their new school, then drove over to her mother's with Missy. George was alone in the house. He had gone down to the cellar to clear the odor with two fans. But when he came down the stairs, there was no trace of any of the terrible stench that had made him vomit the day before.

He sniffed but could find nothing, even when he went directly to the secret red room. George pulled the plywood paneling back open and flashed his light about the red walls. "Damn!" he said. "It couldn't have disappeared just like that. There's got to be an air hole down here somewhere."

George was searching for that possible air vent when Father Mancuso dialed his number. After the meeting, the priest had driven back to his own apartment in the rectory intending to call George with the Chancellors' recommendations. He heard the telephone ring ten times before he finally hung up. Father Mancuso thought he'd try again later when the Lutzes came home.

George was home all right, but he never heard the telephone ring. The door to the basement was open, and usually the ringing telephone could be heard anywhere in the house.

George had no success in finding any opening where the stench could have escaped, but under the area where the front steps to the house had been constructed, he did discover something interesting. When the contractor had laid the foundation for the house at 112 Ocean Avenue, it seemed he had covered over a circular opening with a concrete lid. By squirreling around the dirt piled up against this protuberance, George accidentally loosened some of the old gravel around the base and heard it fall into water far below. He flashed his light and saw the beam hit against a wet, black shaft. "A well!" he said aloud. "That doesn't show up in the blueprints. It must have been left from the old house that was here before."

He returned to the first floor and looked at the kitchen clock. Strange, he thought, it's almost noon and I still haven't heard from Father. I'd better try him myself.

George called the Rectory. The priest picked up on the first ring. George was surprised when Father Mancuso told him he had just called and that there was no answer at the house. Then George asked Father Mancuso when he was coming, and they got down to Father Mancuso's report.

He said he'd been to see the Chancellors of his diocese and repeated their recommendation that George find an organization to conduct a scientific investigation of the house. Father Mancuso gave George the address of a Psychical Research Institute in North Carolina and suggested he get in touch with them immediately. George agreed, but pressed the priest to come to the house.

Not until many months after he and his family had fled 112 Ocean Avenue would George Lutz learn what Father Mancuso had suffered after he originally blessed their house or of his subsequent humiliations and afflictions. Therefore, when Father Mancuso again refused to come to the house, George became confused. He said he really needed him, not some ghost-chasing outfit from somewhere down South. And who, he wanted to know, was supposed to pay for all of this? But after promising to call the parapsychologists and to let Father Mancuso know the results of the investigation, George hung up.

He was still annoyed when he called Kathy at her mother's. George told her what the priest had said, but snorted that he wasn't going to bother with anything like that. But Kathy felt they should pursue the Chancellors' recommendations telling George that he should listen to what the Church suggested.

Finally George agreed, saying he would drive to his office on his Harley chopper and type out the letter to the people at Duke. He didn't tell her he also wanted to talk to Eric, the young fellow at his office who said his girl friend was a medium.

After talking to George, Father Mancuso felt a tremendous pressure lift from his shoulders. Just the fact that he had been able to share his burden with others cleared his head completely for the first time in weeks; the responsibility he had been bearing alone had been taken away by his superiors.

The priest turned to preparing his work schedule for the following week. It took him several hours—until dinner time—to finally nail down the program he wanted for his counseling and for his patients. He ordered Chinese food from a nearby restaurant in the vicinity and wolfed down the meal while reading some clients' case histories.

George rode to his office and mailed the letter to the parapsychologists, using the Chancellors' names as his reference. He didn't really expect an immediate response to his request for an investigator, so he only put a regular stamp on the envelope instead of an airmail one. Then he telephoned Eric's girl friend, Francine.

She was terribly interested in what he had to say. Sure that she could contact whatever—or whoever—was making his and Kathy's lives miserable; she promised to come to the Lutzes' house with her boyfriend in a day or so.

Then the young woman said something that really made George's ears perk up. Out of the clear blue, she mentioned that George should look around his property for an old, abandoned, covered-up well. He didn't admit that he had already found such a place, but asked instead *why* she wanted him to do the searching.

Her answer shocked him: "I think," she said, "that your spirits may be coming from a well. You can cap it off, you know, but I bet if you do find a well under your house, there's a direct passage to it. And somehow, even if it's a tiny crack, that's all it takes. With that, 'it' can climb out when it wants to."

After thanking the girl and hanging up, George made a phone call to the Psychical Research Institute in Durham, North Carolina, and told them of the letter he had just sent. They agreed to send a field investigator as soon as possible. In turn, George agreed to pay the field man's expenses.

Father Mancuso, too, was on the telephone once more that night. The call came after eleven and was, surprisingly, from the priest who had helped him when his car fell apart on the Van Wyck Expressway.

Both clerics recalled the harrowing events of that evening and Father Mancuso asked the other priest whether he had encountered any further trouble after his windshield wipers had gone berserk. "No," his friend said. "That is, not until a few minutes ago." Father Mancuso's heart began to beat loudly against his chest.

"Frank," the other priest continued, "I just got a peculiar phone call. I don't know who it was, but he said, 'Tell the priest not to come back.'"

"What was he talking about?" Father Mancuso asked.

"I asked that. I said, 'Who are you talking about?' The voice only answered, 'The priest you helped.'"

"'The priest you helped?'"

"Yeah. I thought about that after he hung up and I couldn't remember anybody but you. Do you think he really means you, Frank?"

"He never told you who it was?"

"No. He just said, 'The priest'll know who it is.'"

"What did he actually say?"

"He said, 'Tell the priest not to come back or he'll die!'"

18 **January 6 to 7** — Earlier that day, Kathy had returned from her mother's house in time to pick up Danny and Chris at their new school in Amityville. The boys were eager to tell about their teachers, schoolmates, and playground facilities. The yard had been cleared of snow and the children had been able to enjoy some activities outside. Missy, jealous at having to stay home, kept pumping her brothers about what the girls at the elementary school were like.

The whole family ate together at six-thirty. George told Kathy what he had done about Father Mancuso's suggestion, and that he had also spoken to the girl who could contact spirits. Kathy was glad that he had called the parapsychology people instead of just waiting for an answer to his letter. But she wasn't too happy about a stranger coming into her house to talk to ghosts—particularly a young girl like Francine.

After they had finished dinner, Kathy told George she really wanted to return to her mother's until she felt the house was safe to live in. George reminded her that it was ten degrees above zero outside and snow was forecast by morning. Even though East Babylon wasn't too far up the road, he didn't think she could make it from her mother's house back to Amityville in time to get the boys to school in the morning.

Danny and Chris chimed in that they wanted to stay home—they had some homework to do, and besides, their grandmother wouldn't let them watch television after eight o'clock. Kathy finally gave in to their arguments, but felt uneasy about staying in the house another night. She told George she didn't think she could sleep a wink.

Harry had been in the kitchen with them while they were eating, and Kathy had given the dog all the scraps of meat left over from dinner. Before they went to bed, George thought that Harry might be better off staying inside that night. It was bitter cold out and would only get worse if the snow fell. Harry hadn't been served his usual dry food, and George thought the dog might be more alert after having some red meat.

While the boys did their homework, Missy took Harry up to her room to play. But Harry didn't want to stay there. He was nervous and sniveling, Kathy noted, particularly after Missy had introduced Harry to her unseen friend, Jodie. Finally the little girl had to close her door to keep Harry from running out. He crawled under her bed and remained there. Finally Chris came down for him. Harry scampered out of Missy's room and, with his tail between his legs, ran up the stairs to the third floor, where he remained the rest of the night.

At twelve, when George and Kathy finally went up to bed, she went out like a light for the third night in a row, quickly falling into a deep sleep, her breathing heavy. But George, lying on his side with his back to Kathy, was wide awake, his ears alert for any signs of the marching band.

When he first noticed the snowflakes falling outside the windows, he saw it was one o'clock on his wrist watch. The wind was rising, whipping the flakes about. Then he thought he heard a boat moving on the Amityville River. But the bedroom windows didn't face the water, and George didn't feel like getting up from his warm bed to look out from Missy's or the sewing room windows. Besides the river was frozen, so George ascribed the sound to the vagaries of the wind.

At 2 A.M. he began to yawn. His eyes were getting heavy and his body was getting stiff from lying in one position. A short while ago he had looked over his shoulder at Kathy. She was still flat on her back, her mouth open.

Suddenly George had the urge to get up and go to The Witches' Brew for a beer. He knew there were cans of brew in the refrigerator, but he kept thinking that they wouldn't slake his thirst. It had to be The Witches' Brew, and it didn't matter that it was two in the morning, or that it was freezing out. He turned to wake Kathy and tell her he was going out for a while.

In the darkness of the room, George could see Kathy wasn't in bed. He could see that she was levitating again, almost a foot above him, drifting away from him!

Instinctively George reached out, grabbed her hair, and yanked. Kathy floated back to him and then fell back onto the bed. She awoke.

George turned on the night stand light next to him and gasped. He was looking at a ninety-year-old woman —the hair wild, a shocking white, the face a mass of wrinkles and ugly lines, and saliva dripping from the toothless mouth.

George was so revolted he wanted to flee from the

room. Kathy's eyes, set deep in the wrinkles, were look-ing at him questioningly. George shuddered. It's *Kathy*, he thought, this is my wife! What the hell am I doing?

Kathy sensed the fright in her husband's face. My God, what does he see? She leaped from the bed and ran into the bathroom, flicking on the light above the mirror. Staring at her own face, she screamed.

The ancient crone George had seen was gone, her hair was upset, but it was blonde again. Her lips were not drooling any longer, nor was she wrinkled. But deep, ugly lines ran up and down her cheeks.

George, following Kathy into the bathroom, peered over her shoulder at the image. He too saw that the ninety-year-old visage had faded, but the long, black slashes still cut deeply down Kathy's face. "What's hap-pening to my face?" Kathy yelled.

She turned to George, and he put his fingers up to Kathy's mouth. Her lips were dry and burning hot. Then he ran his fingertips gently across the deep ridges. There were three on each cheek, extending from just below her eyes down to just under the jawline. "I don't know, baby," he whispered.

George took a towel from the rack next to the sink and tried to wipe the lines away. Kathy spun about and looked into the mirror. Her scared face stared back at her. Running her own fingers down her face, she began to cry.

Kathy's helplessness stirred George deeply, and he put his hands on her shoulders. "I'm going to call Father Mancuso right now," he said.

Kathy shook her head. "No, we mustn't involve him in this." She looked at George's face reflected in the mirror. "Something tells me he could get hurt. We'd better go and check on the kids," she said calmly.

The children were all right, but George and Kathy were unable to go back to sleep that night. They stayed in their bedroom, with the lights out, watching the snow fall. Every once in a while Kathy would hold her hands to her face, checking to feel if the ridges were still there. Finally the cold dawn broke. The snow had stopped, and there was just enough light for George to make out Kathy when she touched him on the shoulder. "George," she said, "look at my face."

He turned from his position he had taken in a chair near the window and looked at his wife. In the dawn's weak light, George could see that the lines were gone. He put his fingers up to her face and touched her skin. It was soft again, with absolutely no trace of the disfiguring scars! "They're gone, baby," he smiled gently. "They are all gone."

In spite of what Kathy had said during the night, George called Father Mancuso in the morning and caught the priest just before he went to early Mass.

George told him that he had spoken to North Carolina, where a Jerry Solfvin had promised to have an investigator come to the house immediately. Then he brought up the incident of the night before. Father Mancuso was aghast about the second levitation and the alterations of Kathy's face. "George," he said urgently, "I'm worried about what could happen next. Why don't you just get out of that house for a while?"

George assured the priest he had been thinking of doing just that, but first he wanted to see what Francine the medium had to say. Maybe she could help as she had claimed.

"A medium?" Father Mancuso asked. "What are you talking about, George? That's not a scientific investigation."

"But she said she can talk to spirits," George protested. "In fact, Father, do you know what she said yesterday? She told me there's a well hidden under my house. She's right! I found one under the stoop and she's never even been here!"

Father Mancuso became angry. "Listen!" he shouted

over the phone. "You're involved in something danger-ous! I don't know what is going on in your house, but you'd better get out!"

"You mean, just leave everything?"

"Yes, just go for a while," the priest persisted. "I'll talk to the Chancellors again and see if they can send someone, maybe a priest."

George was silent. He had been trying to get Father Mancuso to his house and been refused time and again. The priest's superiors had done nothing but suggest he contact some organization. Finally he had someone who sounded as if she could actually help him and Kathy. Why should he just leave everything and walk out?

"I'll tell Kathy, Father," George finally said. "Thanks." He was about to hang up.

"George, there's just one more thing," said Father Mancuso. "I seem to recall that you and Kathy were into Transcendental Meditation at one time."

"Yes, that's right."

"Do you still practice that?" the priest asked.

"No—yes. Well, we haven't really kept it up since we've moved here," George answered. "Why?"

"I was just curious, George, that's all," Father Mancuso replied. "I'm glad you're not doing it now. It might have been making you susceptible."

Right after talking with George, Father Mancuso called the Chancery in Rockville Centre. Unfortunately, Chancellers Ryan and Nuncio were unavailable and their secretary could only promise to have them call the following day. The priest was extremely agitated and prayed that things would not continue to deteriorate until the Church could bring its forces to bear against the evil that gripped 112 Ocean Avenue.

In his compassion for the Lutzes' plight, Father Mancuso forgot about his own dilemma. But in a few min-utes, he was violently reminded that he too was subject to the unrelenting influence. He began to shiver and shake. His stomach heaved and his throat tightened. The priest sneezed, and his eyes watered; he sneezed again and saw blood on the tissue. Chancellor Ryan's warning, "Don't involve yourself any more!" flashed across his mind. But it was too late. Father Mancuso had all the signs of another attack of the flu!

Later that evening Eric, the young engineer who worked at George's company, arrived at the Lutzes' home with his girl friend Francine. George immediately hustled the young couple out of the bitter cold and into the living room to warm themselves in front of the big fire.

They brought an infectious cheerfulness that had been missing at 112 Ocean Avenue. George and Kathy responded and soon the four were chatting away like old friends. But under George's exterior warmth, there was an urgency. He wanted Francine to look over the house.

As he was trying to turn the conversation around to her experience with spirits, Francine beat him to it. Suddenly she got up from her seat on the couch and motioned to George. "Put your hand gently over here," she said. George bent over and waved his hand where she had pointed. "Do you feel the cold air?" Francine asked.

"Slightly," George answered.

"She's been sitting here. Now she's left. Now follow the couch. Feel it over here?"

George put his hand near a pillow. "Oh, yeah, it feels warm."

Francine beckoned George and Kathy to follow her. The three entered the dining room while Eric remained in the living room by the fireplace. Francine stood next to the big table. "There's an unusual odor here," she said. "I can't quite place it, but it's here. Whew! Do you smell *that*?"

George sniffed. "Yeah, right here. It's a smell of perspiration."

The girl headed for the kitchen, but hesitated before

159

going into the breakfast nook. "There's an old man and an old lady." "They are lost spirits. Do you smell the perfume?"

Kathy's eyes widened. Quickly she looked at George, who shrugged. "Evidently these people must have had the house at one time," Francine continued, "but they died. Only I don't think they died in the house." She turned to George and said, "I want to go to the basement now, okay?"

When George had first spoken to Francine on the telephone, he told her that mysterious things were happening in his house—but without ever really spelling out what the phenomena were, nor what had actually taken place with Kathy and himself. He hadn't discussed the touchings in the kitchen nor the smell of perfume Kathy had experienced. In any case, Francine had said she would rather draw her own conclusions after visiting the house and "talking to the spirits who live there."

Now Francine descended the stairs to the cellar. "The house is built on a burial ground or something like that," she said. She pointed to a large area of the basement where the storage closets were built. "Is that new?" she asked George.

"I don't think so," he answered. "As far as I know, it was all built at the same time."

Francine stopped in front of the closets. "There are people buried right here. Something is over them. There is an unusual odor. This should not be stuffy at all like this." She was pointing directly at the plywood paneling that hid the secret room. "Notice the chill?" Her hands were moving now, touching the wood. "Somebody was murdered, or he could even be buried under here. But this seems like a new part, like a new part has been added on, and over this grave."

Kathy wanted to run from the basement. Her husband noticed her discomfort and reached for her hand. Francine solved their dilemma. "I don't like this spot at all. It's better that we go upstairs now." Without waiting for a response, she turned and headed for the basement staircase.

As they went up to the second floor, Francine's boyfriend Eric joined them. She stood in the hallway, holding on to the banister. "I have to say that when I came up here, there was a whirling sensation. I felt a tightness on the right half of my chest."

"A pain?" Kathy asked.

Francine nodded. "Very slight, very quick. Right as you turn the corner. It disappeared quickly." She stepped to the closed door of the sewing room. "You've been having problems in here."

George and Kathy both nodded. He opened the door, half expecting to find the flies in the room. But there were none, and he and Francine walked inside. Kathy and Eric hung back in the doorway.

Suddenly Francine appeared to go into a trance. Out of her mouth came a different voice, heavier, more masculine: "I would like to make one suggestion to you. Most people find out who their spirits are and they find they like them. They don't want them to get lost or to go away. But in this case, I feel this house should be cleared or exorcised."

The voice coming from Francine began to sound familiar to George. He couldn't quite place it, but he was sure he had heard it before. "Somebody's little girl and boys . . . I see bloodstains. Somebody hurt themselves badly here. Somebody tried to kill themselves or something . . .".

Francine came out of her trance. "I would like to go now," she announced to George and Kathy. "It's not a good time to try to talk to the spirits. I have a feeling I should go. I was born with a Venetian Veil, you know." George didn't know what she meant, but she promised George to return in a day or so—"When the vibrations are better," she explained. The couple departed almost immediately.

Back in the living room, George and Kathy were

silent for a long time. Finally Kathy asked, "What do you think?"

"I don't know," George answered. "I just don't know. She was hitting things right on the head." He stood up to put out the fire. "I have to think about it for a while."

Kathy went upstairs to check on the children. Again Harry was staying with the boys since it was too cold out for even a rugged dog. George made his usual check of all the doors and locks, then turned out the lights on the first floor.

He went up the steps to his bedroom, then stopped before he reached the second floor landing. George saw that the banister above him was wrenched from its moorings, torn almost completely off the floor foundation.

At that very instant, he recalled whose voice had been speaking to him through Francine. It was Father Mancuso!

19 **January 8** — On Thursday, Jimmy and his new bride Carey returned from their honeymoon in Bermuda. They called Kathy from Mrs. Conners', and Jimmy told his sister he would drop over later in the day. One of his first questions was whether she and George had found his $1,500. He was very disappointed when Kathy told him there had been no trace of the envelope.

It had taken George all morning to fit the second floor banister's broken anchor posts back in their sockets. When the boys came down for breakfast, both wanted to help, but George shooed them out of the way, telling them they had to go shopping for new shoes with their mother.

No one—Danny, Chris, Missy, or Kathy—had heard the banister being wrenched off its posts during the night. What had caused this latest damage in the house remained a mystery. George and Kathy had their own ideas, but did not voice them in front of the children.

Finally Kathy gathered herself together and herded her brood out to the van to go shopping. George took the opportunity to call Eric. He reached him at home and asked the young man if Francine had said anything after leaving their home. George was troubled to hear that the girl had been very upset with what she felt in the house. She had told Eric she didn't ever want to go back there; the presence was much too strong. She feared if she tried to talk to whatever was at the Lutzes', she would be in danger of a physical attack.

"Eric," George asked, "what's the Venetian Veil she mentioned just before you left?"

"From what Francine's told me," Eric answered, "that's a caul some babies are born with—a kind of skin covering, like a thin veil, over the face. It can be removed, but Francine says that that person is somehow blessed with a highly developed degree of clairvoyance."

George hung up and sat in the kitchen for over an hour, trying to think of where or how he could get help before it was too late.

Then the telephone rang. It was George Kekoris, a field investigator for the Psychical Research Institute in North Carolina, who said he had been told to contact George and arrange to set up some scientific tests at the Lutz home. Kekoris also said he couldn't make it that day, since he was calling from Buffalo, but would try to get there the next morning.

After speaking to Kekoris, George felt as if he had received a last-minute reprieve. Then, to pass the time until Kathy returned, he busied himself by taking down the Christmas decorations from the tree standing in the living room. Tenderly he placed the delicate ornaments on spread newspapers for Kathy to repack in cardboard boxes, taking special care of his great-grandmother's beautiful gold and silver piece.

All that Thursday morning and afternoon, Father Mancuso nursed his recurrent case of flu. He had resigned himself to this newest affliction as another show of power and displeasure by the evil force he had alienated at 112 Ocean Avenue.

This time there had been no solicitous call by the Pastor, even though Father Mancuso was sure the cleric had been informed of his new illness. He remained in his own apartment, resting in bed, using the medication he had been given on the doctor's previous visits. His fever ranged as high as 104 degrees, his stomach hurt continuously, and as the day wore on, he alternated between chills and sweating. Fortunately no marks had erupted on his palms—a sign that Father Mancuso interpreted to mean that he was receiving a lesser degree of punishment for involving himself again with the Lutzes.

Father Mancuso hadn't even attempted to reach the Chancellors' office again. The priest felt that the aches and pains would eventually lessen if he divorced himself from thinking about the Lutz situation, and so he waited for Father Ryan or Father Nuncio to get in touch with him. At one point during the afternoon, in fact, the priest hoped that the Chancellors would ignore his request for another audience. He passed the time by reading from his breviary.

By four o'clock, Kathy had returned from shopping. Since the Lutzes still had Jimmy's car, there was no way for the honeymooners to travel unless they were picked up. Kathy volunteered to go after her brother and his new wife.

George vetoed her suggestion—the icy roads to her mother's in East Babylon were still in a hazardous condition, and Jimmy's car had a stick shift—a gear system Kathy had never really mastered. George drove instead and was back in Amityville within the hour.

Kathy was delighted to see Jimmy and Carey again and spent the next hours eagerly listening to their account of every single moment they had spent in Bermuda. The newlyweds also had a bundle of Polaroid snapshots to go through with a detailed explanation behind each one. Jimmy didn't have a dime left, he said, but they had memories that would last a lifetime. Naturally they had brought some presents for the children, and that kept Danny, Chris, and Missy out of the adults' way for most of the evening.

Rather than spoil the pleasant visit by recalling their own weird experiences since the wedding, George and Kathy simply shared the excitement of the other two. Eventually Kathy and her new sister-in-law went upstairs to change the linen on Missy's bed. Jimmy and Carey would be staying overnight in Missy's room, while the little girl slept on an old couch in the dressing room down the hall.

Jimmy explained to George his plans for moving out of his mother's house. He wanted to rent an apartment situated exactly between his mother's house and his new in-laws, who also lived in East Babylon; this way, both families would be placated for a while

Everyone retired fairly early. Before turning in, George and Jimmy checked the house inside and out. George showed Jimmy the damaged garage door, but didn't offer any explanation beyond the theory that it was caused by a freak windstorm. Jimmy, who had been victimized of his money by an unknown source, was suspicious of something else, but he too kept silent and followed George as he checked the boathouse.

Back inside, they continued their tour of doors and windows, until both were satisfied with the security of 112 Ocean Avenue. It was eleven o'clock when the couples said goodnight to one another.

George knows that it happened at 3:15 A.M. because he had been lying awake a few minutes and had just checked his wristwatch. It was then that Carey woke up screaming.

"Oh, God, not her too!" he muttered to himself. George leaped out of bed, ran to Missy's room, and snapped on the light. The young couple were huddled together in bed, Jimmy cradling his sobbing wife.

"What's the matter?" George asked. "What's happened?"

Carey pointed to the foot of Missy's bed. "S-s-something was sitting there! It touched m-m-my foot!"

George approached the spot Carey had indicated and felt the bed with his hand. It was warm as though someone had been sitting there.

"I woke up," Carey continued, "and I could see a little boy. He looked so sick! He was trying to tell me to help him!" She began to cry hysterically.

Jimmy shook his wife gently. "Come on, Carey," he said soothingly. "You were probably having a dream, and—"

"No, Jimmy!" Carey protested. "It wasn't a dream! I saw him! He spoke to me!"

"What did he say, Carey?" George asked.

Carey's shoulder's were still shaking, but gradually she looked up from her husband's cradling arms. George heard a noise behind him and a touch on his shoulder. He jumped, then looked around. It was Kathy. Her eyes were misty, as though she too had been crying. "Kathy!" Carey cried.

"What did the little boy say?" Kathy prompted her.

"He asked me where Missy and Jodie were!"

At the mention of Missy's name, Kathy bolted from the bedroom and ran to the other side of the hallway. In the dressing room the little girl was fast asleep, with one foot sticking out in the air. Kathy lifted Missy's blanket and bent her leg back under the covers, then leaned down and kissed her child on the head. George came into the room. "Is Missy all right?"

Kathy nodded.

In about fifteen minutes Carey had quieted down enough to fall asleep again. Jimmy was still nervous, but soon he too drifted off.

George and Kathy had shut the door on the couple and returned to their own bedroom. Immediately she went into the closet and took out the crucifix that hung inside. "George," she said, "let's bless the house ourselves."

They began on the third floor, in the children's playroom. In the eerie predawn silence of the cold room, George held the crucifix in front of him while Kathy intoned the Lord's Prayer. They did not go into Danny and Chris' room; Kathy said they could wait until the next day to bless that room and the ones in which Missy and Jimmy and Carey were sleeping.

They moved on to their own bedroom, and then to the sewing room on the second floor. Warning his wife to be careful of the newly repaired banister, George led the way down to the first floor, still brandishing the silver crucifix as he supposed a priest would during a holy procession.

When they completed their blessing of the kitchen and the dining room, it was just starting to get light outside. Even without turning on the lights, they could see the living room dimly visible before them. George marched around the furniture and Kathy started to recite: "Our Father who art in Heaven; hallowed be thy—"

She was interrupted by a loud humming. Kathy stopped and looked about her. George halted in midstride and looked up at the ceiling. The hum swelled into a jumble of voices that seemed to engulf them completely.

Finally Kathy clasped her hands to her ears to drown out the cacophony of noise, but George clearly heard the chorus thunder: *"Will you stop!"*

20 **January 8 to 9** — Father Mancuso felt too weak to celebrate Mass at the church, so he remained in his quarters, praying at his prie-dieu. The phone rang. It was Father Nuncio calling from the Chancellor's office to say that he and Father Ryan could see Father Mancuso.

The priest pleaded that his illness prevented him from coming to the Chancery, but asked whether he could discuss the Lutz situation over the telephone. Father Nuncio agreed and listened as Father Mancuso related the latest developments at 112 Ocean Avenue. Without hesitation, the Chancellor agreed with Father Mancuso's suggestion that the Lutzes move out of their house for a while. Father Mancuso informed Father Nuncio of his decision not to return to the house in Amityville and said that he would merely relay the message over the telephone.

In Amityville, Kathy and George were still shaken from the previous night's performance by the unseen chorus. She had remained awake, sitting in their bedroom. George returned the crucifix to the closet wall and then he and Kathy held hands, each whispering reassuring words to soothe the other's fright. At eight o'clock, Kathy had risen from the edge of the bed and awakened the children. Jimmy and Carey came out of Missy's bedroom at eighty-thirty, dressed and ready for breakfast.

After speaking to Father Nuncio, Father Mancuso called George Lutz to tell him of the Chancellor's decision. He let the telephone ring for a long time and was ready to give up when George answered. Father Mancuso assumed the instrument was up to its weird tricks, so he was surprised that he had gotten through without interference.

George said that they had just returned from seeing Jimmy off to East Babylon. Then George repeated the results of their impromptu blessing ceremony the night before. Dismayed, Father Mancuso urged George to heed the Chancellors' advice and get out of the house then and there. "And George," he said, "don't ever do that again. Your evoking God's name in the manner you did can only anger whatever is in your house. Just don't do *anything* anymore. It's already completely out of hand . . .".

"Father," George interrupted. "What are you saying?"

The priest hesitated. Had he said too much? The Chancellors had confined any discussion of the Lutzes' case to scientific causes, and there would be a long period of investigation before the Church would acknowledge demonic influence. He hadn't meant to express his own personal fears. "I'm not sure," Father

Mancuso corrected himself. "That's why I plead with you to leave your house now until some determination can be made, scientifically or . . ." The priest hesitated.

"Or what?" George asked.

"It may be more dangerous than any of us realize," Father Mancuso answered. "Look, George, many things happen that none of us can really explain away. I admit I'm very confused about what seems to be an evil force in your house. I also admit that it may be caused by more than our imaginations." The priest paused.

"George? You still there?"

"Yeah, Father. I'm listening."

"All right, then," Father Mancuso began again. "Please get out. Let things cool down for a while. If you get away, maybe we can all think this thing out with more rationality. I'll tell the Chancellors what happened last night and maybe they'll send someone right . . ."

Father Mancuso was interrupted by Kathy's scream over the telephone. George blurted, "Call you back!" and the priest heard him bang down the receiver. He stood there in his living room, wondering what unnatural act was now being played out at 112 Ocean Avenue.

George ran up the stairs to the third floor. When he reached the landing, he saw Kathy in the hallway shrieking at Danny, Chris, and Missy.

George could see why: On every wall in the hall were green gelatinous spots, oozing down from the ceiling to the floor, settling in shimmering pools of green slime.

"Which one of you did this?" Kathy fumed. "Tell me or I'll break every bone in your bodies!"

"We didn't do it, Mama!" all three children chorused at once, dodging the slaps she was aiming at their heads.

"We didn't do it!" Danny yelled. "We saw it when we came upstairs!"

George stepped between his wife and the children. "Wait a minute, honey," he said gently, "maybe the kids *didn't* do it. Let me take a look."

He went up to one wall and stuck his finger into a green spot. He looked at the substance, smelled it, and then put a little against the tip of his tongue. "It sure looks like Jello," he said, smacking his lips, "but it doesn't have any taste at all."

Kathy was calming down after her tirade. "Could it be paint?" she asked.

George shook his head. "Nope." He tried to get the feel of the jelly by rolling it against his finger tips. "I don't know what it is, but it sure leaves a mess."

He looked up at the ceiling. "Doesn't seem to be coming from up there . . .". George stopped. He looked around him as if realizing for the first time where he was. In a rush, he recalled the conversation he had had with Father Mancuso a few minutes before, and the dreaded word "Devil" almost slipped from his lips.

"What'd you say, George?" asked Kathy. "I didn't hear you."

He looked at his wife and children. "Nothing. I was just trying to think . . .". He began to edge the others toward the staircase. "Listen," he said, "I'm hungry. Let's go down to the kitchen and have a bite. Then the boys and me'll come back up and clean up this gook. Okay, gang?"

Jimmy and Carey had arrived back in East Babylon. Carey was happy to be away from 112 Ocean Avenue, even if it meant being at her mother-in-law's. "I felt creepy there, Jimmy," she said, as they got out of their car. "I know I saw that little boy last night, no matter what anybody says."

Jimmy reached out and patted his wife's behind. "Aw, forget it, baby," he said. "It was just a dream. You know I don't believe in that stuff."

Carey squirmed away from Jimmy's touch, looking around to see if any neighbors were watching. But as she was about to go in the door, he grabbed her arm. "Listen, Carey," he said, drawing her close, "do me a favor. Don't mention what happened in front of Ma. She gets very upset about such things. Next thing you know, we'll have a priest over here."

Carey stood her ground. "What about our money you lost at Kathy's? You say that was a dream, too?"

Father Mancuso spent the rest of the afternoon wondering why George hadn't called him back after hearing Kathy scream. At one point, he considered calling Sergeant Giofriddo of the Suffolk County Police to check on the Lutzes. But a policeman ringing their bell out of the blue might cause them even more alarm. Oh, God, he thought, I hope nothing's happened. Finally the priest picked up the phone and dialed George's number.

There was no answer—because the whole family was out back in the boathouse, where the noise of the compressor drowned out the sounds of the rings. George, Danny, and Chris were dumping gobs of green jelly into the freezing water beside their boat. The compressor hose kept churning the substance, mixing it with the icy water so that it was swept below the ice.

As the boys flung it over from the narrow wooden walkway, Kathy was brushing away what fell from their pails. Missy was holding onto Harry to keep the dog out of everyone's way. George worked in silence, trying not to communicate his fears to Kathy and the children. Fortunately for him, Kathy still suspected that the children had been responsible for the mess; she hadn't yet equated the green slime with the other mysterious problems that afflicted the house.

George had been so absorbed in his thoughts that he had completely forgotten to call Father Mancuso back. By that evening, sitting beside the fireplace, Kathy was all for leaving for her mother's. But when she suggested they get out of the house that night, George suddenly went berserk. "Goddammit, no!" he shouted, jumping up from his chair, his face red with rage.

All the pressures that had been building within him finally exploded. "Every goddamn thing we own in the world is in this house!" he stormed. "I've got too much invested here to give it up just like that!"

The children, who were still up, cringed and ran to their mother's side. Even Kathy was frightened by a side of George that she had never seen. He had the look of a man possessed.

Absolutely livid, he stood at the foot of the staircase and screamed so that he could be heard in every room in the house. "You sons of bitches! Get out of my house!" Then he ran up the stairs to the third floor and into the playroom and threw all the windows open wide. "Get out! Get out in the name of God!"

George ran into the boys' bedroom, then down to the second floor and repeated his actions, shoving up each window in every room, bellowing, "Get out in the name of God!" again and again.

Some of the windows resisted his push, and he banged furiously on the frames until they loosened. Cold air poured in from outside, and soon the whole house was as frigid as the outdoors.

Finally George was finished. By the time he returned to the first floor, the anger was leaving his body. Exhausted from his efforts and panting heavily, he stood in the center of the living room, tightly clenching and unclenching his fists.

While George was on his holy errand, Kathy and the children had been rooted to a spot near the fireplace. Now they came up to him slowly, encircled him, and he lifted his arms and embraced all four frightened people.

There was a fifth, very human witness to this tableau. Sergeant Al Gionfriddo, the police officer whom Father Mancuso had wanted to call, had been making a final check of Amityville before he went off duty at nine. As he was passing down Ocean Avenue, the astonishing sight of a madman tearing around in 112, opening windows in the dead of winter, had caused him to brake his cruiser.

Gionfriddo pulled up at the intersection where South Ireland Place cuts into Ocean Avenue, directly opposite the Lutzes'. He turned off his headlights. Something was holding him back from getting out of his car and going up to that front door. He really didn't want to investigate why the owner was behaving like a lunatic. Gionfriddo sat there and watched as a woman went around and shut all the windows in the house.

That must be Mrs. Lutz, he thought. They seem to be all right now. I'll just keep my nose out of it. He sighed and turned over the motor of his car. Keeping his headlights off, the policeman slowly backed down South Ireland Place until he could make a left turn on the street that paralleled Ocean. Only then did he turn on his lights.

Over the following hour, 112 Ocean Avenue warmed up again. The heat from the radiators finally overcame the frigid air that had invaded the house, and once more the thermostat read 75 degrees.

The boys had been dozing in front of the fireplace, while Kathy held little Missy in her arms, rocking the sleeping girl. At ten o'clock she checked the children's bedrooms and decided that Danny and Chris could now go to bed.

Since his tirade, George had been completely uncommunicative, silently staring at his blazing logs. Kathy left him alone, realizing her husband was trying to resolve their dilemma in his own way. After the children were tucked away upstairs, she finally went to him and gently tried to urge him out of the room.

George looked at Kathy and she saw the confusion and anger in his face. His eyes were misty; George seemed to be crying over his frustration. The poor guy deserves a break, she thought. He shook his head at her suggestion to go up to bed.

"You go," he said softly. "I'll be up in a while." His eyes returned to the dancing flames.

In her bedroom, Kathy left the lamp on George's nightstand burning. She undressed, slipped into bed, and closed her eyes. Kathy could hear the wind howling outside. The sound slowly relaxed her so that in a few minutes she began to doze off.

Suddenly Kathy sat bolt upright and looked at George's side of the bed. He still wasn't there. Then she slowly turned her head and looked behind her. She saw her image reflected in the mirrors that covered the wall from ceiling to floor, and she had the urge to get the crucifix out of the closet again.

So strong was the feeling that Kathy was halfway out of bed when she stopped and again stared into the mirrors. Her image seemed to take on a life of its own, and she could hear it saying: "Don't do it! You'll destroy everyone!"

When George came up to the bedroom, he found Kathy asleep. He adjusted the covers about his wife, then went to her nightstand and removed her Bible from its drawer. He turned out his light and silently left the room.

George returned to his chair in the living room, opened the Bible and began at the beginning, the Book of Genesis. In this first book of God's revelations, he came upon verses that caused him to reflect upon his predicament. He read one aloud to himself: "And the Lord God said to the serpent: Because thou hast done this thing, thou art cursed among all cattle, and beasts of the earth: upon thy breast shalt thou go, and earth thou shalt eat all the days of thy life."

George shivered. The serpent is the Devil, he thought. Then he felt a hot blast on his face, and he snapped his head up from the book. The flames of the fireplace were reaching out for him!

George leaped off his chair and jumped back. The fire he had left to die was roaring to life again, the blaze filling the entire hearth. He could feel its searing heat. But then he was stabbed in the back by an icy finger.

George whirled about. Nothing was there, but he could feel a draft. He could almost see it in the form of a cold mist coming down the staircase in the hallway!

Gripping the Bible tightly, George raced up the steps toward his bedroom. The cold wrapped itself about him as he ran. He stopped in his bedroom doorway. The room was warm. Again he was struck by the icy fingers.

George ran to Missy's bedroom and flung open the door. The windows were wide open, the below-freezing air pouring in.

George grabbed up his daughter from her bed. He could feel her little body was icy and shivering. Rushing out of the room, he ran back to his bedroom and put Missy under the cover. Kathy woke up. "Warm her up!" George yelled. "She's freezing to death!"

Without hesitation, Kathy covered the little girl with her own body. George ran out of the room and up to the third floor.

The windows in Danny's and Chris' bedroom, George found, were also wide open. The boys were asleep but burrowed completely under their blankets. He gathered both in his arms and staggered down the stairs to his bedroom.

Danny's and Chris' teeth were chattering from the cold. George pushed them onto the bed and got under the blankets with them, his body on top of theirs.

All five Lutzes were in one bed, the three children slowly thawing out, the two parents rubbing their hands and feet. It took almost a half hour before the children's body temperatures seemed back to normal. Only then did George realize he was still holding onto the Bible. Knowing he had been more than warned, he flung it to the floor.

21 **January 10** — On Saturday morning, Kathy's mother, Joan, received a frantic call from her daughter: "Ma, I need you immediately." When Mrs. Conners tried to question Kathy over the phone as to what had happened she said only that there was no way to explain; her mother had to see for herself. The older woman took a cab from East Babylon to the house in Amityville.

George let his mother-in-law in and hurried her upstairs to Kathy's bedroom. Coming back down, he cautioned Danny, Chris, and Missy to finish their breakfast. When he left the kitchen to join the two women upstairs, the children were unnaturally subdued and meekly obeyed their father. But judging from the way they were eating, they had evidently recovered from their freezing experience the night before.

When George entered his bedroom, his mother-in-law was examining Kathy, who lay on the bed naked beneath her open bathrobe. Kathy watched as her mother's finger traced the ugly red welts that extended from just above her pubic hairline to the bottom of her breasts. The streaks were flaming red as though she had been burned by a hot poker slashed laterally across Kathy's body.

"Ow!" her mother winced, jerking a finger back from one of the welts on Kathy's stomach. "I burned myself!"

"I told you to be careful, Mama!" Kathy cried. "It happened to George, too!"

Kathy's mother looked at him, and George nodded. "I tried putting some cold cream on them," he said, "but even that didn't help. The only way you can touch her is with gloves."

"Did you call the doctor?"

"No, Ma," Kathy answered.

"She didn't want the doctor," George broke in. "She only wanted you."

"Does it hurt, Kathy?"

The frightened girl began to cry. George answered for her. "They don't seem to. Only when she touches them."

Kathy's mother put a hand to her sobbing girl's hair, stroking it gently. "My poor baby," she said. "Don't you worry now, I'm here. Everything's going to be all right." She leaned forward and kissed Kathy's tear-stained face. Then she closed Kathy's bathrobe, softly folding it over her inflamed body. She stood up. "I'm going to call Dr. Aiello."

"No!" cried Kathy. She looked at her husband, her eyes wild. "George!"

George put his hand out to Mrs. Conners. "What are you going to tell him?"

Kathy's mother was confused. "What do you mean?" she asked. "You can see she's burned all over her body."

George was insistent. "But how are you going to explain it to him, Ma? We don't even know how it happened. She just woke up that way. He'll think we're nuts!"

He hesitated. If he told Kathy's mother any more about what had happened during the night, he would have to disclose the demonic events that were plaguing the house. Knowing Mrs. Conners' heavily Church-oriented background, George felt sure that she would insist upon Kathy and the children leaving until she could talk to her priest. George had met the cleric and knew him to be very much like the elderly confessor at St. Martin of Tours in Amityville—unworldly when it came to anything beyond simple parish duties. In reality, George would have welcomed a priest, but not the one from East Babylon. And he did expect to hear momentarily from George Kekoris, the psychical investigator.

"Let her rest a while, Ma," he finally said. "The marks seem to be easing up from what they were before. Maybe they'll go away soon." He was remembering the slash lines on Kathy's face.

"Yeah, Mama," Kathy said, also fearing to involve her mother any more deeply. "I'll lie here a little longer. Can you stay with me?"

Kathy's mother looked from her daughter to George. There's something going on that they're not telling me about, she thought to herself. She would have liked to tell Kathy that she had never liked this house; that each time she was here she felt uncomfortable. She just did not trust 112 Ocean Avenue. Looking back, Mrs. Joan Conners now knows why.

George left the two women upstairs and went down to the kitchen. Danny, Chris, and Missy had finished their food and had even cleared off the table in the breakfast nook. When he came in, there were questions in their eyes. "Mama's all right," George assured them. "Grandma's going to stay with her."

He put his hand on top of Missy's head and turned her toward the doorway. "Come on, gang," George said, "let's go out for a while. We gotta get some things at the store, and I want to stop at the library."

After George and the children had driven off, Kathy's mother left her daughter alone for a few minutes and went downstairs to the kitchen to call Jimmy. Her son would want to know why she had rushed off to Kathy's so hurriedly. Jimmy had wanted to drive Mrs. Conners to Kathy's but she said he should stay at home in case she needed anything from her house.

Over the phone, she told Jimmy that Kathy only had some stomach cramps; she'd call him later when she was about to leave. Jimmy didn't believe her and said he wanted to come over with Carey. He was *not* to come, his mother yelled at him, and he wasn't to bring Carey. She didn't want the report that Jimmy's family was a little crazy to get back to her son's new in-laws.

Kathy, lying in bed, could hear her mother downstairs, shouting into the telephone at her brother. She sighed and opened her robe once more to look at the burning red marks on her body. The welts were still there, but they did seem fainter. Then she tried touching one of the slashes under her right breast. Her finger rested on the ugly spot. It seemed to Kathy that the sensation wasn't as severe as before. The reaction was more like putting her finger under very warm water. Again she sighed.

Kathy was about to close her bathrobe when she sensed someone was staring at her nakedness. The feeling of a presence came from right behind her, but Kathy couldn't bring herself to turn and look. She knew the mirrored wall was there and she was afraid that in it, she would see something terrible. Paralyzed with fear, she was unable to even raise her arms to draw the robe about her. She remained that way, her body completely exposed, her eyes tightly shut, cringing inwardly, waiting for the unknown touch.

"Kathy! What are you doing! You'll catch your death of cold!" It was her mother, back from the kitchen.

Even after the red welts had completely disappeared, Mrs. Conners didn't want to leave Kathy. When George returned with the children, she argued that the whole family should leave 112 Ocean Avenue. *He* could stay if he wanted, but she insisted her Kathy and her grandchildren go.

By then, Kathy was asleep upstairs and after the latest episode, George didn't want to awaken her. "Let her sleep a little longer, Ma," he said. "We'll see about coming over later."

His mother-in-law had agreed reluctantly, getting him to promise to call her the minute her daughter awoke. If you don't, George, I'll be back!" she warned him. He called her a cab, and she returned to East Babylon at four in the afternoon.

At the Amityville library, George had been able to secure a temporary borrower's card and take out one book—on witches and demons. Now that his mother-in-law had gone home, he sat alone in the living room, deep in the subject of the Devil and his works.

It was after eight in the evening before George finished his borrowed book. During the afternoon, Kathy's mother had prepared spaghetti and meatballs that George set out at suppertime. Danny, Chris and Missy ate while George continued reading. The last time he had looked in on Kathy, she stirred a little and he thought she was about ready to awaken from her much needed rest. Now he was in the kitchen and the three children were in the living room watching television.

George had made notes while going through the book, and now he looked at what he had jotted down. On the pad was a list of demons, with names he had never heard of. George tried to pronounce them aloud, and they rolled strangely off his tongue. Then he decided to call Father Mancuso.

The priest was surprised that the Lutzes were still at 112 Ocean Avenue. "I thought you were going to leave the house," he said. "I told you what the Chancellors said to do."

"I know, Father, I know," answered George. "But now I think I know how to lick this thing." He picked up the book from the table. "I've been reading about how these witches and demons work . . .".

Good Lord, Father Mancuso thought, I'm dealing with a child, an innocent. Here the man's house is about to explode under him and his family, and he's talking to me about witches. . . .

". . . And it says here if you hold an incantation and repeat those demons' names three times, you can call them up," George went on. "There's a ceremony in here that shows you exactly what to do. Iscaron, Madeste!", George began to chant. "Those are the names of the demons, Father . . .".

"I know who they are!" Father Mancuso blurted.

"Then there's Isabo! Erz, erz—this one's hard to pronounce. Erzelaide. She has something to do with voodoo. And Eslender!"

"George!" the priest cried. "For God's sake! Don't invoke those names again! Not now! Not ever!"

"Why, Father?" George protested. "It's right here in this book. What's wrong with . . .".

The telephone went dead in George's hand. There was an unearthly moan, a loud clicking, and then just the sound of a disconnected line. Did Father Mancuso hang up on me? George wondered. And what's happened to this guy Kekoris?

"Was that my mother?"

George turned and saw Kathy standing in the doorway. No longer in her bathrobe, she had combed her hair and was wearing slacks and a sweater. Her face was slightly flushed.

George shook his head. "How do you feel, honey?" he asked. "Have a good sleep?"

Kathy lifted up her sweater, baring her navel. "It's gone." She stroked herself. "They're not there anymore." She sat down at the table. "Where are the kids?"

"They're watching television," George answered. He took her hands in his. "You want to call your mother now?"

Kathy nodded. She felt strangely relaxed, almost sensual. Ever since she had the sensation of being stared at in her bed, Kathy had been in a languorous mood, as if she had been completely satisfied sexually. It had even carried over into her recent nap, she mused, when she had unconnected visions of making love to someone. It wasn't George. . . .

Kathy dialed her mother's number while George went into the living room with the children. He heard a loud clap of thunder. Looking out the windows, he saw the first raindrops strike the panes. Then somewhere in the distance, a flash of lightning hit the darkness and again, a few moments later, came another boom of thunder. George could make out the silhouettes of trees swaying in the rising gusts.

Kathy came into the room. "My mother says it's raining cats and dogs there," she announced. "She wants us to use our van rather than have Jimmy come for us."

The rain was coming down much harder now, beating heavily against the windows and outside walls. "From the sound of that," George said, "none of us is going anywhere at the moment."

When she had left her bedroom, Kathy opened the windows about an inch to air out the room. Even if there wasn't much room for water to get in, with the coming storm, she wanted to play it safe. "Danny," she called. "Run up to my room and close the windows tight. Okay?"

George himself ran out to bring Harry inside. In spite of the sheets of icy rain that lashed at him, George could feel the cold spell was breaking up. The rains would wash away the dirty piles of accumulated snow. There was a problem living right on the river though, for such a heavy rainfall could add to the frozen waters and overflow the bulkheads.

George came back inside, with Harry gratefully shaking himself, just in time to hear Danny, still upstairs, cry out in pain. Kathy raced ahead of George up the stairs to their bedroom. Danny stood at a window, the fingers of his right hand trapped under the window. With his left he was trying to push up the heavy wooden frame.

George pushed Kathy aside and ran to the boy who was yelling and trying to pull his fingers free. George tried to slide the window back up, but it refused to budge. He hammered at the frame but instead of releasing itself, the window vibrated, only hurting Danny more. In his frustration, George became furious and started to curse, shouting obscenities at his unseen, unknown enemies.

Suddenly the window came free on its own and shot up a few inches, freeing Danny. He grabbed his fingers in his other hand, cradling them and crying hysterically for his mother.

Kathy took the injured hand in her own. Danny didn't want to open his fist, and she had to shout at him. "Let me *see*, Danny! Open your fist!"

Averting his eyes, the boy extended his arm. Kathy screamed when she saw what his fingers looked like—all except the thumb were strangely flat. Even more frightened by his mother's anguished cry, Danny jerked his hand away.

George exploded. Running like a madman again from room to room, he screamed invectives, challenging whatever was doing this to his family to come out and fight. There was as much of a storm raging inside 112 Ocean Avenue as outside, as Kathy chased after her husband asking him to call a doctor for Danny.

The rage within George soon spent itself. He suddenly became aware that his little boy was hurt and needed medical attention. He ran to the kitchen telephone and tried to call Kathy's family doctor, John Aiello. But the line was dead. As he later learned, the storm had torn down a telephone pole, locking the Lutzes in their house even more effectively.

"I'll have to drive Danny to the hospital," George shouted. "Put his jacket on!"

The Brunswick Hospital Center is on Broadway in Amityville, no more than a mile from the Lutzes' house. Because of the hurricane-force winds raging through Long Island's South Shore, it took George almost fifteen minutes to get there.

The intern on duty was amazed at the condition of Danny's fingers, which were flattened from the cuticle to the second knuckle. But though they certainly looked crushed beyond repair, they were not broken, with no smashed bones or cartilage. He bandaged them securely, gave George some children's aspirin for Danny and suggested they return home. There was nothing more he could do.

By then, the young boy was more frightened from the way his fingers looked than from any pain. While George drove home, he held his hand stiffly against his chest, sobbing and moaning. Again it took George close to twenty minutes to drive back to 112 Ocean Avenue. The winds whipped the front door of the house back against the building, and he had trouble trying to close it behind him.

Kathy had put Chris and Missy in her own bed and was waiting in the living room. She picked up her eldest and rocked him in her arms. Danny finally cried himself to sleep, exhausted by the gruelling pain and fear.

George carried Danny up to their bedroom. Taking off only the boy's shoes, he slid him under the covers next to the other two children. Then he and Kathy sat down in chairs by the windows and watched the rain smash against the panes.

They dozed fitfully all the rest of the night. They had

to stay home—it was impossible to try and get to Kathy's mother or to any other place to sleep—but they were alert to any other dangers that might threaten their children or themselves. Toward dawn both fell asleep.

At six-thirty George was awakened by the rain spattering against his face. For an instant he thought he was outdoors—but no, he was still inside in his chair by the window. Jumping up, he saw that every window in the room was wide open, some frames torn away from their jambs. Then he heard the wind and rain coming through in other parts of the house. He rushed out of the bedroom.

Every room he went into was in the same condition—window panes broken, the doors on the second and third floors smashed open—even though every one had been locked and bolted! All the Lutzes had slept through what must have been a terrible racket.

22 **January 11** — The Lutzes had lived at 112
Ocean Avenue for twenty-five days. That Sunday was
one of the worst.

In the morning, they discovered that the battering rain
and wind of the night before had left the house a complete mess. Rainwater had stained the walls, curtains,
furniture, and rugs, from the first floor to the third floor.
Ten of the windows had broken panes and several had
their locks bent completely out of shape, making it impossible to shut them tightly. The locks to the doors of
the sewing room and playroom were twisted and forced
out of their metal frames; these couldn't be closed at all.
If the family had any intention of leaving for safer quarters, that idea had to be shelved in order to get the
house back in shape and secured.

In the kitchen, some of the cabinets were soaked and warped. Paint was chipped on the corners of almost every cabinet. Kathy hadn't really thought about those problems yet; she had her hands full mopping up almost an inch of muddy water that had accumulated on her tile flooring. She hoped she could dry the floor before the tiles peeled loose from their cement backing.

Danny and Chris had two large rolls of paper towels and were going from room to room wiping down the walls. When they had to reach beyond their arms' length, they used a little kitchen stepladder. Missy trailed along with the boys, picking up the wet towels they discarded and throwing them into a large plastic garbage bag.

George took down every set of curtains and drapes in the house. Some could be machine-washed, and those he carried downstairs to the basement laundry. The others that would have to be dry-cleaned were put in a pile in the dining room, the driest room in the house.

The Lutzes were strangely silent while they worked that morning and afternoon. This newest disaster had only made them more determined to survive in 112 Ocean Avenue. Nobody said it, but George, Kathy, Danny, Chris, and Missy Lutz were now ready to battle any force, natural or unnatural.

Even Harry was putting on a show of toughness. The half-breed malamute was on his lead in his compound, stalking back and forth through the mud, his tail high, teeth bared. The growls and snarls that came from deep within his heavy chest were signs that the dog would tear to shreds the first person or thing he didn't recognize. Every once in a while, Harry would stop his pacing, stare at the boathouse and let out a wolf-like howl that sent shivers down the spine of everyone who lived on Ocean Avenue.

When George finished with the sodden curtains, he began to work on the windows. First he cut heavy plastic sheets to cover the broken panes and sealed them to the window frames with white adhesive tape. It wasn't a pretty sight from the inside or out, but at least it kept out the steadily falling drizzle.

George had guessed right. The temperature had risen with the storm, and it was above freezing. A lot of damage had been done to the trees and bushes along Ocean Avenue, and looking up South Ireland Place, George could see that it too had its share of broken branches lying in the street. He did note, however, that the neighbors on either side of his house had no broken windows or any other exterior damages. Only me, George thought. Terrific!

The locks on the windows and doors were a more difficult matter. George didn't have the hardware to replace the catches on the windows, so he used a pair of pliers to twist off the smashed pieces of metal. Then he hammered heavy nails into the edges of the wooden frames and challenged his unseen foes: "Let me see you pull those out, you sons of bitches!"

The locks to the sewing room and playroom doors he removed completely. In the cellar he found some one-inch pine boards that were perfect for his needs. The doors opened outward into the hallway, so George nailed the boards diagonally across both. For whatever might have remained in the two mysterious rooms, there was no longer a way out.

George Kekoris finally telephoned, saying he'd like to come out and spend a night. There was only one problem—since Kekoris had no equipment with him, the Psychical Research Institute would have to consider the visit an informal one. He would have to draw conclusions without the rigorous controls required for scientific evaluation.

George said that didn't matter; he just wanted confirmation that all the weird events in their house weren't the product of his or Kathy's imagination. Kekoris asked

George whether any sensitives had been there, but George didn't understand what he meant by that term. The field investigator said they would go into that when he came to visit.

Before George hung up, Kekoris asked whether there was a dog in the house. George said he had Harry, a trained watch dog. Kekoris said that was good because animals were very sensitive to psychic phenomena. Again George was puzzled—but at least he had the first tangible evidence that help was on the way.

At three in the afternoon, Father Ryan left the Chancery in Rockville Centre. The Chancellor was concerned about Father Mancuso's mental welfare in the Lutz case, and since one of his duties in the diocese was to minister to the rectories, Father Ryan decided that now would be a good time to visit the Long Island rectory.

He found the bearded priest recovering from his third attack of flu in the past three weeks. Father Ryan said he was well aware of how highly the Bishop esteemed Father Mancuso as a cleric. But he wanted to know if Father Mancuso thought the recurring affliction could be psychosomatic. Wasn't it possible that his emotional state could be influencing his rash of illnesses?

Father Mancuso protested that he was rational, that he still believed that strong evil forces were responsible for his debilitation. He was willing to undergo a psychiatric examination by anyone the Chancellors selected.

The Chancellor made no further demand that Father Mancuso remain away from 112 Ocean Avenue, but stated that the decision would have to be his.

Father Mancuso was surprised and frightened. He understood he was being tested: If he did accept responsibility for the Lutzes, he would have the Chancellors' approbation; and if not, they would understand. But there was no way he was going to involve himself to that extent. He was deeply moved by the anxiety and problems that the Lutzes were undergoing and he could not, in conscience as a priest, simply excuse his own inherent fear, but he *was* terrified.

Father Mancuso finally said that before he made any more decisions in the case, for the Lutzes and for himself, he would like to talk directly to the Bishop. Chancellor Ryan recognized the urgency in the priest's request and said he would be in touch with the superior later in the day. He would call Father Mancuso that evening.

Kathy's mother called her around six o'clock, wanting to know if they were coming to her house to spend the night. Kathy took it on herself to say no: the house was still in a mess after the storm and she would have a lot of washing to do the next morning. And besides, Danny and Chris would have school, and they were missing too many days as it was.

Mrs. Conners reluctantly agreed, but made Kathy promise that she would call if anything out of the ordinary occurred; her mother would then send Jimmy over immediately. After Kathy hung up, she wondered aloud to George if she had done the right thing.

"We're gonna stick it out," he said. "Before you send the kids to bed, I'm going to go through the whole house with Harry. Kekoris said dogs are very sensitive to things like this."

"Are you sure you won't make them mad again?" Kathy asked. "You know what happened when we went around with the crucifix."

"No, no, Kathy, this is different. I just want to see if Harry can smell or hear anything."

"And what if he does? What are you going to do then?"

The dog, still in his aggressive mood, had to be kept on his leash. Harry was very powerful and George had to take a snug grip just to keep from being pulled along. "Come on, boy," he said, "sniff me out something." They went down to the basement.

George removed the leash from Harry's collar and the dog leaped forward. He circled the cellar, sniffing, sometimes scratching at spots along the bottom of the walls. When the dog came up against the storage closet that hid the red room, Harry again sniffed at the base of the paneling. Then his tail dipped between his legs, and he sank to his haunches. Harry began to whimper, turning his head to George.

"What is it, Harry?" George asked. "You smell something there?" Harry's whimpers grew more frantic and he began to crawl backwards. Then he barked at George, stood up, and ran back up the cellar steps. He waited at the top, quivering, until George came up and opened the door for him.

"What happened?" Kathy asked.

"Harry's afraid to go near the secret hideaway," George told her. He didn't put on the leash again, but walked Harry through the kitchen, dining room, living room, and enclosed porch. The dog's spirits picked up and he friskily sniffed around each room. But when George tried to take him upstairs, Harry hung back on the first step of the staircase.

"Come on," George urged him. "What's the matter with you?" The dog put one paw on the next step, but wouldn't move beyond that.

"I can get him upstairs!" Danny shouted. "He'll follow me!" The boy climbed past the dog and beckoned to him.

"No, Danny," George said. "You stay here. I'll handle Harry." George reached down and jerked the dog's collar. Harry moved reluctantly, then ran up the steps.

The dog walked around freely in both the master bedroom and the dressing room. Only when he approached

Missy's room did Harry hang back. George put both hands on the dog's haunches and pushed him, but he wouldn't enter her room. Harry behaved the same way in front of the boarded-up sewing room. Whimpering and whining with fear, Harry tried to wedge himself behind George.

"Goddammit, Harry," he said, "there isn't anyone in there. What's bugging you?"

As soon as Harry came into the boys' room on the third floor, he jumped up on Chris' bed. George chased him off. Shooed out of the room, the dog headed directly for the stairs, passing the play room without so much as a glance. George couldn't catch up with him.

George arrived downstairs behind the dog. "What happened?" Kathy asked.

"*Nothing* happened, that's what happened," he said.

Father Mancuso confirmed his appointment with the Bishop's secretary. The prelate personally telephoned and suggested that if the priest felt well enough to travel, he should be at the Rockville Centre diocese the following morning.

Father Mancuso said that it was only fifteen minutes away, and his temperature was normal. Though high winds were forecast, the weather promised to remain above freezing. Father Mancuso told the Bishop's secretary that all signs pointed to his being there.

At the Lutzes', as the day came to a close, the whole family was again in the master bedroom. The three children were in the bed, and George and Kathy were sitting up in chairs next to the damaged windows. The room seemed overly warm and everyone's eyes had begun to sting. George and Kathy thought it was from fatigue. One after another, they drifted off—first Missy, then Chris, Danny, Kathy, and finally George. Within ten minutes, everyone was fast asleep.

But very shortly, George was rudely shoved awake

by his wife. She and the children were standing in front of his chair, tears in their eyes. "What's the matter?" he mumbled sleepily.

"You were screaming, George," Kathy said, "and we couldn't wake you up!"

"Yeah, Daddy!" cried Missy. "You made Mama cry!"

Not fully awake, feeling almost drugged, George was completely befuddled. "Did I hurt you, Kathy?"

"Oh, no, honey!" she protested. "You didn't touch me."

"What happened, then?"

"You kept yelling, 'I'm coming apart!' And we couldn't wake you up!"

23 January 12 — George couldn't understand. Why did Kathy say he was yelling, "I'm coming apart!"? He knew perfectly well what he had said was "I'm coming *unglued*."

Now he remembered he had been sitting in the chair when suddenly he felt a powerful grip lift up the chair with him in it and slowly turn him around. Powerless to move, George saw the hooded figure he had first seen in the living room fireplace, its blasted half-face glaring at him. The horribly disfigured features became clearer to George. "God help me!" he screamed. Then he saw his own face emerge from beneath the white hood. It was torn in two. "I'm coming unglued!" George yelled.

Now still groggy, he began to argue with Kathy. "I

199

know what I said," he muttered. "Don't tell me what I said!"

The others backed off. He's still asleep, Kathy thought, and he's having a bad dream. "You're right, George," she said gently. "You didn't say that at all." She pulled his head to her breast.

"Daddy," Missy broke in, "come to my room. Jodie says he wants to talk to you!"

The urgency of his daughter's voice broke the spell. George snapped out of it and jumped up, almost bowling Kathy over. "Jodie? Who's Jodie?"

"That's her friend," answered Kathy. "You know—I told you she makes up imaginary people. You can't see Jodie."

"Oh, yes, Mama," Missy protested. "I see him all the time. He's the biggest pig you ever saw." Then she trotted out of the room and was gone.

George and Kathy looked at each other. "A pig?" he said. It struck them both at the same time. "The pig's in her room!" George ran after Missy. "You stay here!" he yelled at Kathy and the boys.

Missy was just climbing on the bed when George stopped outside her bedroom door. He didn't see Jodie or anything like a pig. "Where's this Jodie?" he asked Missy.

"He'll be right back," the little girl said, settling the covers around herself. "He had to go outside for a minute."

George let out his breath. After the weird dream of the hooded figure, George had expected the worst when he heard the word "pig." His neck felt stiff and he rotated it, trying to work out the tight feeling. "It's all right!" he yelled back to Kathy. "Jodie's not here!"

"There he is, Daddy!"

George looked down at Missy. She was pointing to one of her windows. His eyes followed her finger and he started. Staring at him through one of the panes were two fiery red eyes! No face, just the mean, little eyes of a pig!

"That's Jodie!" cried Missy. "He wants to come in!"

Something rushed past George on his left. It was Kathy, screaming in an unearthly voice. In the same move that it took her to reach the window, she picked up one of Missy's little play chairs and swung it at the pair of eyes. Her blow shattered the window and shards of glass flew back on top of her.

There was an animal cry of pain, a loud squealing— and the eyes were gone!

George rushed to what was left of the second-story window and looked out. He saw nothing below, but he still heard the squealing. It sounded as if it was headed for the boathouse. Then Kathy's crying whimper caught George's attention. He turned to his wife.

Kathy's face was terrifying. Her eyes were wild and her mouth was tightly screwed up. She was trying to choke out words. Finally she blurted: "It's been here all the time! I wanted to kill it! I wanted to kill it!" Then her whole body slumped.

George caught his wife and silently picked her up. He carried Kathy into their bedroom, Danny and Chris following. Only Chris saw his little sister get out of bed, go to the smashed window, and wave. Missy turned away only when George called her to come into his bedroom.

In the morning, while George and Kathy were still dozing in their chairs, the children asleep in the big bed, Father Mancuso bundled up and drove to Rockville Centre.

He shivered in the cold, nippy air. Father Mancuso hadn't been outside too often since winter started and after the ride he felt a little giddy. He was grateful when the Bishop's secretary offered him tea. The young priest had often spoken with Father Mancuso and he admired the older priest's legalistic mind. They chatted until the Bishop buzzed.

The meeting was brief—all too short for what Father Mancuso had in mind. The prelate, a venerable, white-haired cleric, was a moralist of national reputation. He had the Chancellors' file on the Lutz case on his desk, but to Father Mancuso's surprise, he viewed the report with reluctance and caution.

The Bishop was very firm about the priest's dissociating himself from the Lutzes and said he'd already assigned another cleric to pick up the investigation.

Father Mancuso had nothing to say. "Possibly you should see a psychiatrist," the Bishop continued.

At that, Father Mancuso became upset. "I will if I may choose my own."

The Bishop read the displeasure in his visitor's manner, and his voice softened. "Look, Frank," he said, "I'm doing this for your benefit. You've become obsessed with the idea that demonic influence is involved. I get the impression that a good deal of it centers around you personally. That may or may not be."

Standing up, the Bishop walked around his desk to Father Mancuso's chair and put his hand on the priest's shoulder.

"Let someone else pick up the burden," he said. "It's affecting your health. I've got too much for you to do here. I don't want to lose you. You do understand, Father?"

On Monday morning, Kathy was determined that Danny and Chris go to school. Ready to fly apart herself, she stiffened her backbone and did her duty as a mother. While George slept on, she awakened the boys, fed them breakfast, and took all three children with her in the van.

George was up when she returned with Missy. As she had coffee with him, Kathy realized he was still in a zombie-like state after the previous night's affair. For the moment, Kathy was determined to be strong for both of them. She talked to her husband in everyday terms, slipping in the reminder that he had to fix the smashed window in Missy's bedroom. Later there would be time to deal with the decision of moving from 112 Ocean Avenue.

Upstairs, George had just nailed plywood over the shattered window frame to protect the room from damage by the weather when Kathy called up from the kitchen that his office in Syosset wanted him on the telephone. The company's accountant reminded George that the Internal Revenue Agent was due to come by at noon.

Not wanting to leave the house, George asked the accountant to handle the tax situation himself, but the man refused. It was George's responsibility to determine how to pay the taxes. George hesitated, certain that something would happen if he left. But Kathy signaled that he should go.

After he hung up, Kathy said that the appointment shouldn't take too long. She and Missy would be all right while he was gone. She would call a glazier in Amityville to drive over and fix the broken panes in Missy's window and throughout the house. Meekly, George nodded at his wife's advice, then left for Syosset. Neither had mentioned Jodie's name.

While Kathy was giving Missy her lunch, George Kekoris called. He was sorry he hadn't been able to get there as he'd promised George, but said he felt he'd picked up the flu in Buffalo. Kekoris' bout of illness had forced him to cancel all his appointments for the Psychical Research Institute. He was sure that he'd be fine by the following day, however, and planned to stay at the Lutzes' Wednesday night.

Kathy half-listened to his explanation. She was watching Missy eat. The little girl seemed to be having a secret conversation with someone under the kitchen table. Every once in a while Missy would extend her hand beneath the plastic tablecloth to offer her peanut butter and jelly sandwich. She didn't seem to be aware that her mother was watching her movements.

From her position, Kathy could see there was nothing under the table, but she did want to ask her daughter about Jodie. Finally Kekoris was finished and she hung up.

"Missy," Kathy said, sitting down at the table. "Is Jodie the angel you told me about?"

The little girl looked at her mother, confusion on her face.

"You remember," Kathy continued. "You asked me if angels speak?"

Missy's eyes lit up. "Yes, Mama," she nodded. "Jodie's an angel. He talks to me all the time."

"I don't understand. You've seen pictures of angels. You saw the ones we had on the Christmas tree?"

Missy nodded again.

"You said he's a pig. So how can you say he's an angel?"

Missy's eyebrows grew together as she concentrated. "He says he is, Mama," she nodded her head several times. "He told me."

Kathy hitched her chair closer to Missy. "What does he say when he talks to you?"

Again the little girl seemed confused.

"You know what I mean, Missy," Kathy pressed her daughter. "Do you play games?"

"Oh, no," Missy shook her head. "He tells me about the little boy who used to live in my room." She looked around to see if anybody was listening. "He died, Mama," she whispered. "The little boy got sick and he died."

"I see," Kathy said. "What else did he tell you?"

The little girl thought for a moment. "Last night he said I was going to live here forever so I could play with the little boy."

Horrified, Kathy put her finger to her mouth because she wanted to scream.

George's session with the IRS had not gone well. The agent had disallowed deduction after deduction, and George's only hope lay in the appeal the agent said he could file. It was a temporary reprieve, at least. After the man left, George called Kathy to say that he'd pick up the boys at school on his way home.

When he arrived after three, Kathy and Missy had their coats on. "Don't undress, George," she said. "We're leaving for my mother's right now."

George and the two boys looked at her. "What happened?" he asked.

"Jodie told Missy he's an angel, that's what happened." She began to push the boys out the front door. "We're getting out of here."

George held up his hands. "*Wait* a minute, will you? What do you mean he's an angel?"

Kathy looked down at her daughter. "Missy, tell your father what the pig said."

The little girl nodded. "He said he's an angel, Daddy. He told me."

George was about to ask his daughter another question when he was interrupted by loud barking from behind the house. "Harry!" he cried. "We forgot about Harry!"

When George and the others reached him, Harry was barking furiously at the boathouse, frantically running around his compound and jerking up short every time he reached the end of his steel leash.

"What's the matter, boy?" George said, patting the dog's neck. "Someone in the boathouse?" Harry twisted out of his grasp.

"Don't go in there!" Kathy yelled. "Please! Let's get out of here now!"

George hesitated, then bent down and snapped the

leash off Harry's collar. The dog leaped forward with a savage snarl and ran out of his gate. The door to the boathouse was closed and the best Harry could do was leap against it. Again he started his wild barking.

George was all set to unlock the door and fling it open. Instead, Danny and Chris ran past him and leaped on Harry, wrestling the big dog away. "Don't let him go in there!" Danny screamed. "He'll get killed!"

George grabbed Harry's collar and helped pull him down to a sitting position.

"It's all right!" Chris kept assuring the powerful, agitated animal. "It's all right, boy!" But Harry would not be calmed.

"Let's get him inside the house," George panted. "If he can't see the boathouse, he'll stop!"

As he and the boys were drawing Harry into the house, a van pulled into the driveway. George saw that it was a window repairman. He and Kathy looked at one another. "Oh, my God," Kathy said, "I forgot all about having called him." They hadn't reckoned on this kind of delay.

His pudgy face and broad accent gave away his Slavic descent. "I figured you folks needed the fixing right away," he said, "what with the bad weather we been having. Yah," he continued as he opened his rear doors, "better to fix now. If everything inside get wet because of outside, it cost you more money."

"Okay, that's fine," George said. "Come on in and I'll show you the windows that got busted."

"The wind the other night, yah?" the man asked.

"Yeah, the wind," George answered.

It was almost six P.M. before the man was done. When the new window panes were scraped free of putty, he stepped back to admire his work. "I'm sorry," he said to George, "I could not fix window in little girl's room. You need carpenter first." He gathered up his tools. "You get him, then I come back, yah?"

"Yeah," George nodded. "We'll get him and you can

come back." He reached into his pants pocket. "How much do I owe you?"

"No, no," the man protested. "No money now. You neighbor. We send bill, okay?"

"Okay!" George said, relieved. His cash *was* very low at the moment.

Somehow the glazier's kindness and friendliness left its mark on their spirits that night. After he left, Kathy —who had been sitting in the kitchen with her coat on all the time he worked—suddenly got up and took it off. Without saying a word to George, she began to prepare supper.

"I'm not too hungry," George said. "A grilled cheese sandwich would do just fine."

Kathy took out hamburger meat for herself and the children. As she worked preparing the meal, she kept Danny and Chris with her in the kitchen, insisting they do their homework in the nook. Missy sat in the living room with George, watching television while he built up a fire.

The glazier had been just the reassurance they needed. After all, nothing had happened to *him* while he was in the playroom or the sewing room. The Lutzes realized that maybe their imaginations were too fired up and they were panicking unnecessarily. All thought of abandoning their home had momentarily disappeared.

Father Mancuso was an individual who despised bullies, be they man, animal, or the unknown. The priest felt that the force that had 112 Ocean Avenue in its grip was taking undue advantage of the fears of the Lutzes and of himself. Before he retired Tuesday night, Father Mancuso prayed that this evil force could somehow be reasoned with; that it should know what it was doing was totally insane. How could it derive pleasure from pain, he asked himself? The priest knew there was only one answer—it had to be demonic.

Just to be on the safe side, George and Kathy decided the children should sleep in the master bedroom again. With Harry inside, down in the cellar, Danny, Chris, and Missy were put to bed. George and Kathy made themselves as comfortable as they could: Kathy stretched out on two chairs; George insisted he was all right with one. He told Kathy he planned to stay awake all night and sleep in the morning.

At 3:15 A.M., George heard the marching band strike up downstairs. This time he did not go to investigate. He told himself it was all in his head, and when he went down, there would be nothing to see. So he sat there, watching Kathy and the children, listening as the musicians paraded up and down his living room, horns and drums blasting away loud enough to be heard half a mile away. All during the maddening performance, Kathy and the children did not awaken.

Finally, George must have dozed off in his chair, because Kathy awoke to hear him screaming. He was yelling in two different tongues—languages she had never heard before!

She ran to her husband's chair on the other side of the bed to shake him out of his dream.

George began groaning, and when Kathy touched him, he cried out in another completely different voice: "It's in Chris's room! It's in Chris's room! It's in Chris's room!"

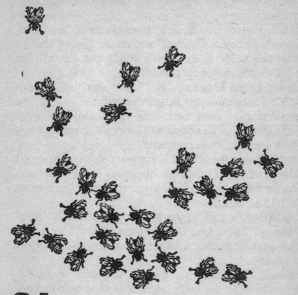

24 January 13 — George is positive he wasn't dreaming. From his position he was sure he could see clear to the boys' bedroom on the third floor. He had been watching a shadowy figure approach Chris's bed.

He tried to rush to his sleeping son's side and grab him away from the menacing shape. But George couldn't get up from his chair! He was pinned to the seat by a firm hand on his shoulders. It was a struggle George knew he couldn't win.

The shadow hovered over Chris. George, helpless, shouted: "It's in Chris's room!" No one heard him.

"It's in Chris's room!" he repeated. Then the pressure on his shoulders lifted and George felt himself being pushed. His arms came free and he could see Chris was out of bed, wrapped inside the dark shape.

George swung his hands wildly about, again scream-ing: "It's in Chris's room!" He felt another violent push.

"George!"

His eyes snapped open. Kathy was leaning over him, pushing at his chest. "George!" she cried. "Wake up!"

He leaped free of the chair. "It's got Chris!" he yelled. "I've got to get up there!"

Kathy grabbed his arm. "No!" She was pulling him back. "You're dreaming! Chris is *here*!"

She pointed to their bed. The three children were under the covers. Awakened by George's shouting, they were now watching their parents.

George was still agitated. "I wasn't dreaming, I tell you!" he insisted. "I could see it pick him up and . . .".

"You couldn't have," Kathy interrupted. "He's been here in bed all the time."

"No, Mama. I had to go to the bathroom before." Chris sat up. "You and Daddy were asleep."

"I never heard you. Did you use my bathroom?" Kathy asked.

"Unh-unh. The door was locked, so I went upstairs."

George went to the bathroom. The door *was* locked.

"Upstairs?" asked Kathy.

"Yeah," Chris answered. "But I got scared."

"Why?" his father asked.

"Because I could look through the floor and see you, Daddy."

The Lutzes remained awake for the rest of the night. Only Missy fell back to sleep. In the morning, George called Father Mancuso.

Minutes before, Father Mancuso had come to a deci-sion. His anguish over the Lutzes' children and their safety had overcome his fear. Feeling he had been a coward long enough, Father Mancuso was now resolved to return to the Bishop and ask that he be allowed to continue communicating with George.

He showered for the first time in days, then prepared

to shave. As he was plugging in his electric razor, Father Mancuso gasped. Beneath his eyes were the same black circles he had first seen at his mother's. The telephone rang at that very moment.

Even before he answered the telephone, the priest knew who was calling.

"Yes, George?" he said.

George was too preoccupied to notice that Father Mancuso had anticipated him. He announced that he and Kathy had decided to take the Chancellors' advice and leave 112 Ocean Avenue. They were going to his mother-in-law's until George could get some kind of investigation going. Too many incidents were beginning to involve the children, and George felt that if he delayed any longer, Danny, Chris, and Missy might be in frightful danger.

The priest did not ask what kinds of incidents, nor did he mention the reappearance of the circles under his eyes. He readily agreed the children's welfare should be everyone's prime concern and that George was right about going. "Let whatever's there have the place," he said. "Just go."

Danny and Chris did not go to school in Amityville that morning. Kathy kept them home again because she wanted to pack as soon as possible. George said they'd leave as soon as he called the police to tell them the family would be away for a while. He also wanted them to have Mrs. Conners' telephone number in case of any emergency. But when he picked up the telephone to dial the Police Department, the line was dead.

When her husband told Kathy the phone was out of order, she became extremely nervous. Hurriedly she dressed the children and then, without taking a change of clothes, herded them out to the van.

George brought Harry from the cellar and put him in the rear of the van. Then he went around the house and checked to make sure all the doors were locked. Finishing with the boathouse, George climbed behind the wheel of the van. He turned the ignition key but the motor wouldn't turn over.

"George?" Kathy's voice quivered. "What's wrong?"

"Take it easy," he said. "We got enough gas. Let me take a look under the hood."

As he got out of the van, he looked up at the sky. The clouds had grown dark and menacing. George felt a cold wind picking up. By the time he lifted the hood, the first raindrops were hitting the windshield.

George never got a good look at what could have caused the van to stall. A huge gust of wind blew in from the Amityville River in the back of the house, and the hood was slammed down. George had just leaped aside to avoid the falling metal when a lightning bolt struck behind the garage. The clap of thunder was almost instantaneous, and the clouds broke in a solid sheet of water that drenched George immediately.

He ran for the front door and unlocked it. "Get in!" he shouted to his family in the van. Kathy and the children bolted for the open door, but by the time he managed to close it behind them, all were soaking wet. We're trapped, he thought to himself, not daring to voice the thought to Kathy. It's not going to let us go.

The rains and wind picked up in intensity, and by one o'clock in the afternoon, Amityville was hit by another storm of hurricane strength. At three, the electricity went out, but fortunately the heat remained in the house. George switched on the portable radio in the kitchen. The weather report said it was 20 degrees and that sleet was pelting all of Long Island. Since the radar showed an enormous low pressure system covering the entire metropolitan area, the weatherman could not predict when the storm would subside.

George dealt with Missy's broken window as best he could, shoving towels into the spaces where it hung away from the frame, then nailing an old blanket over the entire window. Before he had finished, his fresh dry clothes were soaked again.

In the kitchen, George looked at the thermometer that hung beside the back door. It read 80 degrees and the house was getting uncomfortably warm. He knew that with the electricity off, the oil burner's thermostat wouldn't operate. But when George looked again at the thermometer, it was up to 85 degrees.

To cool off the house, George had to have some fresh air. He inched open the windows on the enclosed porch —the only room that faced away from the storm's main onslaught.

From the time the storm broke, it had remained dark outside, and even though it was daytime, Kathy had lit candles. At four-thirty it was as if night had already settled over 112 Ocean Avenue.

Every once in a while she would pick up the telephone to see if it was working again, but she really had little hope that it would be—the storm would prevent any repair crews from going out on call. The children weren't fazed at all by the darkness. They treated the whole affair as a holiday, noisily running up and down the staircase, playing hide-and-seek. Since the boys were much better at hiding themselves, Missy was usually "it." Harry happily joined in the romping, finally irritating George to the point where he cuffed the dog with a newspaper. Harry ran off and hid behind Kathy.

By six in the evening, the storm still hadn't slackened. It was as though all the water in the world was being dumped on top of 112 Ocean Avenue. And inside the house, the temperature was up to 90 degrees. George went to the basement to look at the oil burner. It *was* off, but it didn't matter; the heat continued to rise in all the rooms except Missy's.

Desperate, he decided to make a final appeal to God. Holding a candle, George began going from room to room, asking the Lord to send away whoever didn't belong there. He felt mildly reassured when there was no sinister reaction to his prayers.

After the playroom door had been damaged during the first storm, George had removed the lock. Now as he approached the room to recite his appeal to God, he saw the green slime was back, leaking from the open hole in the door and oozing onto the floor of the hallway. George watched as the pool of jelly-like substance slowly wound its way toward the staircase.

He pulled off the pine boards nailed across the door and threw it open, half-expecting to find the room filled with the slimy material. But its only source seemed to be the empty lock hole in the door!

George gathered some towels from the third floor bathroom and stuffed them into the opening. The towels soon became saturated, but the jelly stopped flowing. He wiped up the slime that had accumulated in the hallway and had managed to flow down the steps. George had no intention of telling his wife about this latest discovery.

All the time her husband was going through the house, Kathy sat by the telephone. She had tried opening the kitchen door a little to let in some air, but even when it was only slightly ajar, rainwater showered into the room. She began to doze from the oppressive heat.

When George finally returned to the kitchen, she was almost fast asleep, resting her head on her arms on the breakfast table in the nook. Kathy was perspiring, the back of her neck damp to his touch. When he tried to awaken her, she lifted her head slightly, mumbled something he couldn't understand, then let her forehead fall back on her arms.

George had no need to check whether the rain and windstorm had let up. Torrents of water were still smashing against the house, and he somehow knew they wouldn't be allowed to leave 112 Ocean Avenue that night. He picked Kathy up in his arms and took her to their bedroom, noting the time on the kitchen clock. It was exactly 8 P.M.

Finally the 90 degree heat got to Danny, Chris, and Missy. Their running about the house most of the day had worn them out, so shortly after George had taken Kathy upstairs, they were ready for bed. George was surprised to find it was somewhat cooler in the boys' room on the third floor. He knew that hot air rises, and on the top floor it should have been well above ninety.

Missy sleepily climbed into bed beside Kathy, but refused to be covered with a sheet or blanket. Before George went back downstairs, she and the boys were asleep.

George and Harry were now all alone in the living room. For a change, the dog didn't seem to be about to fall asleep early but watched his owner's every move. He, too, was suffering from the excessive heat. Whenever George rose from his chair to go into another room, Harry would not follow, but remained stretched out in the cool draft beneath the living room windows.

George thought of running outside to the van to see if it would start. It was still standing in the driveway and George knew its engine would probably be wet by now. But the real deterrent was George's suspicion that once he left, he might not be able to get back into the house. Something within him warned him that he'd never get the front or kitchen door open again.

Suddenly, at ten o'clock, the 90 degree heat began to break. Harry noticed it first. The dog stood, sniffed the air, then walked over to the unlit fireplace where George was sitting, and whimpered. His pathetic sounds broke his master's concentration on the van. George looked up and shivered. There was a definite drop in the house's temperature.

A half hour later, the thermometer read 60 degrees. George started for the basement to get some logs. Harry trotted along behind him to the cellar door, but would not descend the steps with George. He remained in the open doorway, constantly turning his head as if to see if someone was coming up behind him.

George used his flashlight to search out every corner of the basement, but there were no signs of anything unusual. With several logs in his arms, George climbed back upstairs and tried the telephone in the kitchen. It was still dead. He was all set to relight the kindling wood in the fireplace when he thought he heard Missy cry out.

When he reached his bedroom, the little girl was shivering; he had forgotten to cover her when the house got chilly. Kathy on her stomach, was sleeping like a drugged person, not moving or turning in bed. George also tucked blankets about his wife's cool body.

When he finally went back down to the living room, George decided not to make a fire. He wanted to be free to stay near Kathy and the children. Tonight, he thought, I'd better be ready for anything. George put on Harry's long metal leash and took the dog up to the master bedroom. He left the door open, but knotted the leash so that Harry blocked the doorway completely. Then George kicked off his shoes, and without undressing, slid into bed beside Missy and Kathy. Rather than lie down, he sat up with his back resting against the headboard.

At one o'clock, George felt he was freezing. Because of the noise of the raging storm outside, he knew there was no hope of heat in the house that night from the oil burner. He began to weep to himself about the sorry plight he and his family were in. He now realized he should have fled when Father Mancuso originally warned him. "Oh, God, help us," he moaned.

Suddenly, Kathy lifted up her head. While he watched, she got off the bed and turned to look into the mirror on the wall. George saw in the candlelight that her eyes were open, but he knew she was still asleep.

Kathy stared at her reflection for a moment, then turned away from the mirrored wall and started for the bedroom door. But she stopped when she came to an obstacle: Harry was fast asleep, stretched across the threshold, blocking her path.

George leaped from the bed and seized his wife. Kathy looked at him with unseeing eyes. To George, she seemed to be in a trance.

"Kathy!" he cried. "Wake up!" When George shook her, there was no response or reaction. Then her eyes closed. Kathy went limp in his arms and gently he half-pulled, half-lifted her back to the bed. First he sat Kathy down, then straightened her legs so that she was lying flat. Her trance-like state seemed to affect her whole body. She was like a rag doll.

George noted that Missy, in the middle of the bed, had slept through the whole episode. But then his attention was diverted by a movement in the doorway. He saw Harry struggle to his feet, shake violently, and then begin to retch. The dog threw up all over the floor, but kept gagging and trying to force out something that seemed stuck in his throat. Restricted by his leash, the poor dog was only twisting the chain more tightly about his writhing body.

The odor of vomit caused George to gag too. He fled into the bathroom, gulped a mouthful of water, took a deep breath, and came out with towels from the rack. After he mopped up the floor, George untied Harry and set the dog free. Harry looked up at George, wagged his tail several times, then stretched himself out on the floor of the hallway, closing his eyes. "There's not much wrong with you now," George whispered under his breath.

He listened, but everything was quiet throughout the house—*much* too quiet. In a few moments, George realized the storm had stopped. There was no rain, no wind. The stillness was so complete it was as though someone had turned off running water in a sink. There was a vacuum of silence at 112 Ocean Avenue.

With the storm gone, the temperature outside began to drop and in a very short time, the house became ice cold. George could feel the bedroom become even chillier than it had been. He still had all his clothes on when he slipped back beneath the covers.

There was a noise above George's head. He looked up and listened. Something was scraping along the floor of the boys' bedroom. The noise became louder, and George could tell the movement was faster now. The boys' beds were sliding back and forth!

George managed to throw off his covers, but he could not lift his body out of bed. There was no pressure as there had been before when he sat in the bedroom chair. George just didn't have the strength to move!

Now he heard the dresser drawers across his room begin to open and close. A candle was still on his nightstand and he could make out the drawers rapidly sliding back and forth. One drawer would fly open, then another, then the first would bang shut. Tears of frustration and fear flooded George's eyes.

Almost immediately after that, the voices began. He could hear them downstairs, but couldn't make out what was being said. He only knew that it sounded as if a lot of people were thronging on the first floor. George's head began to roll as he tried to reach over and touch Missy or Kathy.

Then the marching band struck up downstairs, its music drowning out the unintelligible voices. George thought he must be in a madhouse. He could distinctly hear musicians parade around the entire first floor—and then their first steps as they began to mount the staircase!

George was screaming now, but he heard no sounds coming from his throat. His body whipped back and forth on the bed and he could feel the terrible strain on his neck muscles as he vainly tried to lift his head from the mattress. Finally George gave up. He realized the mattress was soaking wet.

The beds were banging around above George's head, and the dresser drawers in his room were flying back and forth as the band headed up the steps to the second floor. But that was not all. Despite all the noise, George now heard doors throughout the house beginning to slam back and forth!

He saw the door to the bedroom swing wildly as though someone were yanking it open and then immediately slamming it shut. George could also see Harry lying outside in the hallway, completely undisturbed by the racket. Either that dog is drugged, George thought, or I'm the one who's going mad!

A terrible, blinding flash of lightning lit up the bedroom. George heard the thunderbolt strike something close outside. Then there was a smashing blow that shook the entire house. The storm was back, with torrents of rain and wind lashing 112 Ocean Avenue from top to bottom.

George lay there panting, his heart thumping loudly in his chest. He was waiting, knowing something else was about to happen. Then George let out a horrible, silent scream. Somebody was on the bed with him!

He felt himself being stepped on! Strong, heavy feet struck his legs and body. George shut his eyes. He could feel the pain from the blows. Oh God! he thought. They're hooves. It's an animal!

George must have passed out from fright, because the next thing he remembers was the sight of Danny and Chris standing beside his bed. "Daddy, Daddy, wake up!" they were crying, "there's something in our room!"

He blinked his eyes. In a glance he saw it was light outside. The storm had stopped. The dresser drawers were all open, and his two sons were pleading with him to get up.

Missy! Kathy! George turned to look at them. They were still next to him, both still sound asleep. He turned back to the boys, who were trying to pull him out of bed. "What's the matter?" he asked. "What's in your room?"

"It's a monster!" Danny cried. "He doesn't have any face!"

"It tried to grab us," Chris broke in, "but we ran away! Come on, Daddy, get up!"

George tried. He almost got his head off the mattress when he heard Harry bark furiously. George looked past the boys through the open doorway. The dog was standing in the hallway, snarling and growling at the staircase. Even though he was unleashed, Harry did not head for the stairs, but continued to crouch in the hallway, teeth bared, barking at something or someone George couldn't see from his position on the bed.

With a tremendous burst of determination, George finally heaved his whole body off the mattress. He arose so suddenly that he crashed into Danny and Chris. Then he ran for the open door and looked up at the steps.

On the top step stood a gigantic figure in white. George knew it was the hooded image Kathy had first glimpsed in the fireplace. The being was pointing at him!

George whirled and raced back into the bedroom, grabbed up Missy, and shoved her into Danny's arms. "Take her outside!" he shouted. "You go with them, Chris!"

Then he bent over Kathy and lifted her off the bed. "Hurry!" George yelled after the boys. Then he too ran from the room, Harry following him down the steps.

On the first floor, George saw the front door was open, hanging from its hinges again, torn away by some powerful force.

Danny, Chris, and Missy were outside. The little girl, just awakening, was squirming in her brother's arms. Not knowing where she was, she started to cry with fright.

George ran for the van. He put Kathy on the front seat and then helped the children into the rear. Harry jumped in behind them, and he slammed the door on Kathy's side. George ran around to the other side of the vehicle, jumped in the driver's seat, and prayed.

He jammed in the ignition key.

The motor turned over immediately.

Spraying wet gravel, George backed out of the driveway. When he hit the street, he skidded, spun the wheel, and stepped on the gas at the same time. The van teetered for a moment, then all four tires grabbed and smoke shot up from the rubber treads. In another instant, the van was tearing up Ocean Avenue.

As he steered the van toward safety, George looked into the side view mirror. His house was fast disappearing from his sight. "Thank God!" he muttered to himself. "I'll never see you again, you sonofabitch!"

It was seven o'clock on the morning of January 14, 1976; the twenty-eighth day the Lutzes had lived in 112 Ocean Avenue.

25 **January 15** — That morning, at the very moment the Lutzes were fleeing from their home, Father Mancuso decided to get out of town.

He waited until eleven o'clock, because then it would be eight A.M. in San Francisco, and he didn't want to awaken his cousin too early with a telephone call. The priest announced he was flying West for a vacation. He would leave in a day or so, probably on Friday, January 16.

Father Mancuso hung up, feeling greatly relieved. This was the first positive step he had taken in weeks. The priest reasoned that a week in the California sun could only help his run-down condition and possibly bake the flu out of his system. Let the diabolical powers in 112 Ocean Avenue have the house and the cruel New York winter weather!

He called his office back at the diocese in order to inform them of his plans. They were to reschedule his appointments and duties until after January 30th. He would contact some of his clients in counselling on his own.

As the morning wore on, the priest felt progressively better. He had much to do before leaving, and all his thoughts of the Lutzes were shunted into the background. But at four in the afternoon, George Lutz called from his mother-in-law's in East Babylon. He said he wanted to let Father Mancuso know that he, Kathy, and the children were going to stay there until the scientific investigations were made at his house in Amityville.

"That's fine, George," Father Mancuso said. "But be careful of who goes into the house. Don't make a circus out of this thing."

"Oh, I won't, Father," George replied. "We don't want people trampling all over the place. All our stuff is still there. Nobody gets in unless I say so."

"Good," the priest said. "Just follow up on the parapsychologists. The Chancery says they're the best equipped to investigate a situation like this."

"There's just one thing," George broke in. "Supposing they can't come up with answers. And after last night, Father, I frankly don't think they can. Then what? What happens next?"

Father Mancuso let out a gasp. "What do you mean, *after last night*? Don't tell me you stayed there again?"

There was silence on the telephone. Finally George answered. "It wouldn't let us go. We couldn't get out until this morning."

Father Mancuso felt his palms itch. He looked into his left hand. It was becoming blotchy. Oh no, he thought. Please God, not again! No more!

Without another word to George, the priest hung up. He shoved his hands crossways beneath his armpits, try-

Missy's picture of "Jodie" running through the snow

ing to shield them. He began to rock back and forth on his heels. "Please, please," he whimpered, "let me alone. I promise I won't talk to him again."

George couldn't understand why Father Mancuso had hung up on him. The priest should have been happy that they were out of the house. He held the receiver in his hand, staring at the instrument. "What'd I say?" he murmured.

A sharp tug on his sleeve interrupted George's thoughts. It was Missy. "Here, Daddy," she said. "I made Jodie like you said."

"What?" George asked. His daughter was holding up a paper drawing. "Oh, yeah," he said. "Jodie's picture. Let me see it."

George took the paper from Missy. It was a child's rendering of a pig, distorted, but clearly a five year-old's idea of a running animal.

He raised his eyebrows. "What are all these things around Jodie?" he asked. "They look like little clouds."

"That's snow, Daddy," Missy answered. "That's when Jodie ran away in the snow."

Father Mancuso decided to catch the 9:00 P.M. TWA flight to San Francisco. When the panic after George's call had left him, the priest immediately picked up the telephone and spoke to his cousin's wife. He told her he had changed his mind and would be coming out that night. She agreed to meet him at San Francisco's International Airport.

Father Mancuso packed only one suitcase; called his mother, the diocese office, and a cab company. By eight, he was out of the Rectory and on his way to Kennedy Airport. When the priest checked in at the TWA counter he looked again at his palms. The blotches were gone, but his fear wasn't.

Jimmy and Carey went to stay at her mother's house that night. But before they left, there was a small celebration at Mrs. Conners' house. Because of the dramatic feeling of relief that swept over the Lutzes just to be free of 112 Ocean Avenue, it was practically a party.

George and Kathy now wanted to talk about their experiences, and in her family, they had a sympathetic and credulous audience. Events spilled from their lips in a flood as they tried to explain what had happened to them. Finally, George revealed his plans to rid his house of whatever evil force remained there. He told his mother-in-law and Jimmy that research groups would be invited to participate, but they would have to conduct their investigations by themselves. Under no circumstances would he or Kathy ever enter 112 Ocean Drive again.

Danny, Chris, and Missy were to sleep in Jimmy's room. The boys were exhausted from the harrowing appearance of the "monster" the night before and from the excitement of fleeing to their grandmother's. But they didn't want to talk about the white-hooded demon figure. When George pressed them to tell their version, both boys fell silent and looks of fear came over their faces.

Missy appeared to be entirely unaffected by the whole affair. She adapted easily enough to the new adventure and made herself right at home with a few dolls she had cached at her grandmother's. She wasn't even perturbed when Kathy questioned her further about Jodie's picture. The little girl would say only, "That is what the pig looked like."

George and Kathy took their baths early. Both luxuriated in the hot water and soaked for a long time. It was a dual cleansing: their bodies and their fright. By ten P.M., they were in bed in the guest room. For the first time in almost a month, the Lutzes fell asleep in each other's arms.

George awoke first. He felt as if he was having a dream, because he had the sensation of floating in air! He was aware of his body being flown around the bedroom and then landing softly back on the bed. Then, still in his dreamlike state, George saw Kathy levitate off the bed. She rose about a foot and slowly began to drift away from him.

George reached out a hand to his wife. In his eyes, the movement was almost in slow motion, as though his arm was not attached to his body. He tried to call to her, but for some reason, he couldn't remember her name. George could only watch Kathy fly higher toward the ceiling. Then he felt himself being lifted, and again he had the sensation of floating.

He could hear someone calling to him from a great distance. George knew the voice. It sounded very familiar. He heard his name again. "George?"

Now he remembered. It was Kathy. George looked down and saw she was back on the bed, looking up at him.

He began to drift toward Kathy, then felt himself slowly settling back down on the bed beside her. "George!" she cried. "You were floating in the air!"

Kathy grabbed his arm and pulled him off the bed. "Come on!" she shouted. "We've got to get out of this room!"

As though he was sleepwalking, George followed his wife. At the head of the staircase they both stopped and recoiled in horror. Coming *up* the steps toward them was a snake-like line of greenish-black slime!

George knew he had not been dreaming. It was all real. Whatever he had thought they had left forever back at 112 Ocean Avenue was following them—wherever the Lutzes fled.

EPILOGUE

On February 18, 1976, Marvin Scott of New York's Channel 5 decided to investigate further the reports on the so-called cursed home of Amityville, Long Island. The mission called for spending the night in the haunted home at 112 Ocean Avenue. Psychics, clairvoyants, a demonologist, and parapsychologists were invited to participate.

Scott had originally contacted the recent tenants, the Lutz family, and requested permission to film activities at their deserted house. George Lutz agreed and sat down at a meeting with Scott in a small pizzeria in Amityville. George refused to re-enter 112 Ocean Avenue, but said he and his wife, Kathy, would wait for the investigators the next day at the Italian restaurant.

To provoke the overpowering force said to be within

the house, a crucifix and blessed candles were placed in the center of the dining room table.

The researchers held the first of three seances at 10:30 P.M. Present around the table were Lorraine Warren, a clairvoyant; her husband, Ed, a demonologist; psychics Mary Pascarella and Mrs. Albert Riley; and George Kekoris of the Psychical Research Institute in Durham, North Carolina. Marvin Scott also joined the group at the table.

During the seance, Mary Pascarella became ill and had to leave the room. In a quaking voice, she said, "that in back of everything there seems to be some kind of black shadow that forms a head, and it moves. And as it moves, I feel personally threatened."

Mrs. Riley, in a mediumistic trance, began gasping. "It's upstairs in the bedroom. What's here makes your heart speed up. My heart's pounding." Ed Warren wanted to end the seance. Mrs. Riley continued to gasp, then quickly came out of her trance and back to normal consciousness.

Then George Kekoris, the psychic researcher, also became violently ill and had to leave the table. Observer Mike Linder of WNEW-FM stated that he had felt a sudden numbness, a kind of cold sensation.

Clairvoyant Lorraine Warren finally voiced her own opinion: "Whatever is here is, in my estimation, most definitely of a negative nature. It has nothing to do with anyone who had once walked the earth in human form. It is right from the bowels of the earth."

Television cameraman Steve Petropolis, who had been assigned some scary assignments in combat zones, experienced heart palpitations and shortness of breath when he investigated the sewing room upstairs where the negative force was said to be concentrated. When Lorraine Warren and Marvin Scott went into that room, they both came out saying that they had felt a momentary chill.

Lorraine and Ed Warren also found a source of discomfort in the living room. Mrs. Warren thought some negative forces were centered in statues and nonliving things; "That whatever is here, is able to move around at will. It doesn't have to stay here, but I think it's a resting place." She also thought there was something demonic in the inanimate objects. Mrs. Warren indicated the fireplace and banister on the second floor, without being forewarned of their connection with the Lutzes' problems.

As some people slept in some of the second floor bedrooms, a photographer shot infrared pictures in the vain hope of capturing some ghostly image on film. Jerry Solfvin of the Psychical Research Institute wandered about the house with a battery lantern, searching for physical evidence.

At 3:30 A.M., the Warrens attempted another seance. There was nothing unusual reported, no sounds or strange phenomena. All the psychics felt the room had been neutralized. The atmosphere, they said, simply wasn't right at the moment. But they definitely felt that the house on Ocean Avenue was harboring a demonic spirit, one that could be removed only by an exorcist.

When Marvin Scott returned to the little pizzeria, the Lutzes were gone. By March, they had moved clear across the country to California. They left behind all their belongings, all their worldly goods, and all the money they had invested in their dream home. Just to be rid of the place, they signed their interest over to the bank that held the mortgage. Pending its resale; its windows were boarded up to discourage vandalism and to prevent the curious, the morbid, and the warned from entering.

On Good Friday, 1976, Father Frank Mancuso recovered from pneumonia, and in April, he was transferred by the Bishop of his diocese to another parish. It is nowhere near 112 Ocean Avenue.

Now, Missy gets upset when she is asked about Jodie; Danny and Chris can still vividly describe the "monster" who chased them that final night; and Kathy will not talk about that period in her life at all. George has sold his interest in William H. Parry, Inc. He does hope that those who hear his story will understand how dangerous negative entities can be to the unwary—to the unbelieving. "They *are* real," George insists, "and they do inflict evil when the opportunity presents itself."

AFTERWORD:
A Note From the Author

To the extent that I can verify them, all the events in this book are true. George Lee and Kathleen Lutz undertook the exhaustive and frequently painful task of reconstructing their twenty-eight days in the house in Amityville on a tape recorder, refreshing each other's memories so that the final oral "diary" would be as complete as possible. Not only did George and Kathy agree on virtually every detail they had both experienced, many of their impressions and reports were later substantiated by the testimony of independent witnesses such as Father Mancuso and local police officials. But perhaps the most telling evidence in support of their story is circumstantial—it takes more than imagination or a case of "nerves" to drive a normal, healthy family of five to the drastic step of suddenly abandoning a desirable three-story house, complete with finished basement, swimming pool, and boathouse, without even pausing to take along their personal household belongings.

I should point out, too, that when the Lutzes fled their home in early 1976, they had no thought of putting their experiences into book form. Only after the press and broadcast media began issuing reports on the house that the Lutzes considered distorted and sensationalized did they consent to have their story published. Nor were they aware that so many of their claims would be corroborated by others. In addition to checking their tape recordings for internal consistency, I conducted my own personal interviews with others involved in the case; and indeed, George and Kathy did not learn of Father Mancuso's tribulations until this book's final draft was written.

Before they had moved into their new home, the Lutzes were far from being experts on the subject of psychic phenomena. As far as they can recall, the only books they'd read that might be even remotely considered "occult" were a few popular works on Transcendental Meditation. But as I've since discovered by talking with those familiar with parapsychology, almost every one of their claims bears a strong parallel to other reports of hauntings, psychic "invasions" and the like that have been published over the years in a wide variety of sources. For example:

*The chilling cold that George and others noted is a syndrome repeatedly reported by visitors to haunted houses who sense a "cold spot" or pervasive chill. (Occultists speculate that a disembodied entity may draw on thermal energy and body heat to gain the power it needs to become visible and move objects.)

*Animals are often said to display discomfort and even terror in haunted surroundings. This was certainly true of Harry, the family dog, to say nothing of human visitors who had never entered the house before—Kathy's aunt, a neighbor's boy, and others.

*The window that slammed on Danny's hand has its echo in an English case in which a car door closed by itself, crushing the hand of a woman who was arriving to investigate paranormal reports. Minutes later, during the drive to the nearest hospital, her hand reportedly returned to its uninjured state.

*George's visionary glimpse of what he would later identify as Ronnie DeFeo's face, his repeated awakenings at the time of the DeFeo murders, and Kathy's dreams of illicit lovemaking have their counterparts in a phenomenon called *retrocognition*, in which an emotionally-charged site apparently manages to transmit images of its past to later visitors.

*The damage to doors, windows and bannister, the movement and possible teleportation of the ceramic lion, the nauseating stench in the basement and Rectory are all familiar elements to readers of the voluminous literature about poltergeists or "noisy ghosts," whose behavior has been documented by professional investigators. The "marching band," too, is characteristic of the poltergeist, which is often reported to create dramatically loud noises. (One victim reported the sound of "a grand piano falling downstairs", but with no visible cause or damage.)

Most poltergeist manifestations are said to occur in the presence of a child—usually a girl—approaching puberty. Here, none of the Lutz children seems to have been old enough to serve as the trigger; moreover, most poltergeist antics seem childishly malicious, rather than vicious or physically harmful. But on the other hand, as Father Nicola points out in his *Demonical Possession and Exorcism,* poltergeists sometimes serve as the first manifestation of an entity ultimately bent on demonic possession. The inverted crucifix in Kathy's closet, the

235

recurrent flies, and odors of human excrement are all characteristic trademarks of demonic infestation.

What, then, are we to make of the Lutzes' account? There is simply too much independent corroboration of their narrative to support the speculation that they either imagined or fabricated these events. But if the case unfolded as I've reconstructed it here, how are we to interpret it?

What follows is one interpretation, the analysis of an experienced researcher into paranormal phenomena:

"The Lutz home seems to have harbored at least three separate entities. Francine, the medium, sensed at least two ordinary 'ghosts,' that is, earthbound spirits of humans who—for whatever reasons—remain attached to a particular locale long after their physical death and usually want no more than to be left alone to enjoy the spot they've become accustomed to while on earth. The woman whose touch and perfume were perceived by Kathy (Francine cited 'an old woman') may have been that house's original tenant, who only wanted to reassure the new young woman who found 'her' kitchen such an attractive, pleasant spot.

"Similarly, the little boy independently spoken of by Missy and by Kathy's sister-in-law would probably also have been an earth-bound spirit who—again according to mediums and spiritualists—may not have realized he was dead. Lonely and confused in the timeless world of after-death, he would naturally have gravitated to Missy's room, where he was surprised to find her bed occupied by Carey and Jimmy. But if he asked Carey for 'help,' it was evidently not *he* who was arranging for Missy to become his permanent playmate.

"Rather, the hooded figure and 'Jodie the pig' seem to represent a wholly different class of being. Orthodox demonologists believe that fallen angels can manifest themselves as animals or as awe-inspiring human figures at will; therefore, these two apparitions may have been one and the same. Although George saw the eyes of a pig and hoofprints in the snow, Jodie *spoke* with Missy and thus was no mere animal ghost. And the entity who burned its visage into the fireplace wall and dominated the hallway on that final morning may have simply taken a less frightening shape to converse telepathically with a little girl.

"It seems logical that this entity—together with the voices that ordered Father Mancuso to depart and George and Kathy to stop their impromptu exorcism—may have been 'invited in' during the course of occult ceremonies performed in the basement, or on the house's original site. Once established, they would naturally resist any attempts to dislodge them, and with greater vigor than any ordinary ghost would normally display.

"George and Kathy's inexplicable trances, mood changes, repeated levitations, odd dreams, physical transformations can all be read as symptoms of incipient possession. Some who believe in reincarnation say that we pay for past errors by being reborn in a new body and experiencing the consequences of our actions. But any entity as resolutely malevolent as the ones who tormented the Lutzes would have realized that a return to the flesh might entail retribution in the shape of physical deformity, illness, suffering, and other 'bad Karma.' Thus a particularly nasty spirit might avoid rebirth entirely, instead seizing the bodies of the *living* in order to experience food, sex, alcohol, and other earthly pleasures.

"Evidently George Lutz was not the ideally passive 'horse' for a discarnate rider; the threat to his wife and children galvanized him to fight back. But neither were his unseen adversaries mere ordinary 'ha'nts.' Their unusual strength is suggested by their long-range attacks on Father Mancuso's car, health, and rooms, and by George and Kathy's levitation even after they had fled to her mother's. But why, then, have the Lutzes reported no further trouble after moving to California?

"Another old occult tradition—that spirits cannot extend their power across water—may have some significance here. During the preparation of this book, one of those primarily responsible for it reported feeling weak and nauseous upon sitting down to work on the manuscript—*whenever he did so in his office on Long Island*. But while doing the same task in Manhattan, across the East River, he experienced no ill effects at all."

We're not obliged, of course, to accept this or any other "psychic" interpretation of the events that took place in the house in Amityville. Yet any other hypothesis immediately involves us in trying to construct an even more incredible series of bizarre coincidences, shared hallucinations, and grotesque misinterpretations of fact. It would be helpful if we could duplicate, as in a controlled laboratory experiment, some of the events the Lutzes experienced. But of course we cannot. Disembodied spirits—if they exist—presumably feel no obligation to perform instant replays before the cameras and recording equipment of earnest researchers.

There is no evidence that any strange events occurred at 112 Ocean Avenue after the period of time reported in this book, but this too, makes sense: more than one parapsychologist has noted that occult manifestations—especially those with poltergeist overtones—very often end as suddenly as they began, never to reoccur. And even traditional ghost-hunters assure their clients that structural changes in a house, even a simple rearrangement of furniture, such as would be effected by a new tenant, will bring a speedy end to reports of the abnormal.

As for George and Kathleen Lutz, of course, their curiosity has been more than satisfied. But the rest of us are left with a dilemma: The more "rational" the explanation, the less tenable it becomes. And what I have called The *Amityville Horror* remains one of those dark mysteries that challenges our conventional accounting of what this world contains.

ABOUT THE AUTHOR

JAY ANSON began as a copy boy on the *N.Y. Evening Journal* in 1937, and later worked in advertising and publicity. With over 500 documentary scripts for television to his credit, he is now associated with Professional Films, Inc., and lives in Roslyn, New York.

Praise for

THE WICKED DEEDS OF DANIEL MACKENZIE

"The wonderful, deliciously sexy Mackenzie men have returned! . . . Readers know that they are getting a deep-sigh read that is innovative, engaging, touching, powerful, emotional, and a keeper." —*RT Book Reviews* (Top Pick)

"Adventurous, sexy . . . Ashley has all the elements ready for a fun book. But she adds more when she infuses it with her humor and charm." —*Under the Covers*

THE SEDUCTION OF ELLIOT MCBRIDE

"RITA Award–winning Ashley excels at creating multilayered, realistically complex characters, and the latest installment in her Mackenzie brothers series is a richly emotional treat for fans of tortured heroes. Ashley not only handles Juliana's romantic redemption of Elliot with significant finesse, she also delivers abundant sensual passion." —*Booklist*

"Ashley creates marvelous, unforgettable, and heart-stopping stories with unique heroes. She touches on a multitude of human emotions while never losing sight of the love story. With lush prose and memorable scenes, readers learn how wounded characters can be healed by the power of love. Memorable, remarkable, tender, and touching, here is a book to cherish, reread, and sigh over time and again." —*RT Book Reviews* (Top Pick)

THE DUKE'S PERFECT WIFE

"*The Duke's Perfect Wife* is a sensual, gorgeous story that was captivating from the first page to the very last." —*Joyfully Reviewed* (Recommended Read)

continued . . .

"The unforgettable Mackenzies return as Ashley spins the fourth in the series into another mesmerizing, intensely emotional romance that steals readers' hearts and minds. With her innovative plots and characters, Ashley pushes the boundaries of the genre and creates 'keepers,' because they touch readers on many levels."   —*RT Book Reviews* (Top Pick)

"It's all such a seductive world, you'll get swept away, just as I did."   —*DemonLovers Books & More*

THE MANY SINS OF LORD CAMERON

"Ashley's latest flawlessly written historical romance richly rewards romance readers with its multilayered characterization; sexy, secrets-saturated plotting; sharp wit; and enthralling writing."   —*Booklist* (starred review)

"Passionate, well-drawn characters, breathless romance, and a memorable love story."   —*Library Journal*

"Innovative as ever . . . a beautifully written, tender, touching romance that will leave readers breathless. Her strong characterizations and poignant yet sensual storytelling draw readers into her unforgettable love stories."
                    —*RT Book Reviews* (Top Pick)

"Jennifer Ashley writes very sensual, sexy books . . . If you love the first two books in this series, you will enjoy this one as well. If you haven't tried these, I definitely recommend."   —*Smexy Books*

LADY ISABELLA'S SCANDALOUS MARRIAGE

"I adore this novel: It's heartrending, funny, honest, and true. I want to know the hero—no, I want to *marry* the hero!"   —Eloisa James, *New York Times* bestselling author

"Skillfully nuanced characterization and an abundance of steamy sensuality give Ashley's latest impeccably crafted historical its irresistible literary flavor." —*Chicago Tribune*

"Readers rejoice! The Mackenzie brothers return as Ashley works her magic to create a unique love story brimming over with depth of emotion, unforgettable characters, sizzling passion, mystery, and a story that reaches out and grabs your heart. Brava!" —*RT Book Reviews* (Top Pick)

"A heartfelt, emotional historical romance with danger and intrigue around every corner . . . A great read!"
—*Fresh Fiction*

"For a rollicking good time, sexy Highland heroes, and touching romances, you just can't beat Jennifer Ashley's novels!" —*Night Owl Reviews*

THE MADNESS OF LORD IAN MACKENZIE

"A deliciously dark and delectably sexy story of love and romantic redemption that will captivate readers with its complex characters and suspenseful plot." —*Booklist*

"Ashley's enthralling and poignant romance . . . touches readers on many levels. Brava!" —*RT Book Reviews*

"A story of mystery and intrigue with two wonderful, bright characters you'll love . . . I look forward to more from Jennifer Ashley, an extremely gifted author." —*Fresh Fiction*

"Brimming with mystery, suspense, an intriguing plot, villains, romance, a tormented hero, and a feisty heroine, this book is a winner. I recommend *The Madness of Lord Ian Mackenzie* to anyone looking for a great read."
—*Romance Junkies*

Rules for a
Proper Governess

JENNIFER ASHLEY

B
BERKLEY SENSATION, NEW YORK

THE BERKLEY PUBLISHING GROUP
Published by the Penguin Group
Penguin Group (USA) LLC
375 Hudson Street, New York, New York 10014

USA • Canada • UK • Ireland • Australia • New Zealand • India • South Africa • China

penguin.com

A Penguin Random House Company

RULES FOR A PROPER GOVERNESS

A Berkley Sensation Book / published by arrangement with the author

Berkley Sensation Books are published by The Berkley Publishing Group.
BERKLEY SENSATION® is a registered trademark of Penguin Group (USA) LLC.
The "B" design is a trademark of Penguin Group (USA) LLC.

For information, address: The Berkley Publishing Group,
a division of Penguin Group (USA) LLC,
375 Hudson Street, New York, New York 10014.

ISBN: 978-0-425-26603-8

PUBLISHING HISTORY
Berkley Sensation mass-market edition / October 2014

PRINTED IN THE UNITED STATES OF AMERICA

10 9 8 7 6 5 4 3 2 1

Cover art by Gregg Gulbronson.
Cover design by George Long.
Cover handlettering by Ron Zinn.
Interior text design by Laura K. Corless.

Rules for a
Proper Governess

Chapter 1

His voice drew her, and Bertie wanted to hear more of it. She leaned forward in the balcony to watch the man standing upright and arrogant, one hand touching an open book on a table in front of him, the other gesturing as he made his argument.

The villains Bertie knew called the barrister Basher McBride, because Mr. McBride always got a conviction. He wore one of the silly wigs, but his face was square and handsome, and far younger than that of the judge who sat above him. A wilted nosegay reposed in a vase in front of the judge, both judge and flowers looking weary in the extreme.

The case had caught the attention of journalists up and down the country—the sensational murder of a lady by one of her downstairs maids. The young woman in the dock, Ruthie, had been accused of stabbing her employer and making off with a hundred pounds' worth of silver.

Bertie knew Ruthie hadn't done it. The deed had been done by Jacko Small and his mistress, only they'd set up Ruthie to take the blame for it. Bertie had known, had heard

Jacko's plans, but did the police listen to the likes of Roberta Frasier? No.

Not that Bertie was in the habit of talking to constables most days. She stayed as far away from them as possible, and her dad and Jeffrey, Bertie's self-styled beau, made sure she did. But she'd tried for Ruthie's sake.

Hadn't mattered. They'd arrested Ruthie anyway, and now Ruthie would get hanged for something she didn't do.

The handsome Basher McBride, with his mesmerizing voice, was busy making the case that Ruthie *had* done it. Ruthie couldn't afford a defense, so she was here on her own in the dock, thin and small for her age, a maid who'd been in the wrong place at the wrong time. Bertie could only clench her fists and pray for a miracle.

Mr. McBride, despite his dire statements, had a delicious Scots accent. His voice was deep and rich, rolling over the crowd like an intoxicating wave. Even the bored judge couldn't take his eyes off him.

Mr. McBride had broad shoulders and a firm back, obvious even in the black robes. He was tall, dominating all in the room, the strength in his big, bare hands apparent. He looked as though he'd be more at home out on a Highland hillside, sword in hand as he fended off attackers. One glare from those gray eyes, and his attackers would be running for their lives.

His accent wasn't so thick Bertie couldn't understand it, but his *R*s rolled pleasantly, and his vowels were long, especially the *U*s.

"If your lordship pleases," Mr. McBride said, his voice warming Bertie again, "I would like to call Jacko Small back to the witness box."

Bertie swallowed, nervous. Jacko had already given evidence that he'd found the body in the sitting room of the London house, then seen Ruthie down in the kitchen, crying, with blood on her apron. The silver had been gone, and no one had found it, so Ruthie must have hidden it somewhere, hadn't she? The police had tried to get its location out of her, but of course Ruthie hadn't known, as she hadn't stolen the silver in the first place.

The judge sighed. "Is it *relevant*, Mr. McBride? This witness has already told us his version of events."

"One or two more questions, your lordship," Mr. McBride said without hurry. "You will understand my reasons in due time."

In duuui time. The vowel came out of his mouth with a round, full sound.

Jacko came back in, was reminded he was under oath, and faced Mr. McBride with all innocence on his face.

"Now, then, Mr. Small." Mr. McBride smiled pleasantly, but Bertie saw a gleam in his eyes that was a cross between anger and glee.

Now what was he up to?

"Mr. Small," Mr. McBride said smoothly. "You say you opened the door of the sitting room to find the lady of the house on the floor, her dress covered in blood. You'd been asked to refill the coal bin on your return from your day out and had gone up there to do so." Mr. McBride glanced down at the notes on his bench. "That day was the seventh of July. The middle of the afternoon, in the middle of summer. Quite the warmest day anyone could remember, the newspapers reported. A bit too warm for a fire, wouldn't you say?"

Jacko blinked. "Well . . . I . . . the nights were still nippy. I remember that."

"Yes, of course. Bloody English weather. Begging your pardon, your lordship."

People tittered. The judge scowled. "Please get on with it, Mr. McBride."

"You say in your statement that you saw quite a lot of blood," Mr. McBride said, not missing a beat. "On the sofa, on the floor, smeared on the door panels and on the doorknob."

"'Sright." Jacko put his hand to his heart. "Gave me a turn, it did."

"So you fled the room and went down to the kitchen, where you saw the accused wearing an apron stained with blood. *She* says she got the blood on her because she thought she'd help out the cook by stuffing the chickens for dinner.

The chickens were still a bit bloody, and she wiped her hands on her apron. Correct?"

"It's what she said, yeah."

"Now, I need your help, Mr. Small. I must ask you a very important question, so think hard. Was there any blood smeared on the doorknob of the door to the back stairs?"

Jacko blinked again. He obviously hadn't rehearsed this question. "Um. I don't think so. I can't be sure. Don't remember. I was, you know, in a state."

"But you remember distinctly the blood on the doorknob in the sitting room. You were quite poetic about it."

More titters. Jacko looked flustered.

What the devil was Mr. McBride doing? Bertie's gloved hand tightened on the railing. He was supposed to be proving Ruthie did it, not that Jacko lied. Which Jacko had, of course, but how did Mr. McBride know that?

Besides, it wasn't his job to expose Jacko. Bertie knew from experience that courtrooms had procedures everyone followed to the letter. It was as if Mr. McBride had stepped onstage and started playing the wrong part.

"Was there blood on the doorknob to the back-stairs door?" Mr. McBride repeated, his deep voice growing stern.

"Um. Yeah," Jacko said. "Yeah, now that I recall it, there was. Another big smudge, like in the sitting room. I had to touch it to open it. It were awful." A few of the jury shifted in their seats in sympathy.

"Except there wasn't," Mr. McBride said.

"Eh?" Jacko started. "Whatcha mean?"

"The door to the back stairs, or the green baize door as it is also known, had a broken panel. It had been taken away, since it was a quiet day, to be mended. There was no door that day, not for you to open, nor for the maid to smear blood on."

"Oh." Jacko opened and closed his mouth. "Well, I don't really remember, do I? I was, watcha call it . . . agitated."

"Though you remember in exact detail the placement of every item and every bloodstain in the sitting room. The accused says she didn't see you at all that day, and never knew about her employer's death until the police arrived. I'm going to suggest you went nowhere near the kitchen and never saw the accused. I suggest you left the sitting room and the house entirely, returned later, found the police there, saw them taking away the accused and her bloody apron, and came up with the story about seeing her."

Jacko looked worried now. "Yeah? And why'd I come back, if I'd killed the old bitch?"

The judge looked pained. Mr. McBride's eyes took on a hard light. "You knew that if you'd disappeared entirely, you'd be screaming your guilt. I suggest you left to dispose of the silver and returned as though you'd been gone all day. And never did I suggest, Mr. Small, that you committed the murder."

Rustling and muttering filled the courtroom. The judge looked annoyed. "Mr. McBride, do I have to remind you that the witness is not on trial?"

"No, he's not," Mr. McBride agreed. "Not yet."

Another round of laughter. Jacko's face was shiny with sweat, although it was nippy in here on this winter day.

"I am finished with the witness, your lordship. In my summing up, I will be putting the case that what we have here is not a conniving young woman who killed her employer, smeared blood all over the room, and then remained quietly in the kitchen with an apron covered with the same blood—and, I might add, no time to dispose of the missing silver. I am instead going to put forth my belief that another person must have had much better opportunity, and strength, to commit the crime, and that we are coming dangerously close to a miscarriage of justice. Perhaps your lordship would like to retire briefly and prepare for my outrageous statements."

The judge growled as laughter began again. "Mr. McBride, I have warned you about your behavior in my courtroom before. This is not the theatre."

Oh, but it was, Bertie thought. Only the play was real, and the curtain, final. Mr. McBride knew that too, she sensed, despite his jokes.

"You are, however, correct that I would like to recess briefly to gather my thoughts," the judge said. "Bailiff, please see that Mr. Small does not leave."

The judge rose, and everyone scrambled to their feet. The judge disappeared through the door into his inner sanctum, the journalists rushed away, and the rest of the watchers filed out, talking excitedly.

Bertie looked over the railing at Mr. McBride, who'd sat down, pushing his wig askew as he rubbed the sunshine-colored hair beneath it. The animation went out of his body as the courtroom emptied, as though he were a marionette whose strings had been cut.

He glanced around and up, but not at Bertie. Mr. McBride looked at no one and nothing.

Bertie was struck by how empty his face was. His eyes were a strange shade of gray, clear like a stormy morning. As Bertie watched, those eyes filled with a vast sadness, the likes of which Bertie had never seen before. His mouth moved a little, as though he whispered something, but Bertie couldn't hear what he said.

Bertie remained fixed in place instead of nipping off for some ale, her hand on the gallery's wooden railing. She couldn't take her eyes off the man below, who'd changed so incredibly the moment his performance had finished.

Mr. McBride didn't leave his bench until the judge returned, and the courtroom started up again. Then he got to his feet, life flowing back into his body, becoming the eloquent, arrogant man with the beautiful voice once more.

The judge signaled for him to begin. Mr. McBride summed up his case so charmingly that all hung on his words. The jury went out and returned very quickly with their verdict about Ruthie, *Not guilty*.

Ruthie was free. Bertie had hoped for a miracle, and Mr. McBride had provided one.

After much hugging, Ruthie left Bertie and went home with her mum. Bertie found her dad and Jeffrey waiting for her outside the pub across the street. They were furious. Jacko was Jeffrey's best mate, and Jacko had just been arrested for murder and taken away by the police.

"'E's to blame," Jeffrey said darkly, jerking his chin at Mr. McBride, who was walking out of the Old Bailey, dressed now in a normal suit and coat. Once again, Bertie noted how Mr. McBride had changed from a man who commanded a room to a man who looked tired of life.

The afternoon was cold, darkening with the coming winter night. Bertie rubbed her hands together in her too-thin gloves and suggested that her dad and Jeffrey take her into the pub and buy her a half.

"Not yet," Bertie's dad said. "Just teach 'im a lesson, Bertie. Go on now, girl."

Girl, when she was twenty-six years old. "Leave him alone," she said. "He saved Ruthie."

"But got Jacko arrested," Jeffrey growled. "Whose side are you on?"

"Jacko *killed* the woman," Bertie said. "He's a villain; he always was. I say good on Ruthie."

Jeffrey grabbed Bertie by the shoulder and pushed her into the shadows of the passage beside the pub. He wouldn't hit her in public—he'd take her somewhere unseen to do that—but his hand clamped down hard. "Jacko is my best friend," Jeffrey said, his breath already heavy with gin. "You get over to that fiend of a Scottish barrister and fetch us a souvenir. We deserve it. The traitorous bastard was supposed to take Jacko's part."

Jeffrey's grip hurt. Bertie knew if she protested too much, both Jeffrey and her dad would let her have it. But she couldn't do this.

"That fiend of a Scottish barrister is very smart," she argued. "He'll catch me, then *I'll* be in the cell with Jacko, waiting to go before the magistrate."

Bertie's dad leaned in, his breath already reeking as well. "You just do it, Roberta. You're like a ghost—he'll never know. And if he *does* see you, you know what to do. Now get out there, before I take my hand to you."

They weren't going to leave it. In their minds, Mr. McBride

was the villain of the piece and deserved to be punished. If Bertie refused, her dad would drag her away and thrash her until she gave in. If Mr. McBride went home while Bertie was taking her beating, her dad would make her wait here every afternoon until Mr. McBride returned for another case.

Either way, Bertie was doing this. One way would simply be less painful than the other.

Bertie jerked free of Jeffrey's hold. "All right," she snapped. "I'll do it. But you'd better be ready. He's no fool."

"Like I said, he'll never see ya," her dad said. "You've got the touch. Go on with you."

Bertie stumbled when her dad pushed her between the shoulder blades, but she righted herself and squared her shoulders. Taking a deep breath, she walked steadily toward where Mr. McBride stood waiting, his sad face and empty eyes focused on something far, far from the crowded streets of the City of London.

~~~~~

Sinclair McBride pulled his coat close against the icy wind and drew his hat down over his eyes.

Remember Sir Percival Montague, Daisy? he asked the gray sky. *Well, I potted him good today. Old Monty was nearly rubbing his hands, wanting to pronounce sentence of death on that poor girl. Bloody imbecile. She was no more guilty than a newborn kitten.*

The sky grew darker, rain coming with the night. So damnably cold here, not like the blistering heat of North Africa, where Sinclair had done his army time. His younger brother, Steven, was always trying to talk Sinclair into traveling with him—Spain, Egypt, back to Rome at least, where winters were balmy.

But there was the question of Andrew and Caitriona, Sinclair's very interesting children. Sinclair couldn't bring himself to foist them on Elliot and Juliana while he traveled the world. His brother and sister-in-law were starting their own family, their own life, and needed time alone. *Take them with me?* Sinclair had to smile. *Wouldn't that be an adventure?*

Sinclair imagined his two terrifying bairns on trains, carriages, carts, all the way to Italy. No, not the best answer.

Thinking about Andrew and Cat helped him avoid the one thought Sinclair had been trying to banish all day. Now as he stood in the cold, waiting for his coachman to bring the landau, the thought came unbidden.

Seven years to this day you left me, Daisy.

Margaret McBride, Maggie or Daisy to those closest to her, had died of a fever that threatened to take Sinclair's children as well. Seven years ago today.

My friends and family expect me to move on, can you believe it? But they've not had the loves of their lives ripped away from them, have they? They wouldn't say such bloody daft things if they had.

"Moving on" sounded like forgetting all about Maggie, his wife, his lover, his helpmeet, his best friend. *And I'll never do that.*

Maggie didn't answer. She never did. But it didn't matter. The comfort Sinclair drew from talking to her, out loud or inside his head, was some days the only thing that kept him sane.

When you're ready for me to move on, I know you'll tell me. Another gust of wind had Sinclair grabbing for his hat and clenching his teeth. Where the devil was Richards with the coach? *I trust you, Daisy . . .*

The crowd was thick, everyone in London going home for the night. Sinclair held on to his hat as he was buffeted. Richards was taking a damn long time. Sinclair wasn't usually in a rush, but tonight was bloody cold, and the rain was starting to come down in earnest.

A shove and a thump sent Sinclair a swift step forward. A young woman had stumbled into him, her shoes skidding on the wet pavement. She struggled to keep her feet, and Sinclair put a steadying hand under her arm.

"Easy now, lass," Sinclair said.

She looked up at him . . . and everything stopped. Sinclair saw a dark hat covered with bright blue violets, then eyes of the same blue—clear and warm in this swirl of gray. The young woman's face was round, her nose slightly tip-tilted, her red lips curving into a charming smile.

He'd never seen her before, and at the same time, Sinclair felt a jolt rock him, as though he'd been waiting for years for this encounter. The two of them stood together in a warm stillness, removed from the rest of the world as it rushed around them.

"I'm *that* sorry, mister," the young woman was saying. "Some bloke put his elbow right in me back, and me feet went clean out from under me. You all right?"

"I'm whole." Sinclair forced himself back to the cold of the real world, and studied her with his professional assessment, honed by a long career of watching criminals. She wasn't a street girl. Game girls had a desperate look, and were too eager to be seductive. *Want me to make ya feel better, lamb?* was the cleanest of the offers Sinclair had gotten as he strode through London's streets.

This young woman was working-class, probably on her way home after a long day's drudgery. She wasn't dirty, but the sleeves of her velvet jacket were frayed at the cuffs, her gloves threadbare and much mended. Poor, but making the best of it.

Still, she didn't have the downtrodden appearance many factory women had. Her smile was sunny, as though telling the world things could be better if given a chance.

"Well, that's good," she said. "'Night, mister. Sweet dreams."

Another smile, and in the sudden flare of an approaching light, all Sinclair could see were her eyes.

Deep and blue, like the depths of the ocean. The Mediterranean could be that color. Sinclair remembered southern Italy and its shores from his leave time, when he'd been in the army and traveling the world. He'd known peace there.

This young woman with her blue eyes was beautiful, with a beauty that went beyond her shabby clothes and working-class grin. She was a vision of light in the darkness, in a place where darkness had lasted too long.

Someone else shoved him, and Sinclair turned to step out of the way. When he looked back for the young woman, she was gone. He blinked at the empty space where she'd been, then lifted his gaze and spied her slipping through the crowd, the violets on her hat bobbing.

The detail of her ridiculous hat kept Sinclair from believing he'd dreamed her. But of course he hadn't. Visions of beautiful women were of golden-haired sirens with perfect bodies, strumming on lyres perhaps, luring men to their dooms. Sirens didn't have lopsided smiles and plump faces, and blue eyes that pulled Sinclair out of his despair, if only for a moment.

But she was gone now, vision or no, and Sinclair needed to go home. Andrew and Cat would have locked their new governess into the cellar by now, or accidentally burned down the house. Or both.

They didn't *mean* to be bad, his little ones . . . Well, mostly they didn't. One of the governesses had claimed that Andrew was possessed by the devil. She'd even offered to contact a priest she knew who could have him exorcised. That governess hadn't lasted more than an hour.

A clock struck. Sinclair, out of habit, reached for his watch to compare the time. His watch always ran a few minutes fast and having it repaired made no difference. Buying a new watch was out of the question, because Daisy had given him this one . . .

Which was no longer in his pocket.

Reality rushed back at Sinclair with an icy slap. His gaze went to the violet-covered hat as it disappeared around a corner.

Good God, how stupid had he been? He hadn't pegged the young woman as a pickpocket, because pickpockets usually didn't stop for a chat. They stole and slipped away before the victim was aware.

Her bad luck someone had tripped her. Or had it been luck?

All this went through his head as Sinclair whirled around and strode after the woman, his feet moving faster and faster as he went. Gone was any thought of finding his coach and going home. Nothing mattered but getting that watch back. Sinclair would find the young woman and take it away from her, even if he had to chase her to the ends of the earth.

Chapter 2

Basher McBride was coming after her. Bertie had twigged he was much too smart not to notice if she lifted his timepiece, but she'd told herself not to be a coward. Now she knew her folly, because he was chasing her, and he'd have her nicked in a heartbeat. She should have stuck with taking his handkerchief and been done.

But she'd wanted Mr. McBride to look at her. To see those eyes, gray like the sky before dawn, to hear his rumbling voice. She'd warmed all over when the syllables had poured onto her—*Easy now, lass*.

She'd lingered too long to admire him, and now he was coming. Bertie picked up her pace and dashed around another corner. She knew London better than most, and she could lead him on a merry chase. And if Bertie couldn't shake him . . . well, she'd know where to run.

She scooted into the backstreets behind the grim walls of Newgate, ducking into the warrens and winding streets, lanes so narrow they blotted out the last streaks of light in the sky.

These passages were filled with trash, rats, and layabouts. A few of the men lolling in their gin-soaked stupor tried to grab

Bertie's skirts as she went by, but Bertie expertly twitched away from them and kept on running.

Bertie risked a dash across Aldersgate Street and back into the narrower lanes beyond. She jumped over a vagrant who looked to be far gone on opium, her bootheels clicking on the hard-packed street.

And wasn't it just her luck? The Scottish bloke was keeping up with her. A swift glance behind her as she rounded a corner showed McBride running after her, his body moving with athletic competence as he ducked and swerved around carts, dung, and vermin, both human and rodent.

Bertie's breath was coming fast, her corset too tight to keep this up for long. Blast the man. He should be giving up by now, toddling off to his comfortable home in Mayfair or Belgrave Square or wherever he laid his pristine head to rest.

She remembered how he'd stood straight and tall in front of the judge, taunting the old misery, turning the verdict around to surprise them all. Basher McBride's arrogance had rolled off him, with even the judge grudgingly conceding to him.

But then, as soon as his performance was over, all that arrogance drained out of him, leaving Mr. McBride an empty shell. Until now, of course. His energy was back, focused on chasing Bertie and dragging her off to a constable.

Not that, never that. Bertie didn't particularly want to finish her life at the end of a noose. The jury might be sympathetic that Bertie was forced to pickpocket by her father—if they believed her—but that would only mean she'd be transported across the ocean to someplace she knew nothing about or locked up in a grim and terrifying prison.

She should have been able to slip away from him by now, but Mr. McBride was keeping her in sight, whichever passage she took. Bertie knew she'd have to lure him to The Trap, whether she liked it or not, or she'd never get away from him.

That's how she thought of it—*The Trap*—with capital *T*s outlining the jaws of it. No one escaped it, not easily anyway. Mr. McBride was smart—he'd run the other way as soon as he saw what was what, and leave Bertie alone.

"Oi!" she shouted when she was within three feet of the place. "It's Bertie! I'm coming in!"

A door in a squalid wall in a dark alley swung open, and Bertie leapt over the doorsill. She swept up her skirts as she landed, careful not to turn her ankles in the rubble.

Beyond the door was an empty space where a house had stood, pulled down or fallen down long ago. The lot was surrounded on four sides by other buildings that soared five and six stories to the sky. No windows faced the place, nothing to reveal the secrets of the inner emptiness. The space was lit right now with a fire built in the remains of an old stove, and with lanterns of the men and boys who liked to gather here.

The Trap was to be used in dire emergency, when a pursuer became too keen or bullies from another neighborhood strayed too close. The men and boys who made The Trap their haven were usually armed, usually drunk, and always ready to have a go at whoever was mad enough to come through the door.

Bertie fled through the lot, which was strewn with stones and broken bottles, skirting the pile of old rubbish in the middle. A smaller door led out the other side to another passage, where Bertie could slip away and go home.

She turned around to take one last look at her handsome Mr. McBride, to glimpse him again before he sensibly fled.

Except, he wasn't sensibly fleeing. Mr. McBride came on inside, firelight shining on his light-colored hair, his hat gone who knew where. He showed no fear about the toughs who were converging on him, and when he spotted Bertie on the other side of the lot, he roared, with a voice that rang like a warrior's, "Stop her!"

The toughs blinked, not used to victims who didn't scramble away from them in terror. Mr. McBride started around them, straight for Bertie. The lads came out of their shocked state by the time McBride was halfway past the mound of junk, then they struck.

"Aw, bloody *hell*!" McBride's rich Scots rang out, and he grabbed a rusted iron bar from the pile. Before Bertie's stunned eyes, Mr. McBride turned to face the onslaught and started fighting back.

The youths and men charging him had knives, clubs, or coshes. Mr. McBride parried their blows, thrusting and beating at them as they beat on him. Iron rang against steel, and one of the youths cursed as his knife went flying. Mr. McBride had the advantage against the knives, having chosen a bar long enough to keep them back. When they figured out how to get under Mr. McBride's reach, however . . .

They were going to kill him.

These toughs were thieves, murderers, or the sons of such. They'd killed before, wrapping up a body and tipping it into the Thames, with the police none the wiser. Never mind that Mr. McBride was obviously a toff in his fine clothes—they'd kill him, strip him, divide up the spoils, and go for a gin.

Why the devil didn't he just *run*?

Bertie came pounding back to him. She dove around the flailing bars, earning her curses from the youths yelling at her to get out of the way, and closed her hands around Mr. McBride's arm. She found beneath the expensive cloth strength that matched the iron bar he wielded. Mr. McBride started to shake her off, but Bertie dug deeper.

"This way," she shouted. "Run!"

"Get out of it, girl!" one of the toughs yelled. "Fair game."

"No, you leave him be! Come *on*."

She jerked at Mr. McBride, who finally saw wisdom and came with her. The lads, enraged she was depriving them of their fun, poured after them. Bertie ran out the narrow door on the far side, jumping over the sill to the street. Mr. McBride had to turn and fight at the last moment, buffeting back two lads who'd grabbed his coat. The coat tore, but stayed on, and McBride swung away and followed Bertie.

Bertie slammed the door. She grabbed the iron bar from Mr. McBride's hands and wedged the door shut, though she knew it wouldn't hold for long, and the lads could always go around the other side.

She seized him by the sleeve and started running. McBride ran with her, his strides strong.

It wasn't long before Bertie heard the youths coming. A few would give up, losing interest, but some would be determined. Jeffrey's mates loved a good fight, and they'd want to divide up the spoils they found on Mr. McBride.

"This way," Bertie urged as she dove around a corner.

There was one place in all of London Bertie could go. No one else knew about it but her—not her dad, not Jeffrey, not her own mates. Taking Mr. McBride there was a risk—he could have the constables raid it when she let him go—but maybe it would be worth the sacrifice. This courageous, handsome Scotsman didn't deserve to be beaten to death by East End thugs.

Bertie ran for the end of an alleyway that looked as though it went no farther. Mr. McBride started to argue, but Bertie put her finger to her lips and pulled him around a hidden corner, then down a slippery set of stairs and through a noisome passage. Finally, Bertie squeezed into a space that led between the backs of buildings, corners poking out and seeming to block the way. Bertie had discovered long ago that a lithe young woman *could* push through here and find a refuge.

Mr. McBride grunted a bit as he struggled through the narrower parts, then popped out like a cork behind Bertie as she opened a half-size door and ducked through. This door had led to an old scullery and kitchen for a house that had once been large and fine. But the room had been walled off long ago as the houses had been changed, pulled down, or rebuilt, and this corner of the cellar was lost and forgotten.

"Mind your head," Bertie said.

At the same time she heard a thump and Mr. McBride growled, "Thank you, lass. Very timely."

They went down a set of stairs in the pitch dark, Mr. McBride with a heavy hand on Bertie's shoulder. "Seventeen of 'em," she said, and started counting off.

Mr. McBride's hand was firm, spreading heat beneath her worn velvet coat and wool bodice. Strong too, his fingers blunt and gripping hard.

At the bottom, they went through another door, then Bertie told him to stay put while she groped for the matches she kept on a shelf and started lighting lamps. She had three lamps down here now, which threw a rosy glow over the crumbling bricks and fallen beams that littered the triangular room.

A pile of cushions, carefully formed into the approximation of a sofa, stood against the most solid wall. Bertie had covered it with shawls and blankets, and set up a small folding table near it, strewn now with newspapers and magazines she'd managed to smuggle down here. The passage above was too narrow for her to bring in much furniture, but she'd made the place as cozy as she could. She'd carried down small rugs over the years, overlapping them to keep her feet off the cold, damp floor.

Mr. McBride remained in place by the door until Bertie's lights strengthened. She'd need more kerosene before long, she saw.

The large man was out of place down here, that was for certain. His head touched the ceiling and he had to duck under the few beams that remained. He looked around the room in wonder, then his gray gaze landed on Bertie and pinned her as hard as he'd pinned Jacko in the dock.

"Are ye mad, lass?" he asked. "You stay down *here*? This ceiling could fall upon you any second."

Bertie shivered as his rumbling, delicious voice filled the space. "Hasn't in sixteen years," she said stoutly. "And probably stood up a long time before that. Solid houses in this part of London."

"Whichever part it is," Mr. McBride said, half to himself. "Why'd you save me from those lads, woman, when ye'd led me to them in the first place? Why not let them beat me to a bloody pulp?"

Bertie folded her arms, spending a moment letting his Scottish consonants and vowels flow over her. "Well, you were supposed to run away, weren't you?" she asked. "You thought you could take on eight street toughs by yourself? You have to be daft as a brick."

"No, I wanted my watch." Anger flared anew in his eyes, never mind that he was down here at Bertie's mercy with no idea where he was, no help at hand. But *he* was the one in command, Bertie knew. Not her.

Mr. McBride pointed a strong finger at her. "Which you

stole, right out of my waistcoat while I stood gawping. Give it back to me, and I'll say nothing."

━━◦

Sinclair watched the young woman's face flush in the candle-light, her guilt pure and simple. She swallowed and took a step back, rubbing her arms. She still wore the hat with the absurd violets, which was now hanging half over her right ear.

"Give me the watch, and I'll leave you be," Sinclair said, trying to gentle his voice. "No constables, no dock, though you are a bloody little tea leaf."

She didn't look impressed he knew rhyming cant: *Tea leaf—thief*.

"Why'd ya help Ruthie?" she asked.

Sinclair had difficulty catching his breath. It was close down here, the biting wind shut out. It took him a moment to realize that by *Ruthie* she meant Ruth Baxter, the kitchen maid who'd stood in the dock at the Old Bailey not an hour ago. Already the details of the trial were fading, a trial that would be put down as a loss to him, but Sinclair didn't care.

"Miss Baxter was innocent," he said. "Why should she go down for it?"

"'Cause you're a barrister, hand-in-glove with the judges."

This young woman had a lot to learn about the common courts. Old Monty and Sinclair had been butting heads since Sinclair had first put on a wig. "Miss Baxter couldn't afford a defense. I knew she was innocent when I looked at her, and I knew Mr. Small was guilty. What does this have to do with my watch?"

"Well, Ruthie's a pal of mine, ain't she?" The young wom-an's eyes were deep blue in the candlelight. "Thank you."

"So, you decided to show your gratitude by pinching my watch and leading me into the arms of your ruffian friends?" He made a noise of disbelief. "If that's your method of thank-ing a man, I'd hate so see ye when you're annoyed with him."

She didn't smile. "I told ya, you were supposed to run. They'd have gutted you. What were you thinking? You should have just let it go."

His temper splintered. "Why the hell should I? It's *my* watch. My wife gave it to me."

The young woman took a step back as Sinclair's voice rose. "Yeah? You're a rich bloke. Have her buy you another one."

"I cannae, can I?"

"Why not?"

"Because she's *dead*!"

The words rang against the low ceiling and the uncaring stones, and suddenly, Sinclair couldn't breathe at all.

He'd never, not even the day she'd slipped away, declared flatly that Daisy was dead. Sinclair shied from the word. He'd said *passed, left him, was gone. Dead* meant too much finality, it meant dust and no return.

Sinclair struggled for air. "She's . . ."

He felt wetness on his face. Bloody hell. He hadn't wept either. Not really. To weep for her meant she was never coming back.

"She's . . ."

The world rushed around him, spiraling down into a single point, stifling. Blackness filled his vision, a pressure in his ears grinding out his strength. His knees were bending, and a void opened to pull him inside . . .

He blinked and found himself half lying, half sitting across the cushions piled on the floor. The young woman sat beside him, her hat gone to reveal rich dark hair, worry on her face.

"You all right, mister?"

This was the second time she'd asked him that tonight, as though sweetly concerned. She was a thief, had murdering friends, had brought him to this hole only God knew where to do God only knew what, and yet she asked with anxiety whether he was well. She'd dragged him to this sofa, he realized. Sinclair must have fallen nose-first on the floor, and she'd pulled him to the cushions and made sure he woke up.

"Damn it, woman." Sinclair put his arm behind his head and glared at her. "What am I to do with you?"

She stared at him in wide-eyed contemplation for another second or two, then she leaned swiftly to him and kissed him on the mouth.

Chapter 3

Sinclair's breath went out of him again. He was surrounded by her lush warmth, her wool skirt falling over his legs and thighs, her bosom pressing his chest through his coat. The tip of her nose brushed his cheek, her lips soft on his mouth.

The kiss was unpracticed, even clumsy, telling him far more certainly than anything else that she was an innocent. She had no idea how to kiss a man, no idea how to part her lips to let him take his pleasure. And yet her kiss was welcoming, erotic, a taste of desire Sinclair couldn't ignore.

He found his hand stealing to the back of her neck, moving under her heavy braid, pressing her closer. Sinclair felt her start of surprise as he pulled her to him, then her body responded. She closed her eyes, shutting out the lovely blue, as she flowed into him and kissed him back.

Sinclair's arousal roared to life, the part of his body he tried to neglect becoming achingly stiff.

Why not? This young woman was lovely, willing, had brought him here. If she wanted to rob him of everything when they were done, so be it.

Sinclair could lay her on this couch, rid himself and her

of bothersome clothes, and drive into her. It wouldn't take long, and for one glorious moment, Sinclair could lose himself in the mind-blanking palliative of coupling.

The young woman made a faint noise in her throat. Sinclair realized he'd started shifting to take her down to the couch.

The noise snapped him back to awareness. What was he doing? She was innocent—at least of bodily passions. Other men might not care, deciding that the kind of woman she was and where she lived gave them the right to take her body, but Sinclair could never be that callous.

He let her go abruptly and sat up. She blinked at him from where she'd slid down on the cushions, delightfully mussed and not calming his hardness one bit. She watched him a moment longer then gave him a shy smile.

Shy. Not coercive or coy—she wasn't selling herself for the watch. Sinclair had no idea why she'd kissed him, but it hadn't been because she'd sought favors.

Under his scrutiny, the young woman's face flamed. "Now you'll be thinking me a tart," she said, sitting up and brushing back a lock of hair. "But I just wanted to kiss you, all right?"

Sinclair had wanted to kiss *her*. He still did. "I told you, I'm not a judge." His arousal continued pounding, wanting release, very unhappy he'd let her go. "The only thing I know about you is that you're a talented pickpocket, and you'll be giving me back my watch."

He held out his hand, amazed it was rock steady, his tight leather gloves whole even after the fight in the abandoned lot. The young woman eyed his palm in trepidation while she chewed on a corner of her lip.

She shouldn't do that. The nibbling made her lip red, made Sinclair remember her lips against his, spiking his need to taste them again.

"The thing is, Mr. McBride," she said, oblivious to his torment. "If I go back home without something from you, my dad will beat me rotten. I'd rather he didn't, if you don't mind."

Sinclair's focus returned, her words making his anger rise. "Why should he beat you?"

"He's put out because you got Jacko arrested. He sent me to teach you a lesson."

"Did he, naow?" He heard the broad Scots come out of his mouth, as it always did when he grew enraged. "Tell me who your father is, and he'll be in Newgate before the night's out."

She was already shaking her head. "I don't think I'll do that." She dipped her hand into a pocket in her skirt and pulled out the familiar shape of Sinclair's watch. "I have to say, it's a fine piece."

"I know it is." In one swift move, Sinclair reached for the watch and yanked it from her grasp.

"Oi," she said, indignant. "You . . ." She glared at him, outraged, but with fear behind her anger.

Sinclair let out his breath in relief at the weight of the watch in his palm. The watch was intact, all as it should be.

He believed her when she said her father would beat her if she didn't bring something home to him. Men in this part of London often sent their sons and daughters out to steal for them, or their daughters to walk the streets. These children had nowhere to go and no one to turn to, and many of them thought it fine to go out and earn some dosh to help the family.

This young woman was a bit older than many of the game girls, but if she still lived at home with her father, taking care of him, he'd have the upper hand. Englishmen set such store on women having little power and money, living only to serve the males of the family. Sinclair could never understand why—he'd seen so much grief come of it.

He slid the watch into his waistcoat pocket, keeping a close eye on the young woman's hands as he did so. She'd taken what she'd wanted when he'd been oblivious on the street, and there was nothing to say she wouldn't try again.

Sinclair pulled out a coin and held it toward her. "Will this assuage your bastard of a father and make him spare the rod?"

The woman's blue eyes went wide. Sinclair clasped a gold sovereign between his fingers, enough to pay for an East End family's meals for a long while.

"You really are a madman," she said in awe.

"Take it," Sinclair said. "Before I change my mind."

The young woman stared at the coin for a long moment, but she had no greed in her eyes. Amazement, yes, and wariness, but no greed. She knew she'd be handing over the sovereign to her father, keeping nothing for herself.

"What's your name?" Sinclair asked her.

She gave him a sudden smile, one that lit up her eyes and made her beautiful. "Now *that* I don't think I should tell you. Even if you were good to Ruthie an' all."

Fair enough. She reached for the coin, but Sinclair pulled it back. The young woman made a noise of protest, and Sinclair shook his head.

"This is also your fee for taking me out of here and leading me back to a street I can recognize. Can you do that?"

"'Course I can." She looked proud. "No one knows London better than me."

Sinclair believed her. She'd brought him across the city and into the East End without faltering, ducking around dark corners with complete confidence.

Sinclair took her hand in its worn glove and pressed the gold coin into it. "Show me, then."

Another sunny grin, and she swung to her feet with energy, her wool skirts brushing his legs. Sinclair started to rise with her, still dizzy from the chase, her kiss, the closeness of the room, and whatever noxious gas was down here that had made him light-headed. This place really wasn't safe for her.

The young woman steadied him on his feet, then blew out the lamps around the room, plunging them into gloom.

Before Sinclair could wonder whether she'd simply leave him there in the dark, ripe for the plucking, her warm hand found its way into his. "Come on, then," she said.

⌖

Bertie pulled Mr. McBride out into the dark streets, the sun long gone behind the buildup of clouds. His hand remained in hers as she towed him along, and his warm strength came to her, making Bertie's heart bang in a strange way.

Jeffrey Mitchell was supposed to be Bertie's beau, the man she'd eventually marry, whenever Bertie's dad decided he could let her go. When she'd been younger, Jeffrey's rough charm had seemed exciting to her, but that had quickly faded as she'd grown old enough to know better. Certainly Jeffrey had never made Bertie's heart go all achy and pounding. Bertie had never had the impulse to kiss Jeffrey more than a peck good-bye—not that Jeffrey would try more with Bertie's dad next to him at all times.

Kissing Mr. McBride had been more than an impulse. A need had gripped her, and Bertie had launched herself at him, wanting to kiss the mouth that spoke those rich Scottish syllables.

She'd about fallen through the floor when he'd cupped her neck and pulled her closer to make the kiss deeper. She'd wanted to respond, to lay herself against him all the way and see what it felt like to be cradled by his hard body.

When he'd pulled back, Bertie feared she'd disgusted him, that he'd think her a game girl. She wasn't, and she wanted him to know that. But for one wistful moment, Bertie had wished very much she *had* been a tart. Only for him, mind.

Bertie led him up another set of steps, the sounds of busier streets coming their way. It was foggy here, nearer the river, the lights of working London obscured by gray mist.

Her hand tightened on his. In a moment, Mr. McBride would snatch himself away and jog off, lost to the fog and Bertie forever. She wanted to hang on to him as long as she could.

She knew she had to let him go, though. Mr. McBride didn't belong in this world. Bertie wagered he lived in a fancy house in some posh square, with a passel of slaveys to look after him. His fine clothes, neatly shorn hair, and polished boots told her that.

Bertie pulled him to a halt at the top of the stairs, in the shadow of a wall. "This street will take you to Fenchurch," she said quietly. "See, there's St. Paul's." She pointed to the ghostly dome outlined in the fog. "Think you can find your way from there?"

"Yes." The word came with conviction. Mr. McBride was back in his own world now, arrogance and confidence flowing into him as it had when he'd stood up and looked the judge in the eye.

Mr. McBride ran a hand through his hair, the light from the main street glittering in droplets the mists had left. "My coachman must be driving up and down the lanes, searching frantically for me. He always thinks I'm going to top myself if he's not right next to me."

Bertie thought of the emptiness she'd seen inside Mr. McBride as he'd waited for the court to reconvene and again when he'd stood in the street outside the Old Bailey. She'd seen that bleak look before—in lads who knew there was nothing left in life for them, in girls who'd got themselves bellyful by men who didn't want them. "Are you?" she asked anxiously. "Going to top yourself?"

Mr. McBride pulled his gaze from the bulk of St. Paul's to look down at her. She loved his eyes—a smoky gray that sparkled like diamonds in this light.

"Of course not." He sounded annoyed. "I have wee ones at home. I'd never leave them."

His voice rang with indignation, and Bertie relaxed. Whatever else went on in this man's head, he wasn't about to deliberately do harm to himself.

His expression softened with the beginnings of a smile. "If something happened to me, Andrew and Cat would have to live with one of my brothers or my sister. I couldn't be so cruel to them—my brothers and sister, I mean."

Bertie grinned. "Are they lively then? Your kids?"

"Lively. That's a good word for them." He reached to touch his hat, then remembered it wasn't there, lost in his pursuit of Bertie. "Good night, Miss . . . Anonymous. Go home and stop picking pockets. If I catch you again, I *will* drag you to a magistrate. If your father demands you do it for him, you fetch a constable and tell him to send for me. You're a grown woman. You do as *you* please, not your dad."

He looked at her hard as he said this, his gaze flickering briefly to her bosom, which rose inside her tight corset.

"Right," Bertie managed to say.

He gave her a curt nod. "Good night, then." Mr. McBride slid his hand out of hers and turned away.

Bertie's heart squeezed into a tight mass of pain as he took a step away from her, and another. In a moment, he'd be swallowed by the night and the fog, gone forever.

Bertie ran a few steps after him, grabbed his hand, and pulled him back to her. As he swung around in surprise, Bertie seized the lapels of his cashmere coat, jerked herself up on tiptoe, and kissed him.

Mr. McBride stood still against her assault for one short moment, then he slid both arms hard around her and scooped her up to him.

He slanted his mouth across hers, parting her lips, his tongue sweeping inside to give her a heady taste of him. Bertie moved her tongue clumsily against his, a pleasing shock searing through her cold body. His mouth was hot, lips strong, his arms around her never letting her fall.

The kiss went on, Mr. McBride drawing her with him into the shadows. He was so strong, but his strength protected and shielded, it didn't demand and frighten.

Bertie kept hold of his lapels, hanging on as though she'd float away if she let go. His body was hard against hers, his tallness bending her back. Bertie fancied she spun around with him, the two of them in their own private dance, the hum and rush of the city circling them in one glorious, colorful stream.

Mr. McBride broke the kiss, his breath fogging in the cold. He still had hold of her, his arms around her keeping all bad things from her.

The look in his gray eyes was one of anguish and at the same time, need. Hunger. Bertie's heart beat rapidly, and her legs were shaking. She felt him shaking too, even though he was solid and unfaltering.

Then his jaw tightened, and Bertie saw him deliberately suppress the light in his eyes. He steadied Bertie on her feet and unhooked her fingers from his coat, leaving her cold and bereft.

With a final look, without a good-night this time, Mr. McBride turned and strode away. Out toward Fenchurch Street he went, meeting with the mass of London, who swept him up with them into darkness and heavy mist. Then he was gone.

Sinclair lay back with his hands behind his head and contemplated the ceiling. Hours he'd lain here after he'd persuaded himself to go to bed, wide awake. His thoughts, which usually wandered during his bouts of insomnia, had fixed on one thing—kissing the pickpocket.

A lady with an upturned nose and eyes the color of a summer sky. The warmth of her lips lingered on his, even after hours had gone by. No matter how much Sinclair told himself to stop his spinning thoughts and sleep, he couldn't push past the soaring joy of those stolen kisses.

Not stolen—she'd leapt on *him*, twined her body around his, and kissed him senseless. Twice. Every pressure, every movement of her mouth, every stroke of her fingers was imprinted on Sinclair forever.

An anonymous pickpocket with a sunny smile and very blue eyes, whom he'd likely never see again.

No . . . The efficient man inside Sinclair who was able to gather, store, and understand facts in lightning succession began to sort things through. His rapid thinking and spot-on conclusions were what made him feared in the courtroom, won the grudging respect of judges, and terrified suspects in the dock.

The young woman had said she was a friend of Ruth Baxter, for whom Sinclair, or at least his junior clerk, Henry, had all the particulars. Miss Baxter would know who the young woman was, where she lived, and what her circumstances were. Sinclair could track her down within the day and . . .

What?

Thank her for the kiss? Give her more money? Advise her how to get away from her brute of a father?

Did the woman have a job, or was picking pockets her main source of income? Had she lied to grab Sinclair's sympathy when she'd said her father sent her out to steal? Or was it the truth—because, of course, pickpockets were the most honest people on the streets.

At the very least, Sinclair could make certain her father left her alone. The young woman was of age—the plump firmness of her body, the tiny lines that feathered the corners of her eyes, and the worldly look in those eyes told him that. She was innocent of carnality, but that didn't mean she was a child. She should have real employment, or someone looking after her. *Something.*

The heady wash of the kiss erased Sinclair's common sense for a moment, and when his lust cleared again, he laughed at himself.

He'd never be able to track down the girl. Ruth would not give her friend over to a barrister of all people, no matter how grateful she was to Sinclair for setting her free. The girl with the violet-blue eyes would disappear into the endless drive of London. Sinclair would go back to his chambers to look over briefs, prepare for his next session in court, and try to push aside the pain that accompanied his life every day.

That, and . . .

"Papa!" A cannonball landed on his bed, one with small arms and legs, tow-colored hair, big gray eyes, and a wide smile.

Sinclair succumbed to his son's enthusiastic hug then pushed him back. "It's the middle of the bloody night, Andrew," he rumbled.

Andrew shook his head in enthusiasm. "No it isn't. It's five o'clock in the morning, and our new governess smells funny."

Chapter 4

"No, she—" Sinclair stopped. He couldn't deny that he got a whiff of cod-liver oil every time Miss Evans walked by him. "It doesn't matter. Miss Evans is your governess. No tormenting her, no toads in her bed."

"No toads," Andrew said in perfect agreement. Andrew had the sunniest disposition of anyone Sinclair knew, and also could cause more trouble than the most hardened criminals Sinclair had ever faced. "It's too cold for toads," Andrew went on. "But I found some beetles in the cellar."

Sinclair gave him a stern look. "No beetles, no roaches, no spiders. No insects or arachnids of *any* kind. Understand?"

Andrew didn't look contrite. "Yes, sir."

Sinclair remained wary. He knew if he didn't catalog specifically what Andrew shouldn't do, the boy would come back to him later. *But you didn't say no goldfish!*

Sinclair found matches on the bedside table and lit the lamp. His son, eight years old, already had the leggy, raw-boned look of the tall Scotsman he'd become. He had fair hair and gray eyes, a pure McBride.

The lamplight also fell on the photograph of Maggie

McBride—Daisy—with her dark hair and laughing eyes, the blue of them obscured by the sepia photograph. Sinclair's daughter, Caitriona, had the same eyes.

Andrew climbed over his father, picked up the photograph, and gave it a kiss. "'Morning, Mum," he said, and put it back down.

He flopped onto the mattress, ready to snuggle in and continue his sleep. Sinclair knew bloody well Andrew had sneaked out of the nursery, so there would be uproar when he was found missing, but Sinclair didn't have the heart to send him back. Andrew closed his eyes and made a good impression of a loud snore.

Sinclair lifted a handkerchief and wiped Andrew's wet kiss from the photograph. He'd had to replace the glass in the frame a few times because of Andrew's enthusiasm, but it didn't matter.

The thing is, Daisy, Sinclair said silently, setting down the photograph and tucking the covers around his son, *I think you would have liked her.*

She was out in the city somewhere. One in hundreds of thousands of souls, a young woman with violet eyes and a warm smile, who kissed like fire. Sinclair would probably never see her again.

⁓

Bertie watched Mr. McBride emerge from his house on Upper Brook Street, a posh address, and no mistake. She munched the hot chestnuts she'd bought from a vendor, keeping her fingers and mouth warm as Mr. McBride turned to say something to a broad-shouldered Scotsman who'd followed him out.

The two men were about the same size, but the second one had flame red hair and wore a Scottish kilt and the coat of a slavey—maybe he was what they called a gentleman's gentleman, a Scottish version of one. Ruthie had told Bertie that valets could be so haughty and correct you'd think *they* were the duke or baron. This one wasn't so haughty—he looked more like a fighting man stuffed into a suit and not liking it. He growled something at Mr. McBride, and Mr. McBride growled right back. Good for him.

The red-haired Scotsman stepped aside as a coach came rattling up. The red-haired man opened the door for Mr. McBride, still scowling mightily, and Mr. McBride tossed a case inside the carriage.

"Leave it, Macaulay," Mr. McBride snapped and hauled himself up into the coach.

The door shut and the coach jerked forward. Mr. McBride settled back into his seat, not looking out the window. Except for his liveliness when he'd snarled at his servant, he'd taken on the awful blankness again.

Bertie watched the coach until it turned down Park Lane and was lost to sight. She knew where it was going—every day Mr. McBride climbed into his carriage with a valise of sorts and headed off to his chambers in Middle Temple, which was located near where the Strand became Fleet Street. The Middle and Inner Temples consisted of narrow lanes of rigid brick buildings, all with fine-painted doors and windows, all holding barristers and clerks working their hearts out to bang up criminals like Bertie, her father, and Jeffrey.

Mr. McBride's chambers were in a little square called Essex Court, in an elegant building with a fanlighted door, which matched the style of his Mayfair home. Both chambers and house spoke of money, and lots of it. Maybe the whole McBride family was as toffy as he was, or else Basher made quite a few bob sending murderers to the noose.

Bertie had discovered where Mr. McBride worked and where he lived from careful research. The day after her encounter with him, she'd seen him come out of the Old Bailey after a morning in court, but this time he'd stepped directly into his smart-looking coach. Bertie had been on her own—no dad or Jeffrey to tell her to rob the man again—and she'd found herself walking after the coach, which crawled at a slow pace through London's jammed streets. Easy for Bertie to keep it in sight.

The coach hadn't gone far down Fleet Street before turning off toward the Temples, stopping to let out Mr. McBride

on a narrow lane. Mr. McBride had walked from there, and
Bertie had pattered behind him, not too close.

Mr. McBride had never seen her. He'd gone into the fine-
looking building that housed his chambers, greeting another
barrister and a harried-looking clerk on the doorstep.

The other barrister had slapped Mr. McBride on the
shoulder and laughed. "The legend of the Scots Machine
grinds on. The newspapers love you, old man. Standing up
for the downtrodden, potting the true killer between the
eyes, making old Percy Montague snarl at you—the ladies
will love you even more now."

The clerk wasn't as informal, but he nodded and said,
"Good on you, sir," with much admiration. "Your new brief is
on the mantelpiece, and you've got a conference at three."

"No rest for the wicked," Mr. McBride said, tipped his
hat, and went on inside.

Bertie had ducked out of the way as the barrister and clerk
walked on together. Other barristers were going in and out of
the houses around her, and staring at her, these stiffest of stiff
men in their black suits, coats, and hats. Bertie was out of place
with her worn coat and scuffed boots, even if her hat was new.

Her father had been so happy with the sovereign Bertie had
brought him that he'd given her a few half-crowns as a reward,
telling her to enjoy herself. Bertie's dad was always cheery
when he was rich. He'd been chuffed enough to forget that
Jacko Small was now in the Bow Street jail, waiting to be
shuffled to Newgate to await trial. Jeffrey was still angry about
it, though, so Bertie had avoided *him* and gone shopping.

Why she'd decided to leave the hat shop and make her
way to the Old Bailey she wasn't certain. She'd told herself
she'd never got her half-pint yesterday, so she might as well
go back to the pub there and treat herself and have some
dinner, but once she'd caught sight of Mr. McBride, her feet
simply followed his coach.

What made her return to the Temple after more shopping
later, she didn't know either. She'd missed Mr. McBride leaving that day, but the next afternoon, Bertie spied him walking
to his coach, a big bundle of papers under his arm in addition

to his valise. The coachman asked him where he wanted to go, and Mr. McBride simply answered, "Home."

The sun had already set by this time, the streets dark and chilly, but Bertie had tramped along after the carriage until it had turned onto the Strand and become lost to sight.

Her heart had sunk—she'd never find him in that mess— but she had the good fortune a moment or so later to run smack into the clerk she'd seen on the doorstep of Mr. McBride's chambers the day before. The clerk was only about as tall as Bertie and a bit younger, but he was wiry, with thick dark hair and blue eyes that looked friendly.

The friendly light was the only reason Bertie took a chance and said, "I say, was that the one they call Basher McBride getting into that coach? I've heard all about *him*."

"*We* call him the Scots Machine," the clerk said proudly. "I'm his clerk. Well, one of his junior clerks. He's the bright star in our chambers—a QC. He'll be a judge one day, mark my words."

"Fine coach, and all," Bertie said, plying her smile. "Beautiful horses."

"Matched grays, pure bloodlines. He searched all over the country for those. Of course, his sister's married to Lord Cameron Mackenzie, who knows horses. All his win races, they do."

"Do they?" Bertie's smile deepened. "I'll remember that. I like a flutter, now and again."

"Then take it from me—put your money on Lady Day or Night-Blooming Jasmine in the mare races, and you won't go wrong."

"Lady Day or Night-Blooming Jasmine. I'll remember when I'm in the Royal Box at Ascot." Bertie winked. "Think they'll like me new hat?"

She laughed, and the clerk laughed with her. "It's fetching enough," the clerk said, thoroughly thawed now. "But even the royal family will lose if they don't wager on Lord Cameron's horses."

"He's Mr. McBride's brother-in-law you say? A lordship?"

"Lord Cameron married our Mr. McBride's sister. Scots,

the lot of them." The clerk shook his head, as if to say Mr. McBride would be perfect in his eyes except for that one little flaw. "Mr. McBride lives in London much of the time, though he has a big house in Scotland—he's grown such a large practice here. Wouldn't be surprised if he didn't become head of chambers soon."

"He must live in a grand London house then," Bertie said, at last getting to what she wanted to know.

The clerk had well warmed to her now. "He does. I've been once. Big house in Mayfair, near to Grosvenor Square. So many rooms, huge staircase—I had to describe the whole thing to my mum at least a dozen times."

Bertie asked him a few more questions, but either the clerk didn't remember the exact address or he had no intention of letting on what it was. But it was a start.

"I say," the clerk said, stepping closer to Bertie. "I'm off home now. Maybe I can stand you a half in the pub at the end of the road?"

Bertie put on her warmest smile. "That's kind of you, but I have to be getting home to me dad. He's a right bear when he doesn't get his supper on time, and he's got the biggest fists, I have to tell you. Like that." Bertie held up both hands, showing an exaggerated size of her father's. "Nice chatting with you."

The clerk looked suitably alarmed by thoughts of her violent father, even though he expressed disappointment. He tipped his hat, and the two of them parted.

It had been too late to rush across London that night and track down the house near Grosvenor Square—Bertie hadn't been exaggerating about her father's temper when he didn't have his supper on time.

The next day, then, Bertie made her way to the heart of Mayfair, rambling along the roads that connected directly to Grosvenor Square. The square itself was bounded by four wide streets; in the center was a large stretch of green with trees, surrounded by a fence with a big gate. A nice little piece of countryside for those who lived on the square to enjoy.

Three days Bertie had come to the square and wandered the streets, looking for any sign of Mr. McBride. She was careful to pretend she was a slavey on an errand or out shopping, so no constable would arrest her as a girl on the game. She'd die of mortification if she were taken for a prostitute, and her dad would thrash her good before she had a chance to prove her innocence.

Apparently, she looked respectable enough, because the constables left her alone and no one along the busy streets complained about her. It was early on the third day of her investigation that she stood eating chestnuts and watched Mr. McBride emerge from his very tall, very elegant brick house on Upper Brook Street, which led from the west side of Grosvenor Square.

The ground floor's large bricks were painted white, which made the black door with fanlight all that more sharp. The tall windows didn't have arches over them, but they were regal, becoming smaller on each story as the house climbed—at least five floors that Bertie could see. Delicate wrought-iron railings ran across the windows of the first floor rooms, while the ground floor was encased in a more functional railing, with stairs that ran down to the scullery and kitchen.

While Bertie stood eyeing the house after Mr. McBride had ridden away, absently popping another chestnut into her mouth, the red-haired Scotsman, Macaulay, turned her way. His blue gaze bore into her so fiercely that Bertie almost swallowed the chestnut whole.

She quickly assumed a nonchalant look and hurried across the street and down toward Park Lane. Just a harmless young woman, she made herself convey, taking a day out to see the sights. She felt Macaulay watching her, but by the time she was brave enough to turn back, he was gone, the door of Mr. McBride's house shut.

Bertie didn't trust that the man wouldn't be peering out the windows, so she turned her steps to Hyde Park, on the other side of Park Lane. A gate not far from Upper Brook Street led into the park, and Bertie kept up her rapid pace as she went through that gate, finishing off her chestnuts and crumpling the paper into her pocket.

Even in winter, Hyde Park was a vast expanse of lawn

dotted with trees, a relief to eyes accustomed to jammed-together gray houses and teeming streets. Bertie liked to come up to the park when she had the time, to look at the flowers in summer, the trees turning colors in autumn, and the horses trotting along the Rotten Row any time of year. She liked Regent's Park even better, with its avenues of flowers and sloping lawns, but she couldn't get that far north very often. How splendid it must be to live in the big houses around here and have this park nearly outside the front door.

"Master Andrew!" A sharp voice cut through the winter air. "You come back here! At once!"

A small object burst past Bertie from behind her, a red hat flying from a little head to reveal hair the same color as Mr. McBride's. The hat belonged to a boy in a handsome coat, knee breeches, white stockings, and sturdy boots. Bertie was nearly knocked off her feet by this missile, his small arms and legs pumping, but she sidestepped and spun in place, catching her balance and preventing a fall.

A woman in black panted after the boy. She was hampered by the heavy coat she wore, and a hat with a small veil was slipping over her ear.

"I beg your pardon, miss," she said as she caught up to Bertie. Then the woman gave Bertie a quick once-over, taking in her well-worn clothes and straw hat, realized she wasn't an upper-class miss, and changed her tone. "You ought to keep out of the way," she snapped. "What are you thinking? Master Andrew!" she called again, and loped away after the boy.

A little girl walked down the path after the woman. The girl was about eleven, Bertie would judge, but she was dressed like a fashion plate. She wore a fur jacket over a dark blue dress that had a little bustle in back and a skirt with many flounces reaching just below her knees. She wore fine white stockings, a bit too thin for running around the park in this cold, Bertie would have thought. Completing the ensemble was a pair of ivory-colored button-up shoes and a fur hat that looked silky soft. From under the hat cascaded thick dark hair, wonderfully curled.

The girl walked slowly, almost primly, and she hugged a

large doll with dark curls to her chest. The girl could be a porcelain doll herself with her pink cheeks, blue eyes, and elegant clothes.

The girl didn't acknowledge Bertie at all but simply walked along after the nanny or whatever she was. The emptiness in her eyes struck Bertie—not only was the girl far too young for that kind of bleakness, but Bertie had seen the same emptiness in another pair of eyes recently—those of the handsome Mr. McBride.

She also remembered Mr. McBride reclining in her secret hideaway, his hand wonderfully warm in hers, as he spoke to her with ease. No one in the wide world had known where they were. In the passage before he'd left her, he'd told her about his children, Cat and Andrew.

"Andrew, *no!*"

Bertie saw why Mr. McBride had said his children were lively. Andrew ceased running in a straight line and dodged left, out through another gate and into the traffic of Park Lane.

The nanny ran after him, screeching as she wove past horses, carts, and carriages. Drivers pulled up, swearing at her. "Are you daft, woman?" "Can't you keep your charge better than that?" "You want to get the lad killed?"

The girl, Cat, stopped at the gate, as though uncertain whether to cross the road or wait for Andrew and the nanny to return. Bertie caught up to Cat and gave her a friendly nod.

"We'd best go after them, I think," Bertie said. "Your nanny will likely fall over dead if she has to hunt you down too."

Cat turned a scornful look up to Bertie, worthy of the judge who'd scowled down at Mr. McBride at Ruthie's trial. "She's our *governess*. I'm too old for a nanny." She looked Bertie up and down. "Who are you?"

"Me name's Bertie. Traffic's cleared a little. Come on."

Bertie caught Cat by the hand and pulled her quickly across the street. The girl kept up, not dragging, her doll held firmly in her arm.

"Bertie's a *boy's* name," Cat said with certainty.

"I know, but it's what me mates call me. My real name's Roberta. Here we are."

Andrew had disappeared down another street. Halfway along was a house covered in scaffolding—the house was being pulled down, or put up, or painted, or some such. In any case, no one seemed to be working on it at the moment.

Andrew took the opportunity to scramble up a short ladder, grab the scaffolding, and start climbing it like a monkey. The little girl shook off Bertie, ran to the ladder, and went right up after him.

Chapter 5

"Come down!" the governess implored. "*Please,* come down."

Andrew and Cat blissfully ignored her. They'd climbed nearly to the top floor, just below the last set of windows, when Andrew sat down on a board, swinging his legs in the empty air. His sister, with more dignity, sat down beside him and twined her leather-clad ankles.

The governess tried to be stern. "Master Andrew, Miss Caitriona, you climb down here this instant!"

Andrew looked over the side and stuck out his tongue. Caitriona said nothing, only stared straight ahead of her.

A crowd had gathered. "You treed them, no doubt, missus," a man said, and guffawed.

"Cheeky beggars," a clerk who'd emerged from a shop said. "You need to take a strap to them."

Another man was more kind. "Wait for the workmen to come back. They'll shift them. No one's in that house, or someone could go inside and get them through the window."

"Where *are* the workmen?" the governess demanded. "Lazy layabouts. They've nipped off for tea, or something stronger, I'd wager. Haven't they?"

"They won't be long," the kinder man said.

"Master Andrew, come *down*." The governess was near to tears.

"Let me." Bertie pushed past the governess, who smelled strangely of fish, and gave the ladder and scaffolding a calculating eye. "The workmen might frighten them anyway."

The governess's look of chill disapproval evaporated with her desperation. "If you believe you can fetch them down, young woman, you're welcome to try."

Bertie pulled off her gloves and tucked them into her pocket. She spit on both palms, rubbed them together, jumped, and caught a horizontal pole of the scaffolding.

She used her feet and legs to carry her onto the first board, then started climbing the bars, moving upward quickly. Such things had been easier when she'd been ten, she reflected as she pulled herself up, but she'd kept herself limber.

"You in the circus?" one of the men yelled from below.

Bertie didn't answer. She knew she could have climbed the ladder, as the children had, but she'd decided that swinging up like an acrobat would better catch their attention.

She was right. Both Cat and Andrew were staring at her, round-eyed, by the time Bertie reached the top board and walked fearlessly down its narrow length toward them.

Bertie sat down next to Andrew with a thump, swinging her legs over the side as he did. She made a show of gazing around her. "Ooh, lovely. Quite a view from up here, innit?"

She could see down the short length of the street and then out across Hyde Park, down to the Row and the houses of Knightsbridge beyond.

"There's the Serpentine," Bertie pointed out. "See?"

Andrew climbed to his feet for a better view. He braced himself on an iron pole, leaning out alarmingly far. Caitriona silently seized the back of his jacket, holding him steady.

Cat had come up here to make sure Andrew didn't fall, Bertie realized. Cat pretended to be sullen, but a truly sullen girl would have walked away or stood below, bored, until her brother was either rescued or had fallen to his death.

"Let's go boating on the Serpentine!" Andrew shouted.

"Sounds a treat," Bertie said. She'd never been boating on the Serpentine but she'd watched others do it while she stood by, envious.

"You're not going boating," the governess called up. "You'll be going back to your studies, Master Andrew, so you can grow up to be a fine barrister, like your father."

Mentioning studies was not the best way to entice a boy home, Bertie thought. Andrew clutched the pole.

"I'm not going to be a barrister," he shouted down. "I'm going to be a ghillie, like Macaulay, and hunt game. Or a soldier, like Uncle Steven, and shoot enemies." He raised an imaginary rifle and made explosive noises as he potted his target, human or animal.

"You come down here at once!" The governess had returned to commanding.

"Might be too cold for boating," Bertie said conversationally. "But maybe not for tea. Do you have tea in the mornings? I bet you have truly wonderful teas, with cakes and buns, with lots of butter and jam."

"No," Cat said without inflection. "Miss Evans makes us take our tea very weak, with no milk or sugar, and only a bit of plain bread, no jam or even butter."

"Oh." No wonder the kids had run away from Miss Evans. She sounded a right tightfisted old biddy. "Well, I've got a few coins in me pocket," Bertie said. "How about tea at a shop?"

Both children stared at her, Andrew with his arm around the pole. "We've never been to tea in a shop," Andrew said. He looked wistful a moment, before his disarming grin returned. "Can it be a great, big tea?"

"As much as you want." Bertie wasn't sure exactly how much it cost to have tea and cakes in a shop in Mayfair, but surely she had enough left for it. She'd planned to have her tea or luncheon out today, like a fine young lady, before heading home to be plain old Bertie again.

"We'll come then," Andrew said, mind made up. "What's your name?"

"It's Bertie."

Andrew laughed. "That's a boy's name."

Caitriona answered for her. "Her name is Roberta, but her mates call her Bertie," she said, proud of the knowledge.

"I can be your mate," Andrew said eagerly to Bertie. "So I'll call you Bertie too." He stuck out a grubby hand. "I'm Andrew McBride. This is my sister, Cat."

"Caitriona," Cat said.

Bertie shook Andrew's hand. "Nice to meet ya."

"Come on," Andrew said. "I want lots of cake."

Bertie barely stopped him from swinging onto the scaffolding below him and climbing down the way he'd come up. There was an easier way down at the ends of the boards, where the scaffolding crisscrossed like a ladder. Bertie led the children that way and climbed down ahead of them. She halted at each level and hung on to Andrew and Cat in turn as they climbed after her, not letting them go on until they'd steadied themselves. At last they reached the lowest board, six feet above the street, with the ladder leaning against it.

Andrew and Cat climbed down the ladder, but Bertie held on to the pole she'd used to scramble up and swung out and to the ground. Her landing was a bit harder than she'd have liked, but she pasted on a smile, shook out her aching feet, and held out her hands to the children.

"We're going to have tea and cakes," Bertie said to Miss Evans, whose face was nearly purple, her hat still hanging over one ear. "Where's the closest shop?"

Miss Evans's mouth puckered up, as though she had something nasty trapped inside her. If she didn't let it out, she might burst. "Tea and cakes?" she repeated in a frosty tone.

"Yeah, that's right," Bertie said. The woman ought to show some gratitude. After all, Bertie had succeeded in coaxing the two children off the scaffolding, making sure they didn't break their necks along the way.

Miss Evans sniffed and righted her hat. "Mind you get them back before their father returns home, or he'll summon the police. They live at 22 Upper Brook Street. Good day."

Bertie's eyes widened. "Where do you think *you're* going?"

"To my agency, to tell them to strike Mr. Sinclair

McBride off their books forever. Thirty-one years I've been a governess, with some of the best families in England. But *they* are not children." She pointed at Andrew with a long, black-gloved finger. "They're *fiends*. I'll not stay another day in that house. Mark my words, young woman, you'll be running for your life. But take them back home first so you don't swing for losing the children of a Queen's Counsel."

With that, Miss Evans turned her back and walked swiftly away. Bertie opened her mouth to call after her, then closed it again. Andrew and Cat were clinging tightly to Bertie's hands, Andrew swaying against her grip.

"Are you our new governess then?" he asked, widening his gray eyes at her. "I like you better than Miss Evans." He leaned into Bertie's coat and sniffed. "You don't smell of cod-liver oil."

"Is that what that was?" Bertie asked, watching Miss Evans's long coat swirl as she strode down the street, dodging past carts and carriages. She could certainly set a brisk pace. "Bit rank, wasn't she?"

~~~~~

The closest tea shop was on Mount Street. The delicate interior had tables with white cloths, fine porcelain china, and heavy silver. The waiter who let them in looked askance at Bertie, but recognized the two children who lived nearby. He put them at a table in the back and brought them teapots and cups, along with a bowl of sugar and a wide-mouthed pot of cream. Bertie asked for cakes and buns, and the man disappeared to fetch them.

Bertie knew the proper way to serve tea. One of the many women who'd come and gone in her father's life after her mum had died had been somewhat refined. This lady—Sophie—had shown Bertie how to wear hats, walk into rooms, shake hands properly, choose her clothes, and pour tea and hand it around. A little deportment never hurt anyone, Sophie had said. Bertie had always wondered where Sophie had learned her good manners, but the woman had never spoken of her past.

Bertie had been fond of her, but inevitably, Sophie had grown tired of her father's bullying and had gone, like all the others.

Bertie blessed Sophie now, wherever she was, because Bertie could now pour tea competently into cups, correctly take up the sugar tongs, and ask in a false posh voice whether they wanted one lump or two. Andrew laughed at her, and even Cat looked fascinated.

As they sipped the first scalding taste of creamy, sugary tea, the waiter returned with a two-tiered serving plate full of cakes, scones, and plump buns. A pot of clotted cream rested in the middle of this bounty.

Bertie stopped herself from squealing in delight, remembering to be dignified. When she had money, she usually went straight to the bakery. Hats, coats, and new boots were necessities, but a scone piled with clotted cream was a luxury. Other women could bleat about necklaces and rings, but give Bertie a fat tea cake, and she was in heaven.

She dipped her hand into her pocket and pulled out her pouch of coins. "How much?"

The waiter blinked once in surprise then gave her a cool look. "I will put it on Mr. McBride's account," he said stiffly and walked away.

"Well, I never," Bertie said when he'd vanished. "I suppose I put my foot in it. An account. How lovely."

"My dad's got them all over," Andrew informed her. "He asks for what he wants, and Macaulay goes round every so often and pays up."

Bertie reached for a cake and slid it onto a plate, which she gave to Cat. She was pleased that Andrew didn't simply snatch the sweets, but waited for Bertie to hand them out. When all had plenty of cakes, with cream smeared over everything, Bertie lifted her fork.

"Macaulay," she said. "What did you call him? A ghillie? What is that?"

Caitriona answered. "A ghillie is like a gamekeeper, but Macaulay isn't *just* a ghillie. He looks after Papa. Minds the house, and the house in Scotland. More like a steward."

"Macaulay does *everything*," Andrew said. "He's Papa's nanny. At least, that's what I call him."

Bertie thought of the big Scotsman and his growls as he loaded Mr. McBride into the carriage. "I shouldn't like to call him a nanny to his face."

"He doesn't mind," Andrew said. "He thinks it's funny."

Bertie couldn't imagine Macaulay laughing, but maybe he had a soft spot for Andrew. It would be easy to form a soft spot for the boy, Bertie thought as she ate. Andrew had a warm spirit in spite of his antics, an open friendliness. Even the waiter gave him an indulgent look.

Caitriona, on the other hand, ate primly, with minimal movements. After her initial explanation about Macaulay, she remained silent. She did say *please* and *thank you*, but so faintly Bertie barely heard the words.

It wasn't shyness, Bertie thought. It was more not wanting to put the effort into talking. Not that Cat could have gotten a word in edgewise with Andrew's chatter, so maybe she'd learned to remain quiet while her brother rattled on.

In all the time they'd been on the scaffolding and here in the shop, Cat had never once let go of the doll. She didn't give the doll its own chair, nor did she pretend to feed it cake and tea as other girls might. Cat kept her arm firmly around the doll but didn't even look at it as she downed every bite of cake on her plate and sip of tea in her cup.

"She's pretty," Bertie said at one point, nodding at the doll. "What's her name?"

Caitriona laid down her fork and put both arms around the doll. "She's Daisy. My mother gave her to me."

The mother who had died, leaving the misery Bertie had seen in Mr. McBride's eyes. Bertie wiped crumbs from her fingers and pulled a locket on a chain from behind her collar.

"My mum gave me this," she said. The silver was slightly tarnished, as much as Bertie strove to keep it clean, and the chain was worn. She opened the locket to show Cat the tiny picture of her mother as a pretty young woman on one side of it, and a thin braid of dark hair on the other. "My mum passed too, so this is very special to me, like your doll is to you."

Caitriona stared at Bertie, then the necklace, then back at Bertie again. She looked stunned, as though it had never occurred to her that other people might have lost someone dear to them, and had keepsakes they hung on to.

Bertie closed the locket and tucked it away. "I wear it always, so it's like she's with me."

Caitriona nodded, and Bertie feared for a moment that the girl would burst into tears. Cat's brow furrowed the smallest bit, her eyes losing focus.

Then she drew a breath, blinked, and the moment passed. She held her cup out for more tea and, after Bertie poured, sipped it delicately, falling silent again.

Bertie didn't pursue it. The poor lass was missing her mum, and that was something Bertie could understand.

Andrew ate most of the cakes. Bertie managed to eat her fill in spite of that, and she lingered over her last scone. This was like a wonderful dream—a warm shop, clotted cream, smooth tea, and no need for money. What a fine world Mr. McBride lived in.

At last the plates were clean, the cups empty, and Bertie knew it was time to go. She took Cat and Andrew by the hands and led them out of the shop and back through Mayfair to Upper Brook Street.

She was sorry the outing was over, but the children belonged at home, and Bertie in the East End. She needed to be back before her dad returned from his work with a house builder, so he wouldn't be angry his supper wasn't waiting for him.

Also, Bertie didn't need Mr. McBride to catch her with his children. He'd wonder what the devil she was doing, and why she was following him about. Bertie wasn't quite sure how she'd answer—she couldn't even come up with an answer that satisfied her.

When they reached the house, the front door was flung open by none other than the large Macaulay. He stared out at the three, giving Bertie such a grim look she was ready to drop the children's hands and flee as fast as she could.

Macaulay looked sharply at Caitriona's hand in Bertie's, his frown becoming even more formidable. Bertie tried to release the girl, but Cat wouldn't let go of her.

Andrew, on the other hand, launched himself at Macaulay, wrapping his arms around the big man's kilted knees. "Miss Evans ran away. Bertie gave us tea and brought us home. *She's* our governess now."

Macaulay's eyes narrowed. He was no fool, and this close, he looked more like a frightening giant than ever.

Bertie swallowed on her dry throat, forcing herself to meet Macaulay's light blue gaze. "They needed a bit of looking after, that's all. Their governess did run away and leave them, the silly cow. But here they are, and I'll be off home now."

Cat made a faint cry of anguish and clung even tighter to Bertie's hand. Andrew turned around to Bertie and shouted at the top of his voice: "No, you have to stay! You're the best governess we ever had! Please, Bertie! *Please!*" His yells grew louder, until he was screeching, the words blurring to incoherence.

Macaulay looked alarmed, his grim expression changing to the perplexity of a man who had no idea how to deal with hysterical children. "Mebbe you'd best stay until himself comes home," he said over Andrew's noise.

"But . . ." Bertie wet her lips. "I'm not a governess . . ." Her words were drowned under Andrew's incoherent screams.

"Doesn't matter," Macaulay said. "Nursery's on the top floor, one below the attics. Best you take them up there."

Other servants were coming to see what was wrong, popping out of everywhere, like rabbits from a warren. Two maids in caps, a woman all in black, and a young man in a stiff suit carrying a bucket of coal—all stopped and stared, concern on their faces.

Andrew's eyes were squeezed closed, his face red, fists balled as he bellowed. Cat shrank into Bertie's side, holding on to Bertie's hand as tightly as she held her doll in her other arm.

"All right, all right," Bertie said quickly. "I'll stay. This is as good a place as any to put up me plates for a while. Andrew, stop that awful screeching. I think me head's being cut in two."

Andrew instantly dropped into silence, opening his eyes and breathing hard. "Your plates?" he asked hoarsely, looking her up and down. "What plates?"

Bertie laughed, the laugh shaky. "Plates of meat—feet. See?"

Andrew gaped at her in fascination then he nodded. "Why do you say it like that?"

"It's a rhyme—kind of a game, innit? So no one knows what you're saying."

Andrew sniffled. "Will you teach me?"

Bertie expected Macaulay to snarl that a gentleman's children didn't need to know any Cockney slang, but Macaulay only looked relieved she wasn't rushing away. "I don't see why not," Bertie said. "Now, show me this nursery."

Andrew let out a triumphant whoop and scampered happily up the stairs. Cat led Bertie after him, still holding hard to her hand.

The other servants watched, eyes wide, jaws slack, but none of them stopped Bertie as the two children led her higher and higher into handsome Basher McBride's magnificent house.

~

Exhaustion. That was key to a night's oblivious sleep. Must be, anyway.

Sinclair laid the thick roll of paper next to him on the carriage seat. The ribbon that had bound the brief slid off to the floor, but he didn't bother to retrieve it.

His head ached. Not only had he been in court every day since the Ruth Baxter case—the day he'd met the pickpocket—he'd received another of the confounded letters.

Your dear departed wife wasn't so sweet and innocent, was she? What part of her dossier would you like me to post to your fellows in chambers, the judges on the bench?

The letter had been printed in angular capitals, like the others. Sinclair had folded it aside to take home, a bad taste in his mouth.

The letters had started coming a year ago, just after Christmas. He'd shown them to Chief Inspector Fellows, his sister's brother-in-law, keeping it all in the family. Fellows was one of the best detectives in Scotland Yard, and he had a quality Sinclair valued—discretion. Fellows had started an investigation but so far had found nothing. The letter writer, as much as he or she threatened, had never followed up on the threats, nor had demanded any compensation for silence.

A lunatic, Sinclair told himself. *One who knows nothing.*

He knew he shouldn't worry, but it rankled. Sinclair had dutifully taken all the letters he'd received to Inspector Fellows, as per Fellows's instruction, all except ones like these. The ones that mentioned Daisy specifically he put into a box at home. They were no different from the others, except in subject matter, and he'd already given Fellows plenty to work with.

He didn't have time to rush to pay Fellows a visit anyway. Sinclair hadn't slept much in the last nights, and tonight he had three more briefs to read. He'd be in his study going over them while the house slept and he didn't.

Just as well. If he went to bed, Sinclair would lie awake thinking of the chance encounter with the blue-eyed pickpocket, or he'd drift off and dream of it.

The dreams took him far beyond the kisses they'd shared. In the dreams, Sinclair would lay her back on her makeshift sofa, the lamps burning softly around them, and unbutton the rather prim dress she'd been wearing.

Underneath she'd be bare, soft and sweet, smelling of warmth and the night. He'd kiss her throat and her bosom as she ran her fingers through his hair.

He'd move down her body, trailing kisses as he went, pushing aside fabric until he found the heat between her legs. In the dreams, he could taste the nectar of her, take in her beautiful scent. She'd groan and shift as he drank her, her movements languid. Once Sinclair was finished, he'd rise over her and slide himself inside.

At that wonderful point, the dream always dissolved, and Sinclair would wake up, half groaning, ramrod stiff, fists balled. He needed release—he'd held himself in too long.

Sinclair had learned after the first few years alone that he could sate himself physically with a woman without engaging his emotions. It had been a relief to discover that—he could calm his libidinous needs without feeling he'd betrayed the woman he'd loved with all his heart.

A week before he'd met the pickpocket, Sinclair's brother Steven and his new wife had introduced Sinclair to a widow his age, Mrs. Thomalin, who'd been charming, pretty, intelligent, and hadn't minded Sinclair kissing her in a private corner of the ballroom where they'd been dancing. He should offer to take her out to a restaurant or some such, and they could return here afterward for a private evening. His servants would never say a word. They were loyal to him—Macaulay and the housekeeper, Mrs. Hill, and the under-servants never told tales about Mr. McBride. Their discretion could be counted on while their master relieved his pent-up desires.

The coach pulled to a halt. Sinclair came out of his stupor and gathered his papers, retrieving the ribbon and tying it around the thick stack. His valise was already full, so he thrust the papers at Macaulay, who'd opened the carriage door for him.

Sinclair's study was on the second floor above the ground floor, a large room in the front of the house. A double door opened from it into his bedchamber, though his bedroom could be entered from the hallway as well. Sinclair liked the private aerie where he could be alone with his thoughts— that is when things were quiet in the nursery above him.

They were quiet tonight. Suspiciously so. Sinclair had left his coat, hat, and gloves downstairs with Peter, the footman, and now he thumped his valise onto his desk. Macaulay laid the armload of papers he'd carried up for Sinclair beside it.

"Where are the urchins, Macaulay?" Sinclair asked him. "Or did Miss Evans give up and slip them a dose of laudanum? I'll have to sack her if she did."

"They're in bed." Macaulay's voice was gruffer than usual. "They had their supper and went to bed, and are now sleeping."

Sounded unlikely. "Don't tell me she truly did give them laudanum."

"No, sir." Macaulay moved uneasily.

Sinclair stopped, and the papers he'd been straightening slipped through his fingers. "Why? Are they ill?" He lived in perpetual fear his children would fall ill again, as they had when their mother had passed. They'd been so very sick, especially Andrew, a baby then. They'd survived it; Daisy had not.

"No, sir," Macaulay said. "New governess. She . . . started today."

"New governess?" Sinclair blinked. "What the devil happened to Miss Evans? Or did Andrew manage to lock her in the cellar? And where did I obtain a new governess, for God's sake? I know I'm not the best of fathers, but I *can* manage to remember when I do and don't hire someone to look after my wee ones."

Macaulay opened and closed his big hands, saying nothing. Odd. Macaulay never had difficulty conveying his opinions on absolutely everything, usually in a loud Scottish growl.

"What is it, man?" Sinclair asked. "I've never seen you at a loss for words before."

Macaulay let out his breath. "I think you'd better talk to her yourself."

"I agree." Sinclair shoved the last stack of his papers into some kind of order. "If the children are tucked up and sleeping, send her down."

"Right." Macaulay hurried off, looking relieved, slamming the door behind him.

Sinclair gave up on his papers and moved to a little table near the window and the decanter of Scots whiskey on it that was always kept full for him. The table had an inlaid checkerboard pattern, and Andrew always begged his father to play chess or checkers with him on it. The last time Andrew had been down here, he'd tried to climb onto the table, and had smashed the whiskey decanter to the floor, sending shards of lead crystal and the best Mackenzie malt all over the carpet.

Sinclair poured a measure of whiskey into a heavy glass and drank it in one go, trying to enjoy the sensation on his tongue. He heard Macaulay's voice on the stairs, the man speaking to someone who wasn't answering. Macaulay's footsteps were firm, those of the governess hesitant, as though Macaulay was having to pull her down here.

Sinclair turned around as Macaulay opened the door so swiftly that it banged into the wall. Macaulay's kilt swung as he pulled the young woman he held by the wrist around him, her dark green wool skirts swirling in ahead of her.

Sinclair dropped the glass. It made a resounding smash, almost as resonant as had the one when Andrew knocked over the decanter. Whiskey stained the carpet anew.

Macaulay, having delivered the goods, turned and fled, slamming the door behind him. The big Scotsman was fearless in the wilds, marching miles alone and facing ferocious beasts without blinking. But when it came to handling governesses, he was apt to go pale, his freckles standing out on his face, and disappear as quickly as he could.

Sinclair was exhausted, unsated, hoping to be drunk, and tired of the mad thoughts that had flooded his brain since the night his pocket had been picked.

He was not prepared to face the pickpocket herself, who stood just beyond the whiskey spots on the carpet of his study, staring up at him with her Mediterranean blue eyes. Her bare hands twined nervously, and her face was strained below dark hair straggling out of her coiffure, but she sent him a cocky grin, one that had kept him awake and hard for six nights in a row.

"Now then, Mr. McBride," she said. "Fancy meeting you here, eh?"

Chapter 6

Sinclair's simmering Scots temper, fueled by fatigue, the be-damned letter, and his aching need, boiled up and exploded. He dragged in a breath and let out a shout that reverberated through the cluttered room.

"What the bloody hell are you doing in my house?"

The young woman blinked and took a step back. But she didn't run, didn't gasp and press her hand to her heart as young women who heard Sinclair shout were apt to. Officers and soldiers alike had blenched when Sinclair had wound up into one of his serious tempers, and scrambled to obey him.

The pickpocket only stared, the red lips he'd kissed parting a little. "I was looking after your little ones, wasn't I? I tried to leave after they went to sleep, but your man, Macaulay, bolted the door, and I couldn't open it."

"Bollocks." Sinclair's body was tight and hot. "You scoot around the streets of London where you bloody well please—I can't believe you couldn't find your way out of a *house*. It's why you're *in* the house I want to know."

"Told ya. Looking after your children. Your governess did a bunk, leaving them to me, if you please. Couldn't see her for the dust, she was running so fast. Did you want me to leave them in the street?"

Sinclair scrubbed his hand over his face. "I have no idea what the devil you're talking about. What are you doing here? In Mayfair? *In my house?*"

Her brows drew together, which made her blue eyes and her round face even more fetching. "I did you a bit of a favor, bringing them home. *And* getting them into bed to stay. I understand that's a chore." Her little smile came back. "Don't know why. They just wanted a bit of a story, and they dropped off, simple as that. But seeing as you're home, I'll be off."

She headed for the door. Sinclair barreled in front of her, turning around at the door and putting his back to it. The young woman halted, her eyes widening.

"You are nae going anywhere." Sinclair dimly wondered why he didn't take her by the arm and march her out into the street—she couldn't be up to any good here—but his body and mouth had taken over. "You are going to tell me how ye got here and why you're upstairs in my nursery telling stories to my children."

Her expression softened again. "You know, I like when your voice goes like that. All rich and lilting."

Dear God. The smile, the warmth in her eyes, was killing him. He was going to grab her any moment, drag her into his arms, and kiss her until he couldn't feel anything. Sinclair had to get her out of here. Had to.

He pressed his back to the door. "You will answer my question."

"Now you sound like you did in that courtroom." She gave him an exaggerated nod. "If your lordship pleases."

Or maybe he'd simply fall down dead. Her laughing mimicry of a barrister bowing to a judge made Sinclair's need for her soar. He was achingly stiff, his throat dry, and cold sweat trickled down his spine.

"You're good at evasion, I'll give you that," he managed to say. "How did you find my house?"

Color flooded her face, and she shrugged. "Happened to be strolling by."

"I see. You happened to stroll out of the East End all the way to Upper Brook Street, did ye? What was the idea, to see what other pickings I had? To bring your friends here and show them the choicest bits? They'll be disappointed. I make a good living, but I'm not a duke. No priceless paintings or silver plate in my house."

The young woman's flush deepened. "I'm not a robber, Mr. Bloody Arrogant McBride."

"Yes, you are. You picked my pocket then led me straight into the arms of thugs ready to beat me down and steal everything you hadn't already."

She twined her hands together. "I know, but . . ."

Sinclair stepped to her, standing right in front of her, his best courtroom sternness in his voice. She didn't back down but stared up at him, nervous though not afraid.

"What am I to think?" Sinclair asked. "I see a pickpocket in my house, with my children, for God's sake, when I don't remember giving her my address. And she's never given me her name."

"It's Bertie." More flushing. "I mean, Roberta. Frasier. Miss. I ain't married."

"Bertie." The name was pert, like her. It went with her laughing eyes, tip-tilted nose, and wide mouth better than the more dignified *Roberta*.

"That's me," Bertie said. "And I didn't come to rob you. I'm inside by accident."

"Oh, ye tripped and found yourself falling through my front door, did ye?"

"Mr. Macaulay told me I'd better stay. And when I tried to leave, your kids . . . whew, they can make a noise, can't they? They've taken a shine to me, but I must seem funny after that stuffed goose, Miss Evans. *She* couldn't enjoy herself if someone tied her down and tickled her with a dozen feathers."

This depiction of Miss Evans, the prim and proper governess from the best agency in London, made Sinclair want to burst out laughing.

What was the matter with him? She was a *pickpocket*, with a father who beat her when she didn't steal and ruffian friends to deal with those who tried to catch her. Sinclair faced women like her in the dock all the time. Most were driven to thieving and prostitution—they didn't know any other way, couldn't even imagine it. Bertie wasn't a game girl, but she was a thief. A charming one, but a thief all the same.

"I know you don't believe me," she was saying. "I wouldn't, if I was you. But someone needed to watch your son and daughter at that moment. Those two can get themselves in a right lot of trouble, can't they? Now they're asleep, as I say, so I'll be going home. If you just step aside so I can get around you, you'll see the back of me forever. Promise."

Sinclair couldn't move. "Don't be stupid," he heard himself say. "You can't go now. It's too late for you to be waltzing through the streets alone."

Bertie blinked in surprise. "What are you talking about? I walk around at night all the time. But if you're so worried, you can call up that fancy carriage of yours. I wouldn't mind riding back to Whitechapel like a princess."

Sinclair shook his head. "My coachman's gone to bed. You'll stay here tonight and go in the morning. No wait—you'll go when I've found another blasted governess. If Cat and Andrew like you, then you can watch them until I bring home the next victim."

Bertie raised her brows at the word *victim,* but Sinclair wouldn't take it back. That was exactly what these poor women were. Sinclair couldn't handle his own children, and everyone knew it.

"And how long will that be?" she asked.

"Damn it all, I don't know. Macaulay will go to the agency tomorrow. I can't. Too many cases to review." Sinclair glanced at his desk piled high with paper.

"Make up your mind," Bertie said, planting her hands on her hips. "You think I came here to rob you, so you want me out. When I say, *fine, I'll go,* you say, *no, stay and look after me children.* I will tell you something Mr. Basher McBride." She moved closer to him, her finger lifted in admonishment. "I don't work for nothing. I get paid an honest wage when I do an honest job. I'll stay and make sure the mites are all right, but you have to make it worth me while. A crown I'll have for it. *And* you won't charge me for breakfast."

"A crown—?"

She looked uncertain. "Too much, you think? All right, a half crown then, but nothing less."

"Good God."

What the *hell* was he doing? Sinclair should wake up Richards, never mind the coachman's sleep, and tell him to haul this young woman back to the gutter from whence she came.

But something told him to do anything to keep her around, to keep her smiling like this at him. Her presence was a warmth in the coldness, light breaking through the ponderous dark.

She was speaking again. "If you hold looking after your children so cheaply, it's not a wonder you got a governess who ran away at the first sign of trouble."

"What are you talking about, woman? I pay my governesses fifty pounds a year. Do you want the position or not?"

Bertie's mouth dropped open, her eyes round. "Fifty *pounds*? Good Lord, I'd put up with the devil himself for that much. Miss Evans is a perfect fool." She blinked again. "A moment, are you offering me a job?"

"I told you, yes, until a new governess can be sorted out. Wages and board, and an allowance for clothes." Her worn frock would have to go—she'd have to look the part. Mrs. Hill would throw a fit, but then she'd rise to the occasion, as she always did. Macaulay, a thoroughly egalitarian man, would shrug and nod, seeing nothing wrong with an East End working-class girl taking care of the McBride children, as long as she could do it.

"Clothes." Bertie looked down at the wool dress, the skirt stained with mud from London streets and rent in several places, including her backside, as though she'd sat on something rough. "What sort of clothes?"

"Ones that don't look as though you've been wrestling dogs in them."

Her smile beamed out like bright sunshine. "I haven't been wrestling dogs. Only your kids."

Did Sinclair want to know what had caused Miss Evans, a

haughty woman, to run off and leave Andrew and Cat with Bertie? Or was it best that the adventure never came to his ears?

He made himself step out of the way of the door. "Mrs. Hill, my housekeeper, will sort you out. You'll take breakfast in the nursery. The governess's bedroom is next to it."

Right above this one, in fact. Bertie looked at the ceiling, already knowing that. Sinclair would be in this study all night, poring over the briefs, knowing that right above his head she was lying in bed, stripped to her smalls, her face flushed with sleep. His hands clenched to hard fists.

"You can go now," he said sternly.

She sent him a narrow look. "You say every different sort of thing at once, don't you? You want me to stay? Or leave?"

"Stay. But not in here."

Bertie looked around the room, taking in the wreck of the desk, the overflowing bookcases, books piled on the desk and the floor, and now the smashed whiskey glass and amber stain on the carpet. "You have a passel of servants downstairs—don't they clean up the place for you?"

"No. That is, yes. They're not allowed to touch anything in here. I might mislay something crucial."

Bertie moved toward the desk, her curiosity apparent. "Some note that tells you a maid with blood on her apron ain't a cold-blooded killer? Amazing how you twigged Jacko did it."

"Wasn't much to it. I've learned to recognize the differences between a violent criminal and an innocent woman."

"Still, it was a bloody miracle, and I thank you for it." Bertie reached to straighten a paper that had come out of one of the briefs, and Sinclair realized it was the anonymous letter.

He caught her wrist. "Don't touch anything."

He found warm, firm flesh beneath her sleeve. Bertie glanced at his hand, then up at his face, her eyes holding wariness but also a softness that called to him. "It's all right," she said, her voice quiet, as though she calmed a frightened animal. "I wouldn't hurt nothing."

Sinclair grunted. What the sound was doing in his throat, he didn't know, but it came out. "Go to bed."

"Will, as soon as you turn me loose."

Sinclair told his fingers to release her, but instead, he pulled her closer, bending her arm until her wrist and his hand were just below her chin. "If I find out you've been playing me," he said, trying to sound severe, "if you've come to take what you want, I won't stop until the weight of the law comes down on you."

The most hardened villains the Scots Machine said that to cringed and mumbled that they'd behave, promise. Bertie only sent him another grin.

"Wouldn't be hospitable, would it? I'm not a robber, Mr. McBride. Not anymore. The watch was a one-off, and I was put up to it."

Bertie spoke with sincerity, innocence in her eyes, but Sinclair knew better than to let down his guard and trust her. If she could keep Cat and Andrew amused for a day or so while he tracked down yet another governess, well and good. The moment she wasn't useful anymore, she'd be gone.

Sinclair abruptly released her. "Upstairs with ye then." His throat dried out as he said the words, and he ended on a cough.

Bertie laughed. Sparkles and sunshine was that laughter. She spun around and walked away from him, heading for the door. Relief.

Before opening the door, however, she turned and came back to him. *God, no. Stay away from me.* Sinclair was so hard he knew he'd never sleep—maybe not for days.

Bertie's smile was wide as she held out a handkerchief to him—*his*, damn it. Plus two loose coins he'd had in his frock coat's outer pocket.

"You're too easy a mark," she said. "I'll have to teach you better."

Bertie pressed the handkerchief and coins into his big hand while he stood, stunned. Then she turned around again, her skirts swishing, and headed out the door. The swinging skirts let him see ankles in lace-up boots and a hint of pale stocking before the skirt fell again, and she was out the door. Gone.

All the air in the room seemed to leave with her.

Mr. McBride went off to work the next morning while Bertie took breakfast with the little ones in the nursery and told them the news that she was to be their governess for a little while. Andrew rejoiced loudly until Bertie had to remind him to sit down and eat the breakfast the maid had brought up on a tray.

Fancy that, maids carrying hot, tasty breakfasts to the likes of Bertie Frasier. The maid had flashed her a sideways glance, clearly wondering at her master's senses, but she was polite as could be as she set down the tray, and friendly with Cat and Andrew.

Breakfast was tea and toast, bacon and poached eggs, with a bit of sauce in a sauceboat to go over it all. The sauceboat was heavy silver and worth a bob. If Bertie had been Andrew's age, when she'd still thought her father walked on water, she'd have alerted him that here was a house where they used expensive dishes for everyday meals—in the nursery, no less.

But Bertie knew her father better now. She didn't want to be like him, and she'd never, ever again steal anything from Mr. Sinclair McBride. Taking his handkerchief and coins last night had been a bit of fun, and she hadn't been wrong—he was too easy. She'd only done it to prove a point, that he needed to be more careful.

While she and the mites breakfasted, she heard Sinclair downstairs, shouting for Macaulay, banging doors. Mr. McBride had a voice that could rattle the ceiling, and even Macaulay couldn't match it. No wonder everyone in court bent before him like reeds in a wind. It was only when Mr. McBride stopped banging about that the emptiness came through.

Bertie found herself listening hard to him, disappointment trickling through her when the front door opened and closed, his voice receding as he got into his coach. Cat and Andrew left the table and headed for the window to watch him go. Hooves clip-clopped as the carriage went away, taking him off to another day at his chambers.

Andrew waved frantically, as though his dad could see

him up there. Caitriona merely looked after the carriage, her doll firmly in the crook of her arm.

The maid returned for the tray, still polite, even with the master gone. No sitting down for a chat, no impertinence to Bertie because she wasn't a real governess. She simply collected the breakfast things, said a thank you to Andrew when he fetched a spoon that had fallen to the floor for her, and walked out again.

"Well then," Bertie said, rubbing her hands. "What do ya want to do now?"

"Play soldiers in the park!" Andrew shouted.

"We're supposed to have lessons," Caitriona said, but wistfully, as though playing soldiers was more appealing to her too.

"Tell ya what." Bertie sat down at the cleared table, which was next to a filled bookcase. "Let's have a story out of one of these books, then we'll go out to the park. I'm supposed to be your governess, and your dad would be angry at me if I didn't have you learn something, right?"

The book Bertie chose was big, heavy, and full of illustrations and tiny, cramped text. Bertie could read just fine, though she had to strain her eyes to do it with this book. The chapter Andrew wanted to hear was about a battle long, long ago in East Anglia, with a woman called Boadicea leading an army against Roman soldiers. Bertie read with interest—it was the first she'd ever heard of it.

"It's a bit like a play, innit?" Bertie asked when they'd read the dramatic end of Boadicea. "With villains and heroes and swordfights—like in a Christmas panto."

"A Christmas what?" Andrew asked, wrinkling his nose.

"Panto—a pantomime." Bertie stared at their blank faces in amazement. "Haven't you ever seen a panto? It's a play, with fighting and mean old villains, a girl in breeches and a man dressed up as a lady, and lots of amazing tricks . . ." She trailed off as both children blinked at her, clearly having no clue what she meant.

Bertie closed the book. "I'm going to have to teach you a lot, looks like. But you'll be teaching me in return, I wager."

Caitriona frowned. "Teach you what?"

"How to be a proper governess. I don't know how to be one, do I?" Bertie winked at them. "I have to rely on you completely."

Andrew grinned. "A governess gives us heaps and heaps of cake and lets us play in the park all day."

"I said a proper governess, Andrew, not a proper fool." Bertie softened the words by ruffling his hair. "Now, then, can I trust you two to behave yourselves while I run off home a minute? I'll be wanting my things."

More puzzlement from both of them. "You can send for your things," Cat said. "Like Miss Evans will send here for hers."

"Send to who? I've only got a few friends I'd trust not to help themselves to what I have, and besides, I don't want to put them out. I didn't get home last night, and my dear old dad will be frantic about me and wanting his breakfast."

"But it's ten o'clock," Cat said. "Our father leaves for work every day at eight."

Bertie grinned. "That's because your dad is a respectable barrister at a respectable office. My dad works for a builder, and sometimes there's work, and sometimes not. Either way, he stays out all night with his friends and staggers in when he pleases. By now, he'll be in a right state."

The two children listened in fascination. "Take us with you," Andrew said, his voice rising.

Bertie felt a qualm. Cat and Andrew, all brushed and combed, were like dainty cakes in a sweetshop window. Cat wore a light blue dress whose little bustle was topped with a big bow that matched the blue bow in her hair. Andrew wore knickers, a pristine white shirt, a jacket, and a little cravat. He'd already managed to rumple everything, being Andrew, but no one could mistake him for anything but a rich and pampered little boy. The street toughs where Bertie lived would eat them both alive.

"No, you stay here and read or something," Bertie said quickly. "I won't be long. I'll go while you're having your lunch."

"We don't have luncheon," Cat said. "We have dinner at one o'clock."

Bertie winked at her. "Well you enjoy your fancy dinner then, and I'll nip home."

Andrew's voice went up in volume. "You shouldn't leave us alone."

Bertie looked at him in surprise. "You're not alone. Goodness, you've got oceans of people living under this roof, haven't you? There's Macaulay and Mrs. Hill, Charlotte the downstairs maid, the lad Peter, a cook and the other maid who comes up here for you . . . what's her name?"

"Aoife," Andrew said. "She's Irish. Mrs. Hill says we have to call her Jane, because Aoife is outlandish, but that's her name, so it's what I say."

From the good-humored twinkle she'd seen in Aoife's eye, Bertie thought she must appreciate Andrew's candor.

"And there's Richards, the coachman," Cat said. "We don't see him much, because he stays in the mews, with the groom and the gardener."

"See?" Bertie said. "All sorts of people. You don't really need me all the time, do you?"

"Yes, we do!" Andrew declared at the top of his voice.

"The others say we're unruly and a handful," Cat said without inflection. "That we're holy terrors, and no one can do anything with us."

"I'm a holy terror!" Andrew shouted. "That's what Richards said when I let out the horses to run free. But it was Cat that opened the door."

Cat took the time to press a kiss to her doll's head, but Bertie saw the flush on her cheek.

Bertie rested her elbows on the table. "Did Richards take the back of his hand to ya?"

Andrew stopped shouting and stared, round-eyed. Cat lifted her head. "No," she said, sounding surprised Bertie would ask.

"Dad would have torn his head off," Andrew said. "The governess we had that week sent us to bed without supper, and Dad sacked her."

"Good on your dad." Even Bertie's father had never made her go hungry as punishment, knowing what it was like to be hungry in truth. Her grandfather, dead before Bertie was born, had spent all his money on drink while his wife and son starved. "Even so, sounds like your dad spoils you a bit."

"He gives us anything we want," Andrew said, his voice getting louder again. "Anything, anytime we ask."

"But he's never home," Cat said quietly.

Bertie thought about how late Mr. McBride had come in last night and how early he'd rushed off again this morning. "My dad stays out all the time too," she said. "But I'll nip home and make sure he's fixed, and be right back here before you know it."

Cat looked down at her doll again. "You won't come back."

The words were quiet, nearly drowned by Andrew bouncing in his chair and yelling again that he wanted to go with her.

Bertie leaned down to Cat until she could look her in the eye. "Now, Miss Caitriona, you put that idea right out of your head. Of course I'll come back."

"If you go, we'll climb out the window and come after you," Andrew said.

Bertie grew alarmed, realizing Andrew might do just that. "No, you won't," she said firmly. "I want to come back here and live with you a spell. Now, we just have to convince Aoife or Macaulay that you'll be fine with them while I'm gone."

"Aoife says naughty children in Ireland get dropped down a well," Andrew said. "But she laughed when she said it, so I don't believe her. And Macaulay gets so *mad*. Mrs. Hill doesn't—she goes all cold and stares at me until I think a ghost has grabbed me. Except she sneaked us cakes when Miss Evans was here."

Bertie's respect for Mrs. Hill grew. But it sounded as though the rest of the household had grown wise to the children's ways and wouldn't be welcoming a chance to watch over them.

"We could stay with Aunt Eleanor," Cat said.

Andrew jumped up on his chair, even more animated than before. "Aunt Eleanor! Say we can, Bertie. Say, say."

Bertie regarded them warily. "Who is Aunt Eleanor?"

"She lives in Grosvenor Square," Cat said. "She's a duchess. She's married to the brother of Aunt Ainsley's husband."

Bertie didn't bother to follow the line of relationship—families in the East End could be extensive and convoluted. As long as you said someone was "our Mary" or "our John," outsiders didn't waste time figuring out exactly who was related to whom. "She a real duchess?" Bertie asked, her interest piqued.

"Uncle Hart is a duke," Andrew said. "The Duke of Kilmorgan. A Scots duke."

"An English duke too," Cat corrected him. "Fourteenth duke of Kilmorgan in the Scottish line, second in the English."

Bertie had no idea what any of this meant, but her interest grew. "I think I'd like to meet a real duchess," she said. "I say we try that."

~~~

The real duchess lived in a mansion not far from Mr. McBride's house. Mrs. Hill, who'd thought taking the children to this duchess a good idea, offered to have Richards bring the coach around, but Bertie saw no reason not to walk. The December day was crisp but bright without many clouds, and the house was only a block or two away.

When Andrew pointed out the house in Grosvenor Square, however, Bertie thought it might have been wiser to roll up in some style. The place was much bigger than Mr. McBride's house, taller and twice as wide. Its grand door was positioned between two columns, and arched windows rose up the walls to a dormer roof far above.

The door was opened by a very stiff and slender young man who didn't grin like Peter at Mr. McBride's house did. He knew Cat and Andrew, though, and ushered the three of them into a wide foyer.

A sweep of stairs with a carved wooden railing wound upward through a lofty hall, large windows on each landing pouring in light. Bertie craned her head to look all the way to the top of the stairs, where a painting on the ceiling showed clouds and flying creatures.

Andrew, next to her, exploded into sound. "Aunt Eleanor! We're staying with you, so our new governess can go home and fetch her things before her dad gets into a right state!"

A door shut somewhere above them. Bertie heard light footsteps, and then a lady, so extraordinarily lovely she might have stepped from a fine painting, started down the stairs, her face alight with curiosity. Her dress rustled as she descended—its skirt had stripes of lighter and darker blue green, with a solid blue green overskirt pulled open to fall in ruffles down the back. Her shining red hair was all braids and curls, probably the latest fashion, though Bertie had no idea, and her long-sleeved bodice hugged a body of curves, not pencil thinness.

Bertie had supposed a duchess would be stout and gray, stern and commanding. Not so this woman. She was young and robust, and she moved with an animation that Bertie found fascinating.

The duchess stepped off the stairs and gave Bertie a stare of frank interest from eyes of delphinium blue. "New governess, are you?" she asked.

"Her name's Bertie!" Andrew shouted. He took a deep breath and threw his head back, so his voice could reach the ceiling many stories above them. "We've come to play with Alec!"

"Well, he'll be awake now, that's for certain," the duchess said, her smile widening. She held out her hand to Bertie. "How do you do, Miss Bertie? Quite an unusual name, I must say. You may call me Aunt Eleanor, as everyone in the family does. The grace-ing and duchess-ing can become a little complicated, so within the family, I am simply Aunt Eleanor. Except to my husband, but one never knows what will come out of his mouth. Fortunately for you, he is not home. What did you say your full name was?"

Chapter 7

Bertie hadn't said, and she cleared her throat, suddenly nervous under the duchess's shrewd gaze. "Miss Roberta Frasier," she said, taking the offered hand. She remembered Sophie's teachings and made a brief curtsy, as gracefully as she could manage. "Ma'am."

Eleanor's grip was strong. She kept hold of Bertie's hand and pinned her with a very thorough stare, her blue eyes bright and assessing. "The governess, yes? You never answered."

Andrew was already halfway up the stairs. "She's the best governess in the world! She's going to stay with us forever!"

"Really?" Eleanor didn't release Bertie's hand. "Andrew, please don't climb on the railing. You know what Uncle Hart said when you fell off last month. Pardon me for saying so, Miss Frasier, but you don't look much like a governess."

"Well," Bertie said, wetting her lips. "Maybe I've just started."

"I see." Eleanor peered at her harder, as though she could read every thought in Bertie's head. A frightening woman, this, despite the fact that she was pretty and smiling. "Caitriona, what say you?"

When Eleanor said the name, *Caitriona*, it rolled off her tongue with a hint of the broad Scots Mr. McBride had. *Scots, the lot of them*, the chambers clerk had said, shaking his head. The only Scotsmen Bertie had met in her life were those that came out of the backstreets of Glasgow to try their luck in London. Much of the time, Bertie couldn't understand a word they said. Mr. McBride and Eleanor spoke more clearly, but with a lilt that proclaimed they certainly weren't English.

Cat gave Eleanor an open look. "We want her to stay."

Eleanor's expression softened as she gazed down at Cat, compassion entering her eyes. "I see. Well, I'm sure that can be managed." She switched her attention back to Bertie, still hanging on to Bertie's hand. "You're depositing them here to be looked after? Where are you going, exactly?"

The keen stare wouldn't let Bertie lie. "Whitechapel. Little lane off it."

Eleanor gave a decided nod. "Well, you can't walk all the way. I'll send for the coach."

Bertie's eyes widened. She imagined the reception of a duke's carriage in the warrens off Whitechapel and St. Anne's Street, where she lodged with her father.

"No, no, I'll take an omnibus," Bertie said quickly. She leaned forward and lowered her voice, conscious of the footman at the door listening as hard as he could. "They'll steal the gilt off the wheels there, and the horses from the harness, before you know where you are."

"That's settled then. Franklin, fetch his grace's coachman," the duchess called to the footman. "He'll be driving Miss Frasier to Whitechapel." She moved her attention back to Bertie. "Or, if you'd like, I can have Franklin go collect your things for you. Save you the bother, and you can stay with Cat and Andrew—Andrew, *what* did I say about the railings?"

"He likes to climb things," Bertie said faintly.

"Doesn't he just. One day, he'll be a famous acrobat and put out his tongue at all of us. Shall you stay and have tea with me, Miss Frasier? Go on, Franklin, there isn't much time."

Much time for what? "No, I'll go," Bertie said, at last withdrawing her hand from the duchess's rather formidable grip. "I'll know what to get. And if my dad's there . . . well, it's best if it's me."

Eleanor's eyes narrowed. "Hmm. Well, I'll send Franklin with you anyway. He's a rather good boxer, though he's such a slim young man. If you need him, you shout for him. But you'd best set off if you're going, before . . . oh, dear. Too late."

Franklin had darted out the front door. As it swung closed, Bertie heard a loud growl, and then a giant of a man shoved the door open again and walked inside. He stopped, greatcoat in hand, and looked around with a stare like an eagle's. He had the most golden eyes Bertie had ever seen, which made him seem all the more eaglelike.

"Hello, my dear," Eleanor said warmly. "This is Miss Bertie Frasier, new governess to Andrew and Caitriona. She's going off to fetch her things, and I of course said she must ride in the coach—Franklin has gone for it. I take from the look on your face that your meeting did *not* go well, but fortunately there is plenty of whiskey upstairs and some nice cakes Cook made for you. Cat and Andrew are staying for tea, so do be kind, Hart, and don't frighten anyone, at least for ten minutes."

Throughout the rapid speech, the Duke of Kilmorgan simply stared at Bertie, pinning her in place as his wife had done. He was a handsome man, no doubt—with dark red hair, a strong face, a solid body, and fine clothes—but a frightening one.

Bertie decided she preferred Mr. McBride, with his sudden smiles and flashes of temper, his bearlike voice, and warmth in his gray eyes. One could be comfortable in Mr. McBride's presence. Bask in it. With the duke, Bertie would have to be on her guard all the time. Not comfortable at all. And yet, Eleanor regarded him with vast fondness even as she babbled at him.

"Uncle Hart!" a voice screeched from above. "Catch me!"

The duke looked up in alarm as a missile dropped at him from the railing half a flight up. "What the devil do you think you're doing?" the duke roared, even as he opened his arms and caught Andrew. Andrew, instead of being alarmed, threw his arms around the formidable man's neck, and laughed.

Eleanor made shooing motions at Bertie. Franklin had

popped back inside, stiff no longer, and waved at her to follow. Bertie cast a worried look at Andrew, but Eleanor shook her head, smiling, and kept flapping her hands, driving Bertie away.

Bertie fled. "Whew," she said to Franklin as he opened the door of a black polished coach. "Are they always like that?"

Franklin smiled politely. "It's a lively house, but they're good people. Won't hear a word against 'em. In you go, miss."

Bertie was right about the reception of the duke's coach in her father's street. It was a fine carriage, right enough; a landau, with lovely horses and a coachman in a red coat and high hat to drive it.

Bertie had never lived anywhere so nice as the inside of that coach. The seats were leather, soft and supple, the walls polished wood, the curtains velvet, and there was carpet on the floor. It was warm too, with boxes of hot coals to keep her feet toasty.

She hated to leave the landau's confines for the chill of the East End street, but Franklin, who'd ridden up top with the coachman, opened the door as soon as the carriage stopped in front of the lodgings where Bertie lived with her father. Every person on the street stopped to stare as Bertie hopped from the coach's step to the door of the house, the footman handing her down like a posh lady.

"Won't be a tick," Bertie said to Franklin, pretending to ignore her neighbors, and went into the house's dim interior.

"Where the devil have you been?"

The bellow came as soon as Bertie opened the door of their flat on the second floor. Gerald Frasier, Gerry to his mates, staggered into the front room, face stubbled with graying beard, his eyes bloodshot. *Hung over*, Bertie thought. *And bad too. Just my luck.*

"I've been working," Bertie said. "Earning an honest living." She ducked past her father before he could grab her and entered her own bedroom, which was sparsely furnished, but clean and neat. Bertie liked everything in its place.

"Working?" Gerry shouted as he came after her. "What'cha mean, working? You were with a man, weren't you?"

"No," Bertie said. The only way to deal with her father when he was like this was to be firm. "You know me better than that." She opened the drawer of her bureau and withdrew clean underthings, which she tucked into a valise.

Her father came close to her, peering at her for signs that she'd spent the night in bed with a man. Gerry was always terrified Bertie would run off with a bloke—one he didn't control. Or be taken by one of the full-in-pocket villains who commanded teams of young thieves and prostitutes around here. Her dad might be a drunken lout, but he didn't want anyone touching his daughter.

The trouble was, Bertie *wished* she'd spent all night with a man—Sinclair McBride. Lying in her bed last night, knowing he was a floor under her at his desk, likely running his broad hand through his shorn hair while he read his papers, had kept her restless. She hadn't been able to cease thinking about how he'd kissed her, or the fire in his gray eyes when he'd planted himself in front of the door of his study and challenged her.

Her father grunted. "What work were you about then?"

"An honest job, I said." Bertie piled more stockings in the valise and opened the drawer to add the picture of her mother. Her mother smiled up at her from the framed photo with all the warmth Bertie remembered.

"Doing what?" Gerry demanded

"Looking after children, if you must know." Bertie added hair ribbons, a brush, and a few toiletries, and closed up the soft case.

"Eh?" Gerry stared. "What do *you* know about looking after children?"

"I've looked after *you* all this time, haven't I?" Bertie gave him a warning look. "They're a good family, so you stay away from them."

Gerry's bloodshot eyes opened wider as he tripped after her to the front room. It was cold in here—her father hadn't started a fire or put on a kettle for tea. Sighing, Bertie detoured to the kitchen to poke the kindling in the stove and throw in a few lit matches. She emptied the tea kettle, rinsed it by pumping water into the sink, filled it, and set it on to boil. She put tea into the teapot, but pouring would have to be up to her father.

"You get a nice hot cup inside you, and you'll feel better," Bertie said, returning to the front room. "And have another sleep after that."

Gerry watched Bertie pulling on her gloves again, then he looked at the valise, and everything came together for him.

"Where the devil do you think you're going?"

Really, he could rival Andrew for noise. "I told ya. I have a job. I have to go back."

"Back where?" Gerry seized her by the arm. "You put away that valise and make me breakfast. Do you hear me? Then you're going down the pub to fetch me some beer."

Bertie drew a breath and summoned her courage. A half hour back here, and already her stay in Sinclair McBride's house was fading like a dream. She needed to hold on to that dream, to get away from this place. She thought about Sinclair's gray eyes, which could turn warm in an instant, and the rumble of his Scottish voice that filled a room. She wanted to hear that voice again. Many times more, before she was done.

"I can't," Bertie said. "I've got a proper job now. For real wages."

"You don't unless I say you have," her father said with a snarl.

Bertie jerked away, picked up the case, and marched toward the door. Her dad came after her. Gerry could be clumsy and slow after a night of gin, but today she was unlucky. He got between her and the door.

"You running away from me to be some man's fancy piece?" Gerry seized her arm again, and this time his grip bit down hard. "The hell you are. You start my breakfast, or I'll beat you black and blue."

"No, you'll let me go!"

Gerry was strong, always had been. But Bertie had

learned, long ago, that if she fought back, and fought hard, she could usually get away. She would run off and hide in her sanctuary until her father calmed down and got into one of his good moods. Wasn't no one more generous than Bertie's dad when he was feeling good. Problem was, she could never be sure when he'd be in a sunny temper, and his good mood always wore off.

"Need any help, miss?" a gravelly voice asked.

The duke's coachman had opened the door—he was a big, brawny man with broad shoulders, a flat face, and giant hands. He looked like a prizefighter and had a powerful voice to match.

"Is this him?" Gerry asked. "Your fancy man?"

Bertie rolled her eyes. "You've got a wild imagination, you have."

The coachman peeled Gerry away from her. He didn't jerk or punch, he just pulled Bertie's father back with one large hand on his shoulder, and Gerry had no choice but to move.

Bertie gave the coachman a grateful look. "Go easy on him, all right? He's always in a bad way after he's had too much gin."

The prizefighter bent his thick neck in a nod but continued to hold her father in place with the strength of a stolid bull.

"Bertie-girl," Gerry yelled as Bertie slipped around them and out the door. He sounded pathetic and lost, as he usually did when coming off a hangover. "You can't leave me. Who's gonna look after me?"

Bertie glanced back from the stairwell. Her father peered at her around the coachman's large arm, his face stark with fear. He really was a hopeless old sot, when it came down to it.

"I'll send Mrs. Lang to look in on you. You know you like her." Mrs. Lang was a publican's widow and worked as a barmaid at Bertie's dad's local. She was one of the few people who could handle Gerry Frasier and his moods.

Bertie made herself turn and head down the stairs, resolutely shutting off the sight of her father and the sound of his pleas.

A street lad was holding the horses when Bertie came

out, and interested neighbors had come out to watch. Franklin helped Bertie into the coach under their stares, both curious and belligerent.

Not many minutes later, the coachman emerged from the house, not looking any the worse for wear. Bertie asked if he could stop the coach at the pub down the lane, and he nodded in his taciturn way and climbed to his perch.

Bertie settled into the seat as Franklin slammed the door, and hugged her valise to her, her fingers cold in her gloves. The ducal coach crunched forward through the squalid streets of her childhood, taking her away.

⁓

The house filled up with people before Sinclair could stop them. He studied the crowd from the double doorway of his ground-floor drawing room, wondering what the devil all of them were doing in London. English society was supposed to be off in the country shooting things or preparing for a country Christmas, but both his front and back parlors, the large doors open between them, were stuffed full of guests.

Sinclair's newest sister-in-law, Rose, had been a duchess—briefly—and Sinclair's sister, Ainsley, had once been a lady-in-waiting to the queen. Between the pair of them, they knew everyone in London, and Juliana, who'd married Sinclair's wild brother, Elliot, was amazingly fond of organizing.

When Sinclair had let slip a few weeks before that he was thinking of inviting people for a gathering before he left for Scotland, the three ladies had become a whirlwind. Tonight, Sinclair barely recognized his own house, which was festooned with ribbons and greenery for QC Sinclair McBride's London Christmas soiree.

The children were upstairs, with Bertie. Sinclair hadn't seen much of his pickpocket these past few days, ever since the night he'd asked her to stay. Many cases were being tried at the Old Bailey this week, the courts hurrying to have them done before they adjourned for the holidays. Sinclair was in court long hours every day, then back in his chambers preparing for more trials well into each night.

Or perhaps he was simply avoiding going home. Thinking of Bertie laughing with his children in the nursery or asleep in the bedroom above his office kept him restless and randy.

Mrs. Hill had promised that either she or Macaulay would return to the agency and bring back a list of potential governesses, but strangely, neither the housekeeper nor Macaulay had found time to do it. Sinclair thought he understood their procrastination. Andrew and Cat had been astonishingly well behaved—for them—ever since Miss Frasier had arrived. The consensus in the house was that, no matter how unconventional Miss Frasier might be, it was worth their sanity to have her here.

Their sanity might be safe, Sinclair thought darkly, but his own was in jeopardy.

Sinclair spied his brother Elliot near the windows and made for him.

"I understand Juliana being here," Sinclair said, scooping champagne from a footman's tray as he neared Elliot. "But you, little brother? You don't like crowds. Or fuss. Or Englishmen." Sinclair took a deep drink of the champagne and tried not to make a face. Whiskey, unfortunately, was nowhere in sight. Juliana, Rose, and Ainsley said that champagne was the thing for a London soiree.

Elliot drank nothing—he simply stood and watched the cream of society talking at length about very little at the tops of their voices. "I could go off into a dark corner and brood, if it would make you feel better," he said.

Sinclair answered with a laugh, happy his brother could joke again. Elliot's scarred face no longer bore the lines of exhaustion he'd worn for years, and the darkness in his eyes had lightened. Elliot had experienced hell as the captive of a particularly brutal tribe in the mountains north of the Punjab, and the McBrides had feared him dead for many months. It would take a long time for Elliot to fully heal, Sinclair knew, but Elliot's episodes of darkness had lessened considerably since his marriage. The fact that Elliot could stand next to Sinclair and smile at his own joke was the greatest gift Juliana had given the McBrides.

"For a time I thought one of us would have to shoot you," Sinclair said, taking another sip of overly sweet champagne. "I'm happy we didn't. Of course, if I drink more of this treacle, I might ask you to drag *me* off and end my misery."

Elliot answered with a laugh, which warmed Sinclair's heart. "If you want to know, I'm here for *her*." Elliot nodded in the direction of a pretty, smiling, red-headed young woman who was at the moment working to sweeten a dour judge who'd been invited to bolster Sinclair's career. Elliot's gray eyes softened. "I like to watch my Juliana shine."

The simple statement made Sinclair's gratitude to his sister-in-law surge.

Elliot's attention was caught by something behind Sinclair. "Careful," he said. "Matchmaking ladies on your blind side."

Sinclair turned as Eleanor, Duchess of Kilmorgan, and Rose, now Mrs. Steven McBride, approached, the two ladies flanking a third woman.

She was Mrs. Thomalin—whom he'd kissed and planned to take to dinner when he had the chance. Mrs. Thomalin was in her early thirties and curvaceous of figure, with a mass of golden hair meticulously braided and curled. Her face held beauty, and her eyes were blue, her smile inviting.

Sinclair also noted, with his barrister's scrutiny, that everything about her dress and hair was done with the utmost attention to the most recent style, though not fussily so. Clara Thomalin had taken care to present a pleasing picture to the world, but she didn't ruin it by constantly patting her hair or clothes to make sure all was well. She was poised and sure of herself.

Sinclair couldn't help himself assessing people—he'd learned to take stock of every facet of a person in the dock and witness box, every reaction, every twitch, every way they carried themselves. He learned them, and then drilled through them to get at the truth.

Therefore, Sinclair saw, penetrating Mrs. Thomalin's smile and polite handshake, that she fully intended to share Sinclair's bed this night.

Bertie watched from the landing between the upper floors as the last of the guests flowed out the door and into the night. Andrew and Cat had sat on the stairs with her for much of the evening, looking down at the throng below. Andrew had laughed at everyone, but Cat only watched quietly, saying nothing.

When the two children began to droop, Bertie took them back to the nursery and tucked them up in bed. Then she'd returned, moving down the stairs as far as she dared before settling in to watch once more.

The duchess, Eleanor, had spied Bertie on the landing and given her a friendly wave. Bertie raised her hand in return, expecting the lady to point her out, or come up and try to talk to her. But Eleanor only turned away with her formidable husband, leaving Bertie safe.

Bertie decided she quite liked the blond Ainsley, Sinclair's sister, who was much like him in her restless movements, her sudden smiles and flashes of frowns. *Changeable*, that was a good word for Sinclair. His brothers Elliot and Steven had the same changeability, though Elliot's was more subdued. He'd been broken at some time, Bertie knew—Mrs. Hill had told Bertie much about the McBrides and their history. For all Mrs. Hill's puckered expressions, she was a ready font of gossip, and all of it interesting.

Bertie did *not* like the woman with her hair all primped who'd been hanging on to Sinclair's arm the latter half of the night. She'd been with him every time he drifted toward the drawing room doorway or into the hall to say good-bye to departing guests. The woman was pretty and dressed like a fashion plate, an upper-class lady, elegant, even regal. A friend of Steven's wife, Bertie gleaned, which meant she was sanctioned by family.

Bertie's heart burned when the footman Peter closed the door on the final guests, but Sinclair and the woman— Clara, Bertie had heard her called—remained in the hall together, arm in arm.

"Go to bed, Peter," Sinclair said. "You've done a good night's work. I'll see to Mrs. Thomalin."

Oh, he'd see to her, all right. Bertie's eyes narrowed. From the sparkle in the woman's eyes, she was looking forward to being seen to.

Peter faded discreetly toward the back stairs, leaving Sinclair and Mrs. Thomalin alone. Mrs. Thomalin turned her face up to Sinclair's, and Sinclair leaned down and kissed her.

Bertie stood frozen on the landing, unable to pull back into the shadows. She couldn't move, fixed in place to watch them kiss—lengthy, experienced kisses, none of the blundering Bertie had done.

Clara lifted her head and gave Sinclair a tender look. Sinclair rested his hand on Clara's chest, much of it bared by her low neckline, and Bertie's heart bled anew.

They were going to share a bed, the one on the floor below hers. Sinclair would strip off his clothes to reveal his fine and handsome body, and he would kiss the shameless Mrs. Thomalin as he undressed her. Mrs. Thomalin would be privileged to see his smile in the dark, to watch his gray eyes lose their bleakness as he laid himself on top of her.

Bertie held on to the railing, as though the floor undulated beneath her feet. She felt a hotness in her eyes and realized she was about to cry. Bertie rarely cried, not even when her dad was at his most brutal. She'd learned to hold it in. But at the moment, her shaking limbs and tight chest told her tears were coming.

Sinclair and Mrs. Thomalin broke off from each other long enough to start for the stairs. Bertie gathered the skirts of her new, gray cashmere dress, and sped silently up the rest of the staircase. She shot into her bedroom, her breath hurting, and closed the door without making a noise.

She stood for a long time in the middle of her bedchamber, her throat working, eyes stinging, fists clenching and unclenching. Her body was so stiff her legs ached.

What was she doing here? In this house, in Mayfair at all? Bertie had allowed herself to be persuaded that she could live here as though she belonged here. But she knew she didn't.

She knew why she'd ignored common sense and stayed—not for the salary or new clothes or the soft bed and warm rooms. Bertie had stayed to be close to Sinclair McBride. She'd wanted to see him every day, to hear his voice and be near him, even if she couldn't have him.

Foolish girl. Living here meant Bertie would have to bear it when a pretty lady like Mrs. Thomalin decided to latch on to him. Sinclair was a man, after all. Most men, in Bertie's experience, didn't remain celibate for long. And what happened if Sinclair decided to marry and give his children a new mum? No woman would want a governess who'd thrown herself at and kissed her husband to go on looking after his children.

Bertie made a move toward her valise. Her worn-out green dress had gone, snatched away by Aoife and quickly sold to a rag and bone man by Mrs. Hill. Bertie had three new dresses now, two gray and one dark blue-and-green plaid. The plaid one was for special occasions, Mrs. Hill had said. But the gowns weren't really hers, and Bertie knew it. Sinclair had paid for them.

She took the underclothing she'd brought from home out of the bureau, leaving the new set of smalls Mrs. Hill had given her behind. Sinclair knew her for a thief, but she refused to rob him as she went, refused to give him the satisfaction. She'd take only her own things, leaving the ribbons and the little brush and comb set Mrs. Hill had also provided. Mrs. Hill, as cold as she pretended to be, had proved to be quite thoughtful, underneath it all.

Bertie shut her valise with a snap, blinking back her tears. She'd go. She'd hurry down the stairs as soon as Sinclair was safely cuddling with Mrs. Thomalin, slip past Peter, and let herself out. Back to the cold darkness of a London winter.

In the next room, Caitriona cried out in her sleep.

Bertie found herself abandoning the valise and any thoughts of escape to hurry to the nursery. What had she been thinking? She couldn't leave them alone, could she? Cat and Andrew needed her—that had been clear from the first day.

Cat was all right, sleeping peacefully by the time Bertie

reached her bed. Whatever dream had disturbed her had gone. Cat's eyes were closed, her breathing even, her arm snugly around her doll.

The doll stared up at Bertie in the light of the low-burning lamp, smiling as though to say all was well—she was standing guard. Bertie pressed a light kiss to Caitriona's forehead and moved across the room to Andrew's bed.

Which was empty. The sheets were rumpled, the pillow dented, and Andrew McBride was nowhere in sight.

Chapter 8

Satiation. That was key. When bodily needs overtook the senses, it was time to relieve them so one could concentrate. Even doctors said that.

Sinclair looked into Clara Thomalin's eyes as he shut the door on his upstairs study, taking in her smile, her blue eyes, her pleasing curves. She was pretty, willing, and as lonely as he was. Nothing wrong with passing a night together. They were grown people, had both been married and could be discreet, knowing the way of the world.

So why did Sinclair feel so much reluctance? This was bodily passion alone—it was for Clara as well, he could see. They'd come together, soothe their desires, and return to everyday life.

Clara's smile widened as Sinclair slid off his frock coat then came to her and put his hands on her shoulders. Her bodice was cut to expose much flesh—shoulders, upper arms, and breasts to just above her nipples. Clara's skin was cool, not much heat in it, and its color was what ladies called alabaster. Pure white, like a statue. A woman who hid herself from the sun.

Was the rest of her body as pale? Clara had very fair hair, true blond, no artifice. Which meant her hair elsewhere wouldn't have much color either.

A contrast flashed through his mind—a young woman with dark hair, pink cheeks, and a mouth widening in delighted laughter. A Cockney accent and a teasing tone while she told him exactly what she thought of him.

Sinclair closed his eyes, shutting out the vision, as his lips met Clara's cool ones. Clara knew exactly how to kiss— her answering pressure was demure enough to indicate she didn't have this sort of liaison all the time, firm enough to tell him she'd shared a bed with a man before and liked it.

No unpracticed but enthusiastic kisses that meant she was excited to be kissing *him*. No shy smile when she drew back, no excited laughter.

Don't think about it. Just get on with it.

Sinclair slid one arm around Clara and pulled her up to him. She wasn't any warmer when closer.

He moved his hand to her breasts. Clara exhaled in satisfaction, but good Lord, this woman's skin was *cold*. Perhaps he should summon a doctor—

Thump. Thump. "Mr. McBride?"

Sinclair ripped away from Clara, his heart banging. She stepped back, startled and flushing. "Who?" she mouthed.

Bertie. The name burst into Sinclair's brain, but he said nothing.

"I beg your pardon, Mr. McBride." Bertie's voice was stiff and stilted, trying to mask the London backstreets in her words. "I need to come in."

"The governess," Sinclair said softly. He put a hand on Clara's chilled shoulder. A shawl—that's what the woman needed. It was December, for pity's sake, and she'd bared a good portion of her body to the winter air. Astonishing she wasn't sniffling with a head cold. "I'd better see to it."

Clara nodded, understanding. She had children, she'd told Sinclair, two grown sons. They'd spent most of their childhood at school and now university. She'd looked surprised when Sinclair had mentioned that Andrew hadn't yet been shipped off to a school.

Sinclair strode to the door and wrenched it open before he remembered he was in his shirtsleeves. Bertie stood on the threshold, her eyes bright, but not with mirth. She took in his loosened shirt and rumpled waistcoat with a look that told him she knew exactly what was going on in here.

"Andrew is missing," she announced.

Clara, hidden from Bertie's view by the door, looked concerned. Sinclair gave her the faintest shake of his head.

"Andrew is frequently missing," he said to Bertie. "Find Macaulay and ask him to help you search the house. Macaulay knows all his hiding places."

"I don't have to search the house," Bertie said. She had so much color in her—dark blue eyes, pretty flush of her cheek, red lips. "I know exactly where he is. If you'll just let me . . ."

Bertie ducked under Sinclair's arm and into the room before he could stop her. Her warmth spilled over Sinclair as she brushed past, and he wanted to lean into her, gathering her heat to him. He'd tumble her mussed hair, bury his face in it.

Bertie walked past Clara, pretending not to notice her, and heaved open the double pocket doors that led to Sinclair's bedchamber. She swept inside Sinclair's bedroom without hesitation, striding straight to his bed.

The room inside was dim, only one gaslight turned low for illumination. Bertie turned the light up with a competent hand, and threw back the covers from a lump in the middle of the bed.

Andrew exploded out of the blankets, launching himself directly at Sinclair, who staggered back as he caught his son.

"Papa!" Andrew shouted, flinging his arms around his father's neck. "I was waiting for you!"

Andrew was so *warm*. Love flooded Sinclair, and he gathered his son to him in a hard embrace. Andrew's love poured back over him, the boy generous with it. Holding him was like waking from a bad dream to relieving reality.

Andrew soon squirmed, not liking to be confined. "Put me to bed, Papa. And tell me a story."

Sinclair was supposed to grow outraged, thump Andrew to his feet, thrust him at Bertie, and snap at her to mind her charges. Banish his only son so that he could get back to the business of carnal satisfaction.

"All right, Andrew," Sinclair said. "I'll take you up."

He glanced at Clara, who looked disappointed but also understanding. The understanding made Sinclair soften a little toward her. She couldn't help that her skin was as cold as a dead fish's.

"Bertie, fetch Macaulay and tell him to see that Mrs. Thomalin gets home. I'll lend her my carriage." Sinclair made a bow to Clara. "Good night, madam."

Clara returned the nod politely, as though they were still fully dressed in the reception room filled with people below. "Of course. Good night, Mr. McBride."

Bertie, again pretending not to notice her, moved past Sinclair and through the door, her skirts holding her heat as they flowed past Sinclair's legs. Sinclair followed her out, carrying Andrew up through the darkness to the bright warmth of the nursery.

By the time Bertie returned from fetching Macaulay and closed the door, Sinclair was tucking Andrew into his bed, the planned night with Clara Thomalin dissolving into nothing.

~~~~~

Bertie sat nearby, mending Andrew's shirt—Andrew ripped his clothes every day, so there was always mending—listening while Sinclair told his son and daughter stories about his travels in the army.

He'd been to Egypt and the Sudan, had seen the wonders of the pyramids and tombs of civilizations long gone. The two children laughed or shivered, depending on the story, hanging on every word their father said. He really had a way with them, Bertie observed as she stitched. Pity he had to shut himself up with his dry papers and his stuffed-shirt fellow barristers all the day long.

After a while, eyes grew heavy and both Cat and Andrew began to yawn. Sinclair kissed Andrew's forehead, then carried Cat, who'd come to Andrew's bed to listen to the stories, back across to her own bed. He laid her in it and tucked the covers around her, making sure to include her doll.

When Sinclair turned to Bertie, however, the fatherliness fled and the sternness of the barrister returned. He beckoned for her to follow him out into the hall and firmly shut the nursery door.

"Andrew wanted to see you," Bertie said quickly, before Sinclair could speak. "You can't blame him."

"I don't. I blame *you*." Sinclair folded his arms and fixed her with a severe look.

A delectable picture he made, to be sure. His shirt stretched across his wide shoulders, cuffs straining over thick wrists. His waistcoat hugged his tight torso, and his open shirt gave her a tantalizing glimpse of brown throat.

"I can't chain him to the bed." Bertie clenched her hands. "Or sleep stretched across the door. Wouldn't matter— Andrew would just climb down the drainpipe. Letting him open the bedroom door himself is safer."

Sinclair's brows drew down, his frown unfortunately making him even more handsome. "I'm paying you to watch them."

"Only until you hire a new governess, you said." Bertie shook her head. "You ain't really angry because I wasn't watching Andrew. You're angry because you wanted to get into that woman's knickers, and I stopped you. A mercy I did, wasn't it? Imagine, you taking her all cooing and sighing into your bedroom and dropping her right down on top of Andrew." She broke off with a laugh. "That would have been something to see."

Sinclair took a step closer and unfolded one arm to point his finger at Bertie's face. His cuff rode up his wrist, revealing a round, puckered scar. "*You* work for *me*. That means what I get up to in my own house is my business, and nothing for you to speculate on. 'That woman,' as you call her, is a friend to my sisters-in-law."

"I saw them bring her in." Bertie cocked her head, studying the tip of his finger. "A tart is still a tart—don't matter that she's in thick with duchesses. I saved you some bother, you know. She'd have found some way to twist you into marrying her so she could get her hands on your money. I've seen her sort before."

Sinclair's mouth tightened. "Mrs. Thomalin is a widow with plenty of money—" He broke off, as though realizing he had no idea of her financial situation. "And I have no intention of marrying—" His words cut off as he drew a long breath. "Anyone."

"In that case, she truly is a tart," Bertie said. *And here's me, pretending I'm all virtuous when I'd give anything to take her place.*

Sinclair's broad forefinger jabbed at Bertie again. "You have no idea what the hell you're talking about."

"Yes, I do. I mean, it doesn't matter if she's upper crust. People are people, ain't they? She wants your body, but she'll take your money too, if she can get it."

"Stop."

"I'm only saying what I see." Bertie made herself shrug. "So you missed taking some time with her. Serves you right for never coming home, and being so grumpy when you do."

Sinclair's face went deep red. Bertie knew she'd gone too far, but the hurt that clenched her insides wouldn't cease. Let him sling her out into the street—Bertie had survived before, and she would again.

With a great empty hole in her heart.

Sinclair took another step toward her, and Bertie moved back, until she found herself pressed into the wall. There wasn't much in the way of furniture on this landing, just bare walls and one gas lamp between the two rooms.

Sinclair hemmed her in, his warmth driving away all chill. She could see nothing but him, hear nothing but his voice, the rest of the world receding into a vague blur.

He was speaking again, saying something-or-other, his broad finger an inch from her nose. He kept his nails nicely trimmed and clean, though his blunt hand was more suited to holding a sword than a pen. "Bertie, you—"

Bertie, her heart thumping, leaned forward and nipped the tip of his finger.

Sinclair froze, words dying, his gray gaze fixing on her mouth closing on his fingertip. His chest rose sharply.

"Bloody hell," he whispered.

The next thing Bertie knew, she was flat against the wall, her hands lifted over her head. Her wrists were trapped in his grip, the wallpaper cool to the backs of her fingers. Sinclair leaned to her, close enough that the barest inch separated their bodies.

Bertie's heart thumped and thudded, her hands confined under his strong, firm fingers. She smelled the cloying note of Mrs. Thomalin's perfume on his clothes along with his crisp male scent and the sweetness of champagne.

Sinclair closed his eyes, head bowing a little, and leaned nearer. "You are so warm."

"Well, it is stuffy in here," Bertie whispered. Sinclair's house shut out much of the winter cold.

Sinclair shook his head, thumbs caressing her wrists. He came closer still, his nose skimming her cheek. "So warm."

Let me warm you then. I've got it to spare.

Sinclair pulled her left hand away from the wall. His long body was nearly against hers, but not quite. A breeze, if there was one, could pass between them. The light pressure of his thighs on Bertie's skirts and his hands on her wrists were their only points of contact.

The gaslight, dimmed for night, burnished the gold of Sinclair's hair as he turned his head. He studied her hand a moment, caressing the back of it with his thumb. Heat streaked down Bertie's arm, straight to her heart.

Sinclair straightened her forefinger and brought it to his lips. He kissed the tip of her finger, then as Bertie had done to him, closed his teeth around it.

Bertie let out a faint cry, more of a gasp by the time it

reached the air. Sinclair nibbled a moment, before he closed
his eyes and drew her finger all the way into his mouth.

Fire poured through her body in a molten stream. She'd
never felt anything like it, and Sinclair was barely doing
anything—sucking on her finger, that was all. But the heat
of his tongue, the pull of his lips, stoked the fires inside her.
Her breasts felt heavy, pushing against the tightness of her
corset.

Sinclair's lashes, like his hair, were light, stark lines on
his sunburned skin. Bertie wanted to draw him to her,
smooth his hair, rub the back of his neck, soothe away all
his lines of pain. But she was afraid to touch him, afraid to
break the spell.

Sinclair stepped all the way against her, the space for the
breeze vanishing.

He might claim he needed warmth, but Sinclair was
plenty warm himself. He let go of Bertie's other hand to
brace himself against the wall, while he licked her forefinger and then pulled a second finger into his mouth.

Bertie's gasp was louder this time, echoing around the
high hall and the carved frieze at the ceiling. Sinclair made
not a sound as his body pressed hers, his mouth working.

The strength of his tongue, the tug on her fingers, turned
Bertie's body incandescent. She knew she ought to jerk
away and tell him to stop—she'd die if he didn't. But then he
might stop.

Her blood felt thick. Nothing else existed, nothing in the
world but herself and this stern, strong man, pressed against
her in the upper halls of his beautiful house.

Bertie couldn't keep from reaching for him. Her fingers
contacted the warm sleekness of his hair, and she caressed
it, trailing her touch to the back of his neck. Sinclair made a
noise in his throat and pushed closer to her.

He lifted his head, his eyes half-closed, and drew his
tongue up Bertie's first two fingers. Then he took a third one
into his mouth. His suckling grew fiercer, as though Sinclair
strove to imbibe her warmth.

Bertie's back was tight against the wall, his weight keeping her there. His mouth was a hot place, tongue caressing, teeth lightly scraping.

It was sensual, erotic, wicked, and yet they were both fully clothed, both standing upright, nowhere near a bed. Nothing improper about it at all. But Bertie's knees were weak, her insides shaking.

She would fall, but Sinclair would fall with her, and he'd stretch on top of her on the floor. All the while, his glorious mouth would squeeze her fingers with heat and not-pain.

His warmth seeped into her, and nothing else mattered . . .

"Papa?"

Sinclair stilled. Everything in the hall stilled with him, as though the moment froze into a crystal shape, captured, unmoving.

After a silent, very long moment, Sinclair slid Bertie's hand away from his mouth, lifted his head, and looked to Caitriona standing outside the nursery door, her braid of dark hair over her shoulder, her doll clutched to her chest.

Between one heartbeat to the next, Sinclair changed from the sensual man taking his time with a woman to the empty shell Bertie had watched him become for the first time in the courtroom. The warmth he'd taken from Bertie dissipated into the darkness.

Sinclair cleared his throat. "Caitriona. I thought you were asleep."

"I had dreams." Caitriona held her doll closer, her serious gaze taking in her father, Bertie close to him, and Bertie's scalding face. "I miss Mama."

"Damn it," Sinclair whispered so softly Bertie barely heard it. Sinclair's hand tightened on the wallpaper, and he lowered it, straightening up to his full height.

He left Bertie's side as though he didn't notice her there. Bertie leaned back against the wall, the only thing holding her up. Her legs surely weren't—they were shaking like stalks of tender flowers in the wind.

Sinclair approached Caitriona and reached for her hand. "I miss her too, Cat."

Caitriona pulled back from him. "I want Bertie."

Sinclair's chest rose with a hard breath and the hand that he'd held out to her clenched. For another frozen moment, no one in the hall moved.

Then Sinclair turned stiffly toward the stairs, not looking at either of them. "Bertie, get her to bed," he said in a hard voice, and he started down, his footsteps heavy in the silence. Bertie and Cat heard him open the door to his study; then the slamming of it echoed up and down the stairwell.

Bertie swallowed, her throat hurting. She made herself push away from the wall and go to Cat. "Come, sweetheart," she said, holding out her hand.

Bertie took Caitriona back to her bed and tucked her in. Cat reached for Bertie as she made to turn away, and something in the child's eyes made Bertie stop. This little girl, since Bertie's arrival, had shown almost no emotions at all—the opposite of Andrew, who could change moods in a flash. Cat only watched everyone else, as though she waited for something, maybe had done so for so long that she'd forgotten what she waited for.

Right now, though, Cat's eyes held fear. Whatever the dream had been, she didn't say, but it was clear she didn't want Bertie to go.

Bertie gave her a smile, unwound herself from Caitriona's grip to pull the armchair to the bed, and reached for the mending basket.

Bertie's hands shook as she started again with the needle, the fingers that Sinclair had taken into his mouth burning like bands of fire.

"Bertie." The word came out cracked, and Sinclair cleared his throat. "Miss Frasier."

Bertie stood in front of Sinclair's desk in his study the next morning, her heart thumping. Sinclair was on his feet on the other side of it. He'd barely glanced up at her from the papers he was reading, or tidying, or whatever he was doing when she came in, and now she waited, her chest tight, for him to continue.

The desk was a solid barrier between them, like Hadrian's Wall, built to keep ancient Scots—Sinclair's ancestors—from overrunning England. At least, that's what the book Bertie had been reading to Andrew and Cat said Hadrian's Wall was about. Sinclair wasn't coming out from behind it, and the desk blocked her way to him.

Bertie's head ached, almost as much as her heart did. Her left hand was stiff, because she'd clenched it in her sleep. Once Cat had been sleeping deeply, not moving in dreams, Bertie had gone to bed, only to lie awake herself. Whenever she did drop off, she dreamed of Sinclair's mouth on her fingers, the warm firmness of his lips, the heat of his tongue. When she woke this morning, she found her hand curled into her palm so hard she'd had to pry it open and rub away the stiffness.

Bertie had emerged from her bedroom, dressed but sandy-eyed, only to be told by Aoife that Mr. McBride wanted a word.

"Did ya want to say something to me?" Bertie asked, not bothering to smooth her speech. Mrs. Hill had been teaching her to talk more properly, but Bertie was in no mood to try this morning. "Aoife said you wanted a dickey bird."

"I do." Sinclair finally looked at her. He had a pen in his hand, but he held it so tightly it might snap in two any moment. "Miss Frasier. My children are fond of you, but I will understand if you would like to go."

Chapter 9

"Go?" Bertie asked in sudden panic. The world seemed to drop out from beneath her feet. "Go where?"

Sinclair's eyes flickered, the warmth that had filled them last night gone. "I mean resign. Give notice. Take yourself elsewhere."

Bertie took a step toward the desk. "Ya want me to *leave*?"

Sinclair studied her for a long time, the mouth that had felt so sinful on his finger tightening. "I'd have thought you would want to go."

"Why?" The word burst out before she could stop it. Bertie's throat was dry, not helping her aching head. "Because I twitted you about your lady, and then threw myself at you?"

The pen fell. Sinclair's fists balled, then he opened them, as though he'd had to force himself to, and cleared his throat again. "No, because I behaved . . . improperly toward you."

Bertie's eyes widened. Improperly? He thought *he'd* been improper? That was a laugh. "You were much more improper with the widow."

A crease appeared between his brows. Why did he not leap around the desk and start shouting at her, instead of holding it in until he cracked? His large body, trapped under layers of his pristine suit, swayed a little, as though he kept himself in place with great effort. "Miss Frasier . . ."

So formal. No longer *Bertie*, but *Miss Frasier*, as though she truly were the governess. "Really," she said. "What you did with me—it weren't nothing."

"It *wasn't* nothing, that's the point." His voice grew a little louder.

"Eh?" Bertie stared at him until his meaning trickled through her numb brain. "No, what I mean to say is . . . I didn't mind."

The crease between his brows deepened. "But you should mind."

"Well, I didn't, and maybe you think that means I'm a tart, like I said that widow was, but—" Bertie cut off her words with effort, no idea why she was babbling. "You didn't do nothing—*anything*—wrong. Didn't even kiss me." But the way Sinclair had suckled her fingers, the way he'd leaned into her, had been stronger than kissing. The encounter had been about bodily passion, a desire she'd never known. She wanted to know it again, and more.

"I'm your employer," Sinclair said in his hard voice. "I consider myself an honorable man, which means I shouldn't have my way with everyone in my house, from the cook to the second housemaid."

"Ooh, I'd like to see you try that with Mrs. Hill." Imagining Sinclair acting like a besotted swain with the coldly haughty housekeeper made a hysterical laugh bubble from Bertie's mouth.

"This isn't funny," Sinclair said, the growl returning to his voice.

"Yes, it is." Bertie took a step toward the desk. "My pal Ruthie told me about a place where she was kitchen maid a long time ago—the man of the house dipped his wick in whichever maid he wanted, and a couple of the footmen too. He never got around to Ruthie, because she told her mum, and her mum took her right out of there."

"Bertie." Sinclair raised his hands. "*Stop.*"

Bertie's tongue tripped on. "Point is, you ain't like that. What's between you and me is . . . between you and me. But if you want me to go, I'll go." She had to swallow on the last words. Her throat hurt so much—maybe she was coming down with a cold.

"I don't." The words came out quickly. Sinclair clenched his fists again, his hands brushing the desk.

Bertie remembered the scar on his wrist his rising shirt-sleeve had showed her last night, and resisted the urge to go to him and push up his sleeve now. She'd lift his tanned wrist to her lips and kiss the scar, maybe lick it. She wondered what he'd taste like.

Bertie felt her breasts tighten, and she tried to banish the vision. She'd never think straight if she imagined such things. "Why'd you ask me to go, then?"

Sinclair let out an exasperated breath. "Damn it, Bertie, I'm trying to be noble."

"Well, don't. It don't suit you. Are you finished? I've got lessons to give."

He rested his fists on the desk, keeping Hadrian's Wall between them. "Yes, yes. Go," he said in annoyance, as though Bertie had come to bother him instead of him sending for *her*.

Bertie made for the door, knowing a dismissal when she heard one, but she lingered, her hand on the porcelain door-knob. "You off to your chambers now?"

"Yes."

"Oh." Bertie tried to think of more to say, so she could stay in this room and speak to him longer, but she came up with nothing. "Well, you have a fine day, then."

"Thank you," Sinclair said. His gray eyes pierced her from all the way across the room. He wanted her gone, no mistake.

Bertie felt as though she should curtsy or something before leaving his presence, but he wasn't a king or duke. Only a man—a tall, handsome, lonely gentleman with a warm and wonderful voice—and she was governess to his children.

How nice it would be if she could hand him his valise in the mornings, wish him a good day, and give him a kiss good-bye. And welcome him back home again with another kiss, he enfolding her in his arms and saying how glad he was to be there.

Bertie had to settle for giving Sinclair a brief nod and gliding out the door, her heart hammering. Sinclair said nothing at all, the session over.

Bertie ran up the stairs, back to her own room, where she had to pace the floor for a time before she calmed herself enough to make her way to the nursery and the lively children waiting for her there.

~

"What is it now?" Sinclair snapped at the clerk who put his head around his door. He looked up from another of the blasted anonymous letters that he'd received this morning, no longer interested in the day-to-day running of the common courts.

"Your meeting with his lordship," his junior clerk Henry said. "If you don't look sharpish, sir, you'll be late."

"Bloody hell."

Sinclair shoved aside the letter that burned his fingers and made himself get to his feet. His entire body felt wrong, his legs stiff. *Not the only thing that's been stiff.* Sinclair had lain awake hard and furious all night and decided it best to send Bertie away. Only way he'd regain any sanity. He either had to take her to his bed and ease his need for her or send her off.

But when he'd summoned Bertie to dismiss her, the sensible thing to do, she'd stood resolutely in front of his desk and looked at him as though he were a fool. She didn't want to leave, and Sinclair didn't want her to go.

She had nowhere to go, in any case, and they both knew it. Her choices were the slums of the East End or another house of some aristocrat who exercised his power over the staff, as her friend had described. Damned if Sinclair would let that happen. Also, Richards had told him what Eleanor's coachman had told *him*, about the dank rooms and Bertie's bully of a father who'd been ready to hold her back when she wanted to leave. Sinclair would never send her back to that.

But he had to do *something*. He couldn't lie awake all night and still be able to give attention to his cases. He couldn't stand up in front of a judge and tell him in the politest possible terms that his lordship was an ass when he was daydreaming about unbuttoning Bertie's new and prim governess gowns.

He could always stay overnight at chambers, Sinclair thought as he snatched up his robes and followed Henry out. He never had, always wanting to return home to his young family, but knowing Bertie slept so near him every night was going to drive him mad.

Henry helped Sinclair settle his robes and look respectable before he strode from Essex Court across the way to Middle Temple Hall. The brown brick building, its white corner trim and windows soot-stained, stood like a cathedral on the green of the gardens, an imposing edifice of the law. The walls told the outside world that here was an important place of learning and weighty decisions. If Sinclair hadn't known many of the men inside it so well, he might believe it.

His lordship, Sir Percival Montague, whom Sinclair had enjoyed confounding over the case of Ruth Baxter, didn't rise when Sinclair entered the room he'd commandeered for this meeting. Sir Percival, Old Monty to both friends and detractors, had a cadaverous look, though Sinclair knew he was fond of meat and drink. He had watery blue eyes in a sunken face, thin lips, grayish skin, and wisps of hair across the top of his balding head.

Sir Percival snapped his fingers at a lackey waiting nearby and signaled him to pour two glasses of sherry. "I'm sorry I have no Scots whiskey," Old Monty said, not looking one bit sorry. "But I like a bit of sherry in the morning. Settles the digestion."

Sinclair thought sherry overly sweet and cloying, but he politely accepted a glass.

"You know why we're meeting," Sir Percival said. He drained his glass and held it up for the lackey to pour more.

"Either you want to admonish me for switching from prosecution to defense in the case of Ruth Baxter," Sinclair said calmly, "or you are measuring my backside for a place on the bench."

Old Monty looked pained. "You always have a blunt way of putting things, McBride. This endears you to some of my colleagues who find you rustic and amusing, but not to me. Take care to remember that. You were perfectly right, of course, in the Baxter case—the man taken in arrest has confessed to all and should shortly meet his maker, or else the bleakness of Dartmoor. But there is no secret that you are moving swiftly in your profession. You're young for a silk, aren't you?"

Sinclair was in his thirties. "I worked hard. Not much else to do, is there?"

"Not really." Monty drank his sherry and held the glass up again to his footman. "I like to see a barrister take keen interest in his work. You're a family man? Married, are you?"

Sinclair had known this man since his arrival at the Temple, but Old Monty was notorious for remembering no detail of anyone else's life, barely even of his own. "I have two children," Sinclair said. "My wife . . ." He stopped, and swallowed. *Forgive me, Maggie.* "My wife passed on seven years ago."

"Ah? Well, I am sorry to hear it."

Whether that was sympathy or he was sorry to hear that Sinclair was no longer married, Sinclair couldn't say. "Thank you," he managed.

"I like to see a barrister settled. A wife keeps a man at home and out of mischief, doesn't she?"

Sinclair decided to nod. Sinclair hadn't always been a dull man confined to his job, as Bertie had implied this morning. Andrew's antics had been inherited—both Sinclair and Elliot had been the wild McBride boys, impossible to tame. Patrick had despaired of them but felt better when they'd each joined the army—Elliot going to India, Sinclair to Africa.

Sinclair had done well as an officer, but he'd retained his wild streak off duty. After Maggie had taken him in hand,

Sinclair had given up such enjoyments as filling an obnoxious English officer's tent with goats. Actually, she'd laughed uproariously when Sinclair had told her the tale. The English officer in question had cruelly beaten one of the Egyptian boys assigned to help him. Sinclair had made sure the goats created the worst possible mess, then took the English captain a little way from camp and explained his feelings, with his fists.

"You're young, as I observed," Monty said. "You can always remarry."

Sinclair's anger stirred. *Of course.* When one wife goes, uproot her and replant another in her place. Choose one that looks well and goes with the furniture.

"Perhaps," Sinclair said without inflection.

"You take my advice, my boy. The committees like to see a man settled. They want no fear of a judge getting into scandal. If you don't mind me saying so, your name is already associated with enough scandal as it is."

Sinclair blinked. "Is it?" He led a model life, at least these days. His liaisons in the last few years had been conducted with utmost discretion.

"Your brothers and sister." Monty put his fingers together, now seeming to remember every detail of Sinclair's life. "One nearly mad, hiding himself in the wilds of Scotland. Then there was your youngest brother and that scandal he recently caused with the Duchess of Southdown. And your sister, of course, marrying into the notorious Mackenzie family. Lord Cameron Mackenzie has a terrible reputation, rumored to have killed his first wife, and there was your sister—a lady-in-waiting to the queen, no less—eloping with him." Monty shook his head. "Some of us on the bench were not keen to even consider you, but there are those who persuaded me to give you a chance."

Sinclair's irritation rose, the darker side of his sense of humor starting to itch. "Maybe you're thinking I should replace my brothers and sister with new ones too." He let his accent grow thick. "Mebbe made to order."

"No use you taking offense, McBride," Monty said, looking down his nose. "It's not bad advice. Marry a respectable young woman, and your wife's family will cancel out any embarrassment yours have perpetrated."

"Debts and credits, eh?" Sinclair asked.

"Exactly." Monty almost smiled. "You have grasped it. I know several eligible young women, from excellent families, who might suit."

"So do my brothers and my many sisters-in-law," Sinclair said, trying to keep the annoyance from his voice. He thought of Clara Thomalin from the night before, with her cold skin and colorless face. Perhaps a fine enough woman, but not as a life mate. "I'm inundated with eligible bloody women."

"No need to swear, though I suppose it's the Scots way." Monty sat back in his chair, lifting his hand in dismissal. "You think on what I've said, McBride. If you want to move up in the world, don't sneer at your betters and their advice."

The lackey understood the cues. He set down the sherry goblet and moved to the door to open it for Sinclair.

Sinclair got himself to his feet and swung around to go, making himself say nothing in response.

He seemed to hear Bertie's voice ringing in his head. *Silly old man,* she'd say when Sinclair told her about it. *He's like a spider, inn't he? Waiting in his web for someone to come along so he can bully him.* And she'd laugh.

Not until Sinclair was halfway back to his chambers, his stride swift, did he realize that he'd pictured sitting down with Bertie and confiding all to her without giving it a second thought.

～

Jeffrey Mitchell had sulked in the pub until late into the night, and this morning, he was paying for it. His head pounded and his eyes ached, and he wasn't happy that the winter day was so bright. Sunshine leaked through even the close-set buildings of Whitechapel to stab at him.

He didn't want to be home, not alone in his tiny lodgings. He didn't want to go all the way to Hackney to see the woman who called herself Sylvie, pretending to be French, even if she was a good ride. She wasn't no more French than

Jeffrey was, but she'd been a whore, and caught more flats with her fake accent and name.

Jeffrey didn't want her, though. He wanted Bertie.

Bertie usually told Jeffrey to go to the devil, but her eyes sparkled when she said it. She laughed a lot—she was a great girl for laughing, was Bertie. She could scold too, but Jeffrey would teach her not to when they married.

And he'd marry her. Didn't matter that she'd run off to be the tart of some rich gent. That couldn't last, and she'd be back. Jeffrey would forgive her, after he pounded her for leaving him. She'd learn not to do that. She'd learn that Jeffrey would take care of her and none other.

A carriage came down the narrow lane. Jeffrey moved close to the wall, hugging it so the big horses and conveyance could move through. When the coach was abreast of him, a man called out the open window. "You. Come here."

Wasn't many back here but Jeffrey, so it was obvious who he meant. Jeffrey moved a cautious step forward. Gentry coves passing through sometimes asked the denizens of the streets to run errands for them, and the denizens, usually needing extra coin, complied. But sometimes gents wanted more than that, especially the ones with unnatural appetites.

"Yes, you," the man went on, leaning out the window. "You'll want to speak to me, because I can tell you exactly what you want to know about Basher McBride."

Jeffrey's caution deserted him. "That bloody Scots barrister? What about him?"

The man beckoned Jeffrey over, and Jeffrey stepped to the coach and peered inside. He tried to see what the man looked like, but the gent had a hat pulled over his eyes. He dressed like any other rich cove—heavy coat against the cold, gloves, walking stick he rested his hand on. The carriage was shining and fine, with a beefy coachman on the box.

"He's got your woman," the man said. "The little pickpocket. She's yours, isn't she?"

Bertie. Jeffrey's heart beat faster. "Yeah, she's mine. Where is she?"

The man opened the door of the carriage. "Come inside," he said. "And I'll tell you all about it."

~~~~~

Bertie settled herself on a bench in Hyde Park and let Cat and Andrew play, keeping a sharp eye on Andrew. Andrew's idea of playing meant running around like a mad thing, chasing birds, yelling, and pointing out things to Bertie at the top of his voice. He'd brought a little boat, which he'd sail in the nearest pond whenever he calmed down. Bertie had learned to let him run first and do more complicated things later.

Cat, on the other hand, spread out a little blanket near the bench, sat her doll down next to her, and proceeded to hand out a pretend tea. Every movement was solemn, no smiling, the ritual rehearsed.

Bertie watched her speculatively. There was something wrong with Cat, something beyond grief for her mother, but she didn't know what. The girl should be rushing after Andrew, or skipping rope, or pushing a hoop, or other things little rich girls in parks liked to do. Instead, she sat very quietly, pouring imaginary tea without showing any real enjoyment. Every morning, the maid Aoife dressed Cat as though she were a doll herself, Cat taking no interest in the proceedings. That was wrong. Every girl, rich or poor, young or old, liked to primp herself. Cat took very good care not to tear her clothes or soil them—unlike Andrew who was determined to ruin a fine suit every day—but that was as far as her interest went.

Cat finished her tea-pouring ritual, as though it had been a chore she needed to get through, then she reached into her bag for a notebook—the one she let no one else see. Her pencil began moving, Cat staring at the pages, but again showing no real interest.

The bench moved as someone plopped down beside Bertie, too close to her. She looked up, and all the breath went out of her.

"Bertie-girl," Jeffrey said as he sent her an evil grin. "There you are."

Chapter 10

Bertie cast a swift glance around her. Andrew was still running, flapping his arms as though trying to fly, and Cat had her head down over her notebook. The kids were safe, she saw with relief, but the mild winter day suddenly became colder.

"What are you doing here?" Bertie asked in a low but fierce voice. "I've got a respectable job now. What do you want?"

"I wondered why you ran off from me," Jeffrey said. "I was that riled at you, Bertie-girl. But now I've twigged to what you were doing. Clever, to get right into the man's house. Send us the word, clear out of the house, and then *we'll* clear it out." He laughed, his ale-soaked breath washing over her.

"No, you won't," Bertie said furiously. "You won't come anywhere near him or his house. I'm looking after his kids now, not setting up a mark for you."

"Load of cobblers." Jeffrey closed the few inches of space between them. "You can pretend all you want, but you ain't respectable. Never will be. All I have to do is slip a nod to a magistrate that you're a pickpocket, and he'll haul you up before him quick as you please. I'll make sure he knows about every bloke you done over and what you took. Bet those gents are still looking for their watches, or purses, or handkerchiefs."

Bertie went even colder. "Yeah? Then you'll have to tell about my dad, because he sold the stuff on. You think *he'll* let you peach to a magistrate?"

Jeffrey's expression grew less certain, but he scowled at her. "Look at you in your fancy gear, watching after brats in velvet collars. I bet his suit and her dress would fetch us enough to live on for a year, not to mention what you've got on your back. You start feeding us the goods, Bertie, or I'll let on to your barrister all about you and what you get up to."

Bertie jerked away to her feet. "He already knows about me. I told him."

Jeffrey gave her a look of disbelief. "You told Basher McBride you were a thief? Couldn't have, or I'd be talking to you in Newgate."

"I did tell him. I didn't rob him the other night—he gave me the sovereign to take home. He's kindhearted."

"And then asked you to look after his get?"

"Yes." Bertie clenched her hands in her new gloves, which were soft leather and not out at the seams.

Jeffrey stared at her, then his face flushed, and he got off the bench to tower over her. "You're getting on your knees for him, ain't ya? You're kicking your feet to the ceiling—and you're trying to tell me you're respectable. You're whoring for him."

"No!" Bertie said. "I'd never . . ." Her face went hot, because she knew she'd bloody well kick her feet up for Sinclair if ever he said the word. Last night, he'd done nothing but suckle her fingers, but he might as well have been at her breast or some other intimate part.

"No," she repeated, making her voice firm. "What do you take me for? Why can't you believe I have a proper job?"

"Because no gent would let the likes of you into his house or near his brats without you paying for it. If he ain't done you, it just means he ain't done you *yet*." Jeffrey grabbed her wrist, the same one Sinclair had held so tightly the night before. "But you're *my* girl, Bertie, and you're coming home with me now."

~~~~~

Sinclair left his chambers earlier than usual, another letter Henry delivered to him in the afternoon changing the entire day. This one wasn't anonymous—Daisy's brother had signed it, proud to throw threats at Sinclair and his family. The trouble was, the threats had teeth. Sinclair wasn't in court this afternoon, thank God, so he packed up his valise and called for his carriage.

When he'd arrived this morning, Sinclair had been contemplating hiding in chambers, sleeping there, anything to stay away from Bertie. Now he knew he never could. After reading his brother-in-law's letter, Sinclair wanted to be home, to surround himself with his children, to reassure himself that they were all right, to reassure *them* that he'd protect them at all costs.

Add to that the thought of Bertie there, and his home beckoned like a refuge. Sinclair wanted to see her, hungered for it. Even if he could only look upon her, listen to her no-nonsense voice and cheeky words, everything would be better. He had enough self-control to keep himself from ravishing his children's governess, didn't he? Sinclair was famous for his self-control, at least these days. His brothers teased him about it.

He reached home, the drive today seeming extraordinarily long. Afternoon sunshine slanted through the windows of the house as Sinclair tossed his greatcoat, hat, and gloves at Peter. The winter day had been mild, as winter in London could sometimes be—blue skies, crisp air, sun shining almost too brightly—but Sinclair was chilled.

The house was quiet, Bertie and his children safely tucked in the nursery, he assumed. Sinclair knew if he went straight to them, he'd alarm Cat and Andrew, who were sensitive to his moods and easily upset. He'd calm himself then go up to the nursery to be a cheerful father coming home from the office to visit his brood.

"I'll be in my study," he told Peter. "Not to be disturbed."

"Yes, sir." Peter smoothed the rumpled greatcoat in his arms and peered at Sinclair. "Anything I can get you, sir?"

"No." Sinclair heard his abrupt tone and strove to soften it. "Thank you."

"Right, sir."

Sinclair took the stairs two at a time, barely out of breath when he reached the second landing. He had whiskey in his study, and plenty of it. Ever since Sinclair's sister had married into the Mackenzie family, Sinclair had a standing order of the best Mackenzie malt, and Macaulay always kept the decanter stocked.

Sinclair strode into the room and slammed the door, making straight for the amber liquid. He sloshed a large measure into a glass, thumped the decanter back down with a clatter, and plunked himself onto the sofa under the tall front windows.

"Hiya," Bertie said next to him.

Sinclair was on his feet as swiftly as he'd sat down, the whiskey slopping out of the glass. Bertie huddled against the end of the sofa, her feet tucked under her, her gray dress rumpled, as though she'd been napping.

Sinclair opened his mouth to demand to know what she was doing in here, then noticed her face. Bertie regarded him without a smile, her expression so sad his heart missed a beat.

He sat back down, thrusting the whiskey glass to a table beside him, his fingers sticky. "Bertie, what is it?"   ·

Tears stood in her blue eyes, not only of sorrow but deep anger. "I have something to tell you," she said. "Something that happened today."

"To the children?" Sinclair asked, alarmed. But no, Peter had been tranquil, even cheerful, and Macaulay hadn't met him at the door to break bad news.

"No, no," Bertie said quickly. "They're fine. Went to sleep already—worn out from the late night last night and a long play in the park today."

"Then what?" Sinclair demanded. Bertie looked morose,

very unlike herself. "Your father didn't come making trouble, did he?"

"No, no. Dad's a lazy lout, if nothing else. Traveling across the city is too much for him. It's Jeffrey."

Sinclair scowled. "Jeffrey? Who the devil is Jeffrey?"

"Thinks he's in love with me. But he just wants my dad to let me marry him so he can have someone to wash his socks."

"Bertie." Sinclair took a deep breath. "Tell me what the hell you are talking about."

Bertie sat up, pushing back a lock of hair that had come out of its braid. "I'm talking about Jeffrey and what he said to me today. He's a villain, a bad one. He boasts a lot, but the trouble is, he's not always just telling porkies for fun. He's dangerous."

"Porkies?" Sinclair tried to focus on what she was saying, and not the fact that the wisps of hair straggling about her face made her even more beautiful. "Lies? About what?"

"About things he's going to do, or wants to do. Sometimes it's idle threats but sometimes it ain't."

Bertie trailed off and wet her lips, making them red and moist. Sinclair's body went tight. "Bertie, will you please come to the point?"

"I'm trying to. Jeffrey." Her face was too pale, her eyes dark in the dim light. "He told me if I didn't go home to him he'd come back with his friends to rob you blind or take your children and hold them to ransom—though I warned him he'd have a bit more than he bargained for if he tried that with Andrew. I got Jeffrey to leave me today, though I think it was more the sight of the nice constable strolling by that persuaded him, but he'll be back. I'm scared about what he'll do."

Sinclair's temper mounted. "He won't do anything. I won't let him. I'll make sure of it."

"Don't dismiss him. He came all the way to Hyde Park, where I was alone with Cat and Andrew. I'm grateful he didn't try anything then, but he likes strength in numbers. He'll do what he said."

"Unless you go back to him?" Sinclair's rage wound higher. "The hell you will. He won't be grateful for it—he'll keep bullying you, threatening worse if you try to leave him again." He came to his feet, unable to sit still any longer. "Bullies never stop, Bertie. They keep at you and at you, unless you face them and spit at them." Sinclair punctuated his words with sharp jabs of his finger. Bertie blinked at him, but she didn't look afraid. Not of him. "I bloody well won't let you go running off back to him if he's that much of a danger to you. You stay here, and help me with what I need you to, and be damned to those who don't like it!"

The world started rocking, the air leaving it. Bertie came to her feet next to him, her skirts making a pleasant rustling sound. "Something else has happened, hasn't it?" she asked in concern. "You're as upset as I am, but not about Jeffrey. We're talking about different things, ain't we?"

"*I'm* talking about my ass of a brother-in-law, damn him. Oh, God, Bertie, what if he's right, and he takes them away from me?"

Sinclair struggled for breath. He'd been like this since childhood—when something bad enough happened, an iron band would wrap around his chest and compress his lungs until he couldn't breathe. He'd learned to hide the malady, especially in the army, teaching himself exercises to suppress it. The first year Daisy had gone, Sinclair had barely been able to breathe normally for any stretch of time. He'd painfully taught himself control again, and the incidents had mostly stopped. Until recently—since he'd met Bertie, in fact.

Bertie reached for his hand, her warm fingers wrapping his ice-cold ones. Her touch broke through the constriction, and Sinclair dragged grating air into his lungs.

"You all right?" Bertie led him one step back to the sofa. "Sit with me. Tell me what happened. What brother-in-law? You mean the lord with the horses?"

"What?" Sinclair made himself suck in another breath as they sank to the couch. "No, not Cameron. My wife's brother, Edward. He wrote me a letter." He touched his breast pocket, the paper inside crackling. He had to wait until he could breathe enough to speak in clear sentences. "A bloody awful letter. Edward never liked me. He blames me for taking Daisy away from him. I met Daisy in Rome, when I was on leave— we were married by the end of the second week we knew each other. Edward never forgave her, or me, especially me. He's pursuing legal means to become Cat and Andrew's guardian. He says he knows it will be difficult, but it's the least he can do for poor Maggie's son and daughter."

Bertie listened in alarm. "Can he do that?"

Sinclair felt his chest tighten again, but he made himself stop. He concentrated on exhaling, letting his lungs draw the air back in on their own. "It's a possibility. A father has full say over his children, but if Edward can make a case that I'm incompetent, that the children would be better off if he and his wife took them in—dear God, Bertie, he could do it."

"The law made me stay with my dad when my mum died," Bertie said. "And he's bloody awful."

Sinclair shook his head. "Edward has much money and influence, many connections. He wants more money still, which is another reason the bastard is after me. If he can mold and shape Andrew, he can go to Andrew with his hand out when Andrew comes into his inheritance." Sinclair scrubbed his hands over his face, his breathing easier now, but bleakness lingered in his heart. "What if Edward's right? Look at me. I'm a wreck of a man. What kind of father have I been? My children are little devils. I love them, but I'm not blind. If I'd paid more attention, Andrew wouldn't be so wild, or Cat so . . . detached."

He found Bertie sitting close to him, her warm skirts spilling over his thighs. "Now, you stop right there, Mr. McBride," she said, her eyes sparkling with anger. "You're a perfectly fine father. You don't beat them, first of all. You give them a good house, and lots of things, and book-learning—at least you try with the book-learning. I didn't have none of that. This Edward can't say your kids are mis-treated, because they ain't. I can see *that*. You're good at laws. You'll best him, I know it."

Her confidence was as warm as her touch. "I'm a barrister," Sinclair said. "An advocate. Not a solicitor. The niceties are beyond me."

"What are you talking about? You stand up in court and tell everyone what's right and what's not."

Sinclair wanted to laugh. "Love, I've known barristers who've never cracked a law book in their lives. They take on pupils to do the legal research for them. To be a barrister you only need a firm resolve, a persuasive way about you, and a large pair of bollocks."

Bertie rewarded him with a brief grin. Her unwavering faith made Sinclair feel a bit better. Gave him hope, let him breathe easier. If Edward wanted a fight, he'd have one.

. Then Bertie's smile dimmed. "If your brother-in-law gets wind that I'm not a proper governess, he'll use that against you too, won't he?"

Her gaze was shrewd. She was right, and she knew it.

Sinclair squeezed her hand. Hers was small, delicate yet strong. These fingers had dipped into his pocket, unhooked his watch, and taken it without him detecting it.

And yet, she had finely shaped hands, skin a bit rough from too much manual work, but he didn't mind. Sinclair lifted her hand to his lips and kissed her fingertips. Last night he'd suckled these fingers. He'd been half-drunk, disgusted with himself, and he'd needed her. He'd craved to have something of her in his mouth, and he hadn't been able to let go of her once he'd started.

"Then we'll make sure he doesn't find out," Sinclair said. "Cat and Andrew need you, and I can't do this without you." He kissed her fingers again, tenderly. "Everything's dark for me, Bertie. But there's a little flicker of light, the tiniest one. It's above me every night, in the nursery and you next to it." He pressed her hand between both of his, drawing in her warmth once more. "Please don't put that light out."

Bertie looked at him for a long time, a swallow moving down her throat. Sinclair knew he asked a lot of her—had since he'd chased her through the dark streets of London, determined to wrench his watch back from her. This morning he'd virtuously thought he could let her go, to prevent himself taking what he shouldn't want.

This evening, he knew his virtuousness was a lie. Sinclair wanted her here, needed her, couldn't let her walk out of his life, no matter what tricks they had to play on the rest of the world.

At last, Bertie smiled. She wrapped her hands around Sinclair's, her dark blue eyes meeting his gaze over their twined fingers. "All right," she said. "You convinced me. We'll draw up the battlements here, and I'll become the best governess London has ever seen. We'll face them together, yeah?"

Easier said than done, Bertie thought the next morning. She knew she had to appear to be a well-read, genteel young lady, fit to take on the task of educating the McBride children. Not the simplest task in the world for Bertie Frasier. She'd have to put her mind to how to go about it, but she was determined to. Nobody was going to take these children away from Mr. McBride, not if she had anything to say about it.

Bertie had begun the habit of taking the children for a walk straight after breakfast, after they waved their father good-bye. She'd found they settled down better to reading and things afterward. The previous governesses had forced them to stay inside until they'd done a certain amount of work, and that hadn't done well, had it?

That morning, in light of Jeffrey's threats, Sinclair had ordered Macaulay to accompany them everywhere, which was fine with Bertie. Though Macaulay still made her nervous, she was sure even Jeffrey would balk at taking on a giant in a kilt.

Macaulay trailed behind them, his usual taciturn self, but Bertie couldn't quite forget he was there. He had a presence, did Macaulay.

He kept his eagle eye on the kids as they played—Andrew running, Cat perched on the edge of a bench writing in the book again. Macaulay had been so silent the entire hour that when he cleared his throat, the sound rumbling up from the depths of his large body, it was as though a volcano had begun to bubble over in the quiet tranquility of the park.

Bertie jumped, but Macaulay only fixed a sharp gaze on her and began to speak.

"I won't lie to ye, lass," he said in his blunt way. "I saw Mr. McBride with you upstairs after his fancy supper night before last, a-kissing ye."

Chapter 11

Bertie's face went scalding hot. Macaulay only watched her, daring her to deny she'd been in Sinclair's embrace, which, of course, she couldn't.

"He weren't kissing me—" Bertie broke off. Explaining what Sinclair *had* been doing would be much more delicate and somewhat embarrassing. "What if he was?"

Macaulay kept his eye on her, the man looking out of place in this tame, manicured park. He'd be more at home striding across sweeping hills, his kilt swinging, his hair ruffled by a wild Scottish wind.

"I don't blame *you*, miss," Macaulay said. "Ye have to forgive him for it."

Bertie blinked, her lips parting at this unexpected turn. She'd been sure Macaulay had been about to blister her with an admonishment. "I have to forgive *him*?"

"Aye. He's not been himself since . . . well, in a long time."

Bertie took a breath, trying to recover from the surprise. "Not since he lost his wife, you mean," she said. Her voice softened. "It was hard on them all, wasn't it?"

"Aye, lass. This has been a house of grief for a long time."

Macaulay shook his head. "He's a good man, is Mr. Sinclair, for all his wild ways."

"Is he wild?" Bertie asked, perplexed again. "But he goes off to a job every day, like a respectable gent."

"*Now*, he does. But I was Mr. Sinclair's batman in the army. We were sent to parts of Africa that would make you wilt away. His men respected him more than anybody, would do anything for him, would die for him. When he was off duty though, whew." Macaulay took on a faraway look, one that held fondness. "He loved his whiskey, Mr. McBride did, and his pranks, especially on English officers who were prats. He'd make them look like fools, but he was so good a soldier his superiors wouldn't punish him. He was a fine officer, though. No one better in a fight, always brought his men home."

Bertie listened, soaking in the information. Mrs. Hill had told her a few things, but this was the first time she'd gotten an outpouring about Sinclair's past. "Why'd he leave the army? If he was so good at it?"

"Met his wife, didn't he?" Macaulay watched Andrew leaping over a series of stones he'd set up. "Miss Margaret was a pretty thing. Miss Caitriona looks much like her."

"I've seen her photo," Bertie said. One smiled from a frame on top of the dresser in the nursery. The picture was grainy and dark, but she could tell that the woman had been quite comely. "Mr. McBride was much in love with her, wasn't he?"

"Aye, that he was, lass. He resigned his captaincy and went into chambers in London—his grandfather had been a barrister there, and they took him on easily enough. Miss Margaret encouraged him, and he started to rise. No telling how far he'll go—all the way to the Queen's Bench, I wouldn't wonder. He grew famous as a junior, and was offered silk pretty quickly. He and Mrs. McBride were a fine couple, loved by everyone they knew."

Bertie's heart squeezed, fully aware Mrs. McBride had been a paragon. "But she died, poor lady."

"That she did." Macaulay's voice went quiet. "It was a long illness, and the two wee ones nearly went with her. Thought Mr. McBride would go himself, of grieving. The problem was, Miss Margaret had tamed him, but I think she tamed him too well. When she was gone, there wasn't much left of him."

"Hardly anything." Bertie's heart ached as she thought of the sadness in Sinclair's gray eyes, as though he waited for some reason to come alive again. "He's all emptied out."

"We look after him," Macaulay said. "Mrs. Hill and me, and the others. We make sure he's all right and doesn't grow too morose. We need you to help us with that."

Bertie nodded. "I will." Of course she would. That's why she'd come, wasn't it?

Macaulay gave her an approving look. "Mr. McBride, he carries on—does his cases and all, and he don't say no to the ladies—but his heart's in the grave." His look turned sharp again. "Remember that."

"Yeah," Bertie said, her own heart seeming to shrink. "I will."

When Bertie returned to the house, she gave the children their regular lessons—the history of Britain, sums from a book of maths, and French. Bertie enjoyed the history, was good at the maths, but let Cat take the lead in French.

She thought about what Macaulay had told her as the children read and wrote, a little lump forming in her throat. The sensations of Sinclair holding her hand yesterday evening when they sat in his study, so chummy, and his mouth on her fingers the night before lingered. Bertie had felt special, singled out, the woman with whom he'd chosen to share his troubles.

Everything's dark for me, Bertie. But there's a little flicker of light, the tiniest one. It's above me every night, in the nursery and you next to it.

And then Macaulay: *He don't say no to the ladies—but his heart's in the grave. Remember that.*

Blast it.

After dinner, when Cat and Andrew had a nap—at least,

they pretended to until Bertie was out of the room—Mrs. Hill sent up word, asking Bertie to come to the library on the first floor.

When Bertie entered the dim room, Mrs. Hill, in her usual severe black, was standing in front of the rows of bookcases that rose to the ceiling. "A governess needs to know what she's teaching her charges," she said as soon as Bertie entered. "I know there's Mangnall's *Questions*, but a solid education is much easier to defend than memorization from an answer book. And if you want an education, my dear, this is the best way to go about it." She swept her hand to indicate the rows of books around them.

Bertie took in the leather-backed tomes that marched along every wall up to the very high ceiling, and quailed. "You want me to read all *these*? Are ye mad? That'll take me the rest of me life!"

"If needs must," Mrs. Hill said in her no-nonsense voice. "Mr. Edward Davies—Mr. McBride's brother-in-law—is determined to take our children from us, and we can't have that. If you have to read every book in this room to fool him into thinking you're a real governess, I will stand here until you do so."

"Oh, Lord." Bertie turned in a circle, taking in all the books, which seemed to spin around her. "What if I don't understand any of them?"

"No matter. As long as, when Mr. Edward is nigh, you can trot out a few phrases such as *Carlyle tells us* . . . or *Herodotus's views on Ancient Egypt are* . . . you'll do well."

Bertie's eyes narrowed. "Do *you* know what's in all these books, Mrs. Hill?"

"Of course not," Mrs. Hill said without shame. "But I'm not pretending to be a governess, am I?"

"I'm not pretending," Bertie said. "I *am* one—now."

"Well, you'd better be one with everything you have, my girl. I don't like Mrs. McBride's brother, I can tell you. The first thing he'll do is send Andrew off to some cold school in the north of England. Porridge three times a day, shivering by himself in a narrow little room, which they say will make a man of him."

Bertie doubted Andrew would stand for being shut by himself in a narrow little room—he'd find some way to pick the lock or climb out the window—but she took the point. "What would they do with Cat?" Caitriona definitely wouldn't benefit from being put into a cold room alone. While Andrew was always trying to burst out of himself, Cat retreated deep inside herself where no one could reach. It would not be best to put her somewhere without warmth, without people who understood and cared about her.

"Miss Cat would be educated in Mr. Davies' home," Mrs. Hill said, her nostrils pinching. "With a governess who'd fill her head with all kinds of nonsense, such as a true lady being too delicate to speak above a whisper and so weak she can barely lift a teacup. Then they'll send Miss Cat to finishing school to complete her ruination." Mrs. Hill's lips pressed together, rage in her eyes.

Bertie liked that rage. "Well then," she said, squaring her shoulders. "I'd best get to reading, hadn't I?"

"Yes." Mrs. Hill gave her a look of vast gratitude. "Thank you, my dear."

"All the same," Bertie said, looking up at the books again, her imagination stirring to life. "I have an idea."

Sinclair left chambers at seven that evening and paid a visit on his way home to Detective Chief Inspector Lloyd Fellows in his comfortable home in Pimlico.

The DCI was one of the Mackenzie clan Sinclair's sister had married into, and the Mackenzie Sinclair felt most comfortable with. Though Fellows, a half brother to the rest of the Mackenzies, had spent his childhood in the slums of the East End, and Sinclair had lived in a well-kept house, raised by his respectable older brother, Sinclair and Fellows had both made their way up in their professions by hard work and bloody stubbornness. Both also were in the business of the law—Fellows caught villains breaking the laws, and Sinclair helped put them away. They shared a mutual respect, as well as a bemusement at being drawn into the very scandalous Mackenzie family.

Fellows had married earlier in the year to the youngest daughter of an earl—Lady Louisa Scranton. Louisa's sister, Isabella, had married a Mackenzie herself—Lord Mac, the painter.

Louisa smiled warmly as Sinclair entered, greeting him with a kiss on his cheek. Her red hair glimmered in the lamplight, and her gown couldn't hide her increasing girth. Louisa was expecting sometime in the early spring.

"Lovely to see you, Sinclair," she said warmly. "How are dear Cat and Andrew?"

"Dear Cat and Andrew are very well, thank you," Sinclair answered, waiting for Louisa to sit before he took the chair she indicated. "They have a new governess they've taken a liking to, and so the house has stayed more or less intact for the last few days."

"Yes, the new governess," Louisa said, giving Sinclair a shrewd look. "Eleanor told us about her."

Sinclair blinked, though he knew he shouldn't be surprised Louisa already knew about Bertie. "It's gone around, has it?"

"In the Mackenzie family?" Louisa shot him another smile and began pouring out tea. "Of course. Everyone from Hart's manservant to Beth's scullery maid knows you've recently employed a young governess with a charming Cockney accent."

"No denying it, I suppose." Sinclair accepted the cup Louisa handed him. "One of the reasons I've come is to ask you to help her," he said to Fellows. "I need you to find out about her relations and keep them away from her. Especially one called Jeffrey. A thug who styles himself her beau."

Louisa's brows rose. "A thug? That sounds ominous. Is he a danger?"

"I don't want him to be," Sinclair said. "Either to my children or to Bertie—I mean, Miss Frasier."

Louisa peered closely at him, noticing the slip. "A very winsome young lady, Eleanor said."

Sinclair flushed, and Louisa smiled at him again and lifted her teacup.

Fellows didn't share his wife's amusement, but he did share her concern. "If he weren't a danger, you wouldn't have come to me," he said. "I advise you to keep your governess and little ones close to home, or don't let them go out without you."

"Exactly why I'm here," Sinclair said. "Macaulay keeps a good eye on them, but I want this man found, warned, stopped." He took a sip of tea. "That and . . . the letters."

Fellows's eyes sharpened. "You've had another?"

"Yes. Same as the others. Full of insinuations."

"Let me see." Fellows held out his hand.

Sinclair shook his head, thinking of the letter he'd slid into the box in his study. "I burned it," he lied.

Fellows made a noise of disapproval. "You shouldn't have done that."

"Trust me, it was the same. In all capitals printed as though he'd used a straight edge to draw them. Ordinary paper, which hundreds of people buy by the score every day. Same nonsense about his intention to destroy me. Any ideas from your end at all?"

Fellows sat back, irritated. "No. And you have no idea how much that galls me."

"Lloyd so hates to be perplexed," Louisa said, her fingers graceful as she held the dainty teacup. They were such a contrast, Fellows and Louisa—he a tall, hard man, she as elegant as the porcelain cup she held. "But he'll find out in the end, I'm sure of it," Louisa finished.

Fellows gave Louisa a look that was supposed to be severe and instead was full of fondness. His gaze dropped to the swell of her belly, which held his first child, and Sinclair watched the hard man soften.

"My wife has much confidence in my abilities," Fellows said. "I've been going through the list of men and women who I think would hold a grudge against you. It is, unfortunately, long."

Sinclair nodded, unsurprised. "I've made sure many a criminal was convicted in the last dozen years—for anything from counterfeiting and fraud, to robbery with violence and murder. It could be any of them, or their families. Basher McBride has made enemies. And I don't want any of them near my family." He pinned Louisa with a stare. "Will you make certain, Louisa, that this bit of intrigue does *not* run around the Mackenzie clan? I don't want Andrew and Cat getting wind of it."

Louisa gave him a nod. "I understand perfectly. I'm sure it won't be long before Lloyd solves the problem."

Fellows gave Sinclair a wry look over his teacup. Fellows had helped Louisa when she'd been accused of a crime, and Louisa was convinced he could help anyone. She wasn't far from wrong—the detective chief inspector usually got his man.

The trouble was, whoever this person sending the letters was worked in the dark, pulling strings, manipulating. The worst kind of criminal, keeping to the shadows while aiming to ruin the lives of others. Give Sinclair a straightforward thug like Jeffrey, who spoke with his fists, or even Edward, who openly threatened Sinclair—Sinclair was much more comfortable with someone he could clearly fight.

Fellows gave Sinclair a nod, and they exchanged a look, two men who understood each other. "I'll see to it," Fellows said.

~~~~

Bertie hurried out into the hall when she heard the front door thud shut. Cat and Andrew were already asleep, and it was well dark. Sinclair was very late getting home, which had Bertie fretting, though she tried to reason that the coach hadn't come home either, meaning the redoubtable Richards was looking after him.

Below her, Sinclair handed his coat and things to Peter, as usual, but not as usual, Sinclair strode into the downstairs drawing room instead of heading up to his study.

Bertie gathered up her gray skirts and hurried down the stairs, passing Macaulay on the way. Macaulay gave her a cautioning look but didn't stop her.

Sinclair had paused at a sideboard in the large room to pour himself a whiskey when Bertie came in. Unlike the clutter of Sinclair's study, the front drawing room was rather empty of furniture. Unusual, Mrs. Hill said, for a Mayfair residence, which could be stuffed full of bric-a-brac and plants, but Sinclair liked to have space for his guests to roam.

"Where the devil have you been?" Bertie demanded as she rushed inside. Her heart beat swiftly with relief to see him whole, and home.

Sinclair swung around to her. He'd yanked off his collar, baring a patch of sunburned throat. He scowled at Bertie and swallowed a dollop of whiskey before he answered. "Visiting friends, who insisted I stay for a cup of tea."

Bertie unclenched her hands. "Sorry, I didn't mean to sound like a shrew. But I was worried about you."

Sinclair gave her a curt nod. "I know you're concerned about Jeffrey, but don't be. I will take care of him."

Her heart squeezed in dismay. Sinclair spoke so confidently, but he had no idea what he was up against. "Oh, you will, will you? He's a first-class villain, Jeffrey is. Even his friends don't trust him. He's got all kinds of tricks, and he likes hurting people."

"My friends are well able to take on someone like him. Trust *me*." Sinclair drained the glass in one long swallow and turned back to the sideboard.

Bertie waited until he'd set the glass down, then she launched herself across the room and got her arms around the startled Sinclair from behind. She pulled him backward and jammed her hand to his throat as though she held a knife.

"Yeah?" Bertie said in his ear, trying to ignore the sleek warmth of his hair so near her lips. "This is what Jeffrey would do to you. If I'd been him, he'd have killed you already. What do you think about *that*?"

Chapter 12

For a moment Sinclair didn't move. His body was solid under hers, hard muscle beneath the giving fabric of his coat. Bertie felt his chest expand with his breath, his pulse thud beneath her fingertips. The contact, this intimate, made her so giddy she almost lost hold of him.

A heartbeat later, Sinclair broke her grip, whirled Bertie around, and had her off him and against the nearest wall before she knew what happened. Sinclair's strong hand was at her throat, his fingers just pressing her skin.

His breath was warm and smelled of whiskey. "*This* is what I do to men who attack me, Bertie. You don't have to worry about me. I can hold my own."

His gray eyes were so near hers, the irises flecked with lighter gray, his lashes as light as his hair. Sinclair's mouth—that firm-lipped mouth that spoke the rich, rumbling words—was very close to her own. If Bertie didn't squirm away now, she'd do something foolish, like kiss him.

She drew a breath, contriving to look intimidated. "I'm sorry. I only meant . . ."

Instantly, Sinclair took his hand from her neck, set her on

her feet, and took a swift step back. "Lass, I beg your pardon. I didn't mean to frighten you . . ."

Bertie spun away, laughing. "You're a soft touch, you are. As soon as a thief starts to cry, you'll apologize and let him go?" She held up her hands. From her fingers dangled Sinclair's handkerchief, his watch, and a small pouch of coins. She grinned her triumph.

"Bertie, you bloody little . . ." Sinclair broke off, glancing at the open door, then crossing to close it. "How the devil did you do that?"

"Easy as winking. You see? You need someone looking after you."

Sinclair came to her, his amazement mixed with irritation. "Show me how you took them. So I can be on my guard."

Bertie returned the watch, coins, and handkerchief to his cupped hands. "Wasn't hard. You were concentrating on your hand at my throat, but all the while, my fingers were sliding into your pockets."

Sinclair tucked his things away. "In other words, while I was trying to put down my attacker, she was busy robbing me."

"Exactly. I was taught never to come out of an encounter without winning *something*. But even if I'd only passed by you in the street, I'd have had something off you. Like I did when I took your watch."

"When you beguiled me, you mean," Sinclair said.

"Beguiled?" Bertie's face heated. "I did no such thing."

"You smiled at me, and made the day better." His voice softened. "On that gray day, I needed a smile."

A small flame burned in Bertie's chest. "My good luck, then. But I could have done it without you noticing me at all, if someone hadn't shoved me into you."

Sinclair's eyes glinted. "I don't believe you. Show me."

"All right. Go on across the room and then walk back toward me."

Sinclair slanted her a look that made fire race through her blood, then he turned and strode across the room. At the far end he turned back and started for her, not allowing her time to prepare.

Didn't matter. Bertie strolled past, pretending she didn't notice him, barely brushing him as she went by. Sinclair stopped at the other end of the room, near the windows. "Well?" he asked. "Another turn?"

"Don't need one." Bertie held up a silver card case that flashed in the lamplight. "Lost this, did you?"

Sinclair's brows came down. "Bloody hell. How did you—?"

"Misdirection." Bertie came to him and handed him the card case. "Put that back in your pocket."

Sinclair dropped it in. Bertie walked past him again, letting her shoulder bump him gently, as she had before. A tiny tap, barely noticed in a crowd.

"See, you turn a little to adjust," she said, stopping the movement. "And the contact distracts you. While you move to keep your balance, I dip inside your pocket and take whatever I can get me fingers around." Bertie pulled her hand out, his card case between her fingers.

"I see." Sinclair's eyes narrowed. "Try it again."

Bertie shrugged, gave him back the case, and walked away from him. This time, when the two passed in the middle of the room, Bertie bumped him a little harder and brushed her fingers over his wrist. Sinclair gave a laugh of triumph and caught Bertie's hand, prying open her fingers.

Her hand was empty. Bertie grinned and showed him what was in her *other* hand, his pouch of money.

"Damn and blast it," he said.

Bertie handed him the pouch. "You're a babe in the woods. Misdirection, like I said."

Sinclair jerked her closer by the wrist he still held. "You cheeky little . . ."

His words died as his gaze met hers, his gray eyes full of longing. Bertie's breath went out of her, as did any laughter.

"Damn you, Bertie," he whispered. Sinclair leaned to her as he spoke, the end of his whisper touching her lips.

His warmth undid her. Sinclair's kiss was light, gentle, belying the strength in the hand that slid to the back of her neck, pulling her close.

Bertie felt herself floating to him, rising up on her tiptoes, seeking him. He kissed her bottom lip, suckling it. As when he'd suckled her fingers, she felt a bite of slight pain, then a flood of fire. Bertie dug her fingers into the sleeve of his coat and held on.

Sinclair pulled back and brushed a lock of hair from her face. His cheekbones were flushed, his eyes, half-closed, gray like smoke. He was a beautiful man, unmarred by the few scars that creased his face, leftover from fighting days.

He touched the buttons at the top of her bodice, and one slid out of its buttonhole. Bertie held still, not daring to breathe, as another button opened, and another.

"Too prim," he said, his rough fingertips on the skin of her throat. "Prim doesn't suit you, Bertie."

"I'm a governess." She could barely speak. "I'm supposed to be prim."

His answering smile, small as it was, made her burn. "If *I* bought you gowns, they'd be bright and frothy, swirling around you like gossamer."

Bertie's mind filled with a vision of herself spinning away, laughing, in light silks like Eleanor wore, floating as she went. Sinclair would catch hold of the loose skirts and pull her back to him, laughing his sinful laugh.

He smiled now, and licked the hollow of her throat.

~~~~~

Taste of sweet, sweet woman. Sinclair's blood heated as Bertie's bosom rose under his touch, the placket opening for him, her scent intoxicating. She was a sweet, plump armful, something to curl up against in the nighttime. Everything about her was strong, a woman Sinclair could hold on to, and yet soft and feminine, a woman for wanting.

Sinclair kissed her throat. Warmth, that was Bertie. When she'd taken him into her hiding place under the street, what should have been tomb cold had seemed plenty hot. Her warmth permeated him now, as it did his house. Coming home hadn't held this kind of joy in a long time.

Her body was a fine place, flattening against his, her breath on his cheek. Sinclair gently eased the bodice apart and kissed the softness of her breast, swelling over her corset. Bertie's fingers slid to his hair, tightening as she drew a quick breath.

Sinclair licked her skin, kissed it. He tasted her longing, and at the same time, her innocence.

He moved his kisses down to the space between her breasts. She was nothing but heat, and he licked that heat into his mouth. Need wound through him, so much need—his cock was hard with it. He wanted to unbutton her bodice to her waist, unlace her stays, spread his hand across her bare back.

If he took her, maybe on the floor of this severe drawing room, would he be finished with her, sated and done?

He didn't think so. Bertie was different. She'd give him her cheeky smile, and he'd never let her out of his life.

Sinclair licked between her breasts again, tasting the salt of her skin, then he lifted his head and kissed her lips. He couldn't get enough of her, savoring her while his need soared.

When Sinclair finally broke the kiss, he had no breath, and he didn't care.

He cupped her shoulders, rubbing his thumbs over the flesh he'd bared. "Bertie." The name itself was cheeky. "Roberta."

"That's me," she whispered. Her eyes sparkled.

"We should button you up again." Sinclair touched his forehead to hers. "But I don't want to."

Bertie's grin flashed. "Mrs. Hill might fall over if she saw."

Sinclair nodded. He wanted to laugh at the image of the stately Mrs. Hill falling stiffly to the floor, but it was all he could do to draw air into his body. He held on to Bertie, knowing he'd be the one on his backside if he let go.

Bertie traced his cheek. "You're a good man, Basher McBride."

"No, I'm not." Sinclair caressed her again. "I follow rules because I have to, but that doesn't make me good."

"You are. You just don't know what to do about it."

Sinclair turned his head and kissed her fingertips. "Oh, I know what I want to do about it." He licked her forefinger. Who cared about breathing?

"I'm right that you're a good man," Bertie said softly. "Don't tell me I'm not. I'm the one who's bad. I stole from you, I followed you home, and I stayed, when it was clear I shouldn't. So I'm going to make this easy for you."

She twined her hand around his, lifted his fingers to her mouth, kissed them, and gently withdrew from his grip.

The heat in Sinclair's veins flared, and then plunged into the coldest temperatures as Bertie turned and walked away.

"Where the devil are you going?" Sinclair's voice was harsh, his breath trying to desert him again.

Bertie swung back, buttoning her bodice. "I'm only going up to my chamber, before Mrs. Hill gives me a lecture."

Sinclair coughed, and made his chest expand with a normal inhalation. "You enjoy confounding me, don't you?" He came to her, trying to remain in control as he reached for her placket and started doing up the buttons for her. "Here, let's fix you. I won't have Mrs. Hill come down on you because of me."

Bertie's smile was soft. "Cheers."

Sinclair buttoned the last button, hiding her from him again. He kissed her lips, lightly this time. If he didn't keep it light, he'd have her on the floor, to hell with Mrs. Hill or anyone else who happened to walk in.

Sinclair deliberately stepped away from her and opened the door. "Go," he said.

"Good night," Bertie answered. She glided out of the room, then she turned around, grinning, holding up his handkerchief and his silver case again.

Sinclair slapped his hands to his pockets. "Wretch!"

Laughing, Bertie came back to him and slid the things into his pockets. Her hands were warm, enticing as they moved on his body, but Sinclair made himself not touch her.

She whirled away again and was gone, the warmth leaving with her. Sinclair watched her skim up the stairs, his body aching and stiff, the night grown cold.

⁓

The next morning, Bertie looked up from the large book she held in her lap when Sinclair shoved open the library door.

Light from the hall haloed him, making his hair glisten golden. He looked like an angel from the pages of an illustrated Bible—one of those big, strong archangels who made everyone tremble.

"What the devil is this?" he demanded.

Andrew answered, his loud voice cutting through Bertie's headache. "We're learning books!"

"What, *all* of you?"

Sinclair's sharp gaze swept around the library, taking in Cat, Andrew, Macaulay, Aoife, Peter, Mrs. Hill, and the cook—who rarely came out of her kitchen—bent over books in various parts of the room.

Bertie placed a ribbon in the tome on the English Civil War, closed the book, and got to her feet. "It was my idea. Don't be angry at them."

The members of Sinclair's household looked up, except for Cat and the cook, who kept reading. Cat had found she liked the books on art best, and the cook was reading hard about constellations of the southern hemisphere.

Sinclair's sharp gaze landed on Bertie. Last night, he'd been tender, smiling, holding Bertie in his strong arms. This morning, he was the barrister again, looking at her as though she were another fool in the dock. "*Your* idea?" he rumbled. "Your idea about what?"

"Making people believe I'm a governess. People like your brother-in-law." Bertie twined her fingers together, suddenly nervous under the unwavering gray gaze. "I knew I'd never be able to read all the books in here myself and remember what was in them. I decided that if each person in the house read some of them, then they could come out with a piece of information at an opportune time, and pretend I taught it to them."

Sinclair kept staring. He could knock a person over with that gaze. He was like a wolf with his eye on a poor rabbit who couldn't get away.

"Pretend you taught it to them," he repeated.

"Begging your pardon, sir," Mrs. Hill said. She'd risen to her feet, folding her hands at her waist and looking so very respectable. "It is not a bad plan. We'd not be obvious about it, of course. But the intent is to make Miss Frasier appear to be very, very clever. Then even if her origins are known, it can be argued she's clever enough for that to be overlooked."

Bertie knew Sinclair heard Mrs. Hill, because a muscle moved in his jaw, but he never looked away from Bertie.

"Aye," Macaulay said, looking up from his book on animal husbandry. "I remember the fuss Mrs. McBride's relations kicked up when you married her. Not only did you marry quick, but they hate Scots. We're trying to keep them from kicking up another stink. Miss Caitriona and Master Andrew belong *here,* with us. We're willing to do anything to make sure they stay."

"I say bugger Uncle Edward!" Andrew shouted. "We love you, and Bertie!"

Chapter 13

"Master Andrew, such language," Mrs. Hill said quickly, but she appeared to agree with Andrew.

Sinclair couldn't wrench his gaze from Bertie. In her demure gray, every hair in place, but her eyes full of merriment, she was both a beauty and an erotic joy. Erotic because he knew what she looked like with the buttons loose at her throat, her hair coming down, her eyes closed in pleasure while she parted her lips for his kisses.

He clenched his hands, tamped down his rising hardness, and made himself look around the room. "Since you're all settled in here, Andrew, you won't want to go out with me then," he said in a dry tone.

Andrew's book flew into the air and came down on the floor with a clatter. "Yes, we do! Are we going to the panto-mime? I've never been to a panto. Bertie calls it a panto."

"Panto's not until Christmas, Andrew," Bertie said quickly. "Starting Boxing Day."

"But we'll be in Scotland then!" Andrew wailed.

Sinclair gave him a stern look. "Bertie, get them into their things and outside. Richards is on his way with the coach."

He delivered his command and swung around out of the room, before he realized he'd called her "Bertie" and not "Miss Frasier," to the great interest of the rest of his household.

The weather was cold today. Rain had come in the night, and though the morning had cleared, a thin sheet of ice lay on roadways. Sinclair watched Bertie settle with Andrew and Cat in the carriage seat opposite his, the glowing box on the floor giving the coach some warmth. Bertie kept Andrew from bouncing on the seat by pointing out interesting things about the coach itself as well as what they passed. Stopped Andrew bouncing a little bit, anyway.

Sinclair enjoyed himself watching her. Bertie regarded everything with lively interest—the most ordinary experience was something fascinating to explore. Sinclair had been dead for so long, he didn't notice much anymore. But today, through Bertie, he saw anew the fine marquetry in his own carriage, the crispness of the bright day outside, and the luxury of the Georgian houses they passed. London could be a beautiful and vigorous place. Hadn't Dr. Johnson said, *When a man is tired of London, he is tired of life?*

Bertie, raised in one of the grittiest parts of the city, looked as though she'd never be tired of London.

Richards took them down Park Lane, past its ponderous mansions with lavish gardens, to Hyde Park Corner and on into the park itself. The coach rolled up toward the Serpentine, and finally Richards halted near one of the walking paths. Sinclair alighted first, lifted down Cat and Andrew, then handed out Bertie.

Andrew danced and bounced on his feet, his energy incredible. Sinclair waved to Richards, and the coachman nodded and slowly drove off.

"Can I run now?" Andrew asked Bertie.

Bertie scanned the park around them, her gaze sharpening as she looked down every path, over every person she saw, checking for enemies. Sinclair had already been giving the place a once-over, and he knew Richards had too.

Finally Bertie, after a confirming look with Sinclair, gave Andrew a nod. "Off you go."

Her eyes on Andrew, Bertie tugged a watch out of her pocket. Sinclair glanced at it, then looked again in surprise. Not a watch, but a chronograph, a device that could record the time of any event. Racehorse trainers used them to clock their horses' speeds. They were highly expensive.

Andrew stopped his prancing, marked a line in the dirt with his toe, then crouched down. As Sinclair watched, mystified, Bertie shouted, "Go!"

Andrew bolted. Bertie had clicked a lever on the chronograph, and she eyed both it and Andrew as the boy hurtled himself along.

Andrew was running, flying. His legs weren't very long yet, but they were long enough. He ran like a deer, sprinting over the ground, gracefully leaping over anything in his way. Cat watched him without expression, her arms around her doll.

Andrew ran past an indeterminate line, then he flung his arms out, his pace slowing. He did a long, running turn, then loped back toward them.

Bertie had clicked the chronograph as soon as Andrew slowed. "Look at *that*," she said, shoving the watch in front of Sinclair.

Twenty seconds. Sinclair didn't know the exact distance that his son had run, but it had been a bloody long way.

"He's amazingly fast," Bertie said. "You should put him into races."

Sinclair frowned even as his pride at Andrew's skill rose. "My son is not a horse."

"Races for humans, silly. I knew a bloke who didn't have two coins to rub together, but he could run like nothing you ever saw. A trainer took him up, and now he goes around the world, winning races and prizes. He lives like a king now."

"Andrew can't run races. He has to go to school. I've delayed too long sending him already." The thought of not having Andrew's voice blasting through the house made Sinclair feel suddenly empty. Cat would feel his absence too. Though she never said much, Sinclair knew she was very fond of Andrew.

Bertie's nose wrinkled. "You mean one of the schools where they'll give him cold porridge three times a day? Mrs. Hill told me about *those*."

"He'll go to one that serves meat and bread at least occasionally," Sinclair said, then he caught Bertie's eye. She looked angry, not realizing he was joking. "Don't worry, I'll make sure they treat him very well indeed. He can run races at school if he wants. You're right, he might be good at it."

"Are you sending Cat off to school too?" Bertie asked. Cat glanced at them, hearing. Bertie had no qualm about discussing the children in front of them. Sinclair could hear her explaining why—*Stands to reason. It's their lives, innit?*

"No," Sinclair said sharply. "Cat will stay home." He refused say farewell to both his son and daughter.

"I want to go to Miss Pringle's Select Academy," Cat said, looking straight at Sinclair. "Like Aunt Ainsley and Aunt Isabella."

"I saw your aunt Ainsley at your dad's do," Bertie said to her. "She looked like a fine lady to me."

Cat nodded solemnly. "She is. She used to pick locks and steal things."

Bertie laughed. "Did she?" she asked Sinclair. "Can I meet her?"

Sinclair frowned. "We'll speak of it later."

"About what? Cat going to this Pringle's place or me meeting your sister?"

"Both."

Bertie grinned. "Well, if your sister's anything like Eleanor, I shall like her."

Sinclair growled again, but he wanted to burst out laughing. Then he wanted to grab Bertie and hug her tight. She had no snobbishness in her, no need to impress those born above her in life. Bertie was frank and honest with all, from duchess to scullery maid.

Andrew made it back to them and declared he was hungry. No surprise, since Andrew was always hungry.

Sinclair took his still-prancing son by the hand and led him back toward the coach. Bertie held her hand out for Cat, and

Cat readily slipped her fingers around Bertie's. Cat trusted so few, and yet she was completely comfortable with Bertie.

"Where did you find the chronograph?" Sinclair asked her in curiosity.

Andrew answered for Bertie, in his usual shout. "Aunt Eleanor! *She* got it from Uncle Cameron. Bertie won't let me play with it."

"Because I want to give it back to your Uncle Cameron in one piece," Bertie said firmly. "But yes, Eleanor lent it to me when I said I wished I had a way to know how fast Andrew could run."

Sinclair pictured Eleanor opening her blue eyes wide as she explained to the rough-voiced Cameron that he should lend an expensive chronograph to a pickpocket from a family of thieves. Sinclair also sensed that the chronograph would be safer with Bertie than with anyone else in London.

Sinclair signaled for Richards, who drove the coach back to them, and Sinclair handed Bertie in. The smile she gave him as she pressed his hand made him know he was lost. Any thought of control—of his life, of his emotions—was utterly gone, never to return.

～

The coach stopped after traveling along Piccadilly, and Sinclair handed Bertie down. She loved how he treated her with as much care as he would a lady like his sister and sisters-in-law. Made her feel special, not shoved aside as she had been most of her life.

Sinclair lifted his children to the ground, then took Andrew's hand and reached to Cat. Cat turned away from him and thrust her hand into Bertie's. Bertie's and Sinclair's eyes met, and Bertie shrugged.

Sinclair turned to the door of the great edifice they'd stopped before, and Bertie saw that it was Fortnum and Mason's.

Bertie's interest quickened. She'd never been inside a department store, had been turned away from one she'd tried to enter by its large doorman. Clean stores full of wares were not for the likes of Bertie Frasier.

This doorman bowed respectfully to Sinclair and opened the door for him, also bowing to Bertie as she swept in with Cat. Funny how clean clothes and being in the company of a rich man changed the way people treated her. As long as Bertie kept her mouth shut, she thought, she'd be fine.

The glittering palace of goods made her want to stop and gape. So many people, so many things, so much *food*. Sinclair led them through to a teashop, already crowded with ladies and gentlemen taking their ease. Sinclair settled them into a table in the corner, and admonished Andrew to at least *try* not to shout everything he wanted to say.

Bertie noted the looks from the other tea drinkers, some disapproving. Children were meant to be kept inside nurseries or schoolrooms, seen and not heard. Daft. Andrew didn't know how not to be heard.

Other looks were more fond for the family on an outing— a dad who cared for his children.

Andrew did keep himself quiet, mostly because he spent the time shoveling as many cakes, scones, and pieces of bread into his mouth as he could. Cat ate daintily as usual, saying little.

Sinclair said little as well, but he was polite, making sure Bertie's plate was full, that his family wanted for nothing. Bertie poured the tea, pretending to be very prim, liking it when Sinclair's eyes twinkled at her.

When they were nearly finished, the freezing tones of a woman cut through the warmth of their domestic moment.

"*Mr.* McBride."

A lady had stopped at their table, two companions behind her. She was not much older than Sinclair, with brown hair and dark eyes, but lines framed her mouth. Her chin was tilted high, as though she'd perfected the art of looking down her nose.

Sinclair's friendliness vanished behind a wash of ice as he rose to his feet. "Mrs. Davies."

Mrs. Davies, eh? Wife to Mr. Edward Davies? The one who wanted to take away Cat and Andrew? A knot formed in Bertie's stomach along with a burn of anger.

Andrew, his mouth full, said, "Mornin' Aunt Helena." Cat gave the woman a silent, expressionless look.

"How are you?" Sinclair asked, with an air that said he only inquired to show his children that a person was polite even to someone he loathed. His voice was brittle, Sinclair having become the cold, empty shell of a man once more.

"I am well, thank you," Mrs. Davies said with poor grace. "You are aware, my dear Mr. McBride, that it is *Tuesday*?"

Sinclair gave her a chill nod. "The day after Monday, yes."

Helena's nostrils pinched. "I thought you'd be in chambers, and the children at lessons." Her sharp gaze took in Bertie in her gray dress and white collar. "This is the governess, I suppose."

"You suppose correctly," Sinclair said, an edge to his voice. "This is Miss Frasier."

Bertie smiled up at Mrs. Davies, contriving to look demure and book-learned. She was unsure whether she should rise from her chair or keep her seat—sitting seemed to be safer, but she could not tell whether this pleased or displeased Mrs. Davies. The woman fixed Bertie with another stare then ignored her utterly.

"I suppose this is a lesson on deportment," Mrs. Davies said. The two ladies behind her looked over Andrew, Cat, and Bertie with interest. No doubt they'd be flapping their jaws about the encounter for the rest of the day.

"No, this is a man having tea with his children," Sinclair said, the edge on his voice sharper.

"After which, you'll be buying them all kinds of things not good for them." Mrs. Davies frowned at the remains of a cake on Cat's plate—Andrew's plate was scraped clean. "Toys and other frivolities."

"No doubt we'll be provisioning ourselves for our trip to Scotland," Sinclair said. "For Christmas."

Mrs. Davies scowled even more. She'd ruin her reasonably good looks if she weren't careful, Bertie thought. She already had lines of sourness around her eyes.

"It is far too cold for them in Scotland," Mrs. Davies said. "I've always said so."

"My house is equipped with the latest modes of heating,"
Sinclair said tightly. "We abandoned peat fires and sleeping
rolled in our kilts last winter."

Mrs. Davies did not appear to be amused. "Margaret's
fate was sealed when she married *you*. I'll not let the same
happen to her children."

Sinclair underwent another transformation—this one from
bleak coldness to rage. He stepped to Mrs. Davies as though
ready to throttle her in the middle of the elegant tearoom.

"Ye leave your hands off my children," he said, towering
over her. "And tell bloody Edward to do likewise. I'll take
Cat and Andrew to Scotland and never bring them back
down, if that's what I have to do to keep them from you."

"Not if the law has anything to say about it." Mrs. Davies
had taken a step back, paling under Sinclair's fury. "Edward
lost his sister because of you. You know it. If you lose your
children as well, it will be your own fault."

Mrs. Davies delivered the last in a decided voice, swung
on her heel, and stalked away. The feathers on her hat
bounced, as did her bustle. Another time, Bertie would have
laughed at the absurd picture she made, but Sinclair stood
frozen, face fixed in cold rage.

Bertie rose to him, touching his arm. "We should go,"
she said in a low voice. "People are staring."

Sinclair jerked, as though he'd forgotten she and his children were there. He looked swiftly at Cat and Andrew, who
were watching him, then around at the full tables of the tearoom. So many conversations were flowing, overlapping one
another, that the gawkers might not have heard Mrs. Davies,
but they were looking their way with interest.

Sinclair signaled the waiter, who nodded back, but instead
of settling up, Sinclair lifted Andrew into his arms and started
out. The McBrides must have an account here too.

Bertie took Cat's hand and followed Sinclair. Richards
was nowhere in sight when they emerged onto Piccadilly,
and Sinclair started walking swiftly down the street, not
waiting. Bertie and Cat had to jog to catch up with him.

Sinclair turned sharply into the Burlington Arcade, with

its shops of splendid silver and jewelry; not the fastest route if he were determined to walk all the way to Upper Brook Street. Bertie knew, though, that Sinclair was moving automatically, his anger taking him along without him realizing where he was going. Bertie had done such things on days when her father had upset her too much to stay still.

Bertie caught up to Sinclair. "She's a cow. Don't listen to her."

Sinclair glanced at her, his gaze chill and remote. "We are removing to Scotland," he said abruptly. "You, Cat, and Andrew are, that is. I have trials to finish. Can you live without the soot of London around you all the time? My house in northern Scotland is remote."

Bertie's heart beat faster. She'd never been away from London in her life, didn't know what anything outside it looked like. The thought of leaving it, without Sinclair, did funny things to her insides. She wasn't afraid to leave London—in fact, the idea was exciting—but leaving Sinclair behind was not.

"Can't we wait until you finish up?" Bertie asked. "Then we can all go together."

Sinclair turned to glare down at her, Andrew watching interestedly from his arm, and Bertie's face scalded. She could hardly tell Sinclair she was afraid she'd lose him if she left, that he'd forget all about her. *He don't say no to the ladies*, Macaulay had said.

Bertie rushed on, babbling a little. "Thing is, I've never been on a train, not that far anyway. Hadn't you better come and make sure I do all right?"

Sinclair gazed down at her, as though he tried to fix on what she was saying. "Safer if you go. For Cat and Andrew as well."

"Yeah? Well, what about you? Who's going to look after you if we all run away to Scotland? And what's to say your Mr. Davies won't send the law up there, to pluck away Andrew and Cat while you're here?"

Sinclair's eyes came back into focus. Ah, she had him now. It was a possibility, no doubt.

"If you stay in London, then you stay home," he said in a

hard voice. "No jaunts to the park, not even with Macaulay. Could you stand it? Being cooped up in the house all the time?"

"I can stay!" Andrew shouted. "I'll run up and down the stairs if I can't go to the park. I'd rather go on the train with you, Papa!"

"Cat?" Bertie looked down at the girl. In the constant worry about making Andrew behave, Cat sometimes got rather left out.

Cat shrugged. "As you like, Father."

Sinclair studied her indifferent face, and his frown deepened. Bertie shook her head the slightest bit at him. Now was not the time to wonder about Cat.

"I have cases scheduled all the way through next week," Sinclair said. "I can't get away before then." He switched his gaze to Bertie, and she tried not to look too eager. "Very well, then, stay in London and wait for me. The Old Bailey adjourns Tuesday next, come what may. Even murderers have to wait when judges want their Christmas."

~~~~~

Sinclair lay awake late that night, gaze on the ceiling, his insomnia reaching out to tap him. He'd slept surprisingly well these last few nights, his mind eager to take him to dreams of Bertie, but the encounter with Helena Davies had left him in turmoil.

Margaret's fate was sealed when she married you. The accusation resounded in his head. Sinclair remembered every detail of Helena saying it, the fix of her eyes, the movement of her mouth, the shrill tone of her voice. Helena had worked to take most of her northern Irish lilt out of her voice when she'd moved to England, trying desperately to distance herself from those Irish who wanted freedom from English rule. As a result, she always sounded wrong and stilted, her words overly pronounced.

Helena had made the same accusation she had today more baldly after Daisy's death, in private—*You killed her.*

Edward had agreed with his wife, still did.

Tonight Sinclair had put out all the lights and pulled the

drapes, so that darkness coated his bedroom, but he turned his head and gazed straight at Daisy's photograph. He knew what he'd see if there'd been light enough—the dark eyes that had looked out at him from the photo had never been accusing, only loving.

She's a cow, Bertie had said stoutly about Helena. *Don't listen to her.*

Bertie had a way of putting things—straightforward, practical, never wavering. Sinclair's first instinct had been to tuck Bertie and his children under his arms and rush them to Scotland then and there. They'd be away from Helena, away from Bertie's vengeful Jeffrey, away from the noise and darkness of the city. Constant, constant noise. Though Sinclair had thought about London's lively side today when they'd gone out, tonight he hated it. He wanted Scotland, his home.

Bertie, on the other hand, embraced London. She was a child of the city, laughing at its inconvenience, blithely walking through smoke, soot, and dirt as though it couldn't cling to her. She was down-to-earth; Sinclair was lost in the fog.

In Scotland, he could be alone with her. No prying neighbors. No solicitors fighting one another to hand him their cases, no judges watching Sinclair to see whether he was worthy to be one of them. In Scotland, in his house beside the deep loch, Sinclair could be truly alone. With Bertie. He needed her. In Scotland, he'd bring her into his life, no matter what.

His thoughts turned to her teaching him about pickpocketing, and he wanted to laugh. Bertie had plucked Sinclair clean each time, showing him he was hopeless before her skills. Distraction indeed.

But he had skills of his own. He'd use them. His body warmed. Bertie would learn just what sort of skills Sinclair had, and what kind of distractions he could cause with them. With luck, they wouldn't see the out-of-doors for days.

Sinclair let his eyes drift closed, ready to let his imagination show him what they'd do, step by slow step.

He opened them the next moment, coming alert.

He'd heard a tinkle of glass downstairs, and a few seconds after that, a muffled thump.

Chapter 14

Sinclair quietly rose, pulled on a dressing gown and slippers, and moved silently from his bedroom into his study. He wasn't afraid—he knew in his blood and bones that there was a threat, but he also knew he could deal with it.

He made his way to his desk, unlocking and sliding out the drawer he always kept in good repair. Inside was a Webley pistol and a box of bullets. Fingers steady, Sinclair loaded the gun, tucked it into his dressing gown pocket, and left the room.

No one else hurried to see what the noise had been. Macaulay slept in a room off the kitchens downstairs, as did the cook and Peter, and they might not have heard. The maids and Mrs. Hill had comfortable rooms in the attics, likely too far away from the lower rooms to have been awakened by the soft sounds.

The house was dark, the stairwell lit by only one lamp, turned low, on each floor. Mrs. Hill liked to save on the gas, so most lights were extinguished when the household went to bed. If anyone got up in the night, rushed about, and tripped, that was their own fault, in Mrs. Hill's opinion.

Sinclair had come to know the stairs well on his sleepless nights, and he traversed them without difficulty. He knew which stair creaked and which spindle on the railing was loose, and how to move past them like smoke.

Down, down, down to the ground floor. He heard no more thumps, but he did hear a clinking sound, coupled with low voices, coming from the dining room.

Sinclair put his hand on his pistol, lifted it from his pocket, and eased open the dining room door.

Bertie stood near the table, watching as a beefy young man filled a valise with silver pieces taken from the open breakfront. The tinkling he'd heard had come from the thief breaking the glass door of the cabinet, which was always kept locked—Mrs. Hill and Sinclair had the only keys. The thump must have been the stout valise being hoisted to the table. The windows on the far end of the room, overlooking the garden, were closed, whole, and unbroken. A kerosene lamp burned at the end of the table, giving a warm glow to the scene.

"I told you, I ain't giving you any more," Bertie said. "You take that and get out."

"For this time," the man said. "I'll be back. You'll have more for me if you know what's good for you, Bertie-girl—and for them."

"No, I won't. You'll get me sacked, and worse. You know my dad will beat you if my wages get taken away, and I tell him it's your fault."

"You listen here." The man, who must be Jeffrey, abandoned the valise and went to Bertie. "You *will* rob this fool blind for us, and if you get caught, it's you what gets to hang. Serves you right for abandoning us. You don't belong here, and you know it, so stop pretending."

"I ain't pretending. The kids like me. I'm good at looking after them."

"You'll have to run sometime. You'll leave them high and dry, just like you did me and your dad, and all your friends. You wouldn't let us have Basher McBride when you led him to my mates, and now you're telling us to leave him alone again. You *are* his tart, I know it. And I'm not having it."

Jeffrey grabbed Bertie by the front of her dressing gown, jerking her to him. She suppressed a yelp, but she fought, fists pounding his shoulders. Jeffrey yanked her dressing gown open . . . and found the barrel of Sinclair's revolver pressed to his head.

"No," Bertie said, fading back in dismay.

Sinclair dug the pistol deeper into Jeffrey's temple. "Let go of her, leave the silver, and get out of my house," he said. "If I ever see you again, I will shoot you. If you don't go, I will shoot you right now. Do you understand me?"

Jeffrey swallowed, his eyes wide, believing. He opened his hands and released the folds of Bertie's dressing gown.

"Out," Sinclair repeated.

Jeffrey kept his eyes on Sinclair's pistol as he backed away. "Right, right, I'm going."

His hand stretched toward the valise as he passed it, and Sinclair took a step toward him. "I said *leave it.*"

Jeffrey clenched his fist, turned swiftly, and made for the window. He opened it easily, climbed through, and disappeared into darkness.

Sinclair shut the window on the freezing draft and found the lock broken, obviously forced by Jeffrey. No matter, he'd have Macaulay repair it in the morning.

Sinclair turned back to Bertie. In the light of the one lamp, her blue eyes were huge in her pale face, lamplight shining on the thick braid of hair that flowed over her shoulder.

"I'm sorry," she was saying. "He came tonight—he said he'd hurt you and the kids, kill you even, if I didn't help him. I thought a bit of silver you never use wouldn't do no harm. He'd be caught as soon as he tried to pawn it, the idiot."

Sinclair didn't hear her. He laid the gun carefully on the table and went to her.

"Never mind." Sinclair brushed back Bertie's warm hair as he drew her close. He kissed the top of her head. "It doesn't matter, lass."

Bertie was shaking, and Sinclair realized after a heartbeat that she was crying. His Bertie, the courageous woman who looked at life and all its grimness with a bright smile, was crying in remorse.

Sinclair tilted her face up to him. "Stop, love."

Bertie's face was wet with tears. Sinclair leaned down and kissed one away, then he kissed her parted lips. She kissed him back, her mouth trembling, her hands curling on his chest. Her warmth wove around Sinclair despite the situation, intoxicating him.

The silence in the house meant they were alone in the night. Sinclair moved his touch to her buttocks, firm and sweet under the gown, his arousal hot and stiff under his loose dressing gown and nightshirt. Nothing existed but her kisses, her unfettered body against his . . .

Ice-cold wind blew into his back as the window slid up again. Sinclair heard the cock of a pistol.

Instinct took over. Sinclair flung Bertie down, the two of them landing on the carpet, limbs tangling. The gun boomed at the same time, and then there was another cry of surprise and pain, one too high-pitched to belong to Macaulay.

Sinclair was on his feet and out the dining room door, snatching up the falling body of Andrew, who had blood on his chest and looked up at his father with confusion in his eyes.

Bertie, her lungs constricting, snatched up the pistol Sinclair had laid on the table and rushed to the window. No one was there. She saw Jeffrey's form vaulting to the top of the high garden wall and over, but he was too far away to stop.

She turned back, discarding the pistol on the sideboard, to where Sinclair cradled Andrew in the doorway. Andrew was still breathing, little gasping pants, blood all over his chest.

"Bertie, help me." Sinclair's voice was harsh.

Bertie fell to her knees. Sinclair ripped open Andrew's nightshirt, exposing his pale chest and a red, gaping wound. Sinclair shrugged off his robe and stripped off his own nightshirt, kneeling in nothing but his underbreeches.

He wadded up the nightshirt and pressed it to Andrew's shoulder.

"Hold that right there," he said to Bertie. "Use as much pressure as you can. I have to take out the bullet."

"A doctor . . ."

"Too long to wait. I've done plenty of field surgery, taken bullets out of my friends."

None of them had been eight years old, Bertie would wager. She obeyed, leaning her weight on the nightshirt, warm from Sinclair and now stained red with blood.

Andrew's eyes were closed, his face waxy. But his chest still rose and fell. That was something. As long as the chest went up and down, Andrew was alive.

Footsteps thumped on stairs, from above and below, the household rushing to see what was the matter. Cat trailed them, gripping her doll in both arms, her face pale.

Sinclair moved the cloth enough to spread the lips of the wound. "Hold him down," he said to Bertie. "I'll need clean water, and a needle and thread," he snapped over his shoulder.

Footsteps pounded again as the servants hurried to obey. Cat sank down on one of the dining room chairs, her blue eyes wide, but Bertie couldn't leave Andrew to go to her.

Sinclair dipped his already bloody fingers into the wound, and in one go, closed his fingers around the bullet and drew it out.

Andrew's eyes flew open, and he screamed. Bertie held him, her heart beating wildly, and wanted to scream with him. Andrew cried out once more, then slumped back to the floor, eyes closing, but his chest rose again with his breath.

Sinclair dropped the bloody bullet onto the rug. A small thing, but too large to be lodged in Andrew's little body.

"More pressure," Sinclair said. He joined Bertie in holding the nightshirt over the wound. Sweat streaked Sinclair's bare arms and chest, in spite of the cold.

Mrs. Hill came hurrying in with a sewing box, Aoife and Peter with water they sloshed everywhere. Mrs. Hill handed the sewing box to Bertie and Macaulay took the pans of water, setting them on the floor. Cloths were already inside.

Macaulay touched Sinclair's shoulder. "Let me, lad. You rest now."

"No," Sinclair said in a hard voice. "I'll do it. Fetch a constable and get after that bastard."

"Already done. Man might be long gone though."

"Doesn't matter," Bertie said. "I know the places he'll go." She relinquished her place to Macaulay, and opened the sewing box and threaded a needle.

A circle of feet and dressing gowns surrounded them, the entire household watching over their favorite boy. Sinclair took the needle from Bertie and instructed Macaulay to keep holding the pad of nightshirt where it was.

Sinclair smoothed out the thread with his fingers, held the lips of the wound together, and plunged the needle into his son. Andrew barely whimpered this time. His eyes remained closed, body limp, as Sinclair, his face tight, sewed up the wound.

The constable arrived, along with a doctor. Bertie only noticed the doctor when a black bag landed on the floor near her. Sinclair closed off the last stitch, carefully cutting the thread with the sharp scissors Bertie handed him.

The doctor, a lean man with a thick beard, bent down to them. "Competent job, Mr. McBride."

Sinclair didn't answer, didn't acknowledge him. The doctor pressed his hand to Andrew's brow, felt his cheeks.

"No fever yet," he said. "But that will come. We need to keep him warm and get him up to bed."

Sinclair kept his hand on Andrew, the needle dangling from his fingers. His gaze was fixed on his son's face, the bleakness starting to come over him again. Bertie took the needle and thread from him and dropped the bloody things into her pocket.

"I'll take him up." Macaulay rose, reaching for Andrew.

"No." Sinclair's answer was vehement. He got to his feet, lifting Andrew gently in his arms. "I'll take him to my bed."

Bertie caught the trailing nightshirt that was still over the wound as Sinclair started for the hall, carrying Andrew. She trotted after them, holding the shirt, as Sinclair went swiftly up the two flights of stairs, through his dark study and into his bedroom.

"For God's sake, put on the lights," he snapped. "Keep it light. And warm. It's too damned cold in here."

Bertie turned up the gas on the nearest lamp and lit it, but she'd turned the gas too high, and it nearly exploded into light. She hastily turned it down then went to the next sconce. The fire in Sinclair's hearth was low, so Bertie poked it to life, adding a bit more coal from the bin.

Sinclair's bed was wide, with a thick mattress and a wooden head- and footboard that curved around the corners of the bed. It was big enough for two, but looked overly large with only one small lad in the middle. Andrew lay so still, his body ghostly white, the color of his skin blending with his hair, light like his father's.

Sinclair sat beside him, still half naked, his muscled back tight, his shoulders rigid. Bertie picked up Sinclair's fallen dressing gown, thick and padded, and draped it over his shoulders. He didn't acknowledge her, his attention only for his son.

The doctor set his bag down on the other side of the bed and bent over Andrew. Sinclair at least let the man examine him, the doctor listening to Andrew's heart and briefly lifting Andrew's eyelids.

"The bullet doesn't appear to have hit anything vital," the doctor announced. He lightly touched the stitches. "Through a fleshy part it looks like. But watch him. If you see blood on his lips, you send for me at once."

Sinclair helped the doctor pull the covers up over Andrew to his chin. He gave the doctor an absent nod, and the doctor turned to Bertie and drew her aside.

"Who are you, young woman?"

Bertie blinked, for a moment not entirely sure. "I'm Bertie. Miss Frasier. I mean, the governess."

"Good, then Master Andrew has someone to look after him." He handed Bertie several packets. "Mix these in water and make him drink it, several times a day. Take the empty packets back to the chemist—he'll make up more for you. Keep Andrew warm and still, very still. We don't need the wound to open and him to bleed. And examine the wound for discoloration. There will be bruising, but we don't want to see streaks of red, especially ones leading toward the heart. That means infection. Can you remember all that?"

"Yes." Bertie swallowed. "Of course."

"Good lass. You're English?"

Bertie spread her hands. "As English as they come."

The doctor nodded and lowered his head to speak to her. "These Scots have odd notions. Make sure Master Andrew has much rest and no cold air. We don't want him to take a chill." He glanced at the bed, where Sinclair was sitting, holding Andrew's hand. "Get Mr. McBride to take some brandy and lie down. He's had a shock."

Bertie managed a nod. "Right you are."

The doctor smiled and patted her shoulder. "Good girl. If Master Andrew takes worse, you send for me at once."

He took up his bag and walked out of the room, nodding once to Aoife, who held the door open for him. Macaulay looked after the doctor with some distaste, no doubt having heard him proclaim that "Scots had odd notions."

Mrs. Hill came bustling in with a decanter in her hand. She fetched a glass from Sinclair's study and brought it back into the bedroom. "Brandy, sir," she said to Sinclair. "Best thing for you. And then you go lie down in the spare bedroom. We'll watch over Master Andrew."

Sinclair didn't respond. He kept Andrew's hand in his, stroking the boy's fingers.

"Let me," Bertie said, reaching for the brandy.

Mrs. Hill shook her head. "You need to look after Miss Caitriona. She's with Peter, but the lad doesn't know what to do. Go on, now."

Caitriona. Bertie's heart gave a guilty thud. In the panic, Bertie hadn't kept account of where the girl was. She'd assumed Cat had followed them all upstairs, but she was nowhere to be seen.

"Right," Bertie said, and hurried out of the room.

Chapter 15

Bertie's heart was like lead as she took Cat by the hand and walked her from the ground floor, where she'd been sitting with Peter, to the nursery. Cat said nothing, quiet as usual, but her hand was ice cold.

Bertie turned up all the lights in the nursery and stirred the fire high. Fear needed to be treated with light and heat, not darkness. When she finished, she found Cat sitting at the table, doll in her lap, her gaze fixed on the fire.

Cat was strikingly different from Andrew in looks—her hair was dark and glossy, her blue eyes framed with black lashes. She took after her mother, Mrs. Hill had told Bertie, and Mrs. McBride's photo confirmed, while Andrew was a miniature of Sinclair.

Bertie ought to give Cat tea or something, but she couldn't find the wherewithal to go back downstairs or even ring for one of the maids. They were upset too. Andrew, for all his tearing ways, was easy to love.

Cat was more of a challenge, the poor lamb. Bertie drew a chair next to Cat's and put her arm around the girl's shoulder. Cat didn't shrug it away, which told Bertie she wanted the comfort.

"Is Andrew going to die?" she asked Bertie in a quiet voice.

Bertie's first impulse was to lie, to soothe her fears and say, *Of course he isn't!* But Bertie had lived with ugly truth all her life, and she'd learned to prefer it. Better to face something straight on than to hide and try to pretend it away. Hurt more when you had to stop pretending, in the end.

"I don't know, sweetie," she said, stroking Cat's long braid. "But your dad will take care of him, and the doctor."

"They took care of Mama too. But she died." Cat's voice was faint. "I don't know what to do."

"Well, not much we *can* do is there? Except hope. And pray."

"I don't believe in God."

Bertie started. Personally, she and God had an off-again, on-again relationship, but to hear it put so baldly, from a child, surprised her. But then, Cat had seen her mother taken away from her and her father become an absolute blank, and no one, divine or human, had been able to stop either occurrence.

"Well, *I* believe it," Bertie said. "I think if one of us does, that should be good enough."

Cat gave her a skeptical look. "When Mama died, a lady from Sunday school told me I should be happy, because it meant Mama had been very good and was let into heaven early. She said the angels hadn't wanted to wait to reward her."

"Oh." *Stupid woman.* What a horrible thing to tell a child! Bertie recalled a story she'd heard at the tender age of six, in which angels watched for children who were exceptionally good, and took years away from their lives so they'd die and go to heaven quicker. Bertie remembered being terrified and trying to be as bad as she could possibly be.

"Don't you worry about that," Bertie said, patting Cat's hand. "That's nonsense, that is. It isn't even in the Bible.

What I remember of it anyway." Not that she'd read any of it herself, but some of the stories from the church her mother had taken her to had stuck with her. "That's ladies who don't know anything, and thinking they're comforting you. I wouldn't take no notice."

"Andrew isn't good," Cat said.

"There you are then." Bertie grinned at her. "He'll be fine."

"But everyone loves him."

"So do you," Bertie said.

Cat's eyes filled with tears, and she nodded.

Bertie drew her close, doll and all. "It's all right, love. You worry about him all you want, and I'll pray. We'll help your dad, and we'll get Andrew better." Then Bertie would hunt Jeffrey down and make him pay. If Andrew died . . .

"Do you love my papa?" Cat asked.

Bertie jumped, but again, she couldn't lie. She gathered Cat closer and rested her cheek on the girl's hair. "Yeah," she said softly. "I think I do."

~~~~~

Sinclair held Andrew's hand far into the night and the wee hours of the morning. When he felt sleep coming upon him, he stretched out beside Andrew, laying his hand on Andrew's chest. If Andrew so much as twitched, Sinclair would wake.

Sleep came in waves. It would surround Sinclair in blackness for a few minutes, then ease up, then sweep over him again. Through it all Andrew never moved.

When morning light came, so did Andrew's fever. Sinclair came wide awake, never feeling his restless night. He commanded cool water to be brought and a tonic called Warburg's tincture. The tincture was meant for malarial diseases, but Sinclair knew by experience it would work to bring down fever. The powders the doctor had handed to Bertie were useless—he knew that too. Good for dyspepsia and not much else.

Andrew, restless, didn't want to swallow the medicine, but Sinclair got it into him. He bathed Andrew's face and hands, changing the bedding himself when Andrew soiled it.

All day Sinclair nursed his son, not knowing what time it was or caring. Somewhere during the day, he let Macaulay talk him into donning a shirt and trousers, but Sinclair saw no reason to dress completely. He napped off and on, felt the deepening of whiskers on his face. He knew others came and went, but Sinclair couldn't pull his concentration from Andrew.

Sinclair always sensed Bertie's presence though, even when he didn't turn his head to look at her, even when she said nothing to him. Cool calm stole over the room whenever she was in it, as though she brought peace and reassurance with her.

When the sun went down, Peter restocked the coal fire, and Macaulay brought Sinclair a cup of beef tea and forced him to drink it. Bertie came in as Macaulay departed.

She didn't speak, only closed the door quietly, made her way to the bedside, and laid the back of her hand against Andrew's cheek. His fever had come down a little, or so Sinclair thought, but he was still far from well.

"Cat is finally asleep," Bertie said. "I gave her some tea with sugar and lots of milk—seemed to do the trick. The poor mite is all in." She touched the bandages on Andrew's shoulder then looked at Sinclair. "So are you, I'm thinking."

"I'll sleep when it's over," Sinclair said sharply.

"I can stay with him. I'll watch him every second, believe me."

"No." Sinclair didn't move from where he sat on the bed. "I don't want to leave, in case . . ."

"I'd wake you. I promise. The minute there's any change."

"No!" The word rang, Sinclair's voice raspy. He shook his head as Bertie's eyes widened. "When Maggie . . . Daisy . . . when she was ill, a nurse stayed with her. The nurse promised to wake me, and she didn't. She thought it would be easier for me. But I didn't . . . I didn't even get to say good-bye."

Sinclair's voice broke and his eyes stung. He dragged in a shuddering breath, dismayed that it shook with sobs.

Bertie moved to him with a quiet rustle of fabric. Her arms

came around him, and Sinclair found himself cradled against her, her cheek on his hair, her hands warm on his back.

She was so strong, this woman who'd come to him out of nowhere. Sinclair had been standing in the cold, all alone. *When you're ready for me to move on, I know you'll tell me,* he'd said in his thoughts to Daisy, and then Bertie had bumped into him.

He hadn't been able to cease thinking of Bertie since. Only his son struggling to live had pulled him away from her.

"I'm sorry," Bertie was saying. "I'll never be able to say, in the whole of my life, how sorry I truly am."

Sinclair gently parted her arms and wiped his eyes. "What are you talking about?"

"This is my fault." Her blue eyes were sad, full of remorse. "If I'd not followed you, I never would have led Jeffrey here, and Andrew wouldn't be hurt. But no, I had to find out where you lived, decided to stay here in your house . . ."

"Why did you?"

Bertie stopped in confusion. "What do you mean?"

"Why did you come here? You'd given me back the watch, I'd paid you to lead me back to familiar streets. I'd thought our contract at an end."

A flush stole over her cheeks, one that rivaled the feverish stain on Andrew's. "I wanted to see you, didn't I? To make sure you were all right."

Sinclair let some amusement trickle through his gut-wrenching worry. "Not to look over what pickings you might get from me? You don't have to pretend."

Her brows drew down. "You still think I came to steal from you?"

"No. Not anymore." Sinclair squeezed her hand. "But when you first found out where I lived, you must have thought me a good mark. Not paying much attention to the world, my nose stuck in my papers. Ripe for the plucking."

Bertie tried to pull from his grasp. "I told you. I wanted to see you again. If you don't believe that, then you don't."

Sinclair lost his smile. "I don't know what I believe anymore."

They watched each other in silence a moment, Sinclair holding her hand as though he couldn't let go. Her stiff fingers relaxed, and she didn't try to pull away again.

"Believe me now," Bertie said. "You need to rest, or you'll get sick yourself. Cat and Andrew don't need to lose you too." She smoothed her free hand along the sheets. "You lie right here beside him, and I'll sit by the bed and watch him like a hawk. The minute he moves, I'll wake you. Can't say fairer than that."

Sinclair met her gaze, her eyes full of sincerity. Ironic that a backstreet London pickpocket could speak more truth than the men of law he worked with every day.

"Your name should be Verity," he heard himself say. "Truth." She was right, he needed sleep.

Bertie wrinkled her nose. "Well, I got *Roberta* hung on me, didn't I? My mum called me Bertie, so that's what I like."

Sinclair let go of her hand. His ached to have to release hers, but she was right—he'd do Andrew no good if he was carted off to a sickbed himself. He lay down, gently, so as not to disturb his son, and Bertie pulled quilts over him.

"I'll be right here," she said. "On the other side of the bed, in that chair. Andrew won't move a hair without me knowing."

Sinclair felt some relief loosen his limbs. "Thank you, Bertie."

Bertie leaned down and kissed his cheek, her loose hair brushing his skin. "It's my pleasure."

Bertie watched Sinclair sleep. Thin winter sunlight touched his hair, as fair as Andrew's, and brushed the lines about his eyes.

He was exhausted. Bertie understood the exhaustion, and his terror. Losing someone was never easy, and never grew easier. Losing your child must be hardest of all. Though Andrew wasn't her son, Bertie knew that if he didn't live, her grief would cut her deeply and never heal.

Sinclair, a strong man, had already suffered much. Bertie remembered what Macaulay had said about Mrs. McBride's death—*When she was gone, there wasn't much left of him.*

Bertie vowed, looking down at Sinclair as he reposed on the bed, that she would make sure he didn't lose any more of himself. No matter what.

Sinclair slept on, the sun rose, and the outside world rumbled around them. Macaulay and Mrs. Hill came in from time to time, both trying to persuade Bertie to relinquish her place, but she refused. She'd promised. Mrs. Hill brought her tea and toast, and Macaulay, blankets, but they seemed to understand. Macaulay tried to keep up his bluff good spirits, assuring everyone that Master Andrew was a tough little lad, but Mrs. Hill's eyes were red-rimmed, her usual briskness absent.

Clocks around the town were striking eleven in the morning when Andrew's eyes fluttered open. He took in Bertie, his father sleeping on his back, arm flung over his face, and said, "That man shot me."

"Andrew, sweetie." Bertie's heart beat swiftly as she touched his forehead. He was still warm, but damp with sweat, the fever broken. "Sinclair." Bertie gently shook him. She hated to wake him, but a promise was a promise. "Andrew—"

Sinclair came awake and sat up in one motion. He turned to Andrew, stark fear in his eyes, and those eyes grew wet as he looked down at his son blinking back at him.

"You had a gun too, Papa," Andrew said, his usually loud voice faint. "Did you shoot him back? Wish I'd seen that."

The doctor, returning to check on the patient that afternoon, expressed surprise that Andrew was alive at all, and put it down to his powders.

"Bicarbonate of soda," Sinclair said in disgust after the doctor left. "My cook could have prepared that, and done a better job of it."

He made Andrew take more of Warburg's tincture to keep

the fever down, as much as Andrew complained of the taste. Andrew also wanted to get up, but Sinclair forbade it. He told Andrew he'd seen many a gunshot wound in the army, and he knew exactly how long a man needed to stay down to heal. Being compared to a wounded soldier made Andrew's grin return, though weakly. But at least he agreed to stay in bed.

Sinclair convinced Bertie to take her turn at sleeping. Bertie rested for a time, but she soon was back in the nursery with Caitriona, who didn't need to be neglected. Once Cat was reassured that her brother would live and get better, she returned to her usual cool indifference, or at least pretended to. The relief in her eyes was evident, but Cat held it in, her earlier need to confide in Bertie gone.

Bertie had never met a child who closed herself away as much as Cat did. Even children Bertie had grown up with— beaten and hungry—had more life in them than Cat. Cat was a lovely little girl, with her ripples of dark hair always topped with a big bow, a matching bow on her fashionable dresses. But the child inside was vastly unhappy.

Cat did her lessons without much interest, the only thing that absorbed her being whatever she wrote or drew in her notebook. When Bertie expressed interest in the notebook, Cat gave her a look of alarm and hugged the book to her chest. She didn't relax until Bertie assured her she wouldn't pry.

The day after Andrew awoke, Sinclair said he was ready to be transferred back to his own bed. Sinclair carried him there himself. A hired nurse settled in to look after him, but Sinclair showed no hurry to rush back to chambers. Later that afternoon, he sent for Bertie to come down to him—not to his study, Aoife said, bringing the message, but to the downstairs drawing room.

When Bertie tripped inside, she found Sinclair not alone. Several large men were with him, two in kilts, one in a severe suit. They looked enough like the Duke of Kilmorgan to be his brothers, which, in fact, they turned out to be.

"This is Detective Chief Inspector Fellows," Sinclair said, indicating the man in the suit. "He wants you to tell him all about Jeffrey and where we'll find him."

Chapter 16

Bertie had twigged that Fellows was Old Bill as soon as she set eyes on him, criminal investigation, no less. She recognized his name—Fellows had been a thorn in the side of East End villains for years. He always got his man, or woman, no matter what.

The way Fellows sized up Bertie with his eagle eyes told Bertie he knew all about her, or at least what she was. What she *used* to be, Bertie corrected herself.

The other two men in the room were as formidable as Fellows, but in different ways. The tallest one was Lord Cameron, the one with the horses. Bertie had seen him at the soiree, and she'd observed the way Sinclair's sister had laid a tender hand on his arm whenever she'd spoken to him. Lord Cameron might be a hard man, but Ainsley obviously loved him.

The other stood a little away from his two brothers and Sinclair, not looking at them. He stared at nothing, in fact, his eyes a blank, and the others didn't seem to find this unusual.

If Bertie told these men where to find Jeffrey, he would go down, she understood that. She saw it in their faces, even of the one who wasn't looking at her. Jeffrey would shiver in jail for a brief time, then be taken out and hanged or banged up with penal servitude for life.

But Bertie's anger against him was strong. Jeffrey had broken into the house of a man who'd done him no harm, had tried to make Bertie help him rob it, and had shot *Andrew*. Didn't matter that hitting Andrew had been an accident; Jeffrey had shot with intent to kill. He'd hurt so many in his life that even Bertie's East End neighbors, who knew Jeffrey well, wouldn't blame her for peaching on him.

"I know all his hiding places," Bertie said readily. "Mind you, he knows I know, so he might not have gone to any of them. Then again, he isn't very wise."

She named them: a deserted house in Spitalfields, rooms in a lane off Whitechapel, and the house of his mistress—a lady Jeffrey didn't think Bertie knew about—in Hackney.

Inspector Fellows gave Bertie a nod when she finished, one that told her he knew exactly what she'd done, and that he respected her for it.

Lord Cameron said, "Good. Then let's go find the bastard."

"I'll get my coat," Sinclair said.

The other Mackenzie, who hadn't spoken a word or even acknowledged the conversation, now looked at Sinclair and said, "Andrew."

Sinclair nodded at him. "Miss Frasier, this is my brother-in-law, Ian Mackenzie. Will you take him up to the nursery to see Andrew?" He hesitated. "Do you want to come hunting with us, Ian? We can wait."

Lord Ian shook his head. He turned his back and crossed the room toward the piano, sitting down on its bench. The others let him go, not trying to persuade him.

"Any hunting will be done by me," Fellows said, giving Sinclair a severe look. "I'm only bringing you along so you can watch the man be arrested. Understand?"

"I heard you," Sinclair said, as though this were part of an ongoing argument. "Bertie . . ." He paused in the doorway and looked at her fully. "Thank you."

"I wish you wouldn't go," Bertie said, chilled. "He's dangerous, is Jeffrey."

"I have to go. You know that."

Bertie shook her head. "No, you really don't. Inspector Fellows is a good copper. He'll find him."

"I know that *here*." Sinclair touched the side of his head, his short hair brushing his fingertips. "But I need to see, to know it *here*." He touched the center of his chest and held her gaze with his clear gray eyes. "Don't worry, love. I'll come home."

The carriage pulled up to the house, Richards at the reins. Sinclair touched Bertie's cheek. His eyes were glittering, the man inside him awake and ready to do battle for his son. She knew she'd never talk him out of it—if this had been a hundred years or so ago, he'd be grabbing his claymore on his way out instead of his coat and hat.

The touch became a caress, Sinclair's eyes holding heat, then he turned away and went out.

"You just make sure you bring him back whole," Bertie said to Inspector Fellows.

Fellows flashed her an irritated glance as he took his coat and hat from Peter. "I will endeavor, Miss Frasier," he said, then went on out the door after Sinclair and Cameron.

Ian Mackenzie was still in the drawing room when Bertie, her throat tight, turned back to it. Ian softly pressed the keys of the piano, playing a trickling tune that Bertie recognized from music halls. Gilbert and Sullivan, the song about the major general.

Bertie went to the piano, jittery and impatient. "You wanted to pay Andrew a visit, your lordship?"

Ian didn't answer, the music continuing. After he'd played about half the song, he said, "When I met my Beth, she taught me to play this. She sat with me at the piano, and I kissed her."

The words were simple, but Bertie saw the look in the big man's eyes as he spoke them. She couldn't help but smile a little. "Aw. That's sweet."

"Fellows wanted to pin a murder on me back then. Beth stopped him."

"Oh." Bertie blinked. "I suppose that's sweet too."

"You will like my Beth." Ian took his fingers from the piano, the music ceasing. "I used to hate my memory. Now I'm glad of it. Things remind me of her." His accent was not as pronounced as Sinclair's, but it was there, the Scots richness running through his words.

"I like that," Bertie said. She too had memories now, of Sinclair and his family, things that would remind her of them. "Andrew's upstairs. If he's not asleep, he'll be trying to bully his way out of bed. He's very hearty, is our Andrew."

Ian lost his faraway look to flash Bertie an ironic glance. She saw intelligence in Ian's eyes, and the depths of him, which she wagered many people would miss. Mrs. Hill had told Bertie about Lord Ian during one of her gossipy moods, how he'd spent time in an asylum, but Bertie saw nothing of the madman about him.

Flashing him a grin, Bertie led Lord Ian out of the drawing room and upstairs to the nursery.

~～

They found Jeffrey Mitchell in Hackney, in the rooms of his mistress. Sinclair had told Richards to drive there first—if Jeffrey thought Bertie didn't know about this woman, he'd likely seek refuge with her.

Fellows didn't bother knocking; he simply had his two burly constables kick the door open. Jeffrey, stirring coals in a rusting kitchen stove, turned on them with the poker.

Jeffrey was fast, beating back the constables with deadly intent. A woman came screeching out of the bedroom in her dressing gown. She didn't bother beseeching them—she grabbed a pan from the stove and threw the hot water in it at the constables. Then she came with the sturdy pan after Fellows, who'd waded in and grabbed Jeffrey.

Cameron stepped behind the woman and seized her, lifting her from her feet as she screamed obscenities. He half threw her onto the sofa, then blocked her way when she tried to get up.

The neighbors were coming, pouring out of doorways and up the stairs to see what was going on. Some cheered on Jeffrey and his mistress; some came to encourage the police. Jeffrey took advantage of the chaos to twist from Fellows's grasp and make for the window. They were one floor above the ground, but Jeffrey shoved open the shutters and jumped.

Sinclair, still in the hall, ran back down the stairs, pushing aside those in his way. He emerged from the house to see Jeffrey dash into a passage that ran alongside the building. Sinclair went after him, reaching Jeffrey as he was hauling himself up a wall at the end to make his escape.

Sinclair grabbed Jeffrey by the leg and yanked him down. The crate Jeffrey had used to boost himself gave way, sending Jeffrey, Sinclair, and crate to the ground. Jeffrey rolled to his feet first and kicked Sinclair in the stomach.

Sinclair's breath went out of him as pain washed through his body. The pain coupled with the annoyed look in Jeffrey's eyes—*annoyed*—made Sinclair's red anger rise.

He'd been in plenty of battles in the heat and desperation of the desert that would make Jeffrey run far and fast. Sinclair and four of his men had once fought their way out of a place where they'd been cut off, out of water, and had only enough ammunition between the five of them for one gun. They'd fought hand-to-hand with some of the best-trained men in North Africa, and they'd won through—to nearly die of thirst picking their way back to camp. But all five had made it.

They'd survived because Sinclair had refused to let them die. Rolling over and giving in wasn't in his nature, no matter what the odds.

His yell of rage boomed through the passage. Sinclair came to his feet and launched himself at Jeffrey, all the grief and anger in him focused on one target—the man who'd nearly killed his son.

Jeffrey fought, first in anger, then in fear and desperation. He wrenched himself away and tried to run, but Sinclair grabbed his coat with both hands and hauled him back. Sinclair threw Jeffrey against a wall and raised his fist to strike, strike, and strike again.

"Leave . . . off," Jeffrey panted, blood spewing onto Sinclair's greatcoat.

Sinclair gave him another furious punch. "You shot my *son,* you filthy bastard. He's eight bloody years old!"

"Didn't mean to," Jeffrey said, words muffled by his broken jaw. "Your fault. Meant to hit you. He shouldn't a' been there."

Sinclair grabbed the lapels of Jeffrey's coat and hauled him up the wall. "It was *you* who shouldn't have been there. You broke in, you shot at me and hit Andrew. *Your* fault, and yours alone."

"No, it were Bertie's." Jeffrey snarled the best he could. "She ran away from me, and you made her your whore, you Scottish pig! If she hadn't left me, nothing would have happened."

Sinclair ground him back into the wall. "Don't blame her for your idiocy, you piece of dung. Don't even say her name."

"I knew it. I knew she were your whore." Jeffrey tried to spit at him.

Sinclair drew back his fist again, but his hand was caught by the large one of Lloyd Fellows, the man's grip amazingly strong.

"Enough of that," Fellows said in his no-nonsense tone. Something clinked, and Fellows had a cuff around one of Jeffrey's wrists. "Jeffrey Mitchell, I arrest you in the queen's name for the breaking and entering of a Mayfair home, the attempted murder of Mr. Sinclair McBride, and the shooting of Andrew McBride, an eight-year-old boy. The jury probably won't have much sympathy for that. I have a police van waiting for you, so we can pay an afternoon call on the magistrate." He gave Sinclair a stern look. "*You*, go home and drink. Make sure he gets there, Cam."

Cameron Mackenzie had come up behind them. "A large whiskey is what I prescribe," he said. He put his big hand on Sinclair's shoulder and steered him from the alley.

Inside the carriage, Sinclair collapsed against the cushions, his breath leaving him. He pulled out a handkerchief and mopped his face, covering the cloth with blood.

"You look bad," Cameron said, his broken-gravel voice too cheerful. "Clean yourself up, and then tell her. Straight out. I don't think she'll be heartbroken that her philandering, murderous beau is on his way to the clink."

Sinclair couldn't speak. He leaned back against the cushions, dabbing at his bloody face, and accepted the flask Cameron handed him in silence. Cameron had an attractive trait—knowing when to talk and when to shut up. Without speaking, the two men traveled back across London, Sinclair letting the whiskey burn deep.

~

Andrew was delighted with the visit from his uncle Ian, though Andrew did most of the talking. He showed Ian his wound, and described the wild gunfight—which he wholly invented—that had led him to being hurt. Ian nodded as Andrew spoke, as though he believed every word. Cat listened, not interrupting, and Bertie pretended to focus on her mending.

Andrew prattled on, his powers of speech recovered at least. "Bertie, you should have seen what Uncle Ian built us last Christmas. It took up a whole room!"

"I liked it," Cat said, so softly Bertie barely heard it. Ian did, and he gave her a nod.

"Will you do something like it again this Christmas, Uncle Ian?" Andrew asked. "Please?"

Ian paused a moment, then said, "Yes."

"Hooray!" Andrew started to bounce, then winced and stopped. "I'll take lots of medicine and get better so I can go to Scotland for Christmas. You'll love Kilmorgan Castle, Bertie."

"A castle?" Bertie said from her chair. "Sounds grand."

"Papa's house is big too," Andrew went on. "By a loch. You'll like it too, Bertie."

"I'm sure I will," Bertie said. "Stop bouncing, Andrew. You'll tear open your wound and have to be sewn up again."

Andrew stilled for about three seconds, then started an animated narrative about the beauties of both Kilmorgan Castle and his father's house north of it, where they'd lived with Mama, and everyone had been happy.

When Andrew started to droop, no longer able to pretend he wasn't hurting and tired, Ian stood up, smoothed the covers over the boy, and started out of the nursery. At the door, Ian looked back and gave Bertie a penetrating stare. Then he walked out and waited in the hall, leaning against the railing of the landing.

Bertie set aside her sewing and went out, closing the door behind her, curious as to what Lord Ian could have to say to her.

The hall was gloomy from the coming evening, the December day short. Ian's eyes, a tawny color that went with his dark red hair, glinted in the shadows.

After Ian had stared at Bertie for a long, silent moment, he said, "Stay with them."

"Cat and Andrew?" Bertie nodded. "Of course, I'll stay. I'm their governess now."

"I mean for always." Ian gripped the railing with his big hand. "You need to stay." He delivered this declaration, then walked past Bertie without speaking another word and went down the stairs.

Bertie watched Ian circle around the staircase and landings, keeping to the exact middle of the stairs, never touching the railings. When he reached the bottom, he opened the vestibule door and front door, blowing a draft up the stairs, then the front door banged, and Ian was gone.

The night was fully dark by the time Sinclair arrived home, Richards having wound his way through London's packed streets. Cameron alighted at Berkeley Square, where he'd hired a house for his family's stay in town, and Sinclair rode on to Upper Brook Street alone.

Macaulay took one look at Sinclair and ordered a hot bath be brought to Sinclair's bedroom. Macaulay wanted to stay and bathe him but Sinclair growled that he was fit enough to bathe himself, for God's sake. Macaulay at last agreed and left him alone.

Sinclair took his time in the bath, scrubbing off the blood and grime, pouring warm water over his hair. He finished, dried, and slipped into a dressing gown, then went upstairs to the nursery while Peter and the maids carried the bath back downstairs to empty it.

The lights were low, and Andrew was fast asleep. Cat was also in her bed, with Bertie reading to her in a soft voice. Sinclair sank down on one of the chairs, barely able to move, waiting until Bertie finished the story.

Once Bertie put the book aside, Sinclair rose and kissed Cat good night, then went to Andrew's bed and dropped a kiss to his son's head. Andrew was mending, and Sinclair said a thankful prayer.

After that, Sinclair took Bertie by the elbow and steered her out of the nursery, all the way down the stairs, through his study, and into his empty bedroom. He closed the door firmly behind them both and turned the key in the lock.

Chapter 17

Bertie's heart beat faster as Sinclair clattered the key to his bureau. He turned to her, the brighter light in this room showing more clearly the bruises and cuts on his face.

She quickly closed the space between them. "You all right? Did Jeffrey do this? What happened?"

"Jeffrey's in jail," Sinclair said, sounding weary. "Carted off by Inspector Fellows to spend the night with the magistrate. You won't have to worry about him ever again, Bertie. I promise you."

Bertie believed him. "Look at you," she said. She touched his face, barely letting her hand make contact. The side of Sinclair's left eye was swollen, the corner of his lip cut, and bruises trailed across his cheekbone.

He stood without moving while Bertie went to the washbasin and wrung out a cloth. She came back and dabbed at his cuts, washing away the new blood. He'd just bathed—his skin was damp and smelled of soap—but wounds like these were easily reopened.

When she reached up to dab his forehead, Sinclair caught her wrist. His eyes were like pieces of winter sky as he fixed them on her. She expected him to push her away, to admonish her, but he didn't. He held her wrist, while water from the cloth trickled from her hands.

"I'll just put this back in the basin," Bertie whispered.

Sinclair didn't let go or appear to hear her. He kept his hand around her wrist, his eyes on her, his gaze holding her more effectively than any shackle.

When he finally did move, it was to take his other hand and brush it through her hair. His fingers loosened pins she'd spent a frustrating time this morning putting in, her thick hair soon tumbling free.

He let go of her hand, and the wet cloth fell to the carpet with a splat. Sinclair continued to pull her hair loose, the mass of it flowing over her shoulders to her waist. Since Bertie had been living here, she'd been able to keep her hair clean, amazed at the different soaps the rich washed themselves with.

Sinclair's short hair glistened with droplets of water, and the dressing gown, though it was fastened, held the warmth of the bare man beneath. Bertie's knees went shaky as Sinclair's large hands pushed back her hair then drifted to the buttons of her bodice.

Bertie could say nothing, do nothing, as Sinclair started sliding the buttons through the buttonholes, one by one, taking his time. Sinclair didn't hold her—Bertie simply couldn't move. Her body crawled with heat—she hadn't been so warm all day. No need to run from *this*.

Sinclair's blunt fingers opened the bodice in silence. The placket parted for his big hands, and he drew his fingers down the corset cover beneath.

Bertie's breath hitched as Sinclair moved his touch down to the cuffs of her sleeves. He undid the faux pearl buttons there, then returned his hands to her shoulders and pushed her bodice open and off. Bertie now stood with bare arms in her corset and its jacketlike cover, and her skirts beneath it.

Bertie reached for the cloth fastenings of Sinclair's dressing gown, her fingers trembling, but he gently pushed her hands aside. He ran his fingers up her wrists, back to her shoulders then down to unhook the clasps of the corset cover and push it away.

When his hands moved to the corset's laces, he kissed her, his mouth insistent, lips opening hers. The laces at Bertie's back loosened, Sinclair's strong hand parting them, then his warmth came to her through the thin fabric of her combinations. He made a noise in his throat as he pulled her closer, his fingers splayed across her back.

Hot and cold sensations chased through Bertie's body. She wanted to fold in on herself, and at the same time, she burned with energy. The corset came away, Bertie's chest expanding as the restricting garment released her.

Sinclair fumbled with the clasps that closed her skirts, and the hooks tore off in his impatience. Bertie helped him push the skirts down, her shaking fingers bumping against his solid ones. Now she was bare to the world except for her combinations, her fine, new undergarments.

Sinclair lifted her into his arms and carried her away from her clothes on the floor. He laid her on the bed, which had been stripped and remade after Andrew was moved upstairs, the tight covers cool against her back. The photo of Mrs. McBride had gone from the bedside table as well, to keep Andrew and Cat company in the nursery.

Sinclair didn't join her on the bed. He stood looking down at her for a long time, his gray eyes still, his breath swift. Bertie curled her fingers on the covers, waiting.

Without taking his gaze from her, Sinclair unfastened his dressing gown and let it drop. His body came into view, hard, tight, and beautiful. Bertie's heart thrummed.

His wide shoulders were sunbaked, the red-bronze color fading to paler skin on the rest of his torso. Blond hair dusted his chest, and his navel was a deeper shadow in the dim room. Another swirl of hair, darker than that on his chest, curled between his legs.

His staff was hard and ready, stiff and long. No need for a lady to tickle him up, as Bertie had heard women say about their men. Sinclair looked down at her, paying no attention to his own nudity, his gaze all for Bertie.

He put his knee on the mattress and climbed onto the bed with her. His hands landed on either side of her head, but he didn't kiss her again. Sinclair only looked at her, his eyes dark in the low light, the same light brushing gold into the unshaved whiskers on his face. He continued to hold her gaze as his hand went to the buttons of her combinations and began unfastening them.

Bertie's heartbeat sped. Cool air touched her skin, the placket parting. Sinclair pushed the combinations' sleeveless top down her body, then lifted her hips to slide the drawers from her legs.

There. Bertie was bare before a man for the first time in her life.

Sinclair nuzzled her cheek, then kissed it, his lips brushing so lightly it might have been a breeze. His hand went to her chest, moving to cup her breast, his thumb on her nipple, his touch a dart of fire.

"I never . . ." Bertie's whisper was loud in the stillness. "I never been with a man before . . ."

"Shh." Sinclair lifted away from her breast, leaving Bertie craving him, and touched her lips. "I won't hurt ye, sweet."

Any Englishness dropped away from him—Sinclair's voice was all Scots. His arms were tight but his hands gentle, his fingertips skimming her face before he leaned in to kiss her again.

Fine heat—Bertie found hard muscle under Sinclair's smooth skin, then the warm silk of his hair, the rough bristles of unshaved beard. The cuts on his face caught at her fingers, as did the swollen bruises. Jeffrey had hurt him.

The thought made Bertie furious. "He shouldn't have done that. I'm sorry."

Sinclair raised his head, eyes glittering in the half-light. "I needed to fight him. We Highlanders like our vengeance."

"But . . ."

"No more talking." Sinclair's voice turned to a growl. "It's only you and me tonight, and the very bad thing I'm doing."

"Not bad." Bertie smiled. "It's not bad at all."

"Yes, it is." Sinclair's answering smile burned her. "But I don't care."

He stilled further talk by kissing her. His mouth tasted of whiskey, his whiskers burned, and he pushed her thighs apart with a firm hand. Bertie held her breath as Sinclair lifted his head, his gaze drawing hers, and began to slide himself into her.

~~~~

Bertie's eyes went wide, the tightness of her telling Sinclair more than words that he was her first. He didn't like the triumph that swelled through him, but he couldn't stop it. She was *his*.

Soft woman met his body, hers moving with its first taste of passion. Sinclair knew he could hurt her without meaning to, so he slid in slowly, letting Bertie get used to him before he went on.

It wasn't easy. The small cry that escaped her lips beat heat through his blood, his need escalating with every heartbeat.

He held off as long as he could, but Bertie slid her hands down his back to cup his hips. "Please," she whispered.

Sinclair dipped his head to the mattress, breathing the warm scent of her hair. "Bertie, what are you doing to me?"

She didn't answer, but her intake of breath was enough for him. Sinclair kissed the curve of her neck, then bit it as he slid himself all the way inside.

Something woke in him, a wild spark that had been dead for a long time. Sinclair felt it race through his body, and his attention focused to one point.

Bertie. *Roberta*.

Sinclair moved his hips forward in one hard thrust, crazed magic entwining him fast.

He remembered how, when facing death on the battle-field, his mind had emptied of all other thought. Fear had fled, and rage, and all he'd experienced was a kind of floating freedom. Hard to come out of that when he was back at camp doing ordinary things; hence his mad pranks and the quantities of drinking he'd done.

His marriage and children had floated him free again, to be dashed to pieces five years later when Daisy had gone. Sinclair had lain in those pieces since, believing himself finished. He went through the motions of daily life, and honed his skills to deadly sharpness, but without much interest. His work filled the hours, made the pain more distant.

At this moment, with this woman under him, all the pieces of himself charged together again. It hurt, more than had Jeffrey kicking him in the stomach in the East End gutter. Pain radiated through Sinclair's entire being, sharp like flesh being pulled from a wound.

A shout came from Sinclair's throat. Bertie's eyes widened— her blue eyes he could drown in. She'd come to him out of the fog, her eyes crystal brightness in a world of gray.

Now she was shining a light so bright it seared him. Sinclair wanted to hide his face and not look. But a Cockney pickpocket was dragging him out of the land of grayness, forcing him back into the fire. And he wanted to run into the flames.

He thrust into her, hearing his shouts, unable to stop himself. The hot ferocity of the coupling boiled around him, ecstasy wound with pain.

Bertie cried out softly, her fingers hard points in his back. Sinclair knew she was unused to a man inside her, and he tried to slow, tried to gentle himself, but he couldn't stop.

He needed to go on, *on* . . .

He heard words come out of his mouth, curses at himself, tears hot in his eyes. He wound tighter as his body pressed down into one need—to be in her, one with her.

Bertie's head went back, her eyes filling with wonder as her first climax hit her. Her thrusts met his, her body knowing what to do, her cries beautiful.

Sinclair was coming now, thrusting into her. He had no idea where he was or when, only that Bertie was hot and welcoming, and he needed her.

Bertie fell back to the mattress, breathless, her skin filmed with sweat. She was laughing.

Sinclair, spent, collapsed on top of her, the wretched tears trickling from his eyes. Bertie smiled at him as she reached up and wiped a tear away.

～❦

Women in Bertie's life had told her that men, after lying *with* a woman, started lying *to* a woman. Men also fell fast asleep right after, paying no more attention to the lady once his bodily needs were satisfied.

Sinclair showed no sign at all of falling asleep. He stretched out, facedown, next to Bertie, watching her with warm gray eyes as he lifted a lock of her hair and let it trickle through his fingers.

Bertie wanted to freeze this moment in time—lamplight touching Sinclair's back and hips, brown against the tangle of sheets, his slow smile, his gray eyes holding sin.

"I couldn't steal anything from you now," Bertie said, her voice shaky. "Nothing on you to take."

Sinclair's smile deepened, crinkling the lines around his eyes, which the bruises in no way marred. "You've stolen something from me, don't worry."

Bertie gave him a mock skeptical look. "You don't mean your watch, do you?"

He made a rumbling noise. "You've stolen all sense of my place in life. I thought I knew the road I was on, but now I have no idea."

Bertie didn't know what he was talking about, but she couldn't help smiling back. "You ain't making any sense."

"I haven't made sense, lass, since you tripped into me outside the Old Bailey." He touched the tip of her nose. "My world turned upside down that evening."

"Well, it hasn't been all that right side up for me either."

Sinclair stroked another lock of her hair. He had a scar on the inside of his wrist, a perfect circle, like the end of a cigar. Bertie touched it. "What happened here?"

Sinclair glanced at the scar, almost as though he'd forgotten about it. "Youthful larks." He shrugged. "Nothing important."

Bertie rubbed the puckered skin. "Must have hurt."

"My language was unfortunate. But Steven was stricken—poor lad didn't realize what would happen." Sinclair was silent a moment, as though remembering that long-ago injury. "Thank you," he said.

"For what?" Bertie should be thanking *him*, for this breathtaking feeling.

"For watching over Andrew. For helping me save his life." Sinclair moved his hand to her shoulder, his touch warm. "You were certainly cool and steady while I sewed up his wound."

Bertie had been anything *but* cool and steady, but she shrugged. "Many's the time I've stitched up me dad when he got himself stuck with a knife. He's prone to picking fights with men stronger than him. Never was very bright, my dad. And he yells a lot more than Andrew."

Sinclair's smile vanished. "I'm glad you're away from him."

"He won't be very happy about Jeffrey. They were great pals, Jeff and my dad, even if Jeffrey was younger." Bertie touched an angry cut on Sinclair's face. "The idea was to have Jeffrey marry me and take over Dad's business when he was gone. I mean the business of robbing and thieving."

"Which you are out of," Sinclair said sternly.

"'Course I am. I'm a governess now, ain't . . . *aren't* I?"

Sinclair laughed. He was beautiful when he did that, especially when it was a genuine laugh. "We'll make you one yet, lass. How is the training going?"

"Coming along. We've got about a quarter of the books read. I like the history ones the best."

He looked interested. "What do Cat and Andrew like to read?"

"Well, Andrew likes the astronomy ones, and so does your cook, by the way. Andrew says he wants to build a flying machine that will reach the stars."

Sinclair's laughter came back. "What about Cat?"

"Not sure. She reads everything, remembers everything, but she doesn't *care*. That's not right, is it?"

Sinclair let out a breath. "Poor Cat. I've not been the best father to her. To either of them."

Now Bertie's anger stirred. "Rubbish. You've been fine. Don't they have a fancy house and fancy clothes and all they want to eat?"

Sinclair slanted her an ironic look. "There's more to being a father than that."

"All I can say is, I wish I'd had a dad more like you. Wouldn't have been knocked about, then, or told I had to marry a bully."

Sinclair rolled on top of her again, his weight and warmth a fine thing. "And you are wise beyond anyone I've ever known. I complain, and you slap me with perspective."

Bertie touched his cheek. "Aw, I'd never slap you."

His eyes heated, showing even more wickedness. "I know that, wretched woman. Come here."

Bertie was already there with him, but he drew her up into his arms. Sinclair's next kiss was hot, his body tight, as he parted her thighs and firmly slid into her, starting the loving again.

～

When Sinclair woke in the wee hours of the morning, Bertie was gone. He stretched his hand to the empty pillow, his blood growing cold when he didn't find her there.

He rose and sought his dressing gown, which had been folded neatly over a chair. He couldn't help a touch of amusement through this alarm. Bertie had tidied up after him.

It was four in the morning by the clock on the bedside table. Sinclair fastened his dressing gown and opened the door to his study to find a lamp burning and Bertie standing at his desk.

His heart beat faster, his breath starting its constriction. Bertie was looking at one of the blasted anonymous letters that must have slipped out from where he'd thrust it among his papers. She raised her head as Sinclair strode in, her eyes wide, shock and anger on her face.

Chapter 18

"Put that down," Sinclair said, unable to stop the snarl. He dragged in a breath, forcing himself to exhale normally. "It's nothing for you to see."

Bertie didn't obey—she never did. "That's vile, that is."

Sinclair came to her and pried the paper from her fingers, her hand warm even in this chill room. Bertie had dressed again, though she hadn't laced and buttoned herself all the way. Her hair hung down her back, loose. Her dishevelment made his blood grow hot, Sinclair's need for her in no way sated.

"Who sent it?" she asked, watching him. "Not your brother-in-law, I take it?"

"No, not Edward," Sinclair said with a snarl. "If I knew who, I'd rid myself of him, wouldn't I?"

Sinclair heard his angry tones but couldn't stop them. He'd received this letter this morning—no, yesterday morning now. Henry had brought him his post from chambers, and this letter had been among it. In the stiffly printed capitals, it said:

That whore you've taken to your bosom will be the death

of you and your children. I know who she is and what she is.
The viper always stings, and its venom is deadly.

"The whore, I take it, is me," Bertie said. "Likewise the viper." She was angry, not distressed, her eyes sparkling with indignation.

Sinclair folded the paper and thrust it into a drawer. "I'm sorry you've been caught up in this. I never meant you to see the letters."

Bertie's brows rose. "You mean there's been *more*? About me?

"About every aspect of my bloody life."

"Oh." Her anger wound down a little. "Are they all like that? What do they want, whoever they are? Money?"

"No." Sinclair shook his head. "He's asked for nothing."

"Ah, you know it's a he, then?"

"I *don't* know," Sinclair said impatiently. "I'm only guessing."

"Hmm." Bertie's look turned speculating. "Are you thinking a woman would write a longer letter and use her own hand? Not sure she would. When you get a threat like that, though, it's usually for money, or for you to keep out of the way of some villain making money. But they haven't asked for nothing?"

"No." Sinclair took the key from his desk, locked the drawer, and dropped the key into his pocket. "We don't know. I've given the letters to Fellows, and he's trying to help me find out who's writing them."

"Bet he's not getting anywhere. Scotland Yard blokes like murders and violent robberies, not taunting letters. But I could give it a go. What did the others say?"

Sinclair's temper splintered at the thought of her tracking down whoever could think up such contemptible drivel. "You'll not be giving anything a go. You'll be taking my children to Scotland when Andrew is well enough to travel."

Her look turned eager. "Andrew keeps telling me about your house there. It sounds ever so nice."

"It is." The loch and hills could soothe him, even if Sinclair had hated the place the first year or so without Daisy.

Too much empty space. "Though we won't have time to go there first. We'll go straight to Kilmorgan for the Christmas gathering."

"The kids too? The duke lets them come?"

"Oh, yes," Sinclair said in dry tones. "Hart likes the house to be overflowing—McBrides, Mackenzies, Scrantons, Ramsays, Fellowses, and anyone Hart wants to sway to vote his way on whatever he's got his party in a froth about. He crams them in."

Bertie bit her lip, her frown charming. "Might be a bit difficult, that. I think the duchess likes me—at least, she's kind to me. Lord Ian said he thought his wife would like me too. But you're saying there'll be English aristos there?"

Sinclair felt a modicum of relief at the change in topic. "Yes, and I don't give a hang what they think of you. They should be grateful I've found someone who can keep Andrew away from the matches."

"It's not the aristos I'm worried about. I think I can learn enough to fool your brother-in-law, and maybe other gents and ladies who don't know me, but if real governesses are there, I won't be able to fool *them*. I'm just a girl from the backstreets, and they'll know it."

Sinclair smoothed back a lock of Bertie's hair, mussed from his bed. "We all have to come from somewhere."

"Not in England. You're either born with a silver spoon in your mouth or in the gutter, and you don't cross the line. A working-class man can learn how to make a lot of money, but everyone knows he's still from the gutter. The sign of a true gentleman is that he don't . . . *doesn't* . . . do any work."

"But I'm not English, am I?" Sinclair traced her cheek. "A fact too many people forget. The next head of clan McBride might be eking out a living in the gutters of some industrial city until enough heirs in his way pass on. Will he be any less able to lead the clan for all that? No—he'll probably do better than someone born to do nothing all day. Do you know what we McBrides call a man who thinks he's too much of a gentleman to work? *Lazy*."

Her smile returned, lighting her eyes. "I like that."

"They don't call me the Scots Machine because I let others labor for me."

Something sly entered her smile. "I could think of another reason for that name."

Sinclair stared at her a moment, not understanding. Then he felt his cheeks burn. "Don't embarrass me. I was . . . needy."

"More like greedy."

The burn worked its way down his body, making his arousal, which hadn't much deflated, grow rigid again. "Greedy, was I?" Sinclair wrapped his fingers around her loose hair and gently tugged her closer. "I think I remember *you* wanting plenty."

"Couldn't help it." Bertie slid her arms around him, her body under her loosened clothes warm and welcoming. "Could I?"

The desk was right there. It was covered with papers, but Sinclair shoved them to the floor and lifted Bertie onto it. Her unlaced and unbuttoned garments came away easily, baring her body to him. The lamplight touched her breasts, the nipples becoming a dark rose red as they tightened for him. The light brushed the hair between her legs, which he could see was already damp. Sinclair let his dressing gown drop to the floor, his hardness tight as he stepped naked between her thighs.

Bertie reached for him, her teasing smile becoming languid as he touched her. They fit together so well, Sinclair thought, as he eased her hips forward and himself into her again.

The soft sound Bertie made caused Sinclair's need to flare white hot. Soon they were rocking together, hands grappling, bodies flushed and streaked with sweat. Sinclair gave himself up to the fire of the moment, as her heat, and the completeness of her, welcomed him back.

～

Bertie barely made it back to her room before the maids and Peter started their morning rounds to deliver coal and stir fires. Bertie was flushed with warmth as she peeled off her clothes, even though her room was cool, only embers in the grate.

She'd just pulled on her nightgown when she heard

Charlotte coming up the stairs with her clanking coal bucket. Bertie hurriedly rumpled her bed and pretended to be just climbing out as Charlotte walked in.

Bertie asked Charlotte to draw her a bath, which the girl did. The hot water stung a bit on Bertie's intimate parts as she lowered herself into it, making her flush more. The last go on the desk had been a bit turbulent, not that Bertie had minded. She'd gone a little wild with the amazing pleasure of it, and Sinclair had laughed. Then he'd stopped laughing as he'd lost himself in passion. Bertie liked how his eyes had gone dark, his touch firm, the strength of him holding her in place as he'd loved her.

If she'd been a genteel young lady, Bertie supposed she'd feel sorrow or shame at what they'd done, but she didn't. Maybe that meant she was truly a tart, as the letter had said, but at the moment, she scarcely cared.

She floated on emotion, the joy of it sliding around her like the hot water of the bath. Yes, she could easily have gotten with child any of the three times they'd gone at it tonight, but the thought only made her excitement grow. Any child of Sinclair's would be welcome, never mind the tiny voice deep inside that told her she was a fool.

Charlotte had left her to enjoy her bath in peace, and Bertie slowly drew the sponge over herself, picturing how it would be if Sinclair did it for her. His hair would be damp from the steam, droplets of water would bead on his skin, and he'd give her his slow, wicked smile that was absent of all sorrow.

Bertie hugged the sponge to her chest. Sinclair was part of her world now, and she wouldn't easily let go of that.

She got out, dried off, and dressed. She'd discovered a few smears of blood on her drawers when she'd taken off her clothes, and had known it wasn't from her menses. Bertie had thought she'd be too old to shed virgin's blood, but apparently not. She wadded up the drawers and shoved them into her laundry bag before Aoife came in to help her lace up. Sinclair's family's laundry was all sent out, so with any luck, no one within the house would see it.

Bertie ate breakfast with the children, Andrew already better than yesterday, well enough to eat everything in sight.

Sinclair, Aoife told her, had decided to go back to his chambers today if only for a little while, now that Andrew was healing and the awful man who'd broken in had been arrested. Sinclair departed without coming upstairs, but he raised his hand to Bertie, Cat, and Andrew looking out of the window, smiling up at them. Then he stepped into his carriage and was gone.

In spite of Jeffrey stewing in jail awaiting his trial, Bertie worried about Sinclair out and about in town. The anonymous letter writer bothered her, and though Sinclair didn't think his brother-in-law had sent the letters, Bertie wouldn't put it past him, or his wife. They might want their mitts on Sinclair's children by hook or by crook.

Bertie was no stranger to people leaving threatening notes—her dad had got them all the time. Mostly they were scrawled on a scrap of paper, short and to the point. *Stay off my patch, or else.* High-end villains liked to lord it over the rest of them, and Bertie's father was often warned. Sometimes the villains didn't bother with notes, just sent in a thug or two to do Bertie's dad over. Jeffrey had urged Bertie's father to give in and simply work for the big villains, but Gerry never would. He hated people telling him what to do.

Once Andrew and Cat were settled in, Bertie went back down the stairs to the next floor and made sure no one was in Sinclair's study before she slipped inside and closed the door.

Sinclair had not only locked the drawer into which he'd dropped the letter, he'd locked all the other drawers too. Bertie pulled out a hairpin and unlocked them again. Why the rich bothered with fancy desks that could be picked with a piece of straw, she didn't know.

Bertie didn't find any more letters until she discovered a box pushed into the back of the bottom drawer, hidden behind other stacks of papers. Bertie set this box on the desk, put her hairpin to work, and opened it.

Inside, she found five folded papers in their envelopes.

The envelopes were ordinary, sold by most stationers. Likewise the sheets of paper. Bertie unfolded each letter, finding the same kind of printing as in the one that called her a viper—the capitals were so precise the writer must have used a straight rule to draw them.

Not one of the missives was very long, and there were five in the box. Bertie made herself read them through, as distasteful as they were.

Every letter was about Sinclair's wife, the late Margaret McBride. *Sweet Daisy wasn't what she pretended to be, was she?* one said. *What did she get up to before she squeezed out your children?* Another, *You know what she was, and how she tricked you into marrying her. Who else would you like me to tell about her past?*

Mean things. And odd. From what everyone in the house had told her about Mrs. McBride, she'd been a fine lady—laughing, sweet, loving to her children. Were the letters lies then? The one about Bertie had implied that she'd do harm to Cat and Andrew. *The viper always stings, and its venom is deadly.*

She'd never hurt them at all, or Sinclair. Never . . .

Bertie swallowed, remembering that her presence had caused Andrew to be shot. Maybe the letter writer was more perceptive than she gave him credit for.

No, that was wrong. These letters were vague hints, allowing the receiver to read into them what he or she pleased. The words about Daisy, Sinclair's wife, could mean anything from she'd been a murderer to she'd lied about where she'd gone to school. By all accounts, everyone in this house had loved Daisy, including Sinclair. He'd loved her desperately.

Bertie thought about the woman smiling out of the photos placed here and there around the house. Mrs. McBride didn't look as though she'd been deceitful whatsoever. Bertie must be ten times as deceitful as *she'd* ever been. What was the writer getting at?

And why, if Sinclair claimed he'd given all the letters to Inspector Fellows, were these five hidden in the box?

Answer: He didn't want Fellows to know about these particular ones.

Which made Bertie wonder—if the letters were lies, why did Sinclair fear others seeing them?

Too many questions, and Bertie might not like the answers. She folded the letters and slid them back into their envelopes, arranging them carefully in the box in the order she'd taken them out. Then she put the box back into the drawer, picked the locks closed, and left the study, her thoughts troubled.

~~~

Andrew recovered enough that, on the twenty-third of December, Sinclair decreed he was well enough to board the train for Scotland.

The train would leave from Euston station and travel all night, putting them in Edinburgh in the morning. From there, they'd take a smaller, slower train to the heart of the highlands and Castle Kilmorgan, arriving in time for the Christmas ball.

Last Christmas, Andrew had been a handful, setting the house into uproar. This year, his convalescence and Bertie's presence might keep him calmer, Sinclair thought. *Might.*

Sinclair booked first-class sleeping compartments—one for himself, one for the children, and one for Bertie. Macaulay and Aoife also traveled with them, leaving Mrs. Hill, Charlotte, and Peter to watch over the house. Their families were in London, and Sinclair never had the heart to take them away for Christmas.

"I have this all to myself?" Bertie asked in amazement as she turned in a circle in the cramped sleeping compartment.

"Best I could do on short notice," Sinclair said. He'd had no need to accompany her, but he hadn't been able to stop himself. "If you need anything, ring for the conductor or ask Aoife or Macaulay."

Bertie turned around again and faced Sinclair, her wide smile in place. Bertie had a new dress for traveling, gray with black piping and black cloth-covered buttons. A subdued garment, but one that looked smart and hugged her curves. Her gray hat's brim turned up to reveal a black lining, and a feather curled from the crown. Eleanor had chosen the hat as a gift, having her favorite milliner make and deliver it. Bertie's joy when she lifted it from of the box had been the same as that of a woman regarding a diamond tiara.

Remembering her delight—Bertie had jammed the hat straight on her head and twirled around with it, laughing— started to make him hard. Sinclair had donned a kilt for this trip to his homeland, and an arousal could be disastrous.

He made himself leave her and return to his compartment with Andrew and Cat, sitting down as the train jolted, getting ready for its long journey.

For her part, Bertie thought she'd never settle in. She'd never been out of London, let alone to Scotland, and anticipating seeing the countryside, from a luxurious train no less, had her in a right state. She was sorry they'd travel at night, but she'd make sure she saw something of Scotland before they shut themselves into the castle.

Aoife popped her head in while Bertie was exploring her compartment, saying that Mr. McBride expected her to join him and the children for supper. Bertie tore herself away from the shining inlay walls, the soft seats, and the amazing little closet that had a sink with running water, and followed Aoife down the narrow passage.

The main compartment Sinclair had taken was quite large. Two wide, velvet-upholstered seats faced each other, the windows had thick curtains pulled over them, and lamps softly lit the compartment. Their meal was delivered to a table in the middle of the compartment, served on china plates with silver cutlery.

"I think I could live forever on a train," Bertie said, looking over the fish in sauce, crisp greens, and buttery potatoes.

"You'd soon grow tired of its rocking," Sinclair said. He ate, but without the enthusiasm of Andrew. He was more like Cat, calmly putting the tasty food into his mouth as though it were nothing out of the ordinary.

"You do everything like that," Bertie said. She hadn't

meant to voice the thought out loud, but the words slipped away before she could catch them. Sinclair looked up at her, his expression still, waiting for her to explain. Bertie drew a breath and said, "You have all these wonders, but you barely notice them. Everything is a delight—don't you know that?"

Sinclair put down his fork and gazed across the little table at her, his gray eyes focused so sharply that Bertie moved a little in her seat. She knew she was being far too impertinent, but she always spoke as she found.

The waiter entering with the pudding ended the moment, and the meal resumed.

Sinclair said good night to his children after that and went off to the smoking car. He didn't smoke, Bertie knew, but she assumed he'd drink brandy and speak with other men there.

Bertie got the children to bed. Aoife would sleep in the bunk opposite their two, watching over them, promising to call Bertie if she was needed. Bertie returned to her own cabin, interested to see that her seat had been turned into a small bed while she'd been having supper.

Now to discover if she could sleep on a train. Everything was so fascinating she might have trouble dropping off, in case she missed something. Sinclair had talked about the train's rocking, but Bertie liked it. The train was like a live thing, clicking along the rails, humming to itself, the whistle's shrill call blasting into the night.

Bertie tried to peer out into the darkness, but could see little beyond her own reflection. She had just dropped the curtain when her door snapped open behind her and Sinclair stepped inside.

He didn't smell of smoke—he smelled like the night, as though he'd walked to the end of the train to watch the track unfold behind them. He said nothing, only gazed in silence at her, his hair glinting in the lamplight, his hands in gloves closing to fists.

"Teach me about the delights," Sinclair said after a time, his voice low. "I can't see the wonders anymore. Show me what you see, Bertie. *Please.*"

Chapter 19

Bertie's lips parted, her dark blue eyes taking him in. The top button of her bodice was undone, as though he'd interrupted her undressing. The thought of her in here alone, slowly unbuttoning and drawing off her clothes, was enough to kill him.

"I don't see much different than you do," Bertie answered, sounding nervous.

Sinclair shut the door behind him and locked it. "Yes, you do, or you would never have said that to me."

"I was rude. My father once had a kind mistress, name of Sophie, who tried to teach me good manners, but I wasn't always best at it."

"I don't give a damn about your manners." Sinclair let the motion of the train ease him onto the edge of the bed, and he pulled Bertie to sit beside him. "Show me what you see."

Bertie stared at him as though he'd run mad, and Sinclair likely had. He'd made his way to the back of the train, standing alone on the observation platform in the freezing cold, but it hadn't cooled his need for her.

He realized tonight he'd been trying to hold on to his control and his life when it was nothing. His grief had made him into an automaton, going through the motions of living, stopping when there was nothing to do. If not for Andrew and Cat, he'd have told Macaulay long ago to prop him up in a square somewhere for pigeons to land on.

Sinclair had told Bertie that she was a flickering light in his life. Now he wanted her to fan that flicker and build it to a roaring blaze.

"What do you mean, what I see?" she asked him, mystified.

Sinclair waved his hand around the close room. "Show me anything."

"Right." Bertie continued to stare at him then she jolted herself and looked around. "Um." She touched the wall next to her. "I think this is beautiful. All these little flowers made of tiny pieces of wood woven together. Took some skill to fashion that, and polish it all nice."

Sinclair took in the marquetry. It was fine, with excellent workmanship, but it didn't make him want to leap up and sing. "What else?"

"Well, the whole compartment. Everything exactly in its place, everything fitting together like a puzzle."

True, but Sinclair had been on so many different trains, from elegant to indifferent to downright squalid. A train's engineering might be precise, but he'd seen too much of it.

"What else?"

Bertie pursed her lips. "You're a hard one to please. There's this." She took his hand, her touch firing his nerves, and drew her finger along his palm. "These gloves fit you perfectly, like a second skin. Your clothes are always well done. And there's this." Bertie released his hand to lift a fold of his plaid. "Never seen a man wearing a skirt before."

Sinclair grew warm. "It's a kilt."

"Yeah." Bertie's smile went wicked. "And don't it look fine on you?"

There it was—the delight snapping its way into him. Not from the manufactured things around them, from Bertie herself.

She rubbed the wool between her fingers, the warmth of her hand touching his bare knee.

"It's McBride plaid," Sinclair said, or thought he said. "The secret of the pattern was kept alive in our clan when traditional dress was banned after the '45."

"Bonnie Prince Charlie and the uprising," Bertie said, looking triumphant. "I've been reading. Your family a part of that?"

"In the thick. My brother Patrick knows the stories. He's the keeper of all things McBride."

"Can't wait to meet him."

Sinclair thought about his rather dour older brother, but decided Patrick would like Bertie. She'd be interested in Patrick's stories, listening with that wonder she was showing to Sinclair. Patrick would enjoy it.

Sinclair leaned closer. "What else?"

Bertie's cheeks went pink. "You trying to make me spill all my secrets?"

"Yes, I am. What else do you find amazing?"

"You," Bertie said, smiles gone, eyes quiet.

Sinclair stilled. "There's not much amazing about me."

"Mmm, I wouldn't say that."

"I would."

Bertie cocked her head. "Are you trying to get me to flatter you?"

Sinclair closed his gloved hands over both her bare ones. "I want to feel again, Bertie. Help me to do that. You started. I want more."

She looked uncertain. "But I don't know how."

"Yes, you do." Sinclair released her, stripped off his gloves, and dropped them to the table. Then he reached for the black buttons of her bodice. "I want to see the wonder of *you*."

Bertie's lower lip shook once, but she reached out and pushed his coat open. "Two can play at that."

Sinclair's already awakened need jumped higher as he slid off his greatcoat and let Bertie help him out of his frock coat. His windblown cravat easily unwound under Bertie's fingers. She popped the stud holding his collar and released the restricting band from Sinclair's throat. Sinclair drew a relieved breath and returned to unbuttoning her bodice.

Joy raced back into Sinclair's world as they undressed each other, fumbling at clasps, ties, and buttons, excitement making them clumsy. Not long later, Bertie sat on the bed in her combinations, while Sinclair was in nothing but his kilt.

He stood up and removed that, liking how Bertie's gaze riveted to him as he unpinned and unwound the plaid.

"Blimey," she said softly.

Sinclair spread the kilt on the bed with unsteady hands. Bertie didn't take her gaze from him. The compartment's lamplight hid nothing of his body, showing all his scars, the burn mark on his arm, and the fact that his cock was hard and lifting high.

The lamplight let him see Bertie as well, as he stripped off her combinations. She leaned back on the bunk, her breasts touched by the golden light, her nipples dark. Bertie's hair, mussed by their playful undressing, trickled across her plump skin.

She was a pleasure to look at. Her belly was a little soft, her hips curving from her waist, the sweet curls between her legs as dark as the hair on her head.

A fine woman, bare for him, in this train rushing into the night. They might as well be entirely alone, he thought, at the same time they were surrounded by so many. Up and down the passage, the compartments were shut, hiding the secrets of those hurrying north for a Scottish Christmas.

Sinclair's fanciful thoughts dissolved to nothing when Bertie reached up and closed her fingers around the tip of his cock.

~

Bertie liked the feel of his arousal, warm and soft, and at the same time, hard under her fingers.

How could Sinclair have thought *anything* in this compartment more interesting and wonderful than himself? He'd encouraged Bertie to sing the praises of the woodwork while *he* was in front of her, smelling of the night and his own intoxicating scent. The hunger in Sinclair's eyes had nearly undone her.

As she squeezed his hardness, Sinclair's large hands bunched into fists. He didn't have the soft hands of a gentleman—he'd fought with these hands, sunburned them, worked them raw. Bertie contrasted that with the skin of his cock, which was hot and smooth, that part of him always hidden from the world.

Beautiful man—he was allowing *her* to see it, to stroke it. Sinclair didn't touch Bertie, only let her explore him all the way up his shaft to the fascinating balls that fit into the cup of her hand.

People through the ages had come up with many terms for what she was touching. Funny ones, like *John Thomas* or *fishing rod*, but those crude phrases didn't do Sinclair justice. His beautiful organ stretched toward her, the blunt tip bumping Bertie's hand as she completed another stroke.

He let her touch a little longer before Sinclair pushed her questing fingers aside and dropped to his knees. He looked her over, his face softening, his voice going low. "How did I stumble upon something as beautiful as you?"

Bertie thrilled to be called so by him, but she only grinned. "*I* ran into you." She ran her hand through his warm hair, burnished gold by the lamplight. "Remember?"

He smiled. Bertie loved his smiles and his laughter—she loved *him*.

And it will be the end of me, a voice inside her said. Too late, much too late to stop now.

"I remember," Sinclair said. "From then on, every bit of control I had in my life was gone."

He bent to her and licked between her breasts, his close-cropped hair tickling her skin. He moved to her nipple, teeth brushing it before he drew it into his mouth.

Bertie's breath caught as the tiny pain washed fire through her. Sinclair closed his eyes and began to suckle her, the same way he'd suckled her fingers in the darkness of his house. The heat inside her shot higher, as she wondered whether, when Sinclair had done that, he'd been imagining doing *this*. She shivered, giddy.

"Harder," she whispered. Why did she want that? "Harder."

Sinclair curled his tongue around her nipple, his lips tightening. His hands went to her waist, a beautiful man doing a beautiful thing. Bertie pressed him closer, wanting his mouth harder on her, needing it. *Don't let me go.*

Sinclair suckled a little longer then pulled away, a sinful glint in his eyes. Bertie's breast felt raw, cold where the air touched the moisture left by his mouth.

Sinclair moved his hands to her knees and pushed them apart. Then he gently pressed her back into the cushions, hooked his hands around her thighs, and lowered himself between her legs. He licked over her opening once then fastened his mouth to it and began to suckle.

Bertie couldn't stop her cry. Wild, hot sensations poured through her, the bright friction of his tongue on the most intimate part of her sending her deeper into the cushions. Bertie's hips moved with his mouth's working, her body instinctively responding.

The train curved hard to the right, the wheels squealing against the tracks. Sinclair put out his strong hand and steadied them both, then, without warning, he thrust his tongue deep into her.

The shrill peal of the train's whistle drowned out Bertie's scream. Sinclair raised his head, his eyes full of laughter. "The train wants to challenge us."

Did it? Bertie pushed her hair from her eyes, her mind muzzy.

"We won't let it win," Sinclair said.

No? Sinclair stood up, lifting Bertie from the bunk. He set her on her feet, then sat down where she'd been, looking splendid, naked against the spread kilt. His cock, ramrod stiff, lifted straight out toward her. "Come here," he said.

"Bit of a tight fit on that bunk," Bertie answered breathlessly. "I was wondering how I'd squeeze in on me own."

Sinclair's smile went wide. "We'll fit, lass, but it's not for the prudish." He seized Bertie by the hips and pulled her onto his lap, facing him. He arranged her so that her knees rested on either side of his thighs, spreading her legs wide.

Sinclair slid a few inches to the edge of the bunk, holding Bertie securely in his large hands. He eased her forward, onto him, the position sending his wonderful stiffness straight inside her. She was already wet and warm with her own moisture and that from his tongue, and he slid in with no impediment.

They were face to face, pressed as tightly to each other as two people could get. The arrangement put Bertie on level with him, where she could see his smile and look into his fine gray eyes.

The train straightened out and picked up speed, the acceleration pushing Bertie at Sinclair, and Sinclair at Bertie. He went deeper still, his smile vanishing. A fine ache rubbed her where they joined, his ministrations having made her swollen and hot, and now pleasured by the whole of him.

Sinclair thrust a little, his hips coming off the bunk. The rush of the train, and its unsteady speed moved Sinclair inside her, as though the train itself coaxed this coupling. They hit another bend, Sinclair holding Bertie firmly against the sway.

He got to his feet, Sinclair lifting her with him, her legs still around his hips. He turned around once with her in the tight compartment until the train bent the other way again. Sinclair gave up fighting the roll and ended up with Bertie's back against the window.

The curtains bowed into the glass with her, the window cool through the fabric. Sinclair thrust hard, again and again, while Bertie held on to him, her head rocking against the window.

She heard her own cries, drowned by the hard *clack-clack* of the wheels and the whistle blowing its warning. Sinclair's head went back, and he clenched his teeth against his own shout. "*Bloody* hell," he said in a grating voice. He made a harsh *ahh* sound as his eyes closed, and he lost his seed into her.

The train swayed the other way, the compartment following

its momentum. Sinclair lost his footing and ended up on the
bunk, Bertie still around him. She kissed his face, which was
wet with sweat, their bodies snug together. Sinclair kissed her
back, tumbling her hair, breathing hard, Bertie laughing.

"Damn, bloody trains," Sinclair growled, then he buried
his face in her neck and held her close.

In the morning, they disembarked at Edinburgh, which was
a bustling city under misty skies. Bertie couldn't see much
of it while trundling from one train platform to the next,
cold rain filming her coat and new hat. In the next train,
Sinclair, Bertie, and the children sat together in another
first-class compartment, Macaulay and Aoife joining them,
as they rolled out of Edinburgh north into the Highlands.

The rain eased back as the city dropped behind, the sun
came out, and sweeping hills came into view, marching
across the horizon, rising into the sky. Valleys dropped away
as the train chugged over bridges. Bertie couldn't drag herself
from the windows as she watched the splendor unfold.

The train stopped at a tiny station marked *Kilmorgan* to
let off Sinclair and family, the only ones to disembark.
Macaulay and Aoife oversaw the luggage being unloaded
while Bertie looked around her with interest.

The village wasn't much, that she could see—a high street
that ran from a small square to the train station. Houses and
shops lined the street, with a smattering of cottages beyond,
and after that . . . emptiness. Green hills rolled to the gray
horizon, the higher hills dusted with snow. The stationmas-
ter, who greeted Sinclair by name, said that snow had been
thin this year so far, but they'd likely get more soon.

"Hooray!" Andrew said. "You'll love to play in the snow
here, Bertie. It's glorious. We'll build a fort and have a battle."

"Not until you're better," Sinclair broke in sternly. "And
you'll be better when *I* say you are. Up you go."

He lifted his son into his arms and followed the station-
master through the tiny waiting room to the front of the station. The lane outside was empty, not a vehicle in sight.

"Do people *live* here?" Bertie asked. There was no sign of anyone, no movement on the road. All the silence made her nervous.

"They do." Sinclair sounded amused. "The village near my own house is even smaller, Miss Frasier of the city."

Bertie suppressed a shiver. "Well, I never," was all she could think of to say.

Sinclair frowned at the empty street. "I hope they remembered we were coming today. I don't want to have to tramp all the way to the castle."

Bertie looked about for a castle perched on a hill. She expected to see a tall stone edifice with battlements poking up from the rocks—like the pictures in the books she'd been reading—but she didn't see anything resembling that. She couldn't see much at *all* beyond this tiny village with no one in it.

Bertie heard the sound of hooves quickly clopping and turned to see a conveyance come around the corner into the square. It was a landau, closed against the cold, pulled by two smart horses trotting at high speed. On the box, holding the reins, was a tall man in a kilt standing up next to the red-coated coachman.

The horses pulled to a halt, with the door of the landau exactly in front of Sinclair and family. The tall man was only a lad, Bertie saw, maybe eighteen or nineteen. He dropped straight down from the box as the landau halted, landing gracefully on his feet with a flutter of kilt.

"Danny!" Andrew yelled from Sinclair's arms. "That was bully driving."

Danny had rawboned strength and the looks of the Mackenzies Bertie had already met—broad-shouldered, dark hair with red highlights, his eyes a bit darker than Hart's, Ian's, and Cameron's. Andrew had told Bertie all about Daniel Mackenzie, son of Lord Cameron, now at university in Edinburgh, the young man full of pranks and larks. Plus he knew all about engines and how to make them go.

"Glad you liked it, Andrew." Daniel reached for Andrew,

and Sinclair relinquished him. "How are you, Miss Caitriona? More and more a beautiful young lady every time I see you."

Daniel's Scottish accent was the most pronounced of the Mackenzies Bertie had heard, and he used it easily, unself-consciously. Cat took the compliment with her usual calm, but she sounded a little more animated when she answered. "Thank you, Master Daniel."

Daniel burst out laughing, a warm sound. "Little minx. The beaus will be breaking their hearts over you in a few years' time. And this is the new governess, is it?" His frank stare landed on Bertie.

"This is Bertie," Andrew announced with his usual volume. "She's going to stay with us forever!"

"No she won't." Cat's soft answer was lost in the coachman's *whoa*, as the horses moved, impatient, but Bertie heard her.

"I see." Daniel's look turned shrewd, and Sinclair moved closer to Bertie.

"You don't," Sinclair said in his barrister's voice. "Are we going to the castle or will we stand at the station freezing all morning?"

Daniel grinned and opened the carriage door. "In ye go. Miss . . . ?" He held out one hand to Bertie, his other arm still firmly around Andrew.

"Frasier," Bertie said in her best ladylike voice. "Thank you, Mr. Mackenzie."

"My pleasure." The laughter and intelligence in his eyes unnerved her.

Daniel said nothing more, only lifted in Andrew then Caitriona, and stood back so Sinclair could enter. Instead of joining them inside, Daniel closed the door and climbed back to the box. He was going to drive them to the castle.

Drive he did. The landau rocketed out of the village and straight up a hill, the carriage listing alarmingly.

Sinclair gave Bertie's hand a reassuring squeeze. "Hart Mackenzie's coachman would never let Daniel take the traces if it weren't safe."

Bertie didn't much agree, though if this coachman was anything like the duke's coachman in London, the man would at least be strong enough to stop the horses running away. She could hope so, anyway.

The ride didn't take long—not the way Daniel drove— and soon they were speeding over a bridge and along a curved drive. A house came into view, a colossus of one. Bertie rubbed mist from the landau's window and stared hard at it.

The house spread itself across a wide sweep of land, one long horizontal wing in front, with hints of more wings flowing out behind it. Glittering windows, dozens and dozens of them, marched across every floor, up to small dormer windows in the attics.

Daniel leapt to the ground as soon as they stopped, and two footmen in dark suits came forward to open the landau's doors. They handed Aoife down from the back with as much courtesy as they did Sinclair and family from inside. Five dogs swarmed out of the house, outflanking the footmen to greet the guests with barks and waving tails.

"This ain't a castle," Bertie said to Sinclair as she stared up at the house. "It's a blooming palace."

"The original Castle Kilmorgan is a ruin," Sinclair said calmly. "This house was built about a hundred or so years ago. The ruins are up there." He pointed east, to a high hill with black rocks tumbled along the top.

"It's a bully climb," Andrew said. His new word was *bully*, Bertie surmised. He must have heard someone in the train or stations using it. "I'll take you, Bertie."

"When you're better," Sinclair said in a hard voice.

Andrew paid no attention. He reached out from his father's arm to tug a footman's sleeve. "I got shot!" he said at the top of his voice. "Want to see?"

Chapter 20

The house was packed. The Christmas celebration preparations were in full whirl, and the ladies of the house caught Bertie up in them. The Mackenzie women were all there—Eleanor, Ainsley, Isabella, Beth, and their children, Louisa plump with her pregnancy. The McBride ladies, Juliana and Rose, were also present with more young ones.

The women ran about like sergeant majors in full command. Dogs burst apart every time the ladies rushed by, then closed in to follow them. The Mackenzie men and Sinclair's brothers seized Sinclair immediately and disappeared with him to some male sanctuary.

Bertie assumed she'd be confined to the nursery to help the nannies with the McBride and Mackenzie children, but it seemed the ladies needed all hands on deck. Bertie barely had Cat and Andrew settled in before she was pulled away by Ainsley—literally pulled by the hand—back to the ground-floor drawing room, which had become tactical headquarters.

Many ladies and gents from the upper echelon of British society had arrived to celebrate Christmas as the honored guests of Hart Mackenzie. The family would remain after Christmas for a private celebration at New Year's, but before-hand, the varied guests expected entertainment.

Bertie was drawn into helping fold paper mums that would shower down during the Christmas ball. Bertie saw that the Mackenzie and McBride wives, as lofty as they were, didn't shove the work onto the servants while they took their ease. They rolled up their sleeves and got on with it.

Lady Isabella, whom Bertie had not met before, had glo-rious red hair, like her sister Louisa, as well as a lovely fig-ure and keen green eyes. Isabella sat down opposite Bertie to help make the flowers, and treated Bertie to her assessing gaze.

"Your gown suits you," Lady Isabella said. "I see Mrs. Hill's hand in it. Sedate but not dowdy. I'd prefer to see you in something blue, though. It will bring out your eyes."

"Leave her be, Izzy," Louisa said, pausing from wherever she was rushing to, an open notebook at her ample abdo-men. "My apologies, Miss Frasier. My sister can't meet a woman without re-dressing her."

"Because I have exceptional taste," Isabella said without false modesty. "My sisters-in-law were in sad shape before I took them in hand. Do let me take you in hand, Miss Frasier. I enjoy it."

Her determination was a bit alarming, but charming at the same time. "I'm a governess," Bertie said, her voice faint.

"Nonsense. When you're teaching the children, yes, you're their governess. On your days out, you're a young lady who deserves a treat."

"But I'm not exactly . . ."

Isabella waved her quiet. "We know all about you. Elea-nor told us."

"She did, did she?" Bertie asked, worried.

"It's settled then. You'll come to my room before the ball, and I'll dress you. Everyone is invited to the Christmas ball, and you'll need something besides governess gray." Isabella rose, taking her finished flowers and giving Bertie a warm smile. "Don't worry; I'll fix you up."

She flowed away. Bertie swallowed and kept folding flowers with fingers that had chilled.

"You'll grow used to Isabella," Ian's wife, Beth, said, sliding in to take Isabella's place. "She loves to direct us all, but she has a kind heart. She provided a way for Ian and I to find each other, and I'm very grateful to her."

"Good on her," Bertie said. But Isabella was a lady, an earl's daughter, and Beth was a lady as well. They all were. Bertie was . . . Bertie.

She liked them, though, she decided. The wives talked openly, inviting everyone into the conversation—maids and Bertie, guests and footmen—all were included. A big, loving family, they were, the kind Bertie had always longed for. If nothing else came from her time with Sinclair, she was going to enjoy this Christmas, and treasure it forever.

She knew things couldn't go on as they were, not for always. Even Cat knew that. At the moment, Bertie existed in a bubble of happiness, where her love for Sinclair and his little ones were the only things that mattered. The rest of the world and its sordidness was outside the bubble. Bertie knew it would come crashing in soon—sharing a bed with Sinclair would have all kinds of consequences, and she wasn't stupid about what they could be—but for now, she determined to let herself enjoy the moments of sweetness.

~~~~~

"I'd like you to let someone else look at the letters," Inspector Fellows said.

He and Sinclair were alone at the windows of the long upstairs hall, while Cam and Mac Mackenzie and Steven and Elliot McBride talked and smoked heavily scented cigars in the sitting area at the other end. Sinclair had never taken to cigars, and Fellows, while he would partake, had little enthusiasm for them, and the two had moved off together.

Sinclair was happy to see Elliot out and enjoying conversation, listening to the others and laughing. He knew Elliot still had episodes from his ordeal in prison—who wouldn't?—but the darkness that had surrounded him every day had dissipated.

Sinclair had lightened too, and he knew exactly why.

"At the moment, I don't care about the be-damned letters," Sinclair said.

"I know, but my copper's mind never shuts down." Fellows gave him the ghost of a smile. "I looked through the list of men and women you've prosecuted over the years, and it's a good long one. Any of them could be hounding you. So I'd like to narrow that down by looking at the letters themselves."

Sinclair's fingers went stiff around his glass of whiskey. "Why? You've already looked at them. The paper and envelopes are ordinary, sold at any shop, we concluded."

"Ordinary to you and me, yes," Fellows said. "The letters printed so we can't recognize handwriting. But the man following you hasn't figured on one weapon in our arsenal—Ian Mackenzie."

Sinclair's unease was erased by surprise. "I know Ian has an extraordinary mind—I've seen what he can do with mathematics, his memory, music. But these papers are blanks, mass-produced. The only significant thing about them are the vile messages."

"Let's let him have a look, though, shall we?" Fellows asked. "You never know, with Ian."

Sinclair shrugged and took a sip of whiskey. "I'm willing. Where is Ian now?"

"In secret negotiation with Daniel, preparing something for the younger generation for tomorrow," Fellows said. He gave Sinclair a dark look. "Yes, we should be worried about that. We can try to run Ian to ground tonight, once the festivities start."

Sinclair gave a dry laugh. "You're optimistic. If we are not present and correct at the supper ball, the ladies will track us down with more ruthlessness than any hardened criminal."

Fellows shared his smile. "That, my friend, is true."

Sinclair took another sip of whiskey, studying Fellows over the glass. "You love it," he said. "You're a part of them now, and you're lapping it up."

Fellows gave him a conceding nod. "The Mackenzie brothers are as loud, foul-mouthed, and arrogant as they ever were." He glanced at the gathering behind Sinclair, and a roar of male laughter punctuated his statement. "But I find them easier to take these days. I find everything easier to take."

"Marriage does that to a man," Sinclair said. "I well remember."

Fellows's look softened slightly—as much as Fellows ever softened—first into fondness for his wife, and then into something like sympathy for Sinclair.

Last year when Sinclair had been here, he'd been morose indeed. This year was different. Bertie had already made it different.

He knew Bertie was in the process of ripping the scars from his wounds and letting the blood flow, but it was a healing flow. Sinclair didn't want to look at what was happening to him too closely, because danger always came when he examined something too minutely. It was enough, for now, to simply bask.

"Christmas morning then," Fellows said. "After whatever Daniel and Ian are putting together to impress the children."

"Give me a signal," Sinclair said. He lifted his empty glass in toast to Fellows, then retreated down the hall to his brothers and brothers-in-law, their laughter, and more whiskey.

~

"I can't wear this." Bertie stared into the mirror in shock.

Beth, next to her, resplendent in Mackenzie plaid, laughed at her. "Why not? You look a picture."

But that was just it. It was a picture.

The young woman who looked out of the large gilt-framed mirror at Bertie was a complete stranger. Ringlets of sleek brown hair brushed bare shoulders, which were hugged by a bodice of light blue silk. The bodice's short

sleeves ended above her elbows in a cascade of ivory lace.
The underskirt was a panel of the same light blue with an
appliqué of vines in darker blue across it. An overskirt of
striped dark and light blue taffeta was gathered back over a
small bustle, the excess fabric left to cascade in soft folds to
a hint of a train.

"It's made over," Isabella said, sounding apologetic as
she rearranged folds in the overskirt for the dozenth time.
"There wasn't time to fit you for anything new. But I think
the effort was worth it."

"Of course it was." Ainsley, as fair and gray-eyed as her
brother Sinclair, winked at Bertie, smiling wryly at Isabella's worry. She held out a pair of delicate high-heeled boots
in white leather. "Try these, Bertie. We went through our
wardrobes to see what might fit you. Eleanor and you seem
to be of a size."

Bertie's eyes widened. "You are all being so kind, but I
can't wear a duchess's shoes."

"Yes, you can." Eleanor followed Ainsley to join in the
admiration. "I bought these long ago but never found occasion to wear them. No reason to have them collecting dust
lying about in my dressing room. Not that they are dusty—I
cleaned them off and polished them to every inch. Or my
maid did. I tried to, but she took them away from me, telling
me I couldn't possibly go down to the ball with boot polish
under my fingernails. Not that there isn't photographing
chemicals under my fingernails—there always is, but that
seems to be fine with her. But boot polish, heaven forbid."
Eleanor threw her hands up in mock horror.

Ainsley guided Bertie to a chair and sat down in front of her.
"She means, *please wear them, Bertie. Someone ought to.*"

Before Bertie could stop her, Ainsley had pushed Bertie's
skirt to her knees and thrust first one boot than the other on
Bertie's feet. Bertie reached down as Ainsley started to lace
them.

"Here, you can't do that," she said nervously.

"Of course, I can," Ainsley answered, not stopping. "I've

been lacing boots for ages. If you bend too far forward, my girl, you'll wrinkle the dress and Isabella will have apoplexy. The maids are busy, and here I am. There, it's done."

Ainsley helped Bertie to her feet and walked her to the mirror again. The McBride and Mackenzie wives gathered behind her in a sea of silks and jewels.

The height lent by the boots made the skirts fall cleanly to the floor and thrust Bertie's bosom out a little. She laughed at herself.

"I look like Cinderella."

"And we're your fairy godmothers," Isabella said, straightening the skirt again.

"*Not* your wicked stepsisters," Eleanor said.

"And you don't have to be in by midnight," Juliana said, fluffing out the lace on Bertie's sleeves. "In fact, it would be rude to leave Hart's ball early."

"You won't lose your slipper either." Ainsley smiled at her in the mirror. "I laced those boots quite firmly."

Eleanor looked thoughtful. "I never did understand the part in the story where the sisters cut off bits of their feet to fit into the shoes. Surely the prince's emissaries would notice them bleeding all over the floor. Unless the sisters had enormous corns, and that's what the writer meant." She grinned at Bertie, the gleam in her eyes belying her prattle.

Cat, who'd been invited to come down and watch the proceedings, sat with her head down over her notebook, her pencil moving. Bertie had hoped she'd take an interest in the pretty dresses, but she only glanced at the ladies in their splendid gowns before returning to her notebook.

When Bertie came across the room to kiss Cat good night, Cat slammed the book closed. Bertie caught a brief glimpse of what was in it, but couldn't decide what she'd seen.

Cat quietly followed the nanny who'd come to fetch her out, and the ladies called Bertie back to try to make her wear a circlet of pearls. Bertie won the argument and stuck with her mother's locket. She needed one familiar thing with her on this mad night.

They'd done something to her. Sinclair gazed at Bertie across the duke's giant ballroom, unable to take his eyes off her. His sister and the ladies had fussed over her, dressing Bertie's hair in whatever style women liked these days, and lacing her into a costly gown. Very pretty. Women enjoyed that sort of thing, but Bertie looked as though she'd swallowed a poker.

Sinclair's brother Elliot handed him a glass of whiskey, breaking his line of sight to Bertie. "Your taste is improving."

Sinclair accepted the whiskey gratefully. "Taste?"

"In women. The last time I stood with you at a supper ball, you had your eyes on a jaded widow eager to drag you off to bed. Your governess has more love for life." He sipped whiskey. "Vibrant, that's the word."

"She's not *my* governess," Sinclair said, his gaze going back to Bertie as the ladies moved her through the room like a current pushing a drifting boat. The Mackenzie and McBride ladies wore plaid, making Bertie's blue and ivory stand out all the more.

Steven McBride, Sinclair's youngest brother, and one of Hart's many aristocratic guests paused next to the brothers as Sinclair spoke. The Englishman, elegant and polished, said, "I say, McBride, don't dismiss her so quickly. Some men *like* that sort of thing."

Elliot, his sun-bronzed face creased with the remains of white scars, scowled at him. "What sort of thing? Beautiful women?"

"Governesses." The Englishman gazed too appreciatively at Bertie. "So ready with their *discipline*." He caught Sinclair's eye. "Not that you are such a man, of course."

Sinclair didn't answer. He didn't know the gentleman, and didn't want to. He fixed his gaze on the Englishman, pinning him as he would a lying witness in the box. Sinclair didn't dare speak, because he knew nothing would come out of his mouth but a foul-worded snarl.

The Englishman looked back and forth among the three brothers, took in their hard faces, and flushed. "Gentlemen, I meant no offense. You Scots are a bit funny about your ladies."

"We're very protective of them," Elliot said, his accent becoming broad. "You'd be wise to remember that, m' friend."

"Right." The Englishman looked Sinclair up and down, then sniffed. "Gratified to have made your acquaintance, Captain McBride," he said to Steven. "Thank you." He nodded at Steven then moved off, bending his body to slide through the crowd.

"You've lost yourself a client," Steven said. He plucked a whiskey from a tray carried by a passing footman and took a deep drink.

"Client." Sinclair dragged his attention back to his brothers, trying to calm his murderous intentions. "What are you talking about?"

Steven took another sip of whiskey. The youngest McBride looked much like his brothers—fair and sunbaked, but ten years younger. He wore a pleased-with-himself look now that he'd found his Rose, only last month that had been. "Chap was in the market for a barrister," Steven said to Sinclair. "Wouldn't tell me why. Looking for the best. Wanted to meet you."

"He should have applied through his solicitor, not directly to me," Sinclair said with a growl.

"He knows that. He wanted to size you up." Steven grinned. "I guess he did."

Sinclair's anger roiled. He was famous for being calm and cool even in the face of the nastiest criminals, but at the moment, he knew he either had to redirect his temper or follow the Englishman and beat his face bloody.

He thrust his half-finished glass of whiskey at Steven. "Excuse me, little brothers," he said. "I'm going to dance with my governess."

Chapter 21

Bertie watched Sinclair come at her, parting the crowd like a determined barge.

Juliana McBride was on Bertie's arm. "Good heavens," she said, watching her brother-in-law draw near them. "What fired off the volcano? He's usually sweet as a lamb."

Didn't Bertie know it? But she'd also seen Sinclair plenty of times red-faced and snarling, his Scots anger stirred to rage.

Sinclair stopped in front of Bertie, looking her up and down, and not in an admiring way.

"What's wrong?" Bertie asked him in alarm. "Has something happened?"

"Of course it hasn't. This is a ball. We will dance." He held out his hand.

"Now, you wait just a minute, Mr. High-Handed McBride—" Bertie's words choked off as Sinclair seized her and started dragging her toward the middle of the ballroom. Bertie looked around desperately for Juliana, but Juliana had vanished.

Sinclair drew Bertie around in a graceful circle, the fine

dress sweeping as it should. His hand went to her waist, and he drew her close.

"Stop!" Bertie said in a frantic whisper. "Or this will be a disaster!"

"Why?" His gray eyes held the severity of Basher McBride, the flint-hard gaze pinning her.

"Because I don't know how to dance. The ladies, they were sweet to dress me up, but it's only show." Bertie gestured to her gown, a lovely thing, but she'd spent all the time she'd been in it so far worried she'd tear or stain it. "Like a shop window with a fancy display, but there's nothing inside the shop."

"It's a waltz," Sinclair said, tightening his grip on her waist. "Three steps. Here we go."

He pushed her right foot backward, then her left foot to the side, a little pause, then her left forward, following the music. His hand was firm on her waist, his other hand warm on hers through their gloves. Sinclair pushed her through the pattern again, rumbling the steps in his fine Scottish baritone.

Memories stirred in Bertie's head. She was a little girl again, she and her mother in their tiny parlor, her mother smiling as she pushed Bertie around the floor. *One, two, three; one, two, three—there, you have it, my lovely.*

Bertie's eyes stung, and her step faltered. Sinclair's brows snapped together. "Don't cry, Bertie. I'm in a foul mood, but it's not your fault. You're doing beautifully."

"It ain't . . . it *isn't* . . ." Bertie swallowed her tears. "Never mind. Don't stop dancing."

Sinclair pushed her around with more exuberance, turning with her in a wide circle. She saw why the uncomfortable skirt had been made the way it was—it floated out behind her, as Sinclair took her around and around the ballroom.

The room began to swirl—it was as though Bertie stood in place, in the arms of the man she loved, while the ballroom whirled around them. Colors flashed, the glittering lights ran together, but Bertie was safe, Sinclair's strong arms holding her. She'd never fall. The boots Ainsley had laced so tightly clung to her feet while Sinclair spun her through the ballroom. Bertie threw back her head and laughed.

"Stop that," Sinclair said, scowling.

"Why?" Bertie floated on pure sweetness, and she wanted to dance and dance. She was Cinderella in truth, and Sinclair was her handsome prince.

"Because it makes me want to kiss you," Sinclair said, his gray eyes stormy. "I want to kiss you, Bertie Frasier. I want to haul you into my arms and never let you go."

Bertie went hot, dizzy. "I wouldn't mind that."

"You would mind it, when you understood, lass."

He was wrong. Bertie wanted to stay inside this bubble—like a scene in one of the snow globes Cat had. They'd be dancing, frozen in time, while the rest of the world went on around them. Bertie and Sinclair would remain together forever, and this joy would never end.

"Happy Christmas!" someone shouted.

The orchestra ceased playing, and cheers erupted through the ballroom. The crowd rushed to the huge foyer, where the flowers Bertie had helped fold were being released, the light things floating down from the landings above. Sinclair caught one and handed it to Bertie—pink, one of the ones Beth had done. Bertie took it reverently, as though it were the most precious thing in the world.

The guests streamed outside—into the freezing cold and snow, no less—to watch fireworks bang and sparkle against the sky. The children, allowed to watch from windows in the gallery, shouted from above, and the dogs, somehow freed from their kennels in the stable yard, barked and flowed among the guests.

This was the perfect time for Sinclair to turn Bertie around in the dark and kiss her, but they were jostled apart. Bertie was swept away by excited ladies she didn't know, who didn't notice there was a governess in their midst.

Bertie looked around for Sinclair and saw him captured by his brothers, Steven's hand on his shoulder. They made a fine sight, the three McBride men in black coats and blue kilts, fair hair pale in the darkness.

Sinclair caught sight of her and smiled. Didn't matter how much space was between them, the smile said. They were still dancing, pulled tight together, while the world rushed by, doing things that were of no consequence at all.

~~~~~

No one had told Bertie that being a lady of luxury could be so exhausting. She crawled in bed in the wee hours, knowing she had to be up again soon. The children would be celebrating their Christmas morning in the nursery, with all the families, and Ainsley had said Bertie should be there. Andrew and Cat would be disappointed if she didn't come.

All the beautiful and strange clothes had come off, taken away by Isabella's maid, while Ainsley's maid had collected the shoes. Unlaced and uncorseted, Bertie took a deep breath and fell facedown onto her bed. One of the kind maids pulled blankets over her and then left her alone.

Bertie expected to lie awake in her excitement, reliving the dance with Sinclair. She'd not been able to have another one with him, with all the Christmas fireworks, games, and the fairly silly skits some of the ladies and gentlemen had put on. The Scottish families had not done much—the English had done most of the celebrating. Ainsley had explained that in Scotland, Christmas wasn't the important holiday— New Year's was. At that time only the family stayed at the castle, but the whole village came up for the festivities, and the revelry would be unlike any Bertie had seen.

Bertie dropped off to sleep almost immediately, however, her body having spent its resources.

She woke again when a strong, warm hand landed on her back. The smell of whiskey and wool assailed her, and the bed creaked, as a man in a kilt sat down on it.

"Happy Christmas, Bertie."

Sinclair's voice was low and rumbling. He stroked her hair, now in a loose braid, and slid a tissue-wrapped box under her hand.

"Oh, no," she moaned. "I didn't get you nothing."

His laughter was soft. "You didn't have to, minx. I thought you might like this."

Bertie's curiosity rose as she tugged at the paper. "You

shouldn't give me presents. All the posh people at this do will gossip like mad."

"Open it, Bertie," Sinclair said, impatient. "It's a private gift between us."

Bertie tore off the paper then opened the lid, looked inside, and drew a sharp breath.

A photograph in a slim frame rested among the tissue paper, a picture of Cat and Andrew. Caitriona sat primly on a chair, every hair in place, her legs in white stockings crossed at the ankle. Her doll smiled serenely from her lap. Andrew sat on the floor with his arm around a large dog— one that lived here at Kilmorgan Castle. Andrew was grinning, and slightly blurry, as though he hadn't held still during the exposure. But the camera had caught him as he was—sunny-natured and busy, while Caitriona's smile was quietly pretty.

A sob caught in Bertie's throat. "It's beautiful. I'll treasure it always. Thank you. I love them so much."

Tears came from her eyes. Sinclair gently took the photo from her and closed it into the box, setting it on her night table. "Shh, lass." He gently rolled her over, the rough wool of the kilt warm through the covers. "Damn it; I keep making you cry. I want to make you smile."

"You do." Bertie wiped her eyes. "You always do."

"Shall I tell you what you do to me?" He lowered himself to her, his body warm with his clothes. "I'm a bit drunk, so I might say too much. I tamed myself, so I could have a family, do everything right. But it went too far, and there was nothing left of me. And then you charged into my life. You ripped the lid from the powder keg. You lit the match. Now I, the model widowed father, want to run rampant like a crazed youth. If you think Andrew unruly, he has a long way to go before he surpasses me."

Bertie started to smile. "I'd like to see that."

"No, you wouldn't. But it doesn't matter. You've made me live again, Bertie, you wonderful, beautiful woman."

He kissed her mouth, a swift, rough kiss before he pulled Bertie up with him and yanked away the blankets. She hadn't bothered with her nightdress, so she was bare, nothing between her and the wool of his kilt.

The kilt held his warmth, but didn't keep out the fact that he was hard underneath it. Bertie, as she kissed him, wormed her hand under the wool, until she found the length of his shaft.

"Damn." Sinclair lifted his head, frowning fiercely, but he kissed her lips again. "What are you doing to me?"

"What you do to me." Bertie stroked his cock, loving the way he groaned as though he couldn't stop himself. "You make me want you."

"And I want *you*." He made another sound in his throat, and shifted his position so she could reach more of him. "Tonight, I wanted to dance you into a corner and peel off that pretty dress, didn't matter how many people were in this bloody house."

"Did you think it was pretty?" Bertie asked, wistful.

"I thought you were beautiful. But we don't need the dress."

"It's gone."

"Good."

Sinclair broke her hold of him, but only to strip off his coat, waistcoat, shirt, and undershirt. Bertie's hands roved his bare shoulders, finding every curve of muscle, tight under his skin.

She thought he'd take off his kilt, but Sinclair only tucked the plaid around her, giving her a wicked smile as he slid himself on top of her.

"Oh." Bertie let out her breath as he pushed inside her, spreading her. He was large and thick, and everything that was good.

He thrust slowly, pausing between each one, letting her feel every inch of him. Gone was the frenzy from the train—they came together in warmth tonight, locked in intimacy.

Sinclair slid his hands under Bertie's hips. He rolled her over on the large bed, still inside her, and eased her upward until Bertie was sitting on him, straddling his thighs.

The position lifted him high inside her. Bertie's head went

back, a cry of pleasure escaping her throat. *This* was why men and women desperately sought passion, this amazing feeling, and the joy of finding it with another person.

Sinclair watched her, his hard-palmed hands coming up to cup her breasts. He teased her nipples with his thumbs, sending dark fire to join the one already incinerating her.

Bertie moaned, rising and falling as Sinclair lifted against her. He slid his hands from her breasts to her hips, encouraging her, until she was rocking shamelessly on him. The movement pressed him even more satisfyingly inside her.

Bertie rode him, her hair tumbling down. She was brazen, she knew, but she didn't care. She loved this man, and she wouldn't throw away the joy he was handing her.

By the time she was crying out, drowning in dark waves of passion, Sinclair had lifted himself onto his elbows, thrusting hard. His skin gleamed with sweat, the plaid bunched around them, the lamplight brushing his body and the gold of his hair.

Bertie never knew when it was over. Her mind whirled away, lost in the incredible delights Sinclair gave her body, but suddenly she was lying full length on top of him, holding him, kissing him. Sinclair was inside her, still hard, but he was spent, his breath coming fast, and he was laughing.

"Happy Christmas," he said, his voice rough.

"Happy . . . Christmas." Bertie's words came out between breaths, then she snuggled against him and let all be well.

~~~

Christmas morning commenced without Bertie having gotten much sleep. Her eyes were hot and sandy, her body a bit sore, but she dressed and made her way to the nursery for the celebration.

The entire Mackenzie and McBride families were there, mothers, fathers, and children. Elliot and Juliana had a half Indian daughter—Bertie had heard the entire tale of Priti's origins from Eleanor. Priti was a beautiful child, bright-eyed and full of enthusiasm for opening Christmas gifts.

She was protective of her half brother, Patrick, who was not even a year old.

Amazing gifts had been showered on the children, from kites to entire armies of toy soldiers to dolls and doll furniture, to a bicycle for Aimee, the oldest Mackenzie at seven. Andrew eyed the bicycle with envy, but forgot about it when he opened his steam train on a track, with an engine that belched real steam.

Cat received jewelry, ribbons, lace, hats, and slippers, from the Mackenzie and McBride ladies, and her doll had a new frock, given to her by Sinclair. The gown was of the latest mode, a burnt orange color trimmed with brown, with a puffed bustle and long sleeves that tapered into ruffled cuffs. Cat touched the dress, thanked her father, and set the box aside.

Sinclair's smile when Cat thanked him was strained. Beth whispered to Bertie later that Cat received a new dress for the doll every year, but never put them on her. Bertie had noted that the doll's clothes never changed—though Cat would undress the doll and let Aoife wash the garments, the same things always went back on again.

Daniel Mackenzie didn't let the dignity of his nineteen years mar his eagerness to help the children open and sort through their mountain of gifts. The children loved him, Bertie saw, the tiny ones crawling over him, the older ones, including Andrew, shouting for his attention. Even Cat, the oldest child present, favored him with her rare smiles.

"What did you do for us this year, Danny?" Andrew yelled at him.

"Thought you'd never ask." Daniel rose to his feet, winked at Bertie, and told the children to follow him—no pushing, no shouting.

They filed out obediently, the older ones quivering in excitement as they ran down the stairs after him.

Ian Mackenzie, who'd left the nursery as soon as his son's and daughters' gifts had been opened, waited for them on the terrace. Snow had fallen in the night, but the clouds had gone, and the December day was crisp and clear. The nannies had made the children stop for coats, and Bertie adjusted mittens on several pairs of hands.

Daniel held his hands up for silence, then spoke. "Those of you who were here for Christmas last year remember the spectacular show put on by his brilliance, Ian Mackenzie, assisted by your humble servant." Daniel pressed his hands to his chest and bowed. The children laughed and applauded.

"Get on with it, Danny," Louisa shouted.

Daniel took another bow. "As you know, I have a fondness for mechanical workings, and Ian has a fondness for precision. He also has a fondness for his children, who are spoiled rotten." Ian's two older children jeered at him, while his youngest, Megan, waved her fists from her mother's arms. "We pooled our efforts to bring to you the launch of the first Mackenzie flotilla—*of the air*!"

Daniel rotated his arms in a wild signal to Ian, who carefully leaned down and pulled some kind of lever half hidden by the terrace's wall.

The pops of small explosions, like miniature fireworks, sounded, making the children jump and squeal, some sticking fingers into ears. Puffs of smoke burst up all along the terrace, and with it, balloons, each about a foot in diameter. Dangling from each was a small box.

The balloons, dozens of them, soared up into the air and headed for the garden. The children jumped and danced, or stared, enchanted.

"Those boxes are my presents to you," Daniel shouted. "Catch them if you can!"

Chapter 22

Another collective cheer, and the children swarmed down from the terrace, racing into the garden, screaming and laughing.

Cameron went off the terrace after his tottering, happy daughter. "Blast you, Danny. I'd dreamt of putting my feet up somewhere warm for the rest of the morning, not rushing around the freezing garden."

Daniel only grinned at his father. "I know your meaning, and you can cuddle with my stepmama later. But it's the bairns' day, isn't it?"

Sinclair said nothing at all, only went after Andrew, who was running hell-bent after one of the drifting balloons. Cat watched with some interest, but she sat down on the terrace wall and took out her notebook.

Bertie sat down next to Cat, and Cat shut the book, as usual. "That was a lovely dress your father gave you for your doll."

Cat nodded. "He has a dressmaker make them. It's very kind."

"Will you show them all to me? I bet you can see the march of fashion all the way back to this one." Bertie touched the dress the doll always wore, which had a tighter skirt and a smaller bustle than the one Cat had received today, the mode of about eight years ago.

Cat gave her another nod. "They're in London. We can look when we get back."

Her answers were polite, but she was impatient, her fingers tightening on her notebook.

"Will you show me what's in there?" Bertie asked, gesturing to the notebook.

Cat shot her a look that was almost fearful. "No."

Bertie's curiosity rose, but she remembered how she'd been at Cat's age, having lost her mother. She'd needed something private, hers alone, and so Bertie had made her hideaway under the street. "It's all right. I won't ask if you don't want me to."

Cat watched the children running through the garden, arms outstretched for the balloons, which were drifting down again. Their parents ran after them, like colorful ducks after their ducklings. Bertie and Cat were relatively alone on the terrace, no one in their corner.

"I don't want anyone to see," Cat said, shifting her doll in her arm. "They'll laugh, or try to make me stop. Even Papa."

Bertie's curiosity rose even higher, but she quelled it. "I won't let anyone look if you don't want them to. Promise. Not if it's that special to you."

Cat shifted the doll again, her brows furrowing as though she debated with herself. Finally, slowly, she opened the notebook, at first holding it so Bertie couldn't see inside. Then she leafed to a page and held it out to Bertie.

Bertie stared at the drawing on the paper in some puzzlement, then she realized what she was looking at. It was Bertie herself, standing in front of the mirror in Eleanor's dressing room, gazing at herself in wonder.

The picture wasn't an exact representation of her, with every line precise—it was more light and shadow than thick lines. Bertie's gown flowed into her body, short, bold strokes delineating where gown ended and woman began. Her face was a suggestion but her eyes held all the amazement Bertie had felt, seeing herself pretty for the first time in her life.

The other ladies were there, squiggles of darkness and light, each of them expressing delight.

"Oh, Cat," Bertie said breathlessly. "This is lovely!"

Cat pried the book from Bertie's fingers. "It's not right. I know I don't draw like the drawing master taught me, but it's how I see things."

Bertie touched the notebook's leather cover. "Are all your pictures like that?"

Cat nodded. "I draw all the time." She flushed. "Sometimes I write little poems about what I draw."

Bertie instantly wanted to read them, but she restrained herself. "Have you ever shown your Uncle Mac any of what you've drawn? I've seen his paintings. They're beautiful, even though some of them are . . . well, blurry."

"He paints like Monsieur Manet and Monsieur Degas," Cat said. "Mrs. Evans said that what Uncle Mac paints is shameful, but I think his pictures are beautiful. But no, I haven't showed him."

"Why not? Maybe he can give you some lessons."

"No!" Cat said in a hard voice. She swallowed. "What if he says they aren't any good? It would be . . ."

She made a helpless gesture as though not knowing how to finish the thought. Bertie believed she understood. If Mac derided Cat's drawings—not that Bertie thought he would— that would take something away from Cat, something she considered personal and precious.

"You can't tell him," Cat said with a scowl. "You promised, Bertie."

Bertie lifted her hands. "I know I did. I'll not say a word. Not unless you want me to."

Cat nodded, though she gave Bertie a skeptical look. Bertie saw she'd have to win the girl's trust in this matter, and she determined to do so.

The picture Cat had done of Bertie was full of vibrancy and strange beauty. She had talent, Bertie was sure of it. Maybe one day, Cat would be ready to share it with the world.

After breakfast, once the adults of the family had rested from
the mad chase of children in the garden, Sinclair went to meet
Fellows and Ian in Ian's wing of the house. Before Sinclair
could shut the door of Ian's upstairs sitting room, it was pushed
open by Bertie, who slid in behind Sinclair without apology.

Fellows raised his brows, but Sinclair answered, "It's all
right. I want her here. She might be able to help."

Fellows pinned Bertie with his policeman's stare but con-
ceded with a nod. Ian, who was leaning on the edge of a
desk, had the letters in his hand and was peering at them in
turn. Sinclair watched him interestedly.

Ian didn't simply read the letters. He held each one an
inch away from his face and scanned the paper, turning it
over and then upside down. He even touched a page to his
nose, as though taking in its scent.

"What do you make of them, Ian?" Sinclair asked.

Ian didn't answer, continuing his scrutiny in silence. After
a few moments, he stood up and laid the sheets out on the
wide desk, making three rows. He stood back and studied the
arrangement, then lifted a few letters and changed their
places with others, neatening the rows again.

At last Ian stepped back and made his pronouncement.
"They were all written by the same person."

Sinclair came to stand next to him—not too close,
because Ian didn't like anyone to touch him without warning. His wife and children could, and his sisters-in-law, but
no others. Even his brothers had to be careful with him. Sinclair noted, however, that Ian didn't seem to mind Bertie
coming close to his other side to look at the letters with him.
Was Ian a madman, or simply crafty?

"I'd worked that out already," Sinclair said with a touch
of impatience.

"They were all written at the same time," Ian went on, as
though Sinclair hadn't spoken. "There are five missing."

Sinclair started. The strange revelation that they'd been
penned at the same time was lost in the cold qualm that Ian

knew Sinclair had kept some of the letters back. What's more, from the look Bertie threw at Sinclair, she knew it too, blast her.

Bertie asked the question Sinclair would have if he could have found his voice. "How the devil do you know all that?"

Ian didn't answer. He touched each page in turn in silence, aligning their corners perfectly with the edges of the desk.

Sinclair couldn't take his eyes from Bertie, who looked delicious in a modest gown of McBride plaid. The dark blue of the plaid brought out Bertie's eyes, the blue-violet Sinclair had first noticed under her god-awful hat in the dirty London street. Those eyes flicked to him now, and Bertie flushed.

Ian lifted the second letter, turned it over, and held the back of it to Bertie. He traced his large fingertip over the indentations of the written letters. In silence, he turned the paper to its front side and traced indentations of *additional* letters, ones that weren't inked. He then lifted the first paper, set it over the second, and moved his finger along those lines again. Bertie made a sound of delight.

"I see." She took the pages from Ian's hand, holding them up to the light. "He had a stack of paper and wrote each message on the top page, which left indents on the paper below." Bertie piled the first three letters together and mimed writing. "The indentations of the first letter fades as it goes farther down the stack, and then the second, and so on. But how do you know they were written at the same time?" she asked Ian.

Ian took the pages from her and laid them out again, still in silence. He didn't answer, Sinclair understood, not because he didn't know, but because he didn't have the words to explain. They jumbled up on him sometimes, Beth had said, and wouldn't come out as he wanted them to. So he remained silent.

"The ink," Sinclair said. "It's faded on each letter by exactly the same amount. The ones I received later aren't any sharper than the earlier ones."

"Except the last one you got," Bertie said. "That one's new."

Fellows gave Sinclair a severe look as Ian continued to lightly touch the pages. "Last one? I don't remember you mentioning this."

"Probably because it was about me," Bertie said before Sinclair could answer. "Nasty thing. It came not long before we left London. But it couldn't have been written at the same time as the others, because I didn't happen along until a few weeks ago."

"Was it delivered to your house?" Fellows asked Sinclair.

"To my chambers," Sinclair said. "Henry brought it to me when I was staying home with Andrew. Yes, it was foul, and mentioned Bertie—if not by name, then by inference. The letter said, *I know who she is and what she is,* though he shied away from specifics."

"Hmm." Fellows looked unhappy. "That means this person is watching you or having you watched. He knows you've taken in a young governess, and he possibly does know where she came from. He prepared the first letters to send out to you little by little, to slowly torment you, but he's taking advantage of opportunity now."

"And I want him found," Sinclair said, his anger rising. "I want my children and Bertie safe."

"I'll find him." Fellows spoke with conviction. "Ian, what about the missing letters you talked about? Do you mean they haven't been sent yet?"

Ian shook his head. He ran his fingers in the space between letters four and five, then seven and eight, then a few more down the table.

Bertie followed him. "I see—you mean the indentations don't match any of the ones here. That's how you know they're gone."

"I have them at home," Sinclair broke in impatiently. "Same writing, same paper."

"I believe you told me you burned one," Fellows said mildly.

Sinclair let out a breath of exasperation. "I kept them in case it turned out they'd help. But I didn't want you to read them, Fellows. I'm sorry."

"Because they're about his wife," Bertie said. "I don't blame him for not wanting anyone to see. Even if what they say ain't—*isn't*—true."

Sinclair felt his maddening rage again. "Bertie."

Bertie looked at him in all innocence. "I know I shouldn't have read them. It was an accident. But it's no use waiting for you to tell me things. I want to help, but you hold everything back."

"I know the feeling," Fellows said dryly.

"Forgive me," Sinclair said, voice hard. "You have enough to go on here. You don't need them."

Fellows nodded once. "Probably not. I'd like the last letter you received though, the one about Miss Frasier, to see how they differ."

"Calls me a viper and a whore," Bertie said readily. "Don't matter to me. I've been called worse. You have to have a thick skin to grow up in the East End." She lost her cheeky smile. "I don't like how it says I'll be the death of them, though. I almost was."

"I've told you," Sinclair said sternly. "That was not your fault, but entirely Jeffrey's."

"Did the letter come before or after Jeffrey's attack?" Fellows interrupted.

Sinclair considered. "I'm not sure. Henry didn't bring it to me until a few days after, but I'll have to ask him when it arrived." He met Bertie's gaze again. "Still not your fault."

"I'd say not," Fellows said. "If this man has been watching you and has the resources, I wouldn't be surprised if he directed Jeffrey to your house, telling him that's where Miss Frasier had gone, and possibly even supplied the gun. That gives me another place to dig—Jeffrey's haunts and his cronies. This man, whoever he is, has much patience and likely a lot of money. I have to wonder what the devil you did to him."

Sinclair shrugged, the movement masking the turbulence inside him. "I've been a barrister for years. Either he or someone he cares for—brother, wife, son, lover—was sent down because of my arguments. That's the problem with crime and its punishment—it touches many lives, not only the victims but the victims' families and those of the criminals as well. If I grew maudlin about it, I wouldn't be able to do my job. Murderers should go down, and their victims should have justice." He let out a breath. "But it's not always that simple."

"No." The word came hard out of Ian's mouth, causing Sinclair and the other two to jerk their gazes to him. "There is always hurt." Ian's fists had balled as though he remembered all the hurt in his life before he'd met Beth.

Bertie put her hand on Ian's arm. Sinclair tensed, wondering what he'd do, but Ian only looked at her, his expression calming. "But there are good people too," Bertie said to him. "I didn't know that until recently. Like your Beth, and Sinclair—Mr. McBride, I mean—and your brothers and nephew. And your wee ones."

Ian smiled at her, his face blossoming into happiness. "My Jamie is a handful." He said it proudly. "My girls too."

"And they're beautiful." Bertie rubbed his arm. "You did good there, Lord Ian."

Ian continued to smile at her, the letters forgotten. He and Bertie shared a long look of understanding, Ian lost in the happiness of the world he'd found as a husband and father.

~~~~~

When the discussion with Fellows ended, Bertie tried to slip away alone, but before she could reach the main part of the house and its long gallery, Sinclair caught up to her. He closed his hand around her arm and pulled her up the stairs to another floor, marched her along a hall and into an empty room. This one was a bedroom, but dust sheets covered the furniture.

Bertie pulled away as Sinclair closed the door, and turned to face him. "Before you start shouting at me, I read those letters about your wife because I wanted to help you. And I was curious." Her face burned. "I'm sorry. They must have upset you."

Sinclair's gray eyes sparkled with anger. "I remember locking them in a box in a bottom drawer of my desk, also locked," he said in a hard voice. "How did you 'accidentally' come to read them? They leapt out of the drawer and floated up to the nursery?"

"No." Bertie clenched her hands. "I searched your desk. I

admit that. You said there'd been other letters, and I wanted to see if they matched the one about me."

"Why?"

Bertie blinked. "Because I want to help, what'cha think? You looked so bleak. Like that." She pointed at his face. "And I wanted to help you."

Sinclair stared at her as though torn between shouting or walking out to storm around someplace else. Bertie had noticed that he could be very eloquent when speaking on behalf of other people, but he was bad at talking about himself.

She gentled her voice. "I know why you didn't want to show the letters to Inspector Fellows. They were full of lies about your wife, and you loved her very much. I know you did. But don't let this person, whoever he is, take her away from you. That's what bullies do—they poison everything in your life before they even take the first swing at you. That way you're already too beaten down to fight back."

Sinclair's gaze sharpened. "You speak from experience, do you?"

She shrugged. "Where I grew up, you were either a bully or you knuckled under. Or you got out. Getting out's the hardest, but the best."

Sinclair looked grim. "Well, you got out. You *are* out, and I'm not letting you go back."

Bertie smiled. "Aw, you're a sweetheart, you are. They call you Basher, but you're brimming with compassion. Don't let this man take that away from you, right? You remember your wife as she was, not these lies."

Sinclair stared at her a moment longer, then every bit of anguish she'd ever seen in him flooded into his eyes. After another few heartbeats, he started to laugh. The laughter was strange, and held no mirth.

"The thing is, Bertie, it isn't lies," Sinclair said. "Miss Margaret Davies—also known as Daisy, my wife—was a thorough scoundrel and a liar. And it's very frightening to me that this man somehow knows all about her."

Chapter 23

Bertie stared at Sinclair in surprise. She thought about the photographs of Daisy McBride, the quiet beauty of her, but with a twinkle in her eyes that said she hadn't been meek and mild. But it was a long way from not being meek to being a scoundrel and a liar.

"What the devil are you talking about?" Bertie asked him.

Sinclair walked away across the room then swung back, the light from the windows silhouetting his tall body and kilt. "When I met Daisy, she was trying to fleece me out of a good deal of cash. She thought me a reckless, stupid soldier on leave with too much money." He let out another harsh laugh. "She was right."

Bertie plopped down on the nearest chair, sheet and all, and a puff of dust burst from it. "Well knock me down with a feather. And here I was thinking she was the model of propriety." Her eyes narrowed. "But wait a minute. She *was* the model of propriety. Macaulay and Mrs. Hill can't say enough good things about her, and the children think she was an angel. Macaulay said she saved you. So which was it?"

"Both. What Daisy was and what she became were two different things."

"I see. No, I don't." She frowned. "You'd better tell me about it, hadn't you?"

Bertie wasn't certain Sinclair would say anything at all. He was a private man, and not happy that Bertie knew as much as she already did. In spite of their fiery nights of passion, Sinclair had the upper hand in her life at present, and she knew it.

Sinclair heaved another long sigh. He came to her, standing over her like a stern bailiff about to take her in chains to jail. Then he leaned to her, lifted her in his arms, turned, and sat down on the chair, settling Bertie on his lap.

"All right, I'll tell you," he said, resting his arms around her. "I'll tell you everything."

Bertie snuggled against him, liking this bit, and Sinclair began his story.

"I was an idiot. A thoroughly wet-behind-the-ears idiot. Daisy came from a very staunch, upright, straitlaced Irish Protestant family—you've seen her brother and his wife. Well, when Daisy was sixteen, she rebelled. She eloped with a rake, who took her to Paris and taught her to be as bad as he was. She was thoroughly in love with him, she told me, found him refreshing after years of being forbidden to speak on Sundays, except for prayers. Her father was a strict and difficult man."

"Sounds like my dad. Except my dad's not religious." Bertie gave him a look. "Seems you like criminals then."

"Hmph. So it seems."

"Go on," Bertie prompted.

Sinclair's arms tightened around her. "I met Daisy in Rome, where she was there with her lover, and as I say, they tried to fleece me. They told me Daisy's mother was very ill—dying—but that Daisy didn't have enough money to go all the way back to Ireland to be with her. A simple story, but I was kindhearted, and stupid. I offered to buy the train and boat tickets for her, but she and her lover—they said they were married—told me they weren't certain Daisy's mother wouldn't be moved to London, and they'd rather not have tickets they couldn't use. A waste of my money, wouldn't it be? So I gave Daisy enough to buy the tickets herself. I was supposed to rejoin my company the day after I last saw them, but there was a delay, and I was granted another few days' leave. That's how I caught them—I saw them in another trattoria, chatting up another fool with the same story."

"Ah." Bertie shook her head. "Bad form, that. You should always move on to a different town once you've finished with the mark. Did they try to run?"

"Yes. I caught both of them in their rooms, where they'd gone to get their things. I was so enraged, I frightened them— they at last recognized the danger of making a fool of a trained fighter who went about armed. I told them I wouldn't hurt them or run to the police if they returned my money and went the hell back to Ireland. They handed me the cash, and I thought that the end of it, but later that night, they followed me to my hotel room, and James—Maggie's lover—shoved her at me when I opened the door. He was still afraid I'd go to the police and decided that a night with Maggie would make me grateful and compliant."

Bertie nodded, even as she felt disgust. "It's what some men think of. Women are there to smile and coerce, or pay with their bodies if need be."

Sinclair gave her a narrow look. "I'm sorry you aren't surprised by it, lass. I was sorry Maggie wasn't either. I was so furious I pulled her inside and locked out her lover. I told her she needed to get away from him, and she broke down and said she'd been trying to do just that. She'd been with him a few years by then and realized what sort of man he was. He'd never legally married her, as much as he'd promised. She begged for my help—money was what she needed, because James never shared the take with her."

Bertie frowned. "How did you know that wasn't another story she made up on the spot? To get more money from you?"

"I didn't. I told Daisy that the best way I could help her was to marry her and take her out of the country. I decided that if she truly wanted to be rid of James, she'd take that chance. To my great surprise, she said yes."

Sinclair stopped, taking a deep breath. Bertie pressed her hand to his chest and found his heart beating hard. She wondered if he'd have one of the breathing spasms she'd seen him go into, but to her relief he drew a long breath without strain.

"What happened?" Bertie asked softly.

Sinclair took another breath and cleared his throat. "I sent for the police and had James arrested. I took Daisy back to my company with me, found the chaplain, and had him marry us. I expected Daisy at every turn to run away from me, now that her lover had been taken, but she never did."

"And she became your wife," Bertie said. "Just like that?"

"Just like that. I told the chaplain and my commander that we'd met in Rome and fallen in love, and everyone believed it." Sinclair paused. "And then, we fell in love."

Sinclair's face changed when he said the words, his love not feigned. Bertie's heart stung.

"It's a sweet story." She touched Sinclair's cheek. "You still love her."

Sinclair looked down at Bertie, his gray eyes quiet. "I've never hidden that."

"What I mean is, I know the love was real. Or else you wouldn't care what Inspector Fellows, or me, found out about her. You're still protecting her. I wager even her brother doesn't know what really happened."

Sinclair shook his head. "He knew Daisy ran away but never who with—she never told them about James. When Daisy contacted her family again, she was with me. Edward concluded that I was the man she'd eloped with in the first place."

"That's why he blames you." Made sense now. "He thinks you're the blackguard, not this James person. Why don't you tell Mr. Davies all about him?"

"The same reason I didn't explain to Fellows. Fellows can be discreet, but I don't need Edward besmirching Daisy's name, which he would. He'd take it as a personal offence that his sister had fallen into a bad life, and condemn her, and me. Such a thing would cling to Cat and Andrew as well, especially Cat."

True. The standards to which middle- and upper-class girls were held were stringent, unmercifully so, which had always made Bertie glad not to be one.

"One of the letters implied that maybe Cat wasn't your daughter," Bertie said. "But I wager she is."

"Cat was born one year and two months after I married Daisy," Sinclair said. "And James had been sent to prison after his arrest in Rome. Apparently he was wanted for many crimes. There is no doubt about Cat." He smiled fondly. "Plus, she is very much a McBride. She reminds me of Steven when he was her age. Steven could be very quiet, even obedient, right before the devil came out. I was more like Andrew, shouting at everyone and running ragged over them."

Bertie liked imagining a wild, blustering, shouting Sinclair. "But people might believe the letters. And the ones about me. Cat having a working-class pickpocket as a governess might look bad for her too."

"I hadn't planned to announce the fact," Sinclair said. "My household staff is so grateful to you for taking care of Andrew and Cat that they wouldn't mind if you were the devil himself. Anything to keep my unruly children tamed."

"I wouldn't say I've *tamed* them, exactly."

"No, but they like you. They listen to you, and even respect you. I have never been good with children, and when I lost Daisy . . ." Sinclair stopped, swallowed. "Perhaps she was a confidence trickster to the end, because I couldn't, for the longest time, let her out of my life."

Bertie drew her hand down the silk of his waistcoat. "We never let go of the ones we most love. They're always there with us, never really gone. As it should be."

Sinclair gave a self-deprecating laugh. "So many say I'm morbid about it."

Bertie shook her head. "You aren't. You get on with your life, work hard, look after your children. You're not like the queen—I hear she sleeps with a plaster cast of Prince Albert's hand. I know she misses him, but that's going a bit far, don't you think?"

Sinclair's sad look faded. "That's what I love about you, Bertie. You have the ability to see things clearly. No fog. You look at a thing, and know it for what it is. I wish you could teach me to do that."

"You know how." Bertie laid her head on his shoulder, and Sinclair kissed her hair. "I've seen you do it in the courtroom, sizing up every person around you."

"Easy when it's someone else's life. Not my own." Sinclair kissed her again. "I'm glad you're here to help me, sweetheart."

Bertie was glad too. "We'll get him," she said. "This letter writer. We'll find him, and then he won't hurt you anymore."

"And I love your optimism." Another amused laugh. "Nothing in Bertie's world is too difficult."

Well, he was wrong about that, but Bertie didn't have the words to explain. She was like Ian, she thought, only knowing how to talk about what was straightforward.

Also, she couldn't think much when her heart was reveling in a warm little glow. One word had started the warmth. When Sinclair had praised her ability to see situations in a clear light, he'd said, *That's what I love about you, Bertie.* Not *like*.

Love.

⁓

Blustery, snowy weather returned for a few days, before giving way again to sunshine. The children, tired of being confined, even to a huge house like Kilmorgan, clamored to go out once the clouds parted. Bertie, also wanting to be free of the crowd—though the English guests had started drifting to the train station after Christmas Day—suggested a walk to the ruins of the old castle.

Daniel had told the children about it with the animation of a born storyteller, including the chill tales of its ghosts. "Great-great-great-grandfather Malcolm and his beloved wife, Mary, are said to walk hand in hand on the battlements, looking down at the country they fought so hard for."

"Rot," Mac Mackenzie said when he overheard. "The old castle was pulled down after Culloden, and Malcolm and Mary started building *this* house. If they haunt anywhere, it's inside here, where it's cozy."

Andrew wouldn't be deterred from exploring the ruins, and Cat, in her quiet way, expressed interest. The entire Mackenzie clan started talking about an expedition, but couldn't agree on arranging a time. They enjoyed arguing endlessly about it, though.

In the end, Sinclair put aside the piles of papers he was reading in preparation for returning to chambers, and took Bertie, Cat, and Andrew to the ruins alone.

The scramble to the top of the hill, over dark boulders and clumps of snow-covered heather, took time and much energy. They were rewarded at the top, however, with a magnificent view.

Bertie spread her arms, gazing across the open valley—Kilmorgan house looking small from here—to the hills beyond. The formal garden behind the manor house flowed out in a pattern of curlicues, like a large flower itself.

"You'd never know it looked like that," Bertie said, pointing it out. "Unless you stood up here. Clever."

"Garden designers in the eighteenth century enjoyed such things," Sinclair said next to her. "Loved secret designs and things that mimicked nature. Meanwhile, nature is everywhere, if you only lift your eyes."

"Don't be a wet blanket. It's beautiful." Bertie swept her gaze across the wonder of the Highlands. "Funny, to be able to see so far, and see so much. Even from a rooftop in London, what you mostly see is other rooftops. And smoke. So much smoke." Bertie inhaled the clean air, not a smokestack in sight.

"I like the change," Sinclair said. "London gives me much, but here, I can breathe."

Andrew, having had enough of standing and admiring the view, split away from his father and Bertie and headed for the ruins. Cat found a boulder, wiped it free of snow, brought out a cloth she'd carried in her little pack, and laid it across the boulder. She settled herself gracefully on this makeshift seat, took out her notebook, and started to draw. Bertie had kept her promise, telling no one of the beautiful picture Cat had shown her, and now Cat sketched without tension.

"Is your house in the Highlands like this?" Bertie asked Sinclair, while they both kept an eye on Andrew.

Sinclair raised his brows, a hint of a smile touching his mouth. "A pile of rubble?"

A square part of the old castle stuck into the sky, a few holes near the top regular enough to have been windows or arrow slits. The base was surrounded by a wall that had fallen into nothing but heaps of stones, some stones still large, others ground down by time, weather, and people who took the broken rocks to repair or build their own houses.

"You know what I mean. Silly."

"It's not like Kilmorgan, no, so don't grow too used to living in luxury. No lavish mansion with two-hundred bedrooms—or whatever number it is. I'm not a duke, only a gentleman descended from landed gentry." He dropped his ironic tone. "It's beautiful, though. The house is graceful, and the hills and loch behind it are like a painted backdrop. I'm always astonished that such beauty exists in the world."

Bertie liked when he became like this, lowering his sardonic facade, and looking around with true enjoyment.

She winked at him. "Is there a monster in your loch?"

Sinclair frowned as though giving true thought to the possibility. "Might be. I sometimes see suspicious bubbles in the middle, even on calm days. Macaulay says it's pike, but who knows? Andrew has watched for hours for tentacles or a head to pop up, but nothing ever has. He's quiet the entire time he watches, which I think is more astonishing than a monster ever could be."

Bertie had to laugh. "Andrew's a good lad. He only needs a way to direct his restlessness. Like in running."

Andrew was running now, on the flatter ground, chasing unknown monsters that lurked among the ruins. Cat ignored him and the view, her head down over her notebook. She looked fetching in her dark blue coat and hat, mittens hanging from her wrists, while her cold-pink hands moved across the page.

"She really does want to go to Miss Pringle's Academy," Bertie said. "She speaks of it often."

"I know." Sinclair sounded resigned. "Andrew has asked me when he can go off to school and join a running team. Not so he can study and learn anything, you understand."

"Of course not." Bertie eyed the two of them, children she'd become so fond of in such a brief time. "When you do send them off, I'll be out of a job." The words came out more forlornly than she'd meant them to.

"No, you won't," Sinclair said quickly.

"I don't think any of the fancy governess agencies will put me on their books, no matter how many references you write." Bertie glanced up at him, but Sinclair was watching Andrew, his face a careful blank. "I've started my own collection, you know. Of rules for a proper governess."

Sinclair still watched Andrew, though she saw his chest rise more quickly. "Oh? And what are they?"

Bertie held up her hand, ticking the rules off on her fingers. "Well, book learning for a start. If a governess is going to teach her charges, she should know what she's teaching them."

"I'll grant you that. What else?"

"She must have the patience of a saint but love the children no matter what. They shouldn't have to behave to earn her fondness."

"Rather like being a father," Sinclair said, slanting her a look. "Anything more?"

"She should find ways to keep them interested in learning, not just beat them with facts. Like making history a string of great stories, not dates to memorize."

"Hmm, I wish you could have given your rules to some of my tutors when I was a lad."

Bertie grinned and touched another finger. "She should

take plenty of exercise with the children and not be upset if they want to run and play. A governess being fit is a help."

The glint of humor had returned to Sinclair's eyes. "You sound like a reformer."

"Do I? It's only common sense. I think your other governesses ran away because they didn't like children. They wanted Cat and Andrew to sit like statues while they talked at them, and got angry if they couldn't repeat the boring details. Heaven forbid either of the kids should have an opinion."

"The world expects children to be seen and not heard, you know."

"Then the world ain't—*isn't* paying attention."

Sinclair didn't answer, but the space had lessened between them. Sinclair's gloved hand touched hers, the backs of their fingers brushing.

Bertie wanted this moment to last—she and Sinclair on the hilltop, almost holding hands, Andrew happily exploring, Cat quiet and content. No dark world, no difference in their stations in life, in their pasts. Effervescent happiness welled up inside her—she could float away on it.

The moment broke when the sound of a hunter's gun cracked the air far away. Hart's ghillie and Macaulay had taken some of the remaining English visitors on a stalk on the other side of the valley. The cold, clear air brought the sounds from miles away.

Andrew stood up on one of the rocks, firing an imaginary rifle. "Take that, Butcher Cumberland. See what you get when you rile a Highlander."

Sinclair left Bertie to climb to Andrew. "Don't fall while you're trying to fight the Battle of Culloden again. And keep in mind we lost, more's the pity."

"Wouldn't have if I'd been there," Andrew vowed. He made more shooting noises.

Cat rose from her seat, tucking away her notebook. "We should help father lure him down, or we'll never get our tea," Cat said, resigned. She took Bertie's hand. "Can we go higher? I want to see."

Bertie kept a firm hold of Cat's hand as they climbed up to Andrew and Sinclair. The castle had been built on a rocky outcropping, giving the defenders a good view over the valley. They'd have seen attackers from miles away, and any opposing army would have been hard-pressed to reach it without harm.

The castle had fallen, so Daniel had told Bertie, not to attackers, but to bored English soldiers after the war with Bonnie Prince Charlie, and to time.

The black rocks were slippery. Andrew stood on a half-ruined wall, Sinclair holding the back of his jacket as Andrew shot at imaginary Englishmen.

Cat, next to Bertie, trod on a slab of loose stone, and lost her balance. Her foot went off the stone, her leg in its knit stocking and fashionable boot catching on a jagged rock below.

Bertie clung to her, and Cat scrambled for solid ground. She was almost up again when her other foot slipped on the snow, and Cat began to plunge downward.

With a cry, she grabbed desperately for Bertie. Bertie, heart pounding, seized Cat with both hands and pulled her to safety, but Cat lost hold of her doll.

The doll's pink china face beamed its perpetual smile as it slipped over the black rocks, and fell, end over end, tumbling down, down, down, toward the jutting stones, gorse, and half-melted snow many feet below.

Chapter 24

A high-pitched keening sounded over the valley. Bertie jerked around, wondering what sort of creature could make such a noise, but the next instant, she realized it was Cat.

The little girl ripped herself from Bertie's grasp and flung herself down on the stones, reaching desperately for the doll that continued to roll her merry way down the nearly vertical hill. The doll was battered from rock to rock, pieces of porcelain flying from her face to litter the hillside.

The doll's wild tumble came to a halt on a rock jutting over the cliff, where she lay like a dead thing, her arms and legs dangling over empty space.

Cat's desperate keening wound into words. "Mama! Mama! *Mama!*"

Sinclair leapt back down toward them, carrying Andrew. "Cat. Sweetheart."

Cat reached toward the doll, her empty hands opening and closing. "Mama! Mama! Mama! Mama! . . ." Her words choked her, the girl barely able to draw breath. "Mama . . ."

"Bleeding 'ell." Bertie stripped off her hat and her coat, jammed her leather gloves more firmly over her fingers, and started scrambling down the tumble of boulders toward the limp body of the doll.

"Bertie!" Sinclair's deep voice bellowed over the continuing cries of his daughter. "Get the hell back here! *Bertie! . . .*"

Bertie climbed down the rocks, hands and feet finding niches to steady her along. She knew she was mad to do it—one slip, and she was over the cliff, down the pretty hill to the rocks below. The view that had seemed so beautiful from the top would kill her.

"Mama! Mama . . ." Cat's continued cries penetrated the silence, punctuated by another *crack* from the guns across the valley.

"I have to be daft," Bertie muttered to herself as she sought the next solid rock with the toe of her boot. "I belong on city streets, I do, trying to make ends meet and keep meself out of trouble. What the blazes am I doing climbing down a mountain in Scotland to rescue a *doll*?"

Bertie knew, however, that she wouldn't climb back up without it. If Cat had been any other little girl, an ordinary child Bertie didn't know well, she'd have told Cat to sod the bloody thing and have her rich father buy her another.

But Bertie had come to know Cat in the last weeks, and she understood exactly what the doll was to her. Bertie's mother's locket swung against her skin inside her bodice— she knew good and well she'd be climbing down these rocks if she'd dropped *it*.

Not everyone had Bertie's climbing skills either, honed from a childhood of getting herself up the sides of buildings and through tiny windows to let her father in a discreet side door. Her dad would never take very much during these jobs, just one or two things that might not be missed right away. By the time people realized they'd been robbed, they couldn't be sure when it had been done or who'd been nearby at the time.

Bertie was a bit past those childhood days, however, and no longer as agile. It had taken everything she'd had to climb up the scaffolding after Cat and Andrew the first day she'd met them. This going was harder, and the rocks seemed determined to cut her hands, the damp to make her slip.

Almost there. At the top of the hill, Cat continued to cry frantically; Sinclair was cursing, his hands full with keeping Andrew from climbing after Bertie.

The doll hung face downward, its pretty silk dress caught on a rock, which was why it had ceased its tumbling. Bertie had to inch her way toward it, holding hard to stones that cut her gloves. She knew she'd never climb out onto the jutting rock—she'd have to hang on here, and reach . . .

She heard Sinclair say, "Bertie," in a tone of terror, anger, and certainty that he was seeing the last of her.

Bertie gripped her handholds tightly and prodded with her boot until she had very firm rock under her foot. Then she leaned out, bracing with her hand- and footholds, and hooked her fingers around the back of the doll's dress.

She plucked the doll from the ledge, much as Sinclair pulled Andrew back by his coat even now, the doll's little gown filthy with mud. Bertie levered herself upright, and thrust the doll inside her coat.

Now to make her ascent. Bertie felt for handholds going up, testing each one before trusting her weight to it. Climbing up was always easier for her than down, mostly because she didn't have to look at the empty space beneath her feet. She went slowly, though, knowing that any misstep could mean her death.

Halfway up, she found chunks of the doll's broken face strewn about the gorse. The poor thing's smile was split in two, but both eyes remained in one piece, gazing at Bertie in cheerful encouragement. Bertie gathered up the bits, dropped them into her pocket, and continued.

She was almost to the top when a pair of strong hands gripped her under the arms and hauled her to solid ground. Bertie landed against Sinclair's large body, and his arms went around her, holding her tight, tight. He crushed her to him with arms as hard as steel, lips in her hair. "Bertie. Damn and blast you . . ."

Behind them, Cat continued to cry, her wailing breaking

into hoarse breaths. Bertie pushed away from Sinclair, but he didn't let go of her hand as they made their way back to Cat.

Andrew was kneeling next to his sister, stroking her hair, his small face troubled. "Don't cry, Cat. Bertie's here. She saved your dolly. See?"

Sinclair gently lifted Cat and drew her into his arms. "Shh. Sweetheart."

"It's all right—I nabbed her," Bertie said breathlessly. "She's a bit worse for wear, but I think we can make her better. Nothing a little glue and needle and thread won't fix. And maybe a good scrubbing."

Cat peeked out at the smashed doll, her eyes red and flowing. "Ma . . . ma." The word came in gasps, Cat sounding more like a tiny child than an eleven-year-old girl.

Bertie smoothed Cat's hair, which was tangled now with thorny twigs and dead leaves. "I know, sweetheart. I know."

Cat pushed herself away from her father to reach for Bertie. Bertie opened her arms and gathered Cat in. Over her head, she met Sinclair's gaze, his gray eyes red-rimmed.

"Is she going to be all right?" Andrew asked in a small voice.

Sinclair took his hand. "I think so, lad. Don't you worry, now."

He squeezed Andrew's hand, but the look he shared again with Bertie was uncertain, and she had to nod back in the same uncertainty.

Sinclair took Bertie and his children not to the shared nursery at the top of the house, but to the suite of rooms he'd been given in Lord Cameron's wing. Sinclair didn't want to have to explain the incident to the contingent of nannies or even to Ainsley and his well-meaning sisters-in-law. Not until Cat was better.

Cat was covered in grime, her face streaked with tears and mucus. Bertie didn't look much better—her gloves in shreds, her gray wool gown torn, her face covered in dirt and little cuts. For once, Andrew was the cleanest of the lot.

Sinclair and Andrew waited rather forlornly in the little sitting room while Bertie ordered up a bath for Cat in the bedroom and bathed the girl herself. When she opened the door later to admit Sinclair, Bertie was damp and flushed, her face scrubbed clean, her bodice unbuttoned at her throat. Bertie told him in a quiet voice she'd take Andrew on up to the nursery, and left Sinclair alone with his daughter.

Cat lay in Sinclair's bed, tucked up in her nightie that a maid had fetched from the nursery. The doll, stripped of the gown it had worn for seven or so years now, was propped next to the washbasin like a war casualty. Bertie had carefully set the pieces of its broken porcelain head beside the tattered body.

Sinclair smoothed the blankets over Cat. "Are you all right now, love?"

Cat nodded. The mad light had gone from her eyes, and she looked sad, ashamed, and a little discomfited. "I'm sorry, Papa."

"Nothing to be sorry about," Sinclair said. "I know she's special to you. Bertie's right—we'll fix her up again."

"She's just a doll," Cat said, her voice listless.

He sat down next to the bed and stroked Cat's hair. She looked so like Daisy, with her dark hair and Irish blue eyes and dark lashes—as the saying went, eyes put in with a smutty finger. Cat had shared her mother's liveliness until that terrible day Daisy went away.

Sinclair took her hand, his heart beating too hard. He wished he could reach that liveliness, bring it to the surface, but he didn't know how. It killed him that he didn't know how.

He could have lost her today, and Bertie—when he'd seen Bertie go over the cliff his entire world had stopped. He might be even now sitting here, wondering that he was still alive without Bertie.

Sinclair cleared his throat and squeezed Cat's hand. "I know she's not just a doll, sweet. Your mother gave her to you, and I know you treasure it."

"Mama's gone."

The dull words struck Sinclair's heart. "I know. And I miss her every day. It's all right to miss her, love."

Fresh tears flowed from Caitriona's eyes, but they were quiet tears, not the crazed sobs of her hysterics. "I don't want Bertie to go. Even if I go to Miss Pringle's Academy, I want Bertie to stay."

"I want her to stay too," Sinclair said, all his heart in the words.

Cat wiped away her tears. "She will," she said with conviction, and Sinclair hoped with everything he had that his daughter was right. He'd make sure of it.

Bertie returned to her own room after she set up Andrew with a bath in the nursery. Andrew didn't want a bath, but he gave in without as vehement an argument as usual. Bertie left him in the care of the nannies and went to her room to plop into a soft chair and let out a sigh.

Not two minutes later, Sinclair slammed his way into her bedchamber without so much as knocking, and Bertie leapt to her feet again. "What's wrong? Is Cat all right?"

Sinclair stared at her as though he didn't understand the question, then he nodded distractedly. "Yes, she's asleep. Aoife is with her."

"Good." Bertie pressed her hand to her heart. "You had me worried, there."

"I had *you* worried?" Sinclair banged the door shut and strode to her, his fury evident. "Devil take you, Bertie, what the hell were you thinking, climbing down that cliff and risking your bloody neck? For a *doll*?"

Bertie gaped up at him. Sinclair's face was blotchy red, his eyes glittering with rage. He wasn't the stern, arrogant barrister, or the empty, unhappy man; this was someone new. Sinclair towered over Bertie, his large hands balled to fists, a furious Scottish warrior barely holding himself in check.

"Her mum gave her that doll," Bertie said faintly. "Of course I had to fetch it back." She put her hand inside her

collar and drew out her locket. "My mum gave me this. You
don't think I wouldn't have been over those rocks in a trice if
I'd dropped *it*?"

"It's worth your life?" Sinclair roared.

"I know it was stupid of me," Bertie said quickly, "but I
couldn't let the poor thing go. You saw what it did to Cat. It
was like losing her mum all over again."

"I know, but damn it, Bertie, don't you dare do anything
like that ever again!"

Bertie put her hands on her hips, her own temper rising.
"Were *you* going to skim down there and get it? We'd have
been scraping you from the rocks for sure. I'm limber, and I
know how to climb."

"I would have fetched Macaulay and some lads to help,
and rope," he shouted. "Not thrown myself over the side and
hoped for the best."

"Macaulay was off showing people how to shoot things,
remember? I wager most of the lads who work here were out
with him. Sun was already gone by the time we reached
home—not enough light left to organize a rescue party. And
there'd be dolly, hanging from that rock all night. Or maybe
carried off by some bird to line its nest. How do you think
Cat would have felt about that?"

"That doesn't mean you should have risked your life for
it!" Sinclair's bellow rivaled the noise Andrew could make.
"It's only by the grace of God you didn't fall, or I'd be out
looking at *your* body on the rocks now, you broken and
gone . . ."

His words choked off, his chest working as he struggled
for air. Bertie reached for him, her own heart hurting. "I'm
sorry. I truly am. You all right?"

"No. Can't . . . breathe." Sinclair backed away, sitting
down hard on her bed, his breath coming in hoarse gasps.
"This happens to me whenever I'm . . ."

Bertie went to him. "Let me help. How can I help?"

"I'll be all right in a minute." But Sinclair's breathing
still came with too much difficulty, his shoulders shaking
with the effort.

Bertie sat on the bed beside him. "Now you close your eyes." She moved her hands up his back in a caress and started kneading his shoulders. "Let me ease you."

"Can't. When I close my eyes, I see . . . you . . . falling away from me . . ."

"But I didn't. I'm here, right next to you." Bertie wriggled her thigh against his. "See? You just let me look after you now."

Sinclair turned his head to look at her. "Bertie . . . damn you."

Bertie climbed up behind him on the bed, put her arms around him, and drew him back to her. He resisted at first, stiff, but then he leaned into her bosom, his eyes at last drifting shut.

"We're all here, safe and whole," she said into his ear. "That's all you need to remember."

She caressed his chest, finding his heart banging hard beneath her hands. She continued to rub gently, kneading his tight muscles, smoothing his shirt over his hot skin. Bertie rested her cheek against his hair, breathing the warmth of it, moving to kiss the scars that decorated the top of his cheekbone.

Sinclair's breathing at last began to slow, the gasps easing, until he drew a long, relieved breath. He coughed once, then he closed his eyes again and lay back against Bertie, relaxing.

Bertie lightly kissed his cheek. His skin was flushed, warm, his whiskers rough on her lips.

When she kissed his cheek again, Sinclair turned his head and met the kiss with his lips.

Bertie stilled, fire rising at his warm breath, the smooth touch of his mouth. Sinclair took over the kiss, parting her lips, sweeping his tongue inside. The icy chill of the wind across the ruins, plucking at her as the rocks cut her hands, vanished under his heat.

The next kiss was a little deeper, Sinclair cupping her cheek. He slowly turned her over onto the downy mattress, sliding on top of her, his breathing no longer ragged.

Sinclair undressed her slowly, with gentle hands. Bertie helped pull his clothes away as well until he was bracing himself over her in nothing but his kilt. Sinclair didn't bother taking off the kilt itself—he simply shoved its folds up as he slid inside her.

He moved slowly, heat building between them, sultry and close like a summer night. His body was touched with sweat, his mouth hot as he kissed her.

The glorious friction of his kilt on her skin, of Sinclair stiff inside her, sent Bertie floating on ripples of joy. She latched her fingers around his shoulders as the ripples lifted her. She saw herself on the mountainside again, only this time, her grip slid away from the rocks, and she fell down, down, tumbling freely as the doll had.

She cried out, but Sinclair was there to catch her, sweeping her up into his strength. He buried his face in her hair as his hips moved, languid pleasure giving way to fiercer need.

"I can't lose you," he whispered. "Never, never, Bertie, lass. I can't."

"I'm here," Bertie said, or thought she said.

You've done something to me, Basher McBride. I'll never be the same again, no matter how far I go or what I do. I'll never be just Bertie ever again. Some part of you will always be part of me.

"Dear God," Sinclair groaned. His thrusts came faster, harder, until both of them were filling the air with cries of need.

They crashed together, their bodies slick with sweat, Sinclair's kisses hot on her flesh. Sinclair drew Bertie to him, holding her solidly, keeping her in safety with him.

~~~

The next day was subdued. The rest of the McBride and Mackenzie families heard the tale of the doll's fate and Bertie's daring rescue. Bertie was celebrated with many toasts to her bravery, and tight hugs from the ladies. "Damn fool thing to do," Hart growled, though he looked at her with new respect.

Ian gave her a quiet nod. "Thank you," he said. His even-handed thanks warmed Bertie more than Mac's and Daniel's wild applause.

"When I pick out a wife, she's going to be just like you," Daniel said, his strong hand on her shoulder.

"A governess?" Bertie asked, giving him a grin. *Or a pickpocket?*

"One who knows the world and isn't afraid of it." Daniel kissed her cheek. "And one as pretty. Mmm, let me just kiss you again."

"No." Sinclair got around Bertie and scowled at Daniel. "Leave her be, Danny."

Daniel only laughed, studied the two of them together, and gave Bertie a big wink. "Right you are, Uncle Sinclair."

Macaulay broke the celebration to hand Bertie a telegram that had come from the train station. Bertie took it in surprise, wondering who'd be telegraphing her, but she stilled when she read the terse words.

"What is it?" Sinclair asked, warming her shoulder as he leaned to read it.

"It's me dad."

Bertie wasn't certain what emotions ran through her. The telegram wasn't from Gerry Frasier—Mrs. Hill had sent it, saying that a woman who called herself Mrs. Lang had come looking for Bertie. Bertie's father was very ill, Mrs. Lang had said, and was asking for Bertie to come.

Sinclair plucked the telegram from her cold hands, read it, and immediately told Macaulay to purchase tickets to London.

~

Bertie had supposed that Sinclair would send her back alone with either Macaulay or Aoife to look after her, but Sinclair packed up the whole family to return with her. Sinclair wanted Cat back in a house she was used to, he said. She'd rest and recover better without the other families hovering around her, even with all their sympathy. Cat was unnerved by it. So London it was for all of them.

Bertie was sorry to leave the families and festivities behind, but she too wanted Cat to rest. Also she did feel anxious about her father. Even if the old sot could be a brute, he was still her dad.

"London at Christmas can be fine too," Bertie told Cat as she settled the girl into the compartment she'd share with Andrew. Andrew was with Sinclair, Sinclair carefully letting him explore some of the train, so Bertie, at her request, could put Cat to bed first. Bertie wanted Caitriona settled in before Andrew bounced around the room with his usual vigor. The stay at Kilmorgan had healed him almost completely.

"Your dad promised to take us to a pantomime," Bertie continued. "One of the lavish ones at Drury Lane. That'll be a treat, let me tell you."

Cat nodded without much interest. Bertie propped the doll, which had been mended by Macaulay and Daniel, on the table near Cat's bunk. The doll's porcelain face had a big crack across it, and she was missing part of her cheekbone, but her blue eyes still shone, and her smile was as wide. Her hair, which had been dark like Cat's, was blond now, her original hair now scattered about the hill below the old castle. Eleanor had found an old wig in the attics at Kilmorgan and had given it to her maids to be cleaned and brushed, then to Daniel to cut up for the doll.

Daniel and Macaulay had done an amazing job, but there was no denying that the doll had been ruined. She was dressed in the brand new frock Sinclair had given Cat this Christmas, her old dress far beyond repair.

Bertie straightened the rust-colored skirt of the doll's gown. "There. She looks a bit tattered, but she's still with us."

Cat only nodded. When the repaired doll had been returned to her, Cat had looked it over, thanked Daniel and Macaulay politely, then set the doll aside and didn't pick it up again. She hadn't carried it with her since, and told the maid to pack it with the rest of her things when readying themselves to leave.

"Bertie," Cat said in a small voice as Bertie continued to

lay out Cat's clothes for the morning. "I know you all think I'm mad, but I'm not. I didn't think the doll was my mother, or anything like that."

"No, sweetie," Bertie said quickly. "I don't think you're mad."

"You do. Or at least you did for a while. Others do. But I'm not. I know she's just a doll."

Bertie left the clothes and returned to the bunk. "Now, you stop this nonsense, Cat McBride. I understand, and so does your dad. I explained that I'd have been climbing down that hill if I'd dropped my locket, and your dad understood, even if he's still riled with me for doing it."

Cat pleated a fold of the sheet. With her hair in a braid, in her white nightgown, she looked like an ordinary child, but her eyes held more sadness than an ordinary child's should. "Mama left Daisy—the doll Daisy—to watch over me, you see. Mama told me so when she was sick. I didn't really understand, but I thought if I kept the doll with me all the time, some part of Mama would be with me too. When I dropped her, when I saw her fall . . ." Cat's throat worked. "It made me realize that Mama was truly gone."

Bertie sat on the bunk next to her. "But she's still watching, you know, your mum is, up in heaven. Mums always look after their kids, don't they?"

"I was only four when Mama died," Cat said. "I didn't know what 'died' meant. It was a long time before I understood she was never coming back. I was very angry, I remember. I was angry at Papa for letting her go." She looked morose. "Is that bad of me?"

"Naw." Bertie had spent years furious at her father, even when it was clear he'd done nothing to cause her mother's death. Her mother had fallen ill of a fever that had invaded most of the streets of the East End, and no amount of nursing by Bertie and her father had been able to save her. "Your dad, he's one of the good ones. He loves you with all his might."

Inspector Fellows had said something like that to Bertie before she'd left for the train station that afternoon.

"I grew up in the gutter, same as you," Fellows had said after pulling her aside. "And in the gutter, a man like

McBride seems like an easy mark. But he's not." He'd fixed her with a sharp look very much like those of his half brothers. "McBride is one of the good ones, Miss Frasier. Never forget that."

Bertie had nodded, agreeing with him, and had started out of the house again, only to be stopped by Ian Mackenzie. "Take care of them," was all Ian had said. He'd given her one of his rare direct stares, then he'd walked away without a good-bye.

"One of the good ones," Bertie repeated.

And I'm in love with him, she continued silently. *This very good man is going to break my heart.*

London greeted them with billows of coal smoke, every house stoking its fires to stay warm. Down in the slums, they'd be shivering and burning anything they could find, in stoves, fireplaces, barrels, and tin coal boxes. In Mayfair, fires danced on bright hearths, and maids brought tea and scones to warm the belly.

Sinclair summoned his coach to take Bertie to visit her dad, and insisted on coming with her.

"You're daft, you are," Bertie said in alarm as he followed her out, Richards waiting patiently on the box. "If Basher McBride is seen about the backstreets of Whitechapel, things will go bad for you."

Sinclair only gave her his scowl. "I'm sure everyone in Whitechapel knows full well you're looking after my children. I'm not letting you go alone, and that's the end of it."

No amount of arguing could sway him. Bertie gave up, knowing they could stand all day on the street and fight about it while the neighbors watched with interest.

Bertie, resigned, let him hand her into the coach, and they set off.

The East End hadn't improved since Bertie had left it. The mud was frozen in streets and lanes, fires burned in barrels

with dozens of men and women standing around them, trying
to soak up the heat. No sun penetrated the gloom of the afternoon, the tall buildings shutting out any hint of light.

The dark and cold struck Bertie harder now, after the
wide-open spaces of Scotland and the splendid comfort of
Kilmorgan Castle. She'd survived here because she hadn't
known any different, but now she did. There was a world out
there, oceans of it, and Bertie meant to see it.

A few of the younger lads of the street were huddled
around the front of the lodging house where her father lived.
They swarmed the coach when it came to a stop, trying to
look pathetic as they held out their hands. The pugilist Sinclair had borrowed from the duke's house in Grosvenor
Square jumped down and tried to scatter them.

"Oi, it's Bertie," one of the boys yelled when the pugilist
opened the carriage door for her. "It's Bertie-girl, dressed up
all swank. Is that your protector in there?" They looked past
her to Sinclair. "Looks like he could spare a bob or two.
Give us a coin, Bertie."

"Why'dya think I came here, to drop all my bread in your
hands?" Bertie asked good-humoredly. "I came to see me
dad. He's poorly."

"He'll fall over dead if he spies you with your posh
coach," another of the lads said. "Come on, Bertie. We're
your old mates."

The pugilist waded among them, the lads diving away
from his bulk without him having to touch them. "Clear
off," he growled, his accent as Cockney as theirs.

"It's all right." Bertie dipped her hand into her pocket and
passed out pennies. "They don't mean no harm. He's not my
protector." Bertie gestured to Sinclair, who'd climbed down
beside her. "You lot leave him alone."

She started through the press of boys to the door of her
old lodgings, and Sinclair came directly behind her, not letting her get more than one step ahead of him. The pugilist
followed as far as the doorway, then turned around and
faced the street, blocking the lads from following them in.

"Why are you coming with me?" Bertie asked Sinclair as

they went up the stairs. "What happened to you not showing your face where it's dangerous?"

"I'm not letting you in here alone," Sinclair growled. "You have no idea what or who is waiting for you."

"I thought you'd at least stay in the coach," Bertie said, throwing him a glare.

Sinclair scowled back. "Then you were wrong."

Maddening man. The door to the rooms on the third floor was locked, but Bertie still had her key. She opened the door and walked inside. "It's me," she called.

Mrs. Lang, a plump woman with dyed black hair and a perpetually red face came out of Gerry's bedroom. "Bertie," she said, smiling a genuine smile. "How grand to see you."

She opened her arms and folded Bertie into a well-cushioned hug. Mrs. Lang always smelled a bit of whiskey, which she liked, and a faint scent that was the fancy soap she saved her pennies for.

"How is he?" Bertie asked when Mrs. Lang released her.

"Not well. He wants to speak to you. Is this him?" She looked around Bertie at Sinclair.

"This is Mr. McBride," Bertie said, a bit stiffly. "My employer."

Mrs. Lang looked Sinclair up and down, her scrutiny admiring. "Well, you're a fine one, ain't you? Very handsome, in that way a Scottish bloke can be. Better wait out here, duckie. Old Gerry might get upset at the sight of you."

Sinclair didn't look happy, but he nodded as he took off his hat. "I'll be right here, Bertie. Shout if you need me." He gave her a look that told her she'd better. He might barge right in if she lingered longer than he liked, in any case.

Bertie gave him a nod, squared her shoulders, and followed Mrs. Lang into the bedroom.

"Well, look at the cat who swallowed the cream." Gerry Frasier, his face grayer than Bertie had ever seen it, gazed at her over the bedcovers. His face was also lined and haggard, but he wasn't hung over. This was true illness.

"How are you, Dad?" Bertie said. She pulled off her gloves and went to the bedside, holding out her hand.

Her father clasped her fingers with his hard ones. "Dying. So nice for me own daughter to bother to come and see me."

"I was in Scotland. I know Mrs. Lang wouldn't a' sent for me if it weren't bad."

"It's bad." The hand that pressed Bertie's was strong, though. "That flash bastard you've taken up with out there? I heard a voice."

"Yeah, he's here. Making sure you didn't set me up."

Gerry looked hurt, but he didn't let go of her hand. "As if I would. I've always been good to you, Bertie-girl, haven't I?"

"No, of course, you haven't. You made me steal for you and smacked me when I didn't do it quick enough. You're an old brute, and I'm well rid of you." She patted his hand, softening the words.

Gerry's eyes moistened. "Well, that's true. But I always looked after you, you know that. Your mum asked me to, before she went. Never let anyone else touch you, did I?"

"No, Dad. You're a regular knight-errant."

Gerry squeezed her hand, looking genuinely remorseful. "I'm sorry about Jeffrey. I never meant him to go after you, with a shooter, no less. If I'd known that, I would have had me mates sit on him until he saw reason. I'd have throttled him meself after, if he hadn't got himself dragged off to chokey."

Bertie believed him. For all Gerry had been hard on her, he'd also been extremely protective. Bertie had no doubt that had Jeffrey not been afraid of her father, he'd have dragged Bertie off to his bed long ago, whether she wanted to or not.

Gerry tugged her closer. "I need to tell you something else, love. I didn't just ask you to come so you could watch your old dad push off. I need to warn you."

Mrs. Lang looked worried, and Bertie felt a qualm. "Yeah? About what?"

"There's villains after you, Bertie. High-end villains."

Bertie studied her father's face. He could be a liar, and a good one, but this time, he had true fear in his watery blue eyes. She glanced at Mrs. Lang for confirmation, and Mrs. Lang nodded.

"What do you mean, *high-end*?" Bertie asked. "Posh gents who have turned to crime, or villains who've come up in the world?"

"The second," Gerry said. "Like Frank Devlin."

Bertie started. "What's someone like Devlin want with me?" Frank Devlin was a very bad man, made a lot of money running housebreakers and street girls, plus a couple of bawdy houses for well-paying customers. He'd never bothered much with Bertie and her dad—they were too low-grade for him, and Gerry had taught Bertie to stay well clear of him.

Mrs. Lang answered. "We don't know. But he's working for someone, and word is that he wants you brought to him. That's why we asked you to come here and see us. Couldn't trust a messenger, not with news like that."

Chapter 25

Bertie came running out of the bedroom, her face pale under the gray hat she loved. "We have to go," she threw at Sinclair on her way past him.

Sinclair caught her by the arm. "Wait. Why? What did he say to you?"

Bertie wrenched herself from his grasp. "Tell you downstairs. When we're out of this place."

She made for the door in a swish of skirts and was gone. Sinclair, instead of following her, strode to the bedroom and went inside.

"What did you say to her?" he demanded of the two in the room.

Mr. Frasier peered at Sinclair from his bed. He didn't look good, but he also didn't look near to death's door. Ill yes, but not fatally. "Mr. McBride, is it? You take good care of my girl, all right?"

"You lured her here," Sinclair said sternly, ignoring him. "Didn't you? What's your game?"

"We had to," Mrs. Lang said, her dark eyes anxious. "We couldn't trust no one to tell her but us. Bertie will explain.

Best you go now. We can't risk anyone knowing we spilled anything to Basher McBride."

"The entire street knows I'm here," Sinclair said impatiently.

"Yeah, but won't be us who told you, will it?"

"If you're in danger, you should leave."

Frasier laughed at him. "I've lived on this street man and boy. Me mates are here, me lady . . . me whole life. I'm not going. I'm proud of Bertie for trying to better herself, but I'm not in a hurry to move far from my local, am I?" Another wheezing laugh. "Fancy me walking into any other pub but me own. They'd take me head off on the spot."

Mrs. Lang held the man's hand. "I'll look after him. You take care of our Bertie."

"I intend to," Sinclair said.

Frasier's voice went stern. "If you don't marry her yourself, you marry her off to someone with plenty of blunt who's good to her. Understand me?"

Sinclair had started for the door, but he turned back, his anger tight. "You beat her," he said clearly. "You used her to rob and steal for you—too afraid to do it yourself, were you? You've forfeited any say in what happens to her. She'll never be hurt again, that I can tell you for certain."

"Just tell Bertie . . ." Frasier said. "Tell her she's a good girl. Always was. Like her mum."

He was a sad old git, Sinclair decided, but Sinclair had seen many a man turn contrite when he thought the end was nigh. Frasier probably did feel remorse, but that didn't excuse what he'd done. "She's a wonderful young woman," Sinclair said. "And she'll live like a princess. Good day to you."

He turned his back on the two and made his way out of the flat and down the stairs. Bertie waited for him in the carriage, the pugilist next to it.

"You took your time," Bertie said as the pugilist opened the door.

Sinclair climbed inside and landed on the seat beside her, her body warm against his. It would be more proper to sit opposite her, but to hell with what was proper. "You don't have to be afraid, Bertie," he said. "Don't let whatever he told you rattle you."

Bertie brushed back her hat's feather. "All I know is, I want out. My dad was good to warn me, but I bet Mrs. Lang made him do it. The old soak doesn't want anything blowing back on him. Well, I'm finished with it all."

"Pleased to hear it." Sinclair tapped on the coach roof for Richards, once the pugilist had slammed the door. "Now, what did he warn you about?"

Bertie related the conversation, and Sinclair listened in growing unease. "I've heard of Devlin," he said when she finished. "Your father's not wrong—he's dangerous. But don't worry about him. I'll have one of Inspector Fellows's men . . ." Sinclair turned his head as he saw what he couldn't believe he saw out of the landau's fogged window. "Richards, stop!"

Sinclair was out of his seat, opening the door of the moving coach even as he heard Richards's *whoa.*

"Here!" Bertie grabbed at Sinclair's coat, her voice rising to a screech. "What are you doing?"

Sinclair shook off her grasp, then his boots hit the pavement just as Richards pulled the horses to a halt.

He'd seen a face up the street, one from his past, though it was not a face he expected. The man belonging to it wore a fine greatcoat and hat, very out of place in this area of workingman's caps and rough jackets.

The man was walking rapidly away. Sinclair ran after him, never minding the swarm of people crowding between him and his mark. "Stop, blast you!" Sinclair yelled at the retreating back.

He heard the click of Bertie's boots behind him, her calls to him. Sinclair didn't respond. He sped his steps, reached the other man, and pulled him around to face him.

The man stared back at Sinclair, not in surprise or shock, but in stark anger. He knew Sinclair would be here, damn him, likely had been following him every step.

"James Maloney," Sinclair said. "What the hell are you doing here, and why aren't you rotting in prison?"

~~~

Bertie paused as she saw Sinclair confront the man. She didn't recognize the gent, but he dressed well, and his face was soft, his body trim and not bent by hard work.

The pugilist behind her caught up, not happy. "Don't like to leave the coach unguarded," he growled.

Bertie understood, but she was too agitated to answer. Sinclair turned aside from the crowd, pulling the man with him. Sinclair's face had gone hard, eyes glittering.

"Now tell me what you're doing here," Sinclair was saying when Bertie and the pugilist reached them. Sinclair held the man by the collar of his coat. "Why are you even in England?"

"What did you think?" The man had a broad Irish accent. "That I'd let you take my Daisy, and that would be the end of it?"

Bertie stared in shock. Daisy? Was this the man, James, whom Sinclair's wife had eloped with all those years ago? Things clicked together, and Bertie stepped forward. "You've been sending the letters, haven't you?" she demanded. "Those bloody awful letters."

"Bertie," Sinclair said, his voice low but firm. "Go back to the carriage."

"Not likely," Bertie said. "Nasty piece of work, aren't you?"

Sinclair shot the pugilist a glare, and the man put his beefy hand on Bertie's shoulder. "Best come with me, miss."

Bertie ducked out from under him. "Should be *him* you're taking hold of, *and* giving him to the coppers."

"Letters?" James gave Sinclair a beatific smile. "No idea what she's talking about." His eyes were innocent, but Bertie was good at seeing through lies, and so was Sinclair. James was handsome enough, with charm in his smile. No surprise Sinclair's wife had fallen for the scoundrel, but she'd soon learned her mistake, hadn't she? "D'ye think I'm foolish enough to leave anything behind to connect me with any letters?" James asked.

Not if he were a good confidence trickster, he wouldn't.

Confidence men always traveled light, ready to throw their worldly goods into a small bag and dash away, leaving no trace of themselves behind.

But then, he might have kept *something* . . .

"Miss," the pugilist said. His hand landed on her shoulder again.

Bertie twisted away. This time she pretended to trip, and landed hard against James. As he started and tried to push her away, her hands went to work.

Bertie spun away, ran a few paces, and turned back, dangling a handkerchief, a slim wallet, a card case, and a watch from her hands.

"I wonder what I'll find in all this?" Bertie asked.

Sinclair looked grim, but also as though he understood why she'd done it. James's smooth smile vanished, then he snarled and started after her.

Sinclair grabbed for him but James leapt away, sliding from his grasp as skillfully as Bertie could have. He rushed at Bertie, and Bertie turned and fled.

She made for the coach, which was sitting a little way down from them, jammed in by traffic. Richards was standing up, looking for them. Before Bertie got halfway to it, James seized her by her coat, hauling her back. Her hat slipped, sagging by its pins over her eye.

Bertie knew the pugilist and Sinclair were steps away, but still she felt a qualm of fear as James pulled her around with unkind hands, shoving her into a noisome passage. Confidence men preferred to fight with their tongues, but when they were put to it, they could be very dangerous, violently so.

James blocked her way out to the busier street where the coach and freedom lay. "Give them back, ye bloody little whore." He thrust his hands inside Bertie's coat, but she'd already secreted her takings in inner pockets. She knew exactly how to stash gear quickly, all the better to run from the constables.

Where was Sinclair? There was a press of traffic and people at the entrance to the passage, but this little artery could be another world—and quiet.

Fear made her act. Maloney might have a weapon on him, and she had no doubt he'd be happy to pluck his things from her dead body.

She kicked him hard, her pointed-toed, high-heeled boot making a formidable weapon. When James bellowed, Bertie followed it up by grabbing him by the hair and pulling him hard to the wall behind her.

While he shouted and scrambled to right himself, Bertie was away.

James recovered swiftly enough to get between her and the street, but such things wouldn't slow down Bertie. She'd been born and bred in these alleyways, and she knew better than anyone how to snake around, losing pursuit, and finding her way to where she needed to go.

She ran, dodging into another passage, jumping over filmy puddles and patches of stinking mud. She kept her hand on her hat as she sprinted. Bertie loved this hat, the gift from Eleanor, and she vowed not to lose it to the grimy streets of London.

She heard James come behind her, his fine shoes grating in the muck. He could run almost as well as Bertie could, unfortunately. Of course, he'd likely become fast from evading the police all his life. Those who learned to move swiftly at an early age survived the longest.

On the other hand, Bertie figured she knew these streets better than any Irish stranger. Sinclair would be coming, and she could lead James to where he'd be caught, unable to get away.

She turned from Whitechapel and plunged south into the warren of lanes and courtyards, heading toward the river. "Lads," she shouted as she raced along. "I'm bringing one in!"

Word would pass ahead of her. Bertie ran as she hadn't run in a long time, though her new boots pinched her feet. Posh shoes weren't made for this kind of flight.

Bertie dashed through frozen filth, the usual detritus of broken glass, stones, splinters of wood, and other trash crushing under her feet. The darkness increased between the close-set houses, mist clinging to her as though it had weight.

She dashed around a corner into a narrow lane, familiar edifices rising around her. She threw open the door that led into the empty space between buildings and leapt over the threshold, not stopping until she'd reached the other side of the big pile of debris in the middle. James came on in after her. But the lads poured out of the corners, street toughs and Bertie's old mates, ready to pound the mark so Bertie could get away.

James went down. He drew a knife as he fell, and Bertie cried a warning.

Sinclair came charging through the door, halting when he saw the fight in progress. He watched for a few heartbeats then made his way around the fracas toward Bertie, his anger palpable.

And then everything stopped. The youths, one by one, looked up and peeled away from James and started off, out the door or climbing over the broken walls, disappearing into the gloom. The afternoon was just light enough for Bertie to see James come to his feet, his long knife glinting in his hand.

Through the door behind Bertie came four men—Frank Devlin and three of his regular henchmen. Devlin was middle-aged, but he'd kept his youthful slimness. He wasn't very tall, but he had a granite-hard face that made men half again his size back down in a trice. It was the eyes, Bertie thought. Light blue, cold, and mean, and holding no compassion whatsoever.

Bertie had only about two seconds to wonder whether it was sheer coincidence that brought Devlin here at this moment, before James said, "I thank you, sirs. I want both of them."

"Damn it to hell," Sinclair said. He grabbed Bertie's hand.

Bertie gave him a brief nod. Only one thing to do. *"Run!"* she shouted.

Sinclair didn't argue. They set off for the door through which they'd entered, Bertie praying Devlin hadn't set other villains to waylay them on this side.

James hurtled himself into Sinclair as they went by. The knife flashed, and Sinclair stumbled.

"No!" Bertie swung around, ready with a kick at James, but Sinclair shoved her onward.

"Don't stop," Sinclair said fiercely. "Run!"

Bertie latched her hand around Sinclair's, and they sprinted along together. She couldn't tell whether the knife had only torn his coat or had gone all the way in. She only knew that lingering to let Devlin and his henchmen grab them while they checked was a bad idea.

Bertie knew the streets, but so did Devlin. Then again, Devlin hadn't kept himself fit these past few weeks by running after Andrew. Sinclair, the former soldier, twisted through the streets with Bertie, moving rapidly but silently.

Bertie knew where they had to go. Around to the lanes near the river, down to the secret, narrow passages. Bertie slid through the tiny lane that led to her hideaway, Sinclair stifling grunts as he followed her around the jutting corners. Sinclair ducked his head this time as they went under the lintel of the door Bertie opened. "Seventeen steps," she reminded him in a whisper.

They were down inside her hidey-hole, the door closed and bolted against the outside world. Bertie groped for matches, finding them right where she'd left them. She lit the lamps and turned back to Sinclair.

She found that he'd staggered to the makeshift sofa and collapsed on it, his hand to his abdomen. Bertie, mouth dry in fear, pulled off her hat and knelt beside him.

"Let me see."

"Not a big wound," Sinclair said, voice tight.

"Don't matter. A thin knife can kill a man. Let me *see*."

Sinclair opened his coat, moved aside his frock coat, then opened his waistcoat and inched up his bloodstained shirt and undershirt. A slice of tight brown skin came into view, and with it a raw, red wound, a hole about a half-inch across.

"Nasty." Bertie grabbed Sinclair's handkerchief from his pocket, folded it, and pressed it to the wound. "Stilettos can go deep, and they're jagged."

"So I feel."

Bertie bit her lip. Knife wounds could be shallow and heal quickly, or they could be deep enough to puncture something vital. Or they could fester. It happened so swiftly, the sickening, and then the man or woman was no more.

"You need a doctor," Bertie said. "And bed."

Sinclair shifted, bringing out another sound of pain. "Two things lacking in this backstreet basement."

"I didn't know where else to go." Bertie rocked a little in worry, still pressing hard on his wound. "Devlin's got men everywhere." She blinked back tears.

"Bertie, it's all right." Sinclair's voice went gentle. He put a steadying hand on hers. "We'll be all right. Richards is looking for us, and Hart's footman too. The coppers walking these streets will notice armed men hunting for us."

"Many of the coppers around here are Devlin's men," Bertie said darkly. "In his pay. They'll likely help him find us."

"Then we'll have to rely on Fellows."

"Who's in Scotland," Bertie pointed out.

"But his sergeant isn't. I asked Fellows to telegraph Sergeant Pierce to tell him about our return to London and your summons by your father. I wasn't happy with it."

Bertie tried to feel relief, but it wouldn't come. "For once, my dad's heart was in the right place, warning me. He hates Devlin with a passion—Dad's scared of him, and he says Devlin ruins our trade, which is true. Since Devlin's hand in glove with the bobbies, they're happy to arrest the likes of my dad, but they'll leave Devlin and his thugs alone."

"Are you sure your father only wanted to warn you?" Sinclair asked. "That he didn't swallow his fear and take money from Devlin for bringing you to him?"

Bertie nodded. "I'm sure. Dad hates Devlin more than he can be angry at me, that's for certain."

"I'm sorry, Bertie." Sinclair stroked the backs of her fingers. "I've dragged you straight into my troubles. It appears that James hired Devlin to try to find you to hurt me. I'd thought James safely in a prison somewhere long ago, or maybe dead and gone, but he must have persuaded the prison governors to let him out. The man always had a smooth tongue."

"Confidence tricksters talk their way out of everything," Bertie said. "They're good at making people believe they can't be that bad. Or that they've changed. They lie, every time."

The handkerchief grew bright red with blood. There

wasn't quite as much blood as Bertie feared, but that didn't mean the wound was trivial.

Sinclair needed to be examined and stitched up. But here they were, stuck down a hole, with men roaming the streets looking for them. Sinclair's face was gray-white, his voice, as reassuring as he tried to make it, dry and growing faint. He might die down here before they could get out. Devlin might give up eventually—depended on how much he was being paid—but it might be too late for Sinclair.

Bertie pulled out her own handkerchief and pressed its pristine white fabric to the wound. Sinclair grunted, body moving. "Am I hurting you?" Bertie asked anxiously. "I'm trying not to."

"You're doing fine, love. Don't be scared. We'll get out of this."

Bertie drew a breath, letting his warm Scottish voice flow over her. "You're good at reassuring me, but I'd rather hear some plans for doing it."

"I'm thinking. Don't rush me."

"Says the man who boasts about his soldiering days, surviving by a hairsbreadth in North Africa."

"I don't boast." Sinclair contrived to look offended. "I tell Andrew stories."

Bertie laughed shakily. "Sounds like boasting to me. All your courage in the face of danger."

"It's a relief that I made it home to have a son to tell the stories to."

"Well, maybe you'll be able to tell him *this* story," Bertie said.

"I will." Sinclair's eyes slid closed, his hand going slack on hers.

She shook him. "No! Stay awake."

Sinclair opened his eyes again, gray slits in the dim light. "I'm alive. Don't worry."

"But you can't go to sleep. Keep talking to me." Bertie's small handkerchief was soon soaked. All she had left was the cloth she'd lifted from James. It was fine linen, expensive, handmade with initials stitched into the corners.

"Talking," Sinclair said. "I've been doing that my entire life. As a child, as an officer, as a barrister. Too much bloody talking."

"I like hearing you talk." Bertie pressed James's clean handkerchief over the bloody hole. "I like your accent, and the way your voice fills up the spaces. It's the first thing I noticed about you, your voice. Standing in that courtroom, looking the judge in the eye, your words rumbling strong as you told him Ruthie didn't kill that poor woman. I couldn't take my eyes off you."

Sinclair's brows twitched upward. "You flatter me."

"I thought you were wonderful. And handsome. And kind. You helped my friend, saved her life. But you looked so empty and sad afterward, not glad you'd been right. I wanted to know why—I wanted to know everything about you. That's why I followed you home."

His eyes went warm, the corners of his mouth twitching. "After stealing my watch. And kissing me, little wretch."

"Couldn't help meself, could I?" Bertie asked. "I had a handsome man hidden away with me. I should have been afraid of you, but I knew you were good inside, all the way through. So I kissed ya." She grinned. "I was right. You *are* good all the way through."

"No, I'm not." Sinclair's eyes drifted closed again. "I have a black heart, love."

"You don't." Bertie pressed harder on the handkerchief. "You have a *good* heart, a caring one. Look at you with your kids, and helping people like Ruthie. And me." He didn't stir, and Bertie's fears came pouring in on her.

"Don't," she said frantically. "Don't die on me and leave me alone. *Please*." She laid her head on his chest while she held the handkerchief to the wound, relieved to hear the slow beating of his heart. "I love you, Sinclair McBride. Don't leave me before I can tell you that."

Chapter 26

Sinclair's head was buzzing, everything seeming far away and small. The only sharp points were the pain in his abdomen, and Bertie's voice. *I love you, Sinclair McBride.*

Bertie. Sinclair felt her warm weight on him, tried to move his fingers to stroke her hair. *I'm all right. I'll be all right. You're with me.*

He didn't hear the words come out of his mouth, which worried him. The knife hadn't gone in that far, had it? The thick wool of his greatcoat and frock coat beneath had slowed the blade. Hell, the thing had had to penetrate five layers of cloth.

But the knife had been sharp, thin, precise. Sinclair could no longer feel his fingers.

"I love you," Bertie said again. "I don't know if you can love me back—if you see me as only a governess, or a pickpocket, or the girl with the funny name. But this girl loves you, and always will. Don't matter if you send me away—I'll always love you."

And I'll always love you. "Bertie." He made his mouth move.

Bertie raised her head, her eyes streaming with tears. "Don't die, Sinclair."

"Trying not to." Sinclair wet his lips. "Say it again."

"What?" Bertie wiped her cheeks. "That I love you?"

"Yes." Sinclair sighed and let his eyes close again.

Bertie shook him, which hurt, damn it. "You stay with me," she said. "I have to get you home."

His own bed would be a much more comfortable place in which to die. Then Sinclair clenched his teeth. No, he wouldn't die, neither here nor in his bed. He wouldn't let James win. The man had ruined Daisy's life—it had taken Sinclair and Daisy years to put it back together again. James could not come in now and wipe all Sinclair cared about away.

He cracked open his eyes. "We need help," he managed to say.

"I know that. But I'm not leaving you here to run and fetch it, and you can't run anymore. It should be all the way dark by now—we might be able to slip through and find your coach."

"Too much of a risk." Sinclair wet his lips again. "Any chance of some water?"

"No. I haven't been back to keep the place up."

"This cellar . . ." Sinclair turned his head to look around and groaned as he pulled at his wound. The walls formed a triangle around the small space, where houses had sealed off the end. Why it was done and whether the current inhabitants knew the space was here could not be said.

"That wall." Sinclair tried to point to his right and gave up. "It leads to another house?"

"Yeah. Used to be one house, it looks like, but broken up into flats now."

"How solid is the wall? Can we break through?"

"Are you mad? Though . . ." Bertie trailed off. "Let me look." Sinclair heard her skirts swish as she walked the small distance from him. He hated her gone, because he was so cold.

"It's brick, but also plaster," she said. "Who knows what's on the other side?"

I'll leap off this bed and break it down, Sinclair told himself. *Any moment now.*

"Let me see what I've got down here." Bertie moved out of the circle of light, and Sinclair heard things clanking and thudding. "The builders of long ago left things lying about. Nothing worth much."

Or she would have taken them home and given them to her father to sell, Sinclair knew. Anything, nailed down or not, could be sold in these streets, including the nails.

"Here's something," Bertie said at the same time Sinclair heard voices above them.

Bertie went absolutely silent. It was uncanny how she could do that—no more rattling of lumber or metal in the corner, no sound of fabric, no words, not even her breathing. She came back to Sinclair, holding something, but Sinclair couldn't make out what it was.

She put her hand to his chest, stilling him, though Sinclair didn't need to be told not to move. Above them, boots thumped, and voices became clearer.

"There's blood," a man said in thick Cockney. "Drops of it. Fresh."

"Down there." The Irish tones of James came through. "Another twenty quid if you make sure he's dead."

"A gentleman and barrister?" said a less thick voice but still a working-class accent. "Not bleeding likely. Having him crawl off to die after you knifed him is one thing. Shooting him deliberately is another."

"Fine. Just the girl then."

"The girl, I can do. Her father's been a pain in my fundament for years, and she'd a nice bit of flesh."

Bertie's eyes were wide with rage. "I'll give him a nice bit of flesh," she whispered.

Sinclair managed to move his hand—his whole arm came alive, energy flowing through him. "No, you start pounding on that wall. If we get trapped in here, we're done."

The banging would attract the men's attention, but they were going to check the cellar anyway. Bertie turned away, hoisting the bit of beam she'd found. Sinclair tried to swing up to help her, and found himself sitting down again.

Bertie hurried to the wall. She looked at Sinclair before

she drew back for the first stroke. "When I said I loved you? I meant it, you know."

Sinclair's lips moved upward in a smile, his heart flooding with warmth. "I mean it too."

Bertie's sunny smile beamed out at him, then his beautiful, tender lady turned around and smacked the post into the wall with a resounding *boom*.

~~~

As Bertie crashed the solid wooden beam into the plaster wall, another shout sounded upstairs, and their enemies started coming down. The door at the bottom of the stairs was locked and bolted, but they could break through. The only question was whether Bertie would—or even could—break through her wall first.

Bits of plaster rained down from her onslaught, old whitewash flaking over her hair and gown like snow. Bertie was terrified, but also glowing with joy. *I mean it too.*

Cryptic words from her dour Scotsman, but Bertie knew how hard it had been for him to say that. Sinclair didn't love easily, but when he loved, he did it deeply.

Bertie kept pounding as the door to the stairs started to splinter. She couldn't turn to see what Sinclair was doing—every second counted. Devlin being too scrupulous—or cautious—to kill Sinclair didn't mean he wouldn't stand by and watch James do it. Sinclair was too injured to fight them all, and Bertie would never win against them.

Which was stronger, a brick and plaster wall or a stout oak door? Bertie would soon find out.

In her favor, the bricks were quite old, the mortar crumbling between them. The plaster soon broke under her onslaught, and then a brick fell through the wall to the other side. Bertie put her hands through and pulled the next brick down, praying that what she found behind those wasn't more bricks.

She felt air. Foul-smelling air to be sure, but air all the same. "I'm through!" She hit the bricks again, rewarded with more falling inward. "It's coming down!"

"So's the door," Sinclair said.

He sounded stronger. But Bertie had seen enough victims of illness and injury who'd rallied before they'd died to take heart. She turned her head to look for him.

Sinclair had managed to get himself off the cushions. He'd upended the small folding table and piled the sofa cushions on top of it. A barricade, but not a very good one.

"Go!" Sinclair shouted at her, just as the door burst open, admitting men and bright lanterns.

Sinclair had something bulky and black in his hand. There was a roar of noise, a flash, a stench of pistol shot. One of Devlin's henchmen cried out.

"You brought your pistol," Bertie shouted.

"Excellent observation," Sinclair said in his biting tones. "Now get through there."

"I'm not leaving you!"

"Yes, you are. Go, before I shove you through with my foot on your backside."

The men in the room, blinded by their own lanterns and the gunshot, took a moment to readjust. Bertie knew that when they did, those who were armed would open fire.

"Bertie, damn you to hell." Sinclair started for her. Which would leave him exposed, and Devlin was shouting at his men to douse their lanterns.

Bertie dove through the opening. She'd done such a thing many times as a girl, throwing herself through windows for her dad, or through holes in walls to escape the approaching bobbies. She landed on a pile of bricks, mud, and slime, hearing the drip-drip of water from a pipe somewhere in the room.

Light flared as a hand thrust a lamp at her, then the hand was gone. Bertie was alone in a cellar full of damp, rotted timbers, and the beady eyes of rats. Behind her, noise filled the room she'd left, and voices.

James's fury. "Get her!"

Devlin, annoyed. "He's got a shooter, you daft Irish bastard."

"How many bullets can he possibly have?"

"Five," Sinclair said clearly. "I have five left. There's five of you, and I'm a dead shot. Want to wager on me missing any of you?"

Bertie froze, unable to move. By the light of her lamp, she saw that the cellar she stood in was small, and about an inch of water covered the floor. A wooden stair on the other side of the room led up to a door. Locked, probably, though it looked flimsy.

Had Devlin sent men around to the other side to wait for them to pop out? Possibly, but then, would Devlin know which house it was? The warrens around here were tricky.

Sinclair was ready to shoot all those men, and risk that he could before they shot him back. *Run!* Bertie's mind screamed at her. *Bring help!*

That would be sensible, but her feet wouldn't move. If she went for help, she'd never be able to get back in time to save Sinclair. Devlin or James would have killed him by then.

What do I do? What do I do? Bertie had only one weapon in her arsenal, the post she held. Unless she could command the rats to attack—Bertie had one giddy vision of the rats swarming in to terrorize Devlin, before her eyes alighted on her second weapon.

Sinclair fired, and another man grunted in pain. "Make him stop!" James cried.

"Damn your hide," Devlin snarled, though whether at Sinclair or James, Bertie couldn't tell.

Bertie ran across the room and up the stairs. She didn't like rats, but she didn't fear them—they were simply trying to survive like the rest of London.

The door at the top was closed fast, but as Bertie yanked at it, she found it was only latched. Another yank tore the latch from the wall on the other side, the piece of metal clinking onto a stone floor beyond.

Bertie opened the door and peered into the passage. All was dark and quiet, but that did not mean the house wasn't inhabited.

Bertie didn't much care at the moment. She raced down the stairs again and snatched up her lamp, rushing back toward the hole.

Sinclair fired again. This time James shouted and cried out. Whether Sinclair had hit him fatally or only grazed him, Bertie couldn't tell, but she had no time for assessment. *I'm a dead shot,* Sinclair had said, with chilling conviction.

Bertie scrambled back through the hole and grabbed Sinclair, who was crouching behind his barricade. The look on his face was that of a grim soldier who knew he would likely fall to his enemy, but who would take as many as he could down with him.

He glared at Bertie when she tugged him, but she didn't wait to explain. Rising, she lifted her lamp high and threw it at their pursuers.

Devlin swore, as did his one thug left standing. Bertie caught up the second lamp and tossed that one as well. The lamps were nearly empty, but there was enough kerosene in them to catch and burn.

Sinclair rose. He fired another shot, then he grabbed the remaining lamp and tossed it into the blaze. It burst with a puff of flame, and then fire and smoke filled the tiny space.

Sinclair's fingers latched around Bertie's arm, and he shoved her back toward the hole. Bertie paused a split second to snatch up her precious hat, then she climbed through. Sinclair followed, turning around to fire one more time before he dove after her.

He landed and rolled, as Bertie had, but instead of leaping to his feet, he groaned and slipped down to the muck. Bertie ran to him. She got under his arm and lifted him, half dragging him to the stairs. Behind them, she heard Devlin yell, "To hell with this. Get up there and around. I *want* them."

Bertie pulled Sinclair up the rickety wooden stairs, praying they wouldn't give way. Sinclair tripped and staggered, his body heavy on Bertie's. She'd left the door open, and she reached it, but Sinclair fell at the top of the stairs.

Sobbing, Bertie got him to his feet. He was half unconscious, snapping awake again as Bertie drew him into the hall beyond.

She slammed the door, though there wasn't much point,

and limped with Sinclair down the hall toward where she thought the front door must be.

Halfway along, Sinclair stopped her. "Bertie." His voice was a little stronger. He turned her to face him. "Bertie, I love you."

Before Bertie could answer, he hauled her to him, every bit of gentleness gone, and kissed her. She was ground against him, Sinclair's hands hard on her, the kiss fierce, savage. He smelled of sweat and blood, fear and worry, but his mouth was a place of heat in the cold darkness.

His teeth scraped her lips as he opened her mouth with his. Bertie sank her fingers into his coat, the hat she'd jammed on her head sliding sideways as Sinclair raked her hair from her face. If she let go of him, she knew, she'd tumble into a mire of despair and never be free. Sinclair was her world now, and Bertie would hold on to him through madness and terror, up again into the light.

The kiss turned deeper, as though Sinclair drew all his strength from Bertie. His strength fed her in turn, fires heating her in the bitter chill of this last day of the year.

Sinclair grunted, faltering, and he broke the kiss. Bertie looked up to see pain in his eyes, his strength depleted, the strain of his wound taking the fight out of him.

"We've got to go," she whispered.

Sinclair put his hand under her chin, his fingers ice-cold, and kissed her lips again. "When you get outside, you *run*. Find Hart's man. He'll look after you."

Fear slashed through her. "I'm not leaving you!"

Sinclair shook his head. "You have to, love. I can't move faster than a snail right now—a very slow snail."

"Then we'll be slow together. Two is better than one. I'm not a precious lady who won't dare soil her lily-white hands—I know how to kick and fight with the best of them."

Sinclair slanted her a look as he put his arm around her shoulders and leaned his weight on her. "Are you sure you're not Scottish?"

"No. But I'm Cockney, and we're pretty tough."

"You are, bless you." Sinclair kissed her on her cheek, which sent her hat sliding again.

Bertie righted it as she helped him down the hall. There was a door at the end, a large thing, bolted shut, but the bolts were fairly new, and a key rested in the lock. Bertie slid the bolts back, turned the key, and pulled open the door. Sinclair smiled grimly at her as they stumbled over the threshold, back into the unwelcoming streets.

Chapter 27

Plenty of people were about, as well as carts, horses, and hawkers. The night had gone dark and icy cold. Lights flashed from carried lanterns, or trickled dimly from windows and lamps along the main street.

"This way," Bertie said.

Sinclair leaned on her, having no idea where she was leading him, but he trusted her. He knew he'd fall over and expire before too long—Bertie was the only thing holding him up. She had more courage than any soldier he'd ever known, and a caring that left no one behind.

The cold was brutal. Snow started to fall as they staggered along, ice under their boots. Sinclair's wound had ceased hurting, which he took to be a bad sign.

"There!" Sinclair heard a man shout.

"Hell and damnation," Sinclair said. "Bertie, *go*."

Bertie gave him an anguished look, but she propped him up against a wall and gave him a nod. Tears wet her eyes, but she understood. Things were different out here—plenty of people surrounded them. The thugs would have to gamble that someone on the street wouldn't come to Sinclair's aid, or Bertie's, while she raced to find Richards and Hart's pugilist.

Another shout went up, but this one the denizens on the streets responded to. *"Fire!"*

Smoke billowed from the passage that led to Bertie's cellar. The walls and floor in there were all stone and plaster, without much to burn, but the wall of smoke was thick, the stench strong.

One thing that could pull Londoners together was fire—even the smallest blaze carried the danger of destroying half the city. The great fire of London two hundred years ago had started not far from here, in fact. Devlin and his men got shoved aside, as people began shouting for buckets and the fire brigade.

Sinclair watched Bertie's gray feathered hat disappear into the throng. She could move, sliding through the crowd, in and out of openings no one else saw. He remembered watching her hat bob along like that the night he'd first seen her, as she disappeared after picking over her mark. Sinclair's heart swelled. His brave, strong, street-smart lady would outwit them all.

Devlin was coming for him, as was James, still standing, though he moved unsteadily. James was truly a bastard. He'd coerced Daisy all those years ago, stealing away a spirited young woman and breaking her into tiny fragments. Sinclair thanked God he'd been able to rescue her from him. Now James wanted vengeance for that rescue, ready to hurt innocent Bertie and Sinclair's children to get it.

Thoughts of Cat and Andrew, waiting at home under Mrs. Hill's care, galvanized him. Sinclair had asked Fellows to make sure constables watched his home, so if anyone tried to slip in while he was gone, they'd be routed.

Sinclair knew now that he'd live. He'd see his children again, he'd bring Bertie home to stay, and James would lose. Again. The man was doomed to lose in the end, because his entire life was a lie. Truth, even ugly truth, always won.

Shrill bells rang as the fire brigade and their terrifyingly large wagon and horses charged down the street. Devlin leapt out of its way just in time, becoming separated from his thugs. Sinclair used the opportunity to stagger down the street, caught up in the crowd like a piece of flotsam.

When he drifted to a halt again, he saw Devlin look around then throw up his hands in disgust. Devlin signaled to his henchmen, and they all disappeared down the street, toward the river and more darkness.

James spotted Sinclair. He came at him, his handsome face smeared with blood, soot, and grime, his eyes full of crazed anger. James knew his hired thugs had left him stranded, but it was apparent he didn't care.

He rushed Sinclair, his knife flashing in the glare of lamplight. "Fucking Scottish pig," he said, and struck.

Sinclair had one bullet left in his gun. He fired.

James's body jerked, but his anger didn't fade. The knife came down, and Sinclair dove wildly out of its way. The blow went slack as James fell, his body crumbling to a heap on the street. The crowd, rushing with buckets toward the fire, leapt over him or stepped right on him, never noticing.

Sinclair managed to drop his pistol back into his pocket before his knees folded, and he slid to the ground next to James. He protected his head with his arms, but he'd be trampled, just like James, nothing left but pale flesh ground into the mud.

He couldn't see whether James was dead or alive. Blood flowed from the wound Sinclair's Webley had made, and James didn't move.

More people rushed past, bumping and buffeting Sinclair, all too worried about the fire to stop and find out if he was well. Didn't even take the time to try to rob him, Sinclair thought with ironic humor. He was losing strength again, the pain of the wound returning. He was wrong—feeling the pain was worse. It made his head buzz, and the city recede again, taking Bertie with it.

"Sir!" Harsh light flashed into Sinclair's face, and a strong hand caught him under the arm.

Sinclair groaned and looked up into the sky-blue eyes of Macaulay, the ghillie come to rescue his laird. Macaulay's freckled face and red hair seemed a long way up, and Sinclair understood now how Andrew felt when he looked up at the giant of a man.

Another warmth came to Sinclair's other side. *Bertie*. She regarded him anxiously with her violet blue eyes. Her hat was straight on her head again, but her nose was covered in soot, which made him want to laugh.

"You are the most beautiful woman in the world," Sinclair said, and he did laugh.

Laughter hurt, but he kept on, as Macaulay and Bertie dragged him to another beautiful sight, his own carriage. Hart's pugilist and Richards reached out to help, and the four of them got Sinclair successfully decanted inside.

Bertie climbed in after him. She landed beside Sinclair on the seat and gathered him into her arms as the carriage jerked forward.

Outside, London clamored, the fire brigade and London's citizens rushing to put out the blaze. Inside the coach, all was calm and sweet. Bertie cradled Sinclair against her soft bosom, and she kissed his lips, his face, his hair. She was crying, but Sinclair was too exhausted to try to figure out why.

Bertie refused to leave Sinclair's side, no matter how often Macaulay, Mrs. Hill, and the surgeon told her to go to bed. She'd nurse Sinclair with her own two hands until he was better, she declared. She'd never give up on him.

She watched anxiously as the surgeon Macaulay had fetched cleaned Sinclair's wound and stitched him up. The surgeon instructed Bertie how to wash the wound and change the dressing, then he mixed up powders and a poultice to leave with her for him. Bertie mentioned Warburg's tincture, which Sinclair had used to dose Andrew, and the surgeon said it couldn't hurt.

Sinclair lay deathly still throughout the procedure, not waking enough to take the morphia the surgeon had brought. The man finished, telling Bertie that when Sinclair woke, she should try to make him eat some broth, to keep up his strength.

The night was long. Sinclair tossed and moaned, his body heating and then breaking into a sweat. He pushed off the covers then shivered, and Bertie and Macaulay patiently tucked him in again.

Macaulay slept on the sofa in the study, and Mrs. Hill came in often. The children wanted to see their father, of course, but Mrs. Hill was keeping them away so they wouldn't disturb him or accidentally hurt him.

"Less distressful for them too, not seeing him like this," Mrs. Hill said, entering near to midnight. "But they're still awake, and they'd benefit from seeing you, Miss Frasier."

Mrs. Hill gave her a pointed look, but Bertie shook her head. "I can't leave him." Her eyes hurt from tears. "Not yet."

Mrs. Hill frowned, then she smoothed Bertie's hair with a gentle hand. "I understand, dear. But they need you too."

Bertie knew she was right. Cat and Andrew must be frightened and worried, knowing their father was in danger of slipping away. Bertie couldn't make them face that alone. "I'll nip upstairs and make sure they're all right," she said, and Mrs. Hill gave her an approving nod.

Mrs. Hill sat down in Bertie's place, and Bertie hurried to her room, her legs weak with exhaustion. She washed her face and smoothed her hair, trying to enter the nursery with some show of confidence.

Andrew threw himself at her, wrapping around her as soon as Bertie walked inside. Cat took Bertie's hand, squeezing hard.

Cat looked different now that she no longer had the doll perpetually in the crook of her arm—she stood a little straighter and some pain had gone from her eyes. The repaired doll sat on a shelf above Cat's bed, dressed in another of the gowns Sinclair had given Cat over the years, her cracked smile still benevolent.

"You'll save Papa, won't you, Bertie?" Andrew demanded.

"Of course she will," Cat answered him. "Just like she saved you, and my dolly. She'll take good care of him."

Cat's voice was firm, that of a sister reassuring her younger brother, but the look she sent Bertie was anxious.

"Cat is right." Bertie stroked Andrew's hair, which was the same color as Sinclair's. "I'll look after your dad proper, don't you worry."

"Macaulay told us he was in a battle," Andrew said. "With guns and everything. Like at Culloden."

"Not like that, Andrew," Cat said with a touch of her usual scorn.

"He was very brave." Bertie shivered, remembering how she'd watched Sinclair collapse on the street, barely able to react to her and Macaulay when they came for him. He'd been bleeding again, blood staining his clothes, her gloves, and the seat of the carriage.

Both children hugged her, then Cat withdrew and wiped tears from her face. "You must go back and look after him. Mustn't she, Andrew?"

Andrew squeezed his eyes shut and clung tighter to Bertie. Cat nudged him, and Andrew jumped.

"Yes, you must look after Papa," he said rapidly, as though Cat had made him rehearse the line.

"I'll take care of Andrew," Cat said. "I'll put him to bed."

Andrew tried not to look dismayed. Bertie kissed both of them. "Thank you. I promise, I'll send for you the moment he's better."

Hours later, she feared the worst. Sinclair muttered in his sleep, shoving away the covers. Bertie changed his bandage, washing the wound, which felt hot. She couldn't make him wake enough to drink the tincture or the powders, so he only tossed more in pain.

He finally quieted when the clocks were striking five. Sinclair's skin was damp but didn't feel roasting hot, and his breathing had become more even. Bertie curled up next to him, pulling the rumpled sheets over herself. She said a little prayer, then her eyes would stay open no longer, and she slept.

~~~

Sinclair woke, moved, and cursed. Pain ripped from his abdomen through to his spine, and he hissed a breath through his teeth.

He relaxed slowly, making himself lie perfectly still. There. If he stayed just . . . like . . . this, the pain was only slightly excruciating.

He heard soft breathing beside him and carefully turned his head. Bertie was next to him, her head pillowed on her arm, her eyes closed. Her hair was a mess, the curls on her forehead damp. Her nose was free of soot now, except for one tiny smudge, and her lips were parted in her sleep.

If Sinclair didn't hurt so much, and could move his body at all, he'd roll over and kiss those pretty red lips. Then he'd brush back her hair and slide on top of her, parting her legs to make sweet, deep love to her as the house slept around them.

Sinclair did hurt, however, so all he could do was look at her. Not a bad thing. Firelight touched her throat, her dress open at the neck, and glinted on the chain of her locket.

Safe. She was safe. James was dead or dying, Devlin would likely go after more lucrative game, and Jeffrey would be sent off to Dartmoor.

Safety. Peace. Bertie had never known it, and Sinclair had taken a long time to learn it. He'd make sure Bertie had it for the rest of her days. He'd go on standing up in court, speaking for those who didn't know how to speak for themselves, helping the innocent and making a case against the guilty. He'd continue working toward being a judge, making Old Monty and his committee happy enough to present him with a position on the bench. Then he'd come home to Bertie and his children every night. Idyllic.

Sinclair knew, though, that he'd never stomach such an ordinary life for long. He'd clung to this routine only because it had helped him bury his grief—being caught up in his work meant he'd never had to take grief out and look at it.

He'd looked at it plenty in that basement with Bertie,

when the men had come through the door, ready to kill her. Sinclair would make sure that never happened, and he'd live his life with her and his children to its fullest. He'd take them to this Christmas pantomime Bertie kept talking about, and then they'd go home to the Highlands for the rest of the holidays, back where he belonged.

Sinclair could move his right hand without too much pain. He lightly smoothed Bertie's hair, loving the soft warmth of it. Bertie was life, and he wanted life with all his might.

Bertie stirred, her eyes fluttering open. Her first puzzled look slowly dissolved, and a little smile moved her lips. Sinclair smiled back.

Bertie's eyes widened, and she sat up straight. Her hand went to his forehead, then his face, then lightly landed on his chest. "You all right? How do you feel?"

"Bloody awful." Sinclair winced at the croak that was his voice. "What about you? Throwing fireballs and breaking through walls, like a warrior woman. I'll wager Boadicea is an ancestor of yours. Though I wager she was never as pretty."

Bertie's cheeks went red. "You're a charmer, ain't you? Bet you won't be so charming while I'm changing your bandage." Bertie sat up, reaching for a pile of cloth on the bedside table.

Sinclair rumbled a laugh. "I was never a good patient, lass, but I won't promise not to seduce you while you're nursing me. With the understanding that I can't carry out anything I suggest until I can move again." Sinclair's breath went out of him as he twitched the wrong way. "Bloody hell."

"You lie still." Bertie grabbed the bandages and hurried around the bed. "I'll try not to hurt you."

She started for the basin in the corner, then halted, her back quivering, and swung around again. "Blast it all, I thought I'd lose you for sure." Tears trickled down her cheeks as she rushed back to him, leaned over him in the bed, and wrapped her arms carefully around him.

Warm goodness. Sinclair lifted his stronger hand and

threaded it through her hair, gently pulling her head back so he could kiss her. This he could do—kissing—without pain . . . as long as he didn't move too much.

Bertie eased away and touched his face. "Thank you for staying alive."

Sinclair tried a smile, though in his heart he was thanking God, Bertie, and his stubborn constitution for not letting him slip away. "Just wait until I'm better, vixen," he said. "I'll show you what I've been dreaming about all night, what I'd do right now if I wasn't in debilitating pain."

"Yeah?" Bertie's word was soft, but her eyes danced with laughter. "Well, maybe I'll show you what I've been dreaming about *you*."

Sinclair's heart beat faster, heat creeping into his body, which had been cold too long. "Then we'll plan an assignation." Sinclair caressed Bertie's face, loving her soft skin, her smile, the beautiful eyes that had snapped Sinclair out of his prison of grief weeks ago and set him on the path to the world again.

Bertie grinned at him. "Too right," she said. "I look forward to it."

Chapter 28

After a week, Sinclair was able to rise from his bed and move about, regaining more of his strength. Bertie watched him anxiously, and so did his children—not to mention Mrs. Hill, Macaulay, the maids, Peter, the cook, and the coachman. Sinclair began to growl that he didn't need to be mollycoddled, but they refused to leave him be.

Inspector Fellows and his sergeant paid Sinclair a visit in the second week, and Sinclair invited Bertie to stay and listen to what Fellows had to say. Sergeant Pierce looked uncertain about her being there, but Sinclair knew she'd played an integral part in bringing James down. She deserved to be in the room. Besides, Sinclair simply liked her near.

"James Maloney survived your shot," the inspector said, his voice as dry as ever. "A resilient man, he is. But he has much ill will from those in the East End—a number of witnesses have come forward to claim they saw him pursuing you, stabbing you, tackling you, and numerous other things. Some went into flights of fancy of things he couldn't possibly have done. The word has gone out, apparently, that Maloney is to fall, and East End dwellers are required to speak up."

"Devlin, possibly," Bertie said. "He doesn't like me or my father, but he hates outsiders even more, especially ones who get him into trouble. He must have decided James's money wasn't worth it, and turned against him instead."

"Bertie has many friends, as well," Sinclair said.

"True," Fellows said. "We can bang up Maloney for assault, attempted kidnapping, paying a known criminal, coercion, and numerous other things. Possibly also for causing you anguish through the letters, though we might have a devil of a time proving that. However, with the things Miss Frasier happened to . . . find . . . inside Mr. Maloney's coat, we can tie him to other confidence games and blackmail. Seems he had several identities, and papers connecting him to victims in France, England, and Prussia. I'm enjoying going through them." Fellows smiled one of his rare smiles. He did love catching a crook.

"Make sure he stays put this time," Sinclair said in his deep rumble. "I don't want him turning up again, trying to make my life and my family's lives a misery."

"No fear," Fellows said. "My case will be very solid against him, and I'll use my influence to get the best prosecutor there is. I'm sorry that barrister can't be you, but you'll make a very good witness."

"That will indeed be a pleasure," Sinclair said. "As long as my late wife's name, and Bertie's, stay out of it."

"Since I don't have hard evidence that he sent the letters," Fellows said, "that won't come up. Trust me, he's done plenty else to fix himself. He's a charmer, but juries don't like tricksters—they'll all have been fooled at one time or another, or know someone who has, and I'm sure they'll see to it that this one, at least, gets his just deserts."

Fellows left soon after, happy to get back home to his wife and put together his case.

⌣

The next visitor to gain entrance was Sinclair's brother-in-law, Edward. Again, Bertie was present, though she wasn't certain she wanted to be for this meeting. Edward put her back up too quickly. Then again, she'd rather be there to make sure he didn't make Sinclair worse.

Sinclair received Edward in his study. Sinclair wore an informal suit, his abdomen bulked by bandages, and he didn't rise from the sofa when Edward came in. Bertie had been reading Sinclair's correspondence out to him, making notes on what he wanted to say in reply. She remained at his desk, pen poised, as the irritating Edward entered.

Edward swept his gaze over her then fixed it on Sinclair, looking him up and down. "I heard you were in a brawl," Edward said coldly. "Somewhere in the gutter. Defending her honor, were you?"

Sinclair gave Edward his stern barrister's stare. "If you don't keep a civil tongue about Miss Frasier, I'll be defending her honor against *you*, and winning."

"I don't brawl," Edward said. He sniffed.

"I don't care," Sinclair said with his impatient growl. "If you continue to insult her, I'll come off this couch and punch you in the nose. What do you want?"

"To see how you are, of course."

Oh, of course, Bertie thought. *Come to kick a man when he's down, more like.*

"I appreciate your concern," Sinclair said. "You may go now."

"I was mostly worried about the children," Edward said, ignoring him. "With you an invalid, my wife and I think it best that we take over the caring of them. Arrange Andrew's school, find Caitriona a proper governess. You may visit them at holidays, of course. I've consulted a solicitor, who assures me such a thing is logical and feasible. They have no mother, and their father is unfit to take care of them. They will be well provided for by me."

Sinclair sat still and listened until Edward finished. How Sinclair didn't come off the couch with a roar, Bertie didn't know.

"I've consulted a solicitor as well," Sinclair said in his reasonable voice, though Bertie heard the bite of fury behind it. "As you know, I am acquainted with many. While it's common for families to take in the children of sisters and brothers, it is entirely the father's and mother's choice if the parents are alive and competent. Since Margaret is no longer with us, I'll have to speak for her. No, my children will not live with you, Edward. I'll not have Cat and Andrew turned into stiff-necked prigs who need a pulley system in order to bow their heads. I have already ensured that if I shuffle off this mortal coil before my children are of age, either my brothers—Elliot, Patrick, or Steven—or my sister, Ainsley, will have care of them. My brothers and sister all have plenty of money and good social standing, and you'll never need to worry about Cat and Andrew with them."

Edward's face suffused with red. "I'll not have my sister's children associated with *Mackenzies*."

"Why not? My sister is deliriously happy, and her children are well cared for." Sinclair sat up straighter. He didn't wince, but Bertie saw the lines around his mouth tighten. "You aren't concerned for your niece and nephew, Edward. You're worried about your own standing. Margaret embarrassed you by running off to find some happiness, and you want to shove Cat and Andrew back into the Davies mold to show the world that your way is right. Sod you, and your wife too. My children are mine, and they're staying with me."

"To become indolent little layabouts?" Edward asked. "There's also some question, I've always known, about whether you married my sister correctly or not."

"I'll show you the license if you doubt." Sinclair's voice hardened. "The marriage was true. I'd think you'd not be so hasty to bastardize your own niece and nephew. But I've decided to make you happy." Sinclair sank back, keeping his gaze firmly on Edward. "Your main objection seems to be that my children are being educated at home. I'll have you know that at Easter, Andrew will be starting at Harrow, and Cat has been enrolled in Miss Pringle's Select Academy, one of the best schools for girls in the country. She'll begin at Easter as well."

Edward blinked in surprise then shot a sharp look at Bertie. Bertie regarded him calmly, the revelation no surprise to her. Sinclair had discussed it with her—and Cat and Andrew—at length. Cat had asked most of all to take drawing lessons. She'd shown Bertie a few more of her astonishing pictures, and she'd shyly agreed to let her Uncle Mac see some of them. Mac had looked at them, been quietly stunned, and told Cat she had the beginnings of great talent. Which had sealed Cat's decision to go to Miss Pringle's and study with the best teachers she could.

"And Miss Frasier?" Edward asked.

"My children will no longer need a governess. Will all that keep you from running to my house every fortnight or your wife accosting me in tearooms?"

Edward still looked surprised, but he wasn't the sort of man to not find something to be annoyed about. "I suppose it will have to do," he said sourly.

"You may of course visit the children on holidays and for school treats," Sinclair said.

Edward made a sound like a grunt, and gave Sinclair a stiff nod. "Very well then. Good day."

He turned around and walked out of the room, to find Macaulay standing slap outside the door holding Edward's hat and coat. Edward was uncomfortable with Macaulay, it was clear as he cringed away from the big Scotsman. Macaulay herded Edward toward the stairs, nearly chasing him with the coat and hat.

"Close the door, Bertie." Sinclair sank back to the cushions, sounding tired.

Bertie left the desk and shut the door, but her anger wasn't assuaged. "He has no call to come here and berate you while you're feeling poorly." Bertie looked at the door, picturing Edward fleeing down the stairs. "No wonder your Daisy ran away from him."

Sinclair grunted a laugh. "I fully understood the first time I met him. She'd simply picked the wrong man to run off with at first."

"She was lucky to find you," Bertie said. She left the door and came to stand in front of the sofa. "Something I've been meaning to ask you. Now that Cat and Andrew are going

away, and they won't need a governess . . ." She drew a
breath. "I'd like to stay on. I can help you write letters, like
today. Or help Mrs. Hill. Or be the cook's assistant, or black
the boots—I'm not particular."

Sinclair watched her without changing expression. "Why
do you want to stay on in my poky house? There's a large
world out there. I thought you wanted to see it."

Bertie swallowed, a little pain in her heart. "Because,
truth to tell, I've got nowhere to go. With Mrs. Lang moved
in with my dad, there's not much room for me. Not that I
want to go back to him at all. If I can't stay here, then can
you at least help me be governess for one of your brothers?
Or housekeeper, or cook's assistant?"

Sinclair let her finish without interrupting, but he watched
her closely. "No, Bertie. I won't get you a place in one of my
brothers' houses. I think you should stay on here. In what
capacity—*that* we must discuss."

Bertie's heart beat faster. "I agree. We should discuss it.
At length."

Sinclair looked her over, a much more welcome scrutiny
than what his brother-in-law had given her. Then he laid his
head back and closed his eyes. "The first thing we should
talk about is your clothes."

"My clothes?" Bertie glanced down at her dark gray
dress, a new one to replace the frock sadly torn on her East
End adventure. "What's wrong with my clothes?"

"You'll need more of them. Much more." Sinclair opened
his eyes a slit, humor sparkling in them. "A wedding dress
first, I think. Have my sister and sisters-in-law find something you'll be so beautiful in I'll forget all my lines when
we're standing in front of the vicar."

Bertie's breath deserted her. The room spun around, as
had the ballroom when they'd danced, whirling faster and
faster until she couldn't think. "Sinclair McBride," she said,
her voice scratchy. "You open your eyes and look at me."

Sinclair did, a grin spreading across his handsome face.

"Are you asking me to marry you?" she demanded.

Sinclair shrugged. "Wedding gown, church, vicar, vows—if

we put it all together, I believe that's exactly what I am saying." He lost every bit of indifference and pinned her with a sharp look. "What answer will you give, Miss Frasier? Remember, you're under oath."

"Damn and blast you." Bertie got herself across the room to him, her shaking legs threatening to collapse under her. She knelt beside him on the sofa, being careful of his wound. "Are you sure? We're not exactly the same, you and me."

"Thank God," Sinclair said fervently. "The women pushed at me are wooden, expressionless, and afraid to say yes or no without permission. You're forthright, honest, courageous, full of life, and my children love you. *I* love you. I remember telling you that before we ran out to meet our maker." Sinclair put his large hand on her cheek, his fingers warm, the chill of his injury gone. "I love you, Roberta Frasier. My Bertie."

Bertie felt herself floating. "I love you too," she whispered.

"Then marry me. Marry me, and to hell with them all."

Bertie nodded, a lump in her throat so tight she couldn't speak. Sinclair's gray eyes were free of emptiness, the bleakness gone. The pieces of the broken man were back together again, Sinclair ready to take on the world.

They'd face it together.

Bertie put her hand in his and drew herself up to kiss him. Sinclair cradled her head and kissed her back, his lips strong on hers, mouth seeking. The kiss went on, happiness flushing Bertie as she realized exactly what was happening. She would marry Sinclair and be his wife, have his warm body beside her for all her days.

She eased back from the kiss and looked into his eyes, her heart in her smile. "Yes. I'll marry you, Mr. McBride."

"Hooray!" The door, which Bertie was certain she'd shut, swung open and banged into the bookcase behind it. Andrew ran in, shouting the word. Cat followed him, her eyes alight with more excitement than Bertie had ever seen in her.

"Papa is going to marry Bertie!" Andrew announced at the top of his voice. He ran out into the hall, yelled it again, then dashed back inside. "Bertie's going to be our mum!"

"We heard you, Andrew," Cat said with big-sisterly annoyance.

Sinclair held his hand out to them. "Come here, you two. Give Bertie a kiss."

Andrew flew at them, flinging himself into Bertie's lap. The sofa suddenly became very crowded as Cat joined them. Andrew kissed Bertie's and then his father's cheek, then he drew back and gave Sinclair a manly handshake.

Cat hugged Bertie. "Thank you," she whispered.

Bertie gathered her in. "My pleasure, sweetie."

"We'll adjourn to Scotland," Sinclair said. "And marry there, in our home in the Highlands." He let out a long breath, then gave Bertie a look that was so loving, she feared she'd burst into tears. "I can recover well there, with you all running around making noise. We'll invite the whole McBride clan, and throw in the Mackenzies too."

"Hooray!" Andrew shouted again.

Sinclair winced at the piercing sound, but he stretched out his arm to encompass Bertie and Andrew too. "Nothing I can't do without my family."

"And *what* a family." Bertie laughed again. "Cheeky and loud, always arguing or pestering you about something."

"If they were quiet and meek, I'd know something was wrong." Sinclair sat up. "Now go on. Start packing. We're off."

Andrew cheered again. He scrambled off the chaise and headed for the door. Cat gave Bertie another hug, then Sinclair, and ran after her brother. There was more spring in her step, a flush of happiness on her face.

"What a family," Sinclair repeated Bertie's words. He drew her close. "What a wife I've chosen. You're going to give me merry hell, aren't you?"

"That I am." Bertie sank into the curve of Sinclair's arm and raised her face to him for another kiss. "You ain't getting away with nothing, Mr. Basher McBride."

"I wouldn't want it to be otherwise," Sinclair said softly. Then he kissed her, and Bertie lost herself in his warmth.

Epilogue

The wedding photo showed Bertie in white, a lace veil trickling to her hips, a large smile on her face. Sinclair stood ramrod straight next to her, holding her arm and trying to look dignified. Caitriona sat in a chair in front of the happy couple, with Andrew standing beside it, a large dog sitting next to him.

The dog was a present from Ian and Beth Mackenzie, a puppy from their estate who'd grown gangly and unruly. Andrew had fallen in love with him on the Christmas visit, and so the dog joined Bertie and Sinclair on their journey to Sinclair's Highland home.

It was March, the Highlands just showing the light green of spring. Bertie loved Sinclair's house the moment she saw it. A large three-story stone structure, it had been built in the late eighteenth century, as Kilmorgan had been, but it was about one tenth Kilmorgan's size, which was fine with Bertie. The house was plenty big to her, and she didn't want to rattle around and not be close to Sinclair or the children. The walls were plain stone with tall windows and red-painted shutters, dormer windows peeking out from the slate roof.

The house sat on the banks of a pale blue loch, with green hills rising around it. Farms filled the valley around the village, as did pastures full of sheep. Fat cows with long hair falling over their faces wandered about, even into the streets of the village and the front door of Sinclair's house. Ospreys soared across the loch, and bubbles did indeed boil in the middle of the water. Bertie and Andrew would have to watch for their very own monster.

The wedding was held at the chapel near the village, with the McBrides—Steven and his wife Rose, who was expecting; Juliana and Elliot with Elliot's daughter Priti and their year-old son, Patrick; and the older Patrick McBride, with his wife, Rona. The Mackenzies were in attendance, from Hart to Ian, with their wives and growing brood of children. Inspector Fellows and Lady Louisa also came, Fellows hovering protectively around Louisa and their newborn daughter, who'd come to them in February. Daniel Mackenzie, filling out more every time Bertie saw him, arrived with Ainsley and Cameron. Twenty years old now, he was full of energy and plans for his future.

The revelry began at the wedding breakfast and lasted all day and into the night. Sinclair told Bertie the festivities would go until morning.

Fiddlers and drummers came from the village to play lively Scottish tunes, and the company danced. Bertie didn't know the dances, but Sinclair pulled her into them, teaching her as they went. Daniel also helped, his exuberance nearly knocking Bertie off her feet.

She danced with almost all the gentlemen—Elliot, Steven, even Patrick, Cameron, Mac, Daniel again. Hart never joined in, they told her, although Bertie caught him with Eleanor in the hall, the two circling around each other in their own private waltz. Ian didn't dance either, but he watched Beth and his children take part, the look on his face one of pure love.

Bertie sat out with Ian when she was exhausted, Sinclair walking Ainsley into another circle. Ian's gaze rested on

Beth as she danced with Daniel, Beth laughing, her cheeks pink, as Danny swung her around.

"I did what you told me," Bertie said to Ian over the music. "I stayed."

Ian glanced at her, taking in her ivory gown, minus the veil now. Bertie thought he'd speak, but he turned back to his wife and the dancers.

"You might not remember," Bertie went on. "You took me aside when Andrew got hurt and told me I should stay with them. It was good advice. I took it to heart."

"I remember." Ian's words broke through hers.

Bertie waited, but Ian was finished. "I understand now," Bertie said. "I know you meant that they needed me to look after them, but I need them too. It goes both ways."

Ian glanced at her, as though he had no idea why she kept speaking to him. The matter was closed.

"I just wanted to say thanks," Bertie said. "You made me think. I'm grateful, is all."

"You love them." The statement was bald, flat, brooking no argument.

Bertie's gaze went to Sinclair, his light hair glinting in the lamplight, as blond as his sister's. He was graceful for a large man, his kilt swaying enticingly as he danced.

"You're right about that," Bertie said. "I love them with all my might."

Ian waited a long moment before he spoke again. "A few years ago, I would have asked how you knew you loved them. Now, I don't have to." His gaze went to Beth again, and Bertie saw his world adjust.

Bertie felt the same adjustment when she looked at Sinclair. Her world had been chaotic, sometimes frightening, but always uncertain. Sinclair was certainty, but not dullness. Never that.

Sinclair caught her eye as he spun Ainsley by the waist and joined the main circle again, and he grinned at her. It was a smile of gratitude and love, as well as one of sinful promise. They hadn't had much time to be alone since they'd arrived, although late last night, Sinclair had entered Bertie's bedroom and made swift and silent love to her. They'd had to be quiet, as the house around them was filled, but the heat of the encounter was still with her.

The dance ended. Ian immediately left the corner to find Beth. Sinclair led Ainsley back to her husband, who was deep in conversation with Elliot, and came for Bertie.

"There's a Scottish tradition of the clan waiting outside the bedroom door for the groom to deflower his bride," he said to her. "With much drinking and shouting to go with it."

Bertie faltered. "Oh, dear."

"I told my brothers and the clan Mackenzie they'd better not try it. So they'll want to cheer us to our bedroom, unless we can get away before they notice."

"Yes, let's." Bertie's face burned. "Please."

Sinclair gave her a quick kiss on the lips, which elicited a shout from the dancers. They were certainly being watched. "You go first. Make an excuse to anyone who sees you. I'll join you. Be casual."

"Oh, you know I'm very good at slipping away." Bertie winked at him. "Raised to it, I was."

Sinclair laughed. "You are so beautiful."

Bertie warmed. "Flatterer."

He kissed the tip of her nose. "Until then."

Sinclair drifted off, allowing himself to be caught by his friends and brothers-in-law. Bertie talked and laughed with the ladies a few minutes, then excused herself to go to the necessary. She declined any company, saying she could find her way in her own house.

Once she'd left the ballroom, she ducked into a side passage and nipped up a set of stairs. The bedroom she'd share with Sinclair was on the first floor, a suite that took up one corner of the house. A lovely place with a view of the loch.

The hall was dim but the sitting room outside the bedroom was lit, as was the bedroom itself. Bertie shut the door and stood for a moment in the middle of the chamber, letting out her breath. Her body hummed—all the dancing, laughter, and tiredness catching up to her.

She was married. Mrs. Sinclair McBride. She could scarce believe it. Cat and Andrew would be her own children. A ready-made family.

Bertie sat down, running her hands along the finery of her ivory skirt. The Mackenzie and McBride ladies had once again enjoyed themselves transforming Bertie from her plain governess attire to a Cinderella gown. Bertie lifted the layers of silk and tulle and the petticoats beneath, stripping off her stockings while she waited for her Prince Charming.

He came in not long later, closing and locking the bedroom door. He leaned against it, letting out a breath of relief.

"Thought I'd never get away. The Mackenzie and McBride men are all madly in love with their wives—you'd think they'd let me be alone with mine."

"They love to tease, your family does."

"They're your family now too," Sinclair said darkly. "I'm not sure whether to congratulate you or express sympathy."

"I don't mind. I've always wanted a big family." Bertie rose, took hold of his broad hand, and placed it on her lower abdomen. "Which will become bigger soon."

Sinclair gazed down at her in no surprise at all, his palm warm through the fabric. "I wondered when you would tell me."

Bertie scowled. "Oh, blast you, I was hoping you'd fall down in a dead faint. Who told ya?"

"No one." Sinclair's shrug was maddening. "I'm good at observing people—I know what it means when a woman is ill in the mornings then eats like a horse the rest of the day."

"A horse?" Bertie planted her hands on her hips. "What do you mean, a horse?" She deflated. "You're probably right; I'm always hungry now. I'm going to be *enormous*."

"I hope so. I want you and our son or daughter healthy." Sinclair lost his smile and stepped close to her. "I'd forgotten what it was to be happy, Bertie. Truly happy all the way through. Thank you for putting the laughter back into my life."

Bertie rested her hand on his chest, feeling his heart beating beneath. No flutters as when he couldn't breathe, no strange pounding as when he'd been fevered. "When I first saw you," she said, "I wanted more than anything to make you smile."

Sinclair rewarded her with one now. "And you've been doing it ever since."

Bertie let her hand stray down his abdomen to his kilt. "Looks like you're doing more than smiling."

"You think I can help it?" Sinclair rested his hands on her shoulders, fingers gripping. "I'm with my beautiful wife, in her wedding dress, on my wedding night. I'm drunk and happy, but not insensible."

Bertie squeezed the very hard thing beneath his kilt. "I can see that. Feel it, rather."

"No more talking." Sinclair leaned close. "I make my living talking. Tonight, I just want . . . *you.*"

"You have me," Bertie whispered. "Forever. Love you, Sinclair."

"*That* you can say, over and over again." He nuzzled her. "I love you too, Bertie."

Bertie again told Sinclair she loved him as he slowly stripped off first her beautiful clothes then his. She said it when he lifted her to the bed and knelt in front of her to kiss his way down her body. And again as he leaned forward and drank her, firelight kissing his bare back and the gold of his hair.

Sinclair laid her on the bed, rising over her, his cock hard against her thigh, while he took her breast in his mouth, licking, suckling. Bertie said *I love you* when he slid himself inside her, his eyes intent on hers, and she said it once more when he began the rocking motion that sealed them together.

She cried it when ecstasy lifted her higher than had the dancing and the fact that she was his wife. Bertie murmured it in a low voice when Sinclair collapsed onto her, gathering her against his sweat-sheened body. He kissed her face, her hair, her throat, and Bertie whispered it to him.

"I love you too, Bertie," Sinclair answered every time. "I love you."

They lay together, curled into each other, one.

Complete.

Dear Reader,

I hope you enjoyed Sinclair and Bertie's story! They were a wonderful couple to write.

The Mackenzies' family saga continues: Watch for the next novel, The Stolen Mackenzie Bride, *and another novella in 2015, as well as print versions of the novellas bundled into paperback form. I will be exploring the Mackenzie family past, present, and future in the stories coming up.*

Meanwhile, please enjoy a peek at the very first novel of the Mackenzies series, The Madness of Lord Ian Mackenzie, *where it all began! Meet Ian Mackenzie, a man the world believes is "mad," and Beth Ackerley, a young widow who sees that there is far more to him than anyone understands.*

Thank you, and all my best wishes,
Jennifer Ashley

"I find that a Ming bowl is like a woman's breast," Sir Lyndon Mather said to Ian Mackenzie, who held the bowl in question between his fingertips. "The swelling curve, the creamy pallor. Don't you agree?"

Ian couldn't think of a woman who would be flattered to have her breast compared to a bowl, so he didn't bother to nod.

The delicate vessel was from the early Ming period, the porcelain barely flushed with green, the sides so thin Ian could see light through them. Three gray-green dragons chased one another across the outside, and four chrysanthemums seemed to float across the bottom.

The little vessel might just cup a small rounded breast, but that was as far as Ian was willing to go.

"One thousand guineas," he said.

Mather's smile turned sickly. "Now, my lord, I thought we were friends."

Ian wondered where Mather had got that idea. "The bowl

is worth one thousand guineas." He fingered the slightly chipped rim, the base worn from centuries of handling.

Mather looked taken aback, blue eyes glittering in his overly handsome face.

"I paid fifteen hundred for it. Explain yourself."

There was nothing to explain. Ian's rapidly calculating mind had taken in every asset and flaw in ten seconds flat. If Mather couldn't tell the value of his pieces, he had no business collecting porcelain. There were at least five fakes in the glass case on the other side of Mather's collection room, and Ian wagered Mather had no idea.

Ian put his nose to the glaze, liking the clean scent that had survived the heavy cigar smoke of Mather's house. The bowl was genuine, it was beautiful, and he wanted it.

"At least give me what I paid for it," Mather said in a panicked voice. "The man told me I had it at a bargain."

"One thousand guineas," Ian repeated.

"Damn it, man, I'm getting married."

Ian recalled the announcement in the *Times*—verbatim, because he recalled everything verbatim: *Sir Lyndon Mather of St. Aubrey's, Suffolk, announces his betrothal to Mrs. Thomas Ackerley, a widow. The wedding to be held on the twenty-seventh of June of this year in St. Aubrey's at ten o'clock in the morning.*

"My felicitations," Ian said.

"I wish to buy my beloved a gift with what I get for the bowl."

Ian kept his gaze on the vessel. "Why not give her the bowl itself?"

Mather's hearty laugh filled the room. "My dear fellow, women don't know the first thing about porcelain. She'll want a carriage and a matched team and a string of servants to carry all the fripperies she buys. I'll give her that. She's a fine-looking woman, daughter of some froggie aristo, for all she's long in the tooth and a widow."

Ian didn't answer. He touched the tip of his tongue to the bowl, reflecting that it was far better than ten carriages with matched teams. Any woman who didn't see the poetry in it was a fool.

Mather wrinkled his nose as Ian tasted the bowl, but Ian had learned to test the genuineness of the glaze that way. Mather wouldn't be able to tell a genuine glaze if someone painted him with it.

"She's got a bloody fortune of her own," Mather went on, "inherited from that Barrington woman, a rich old lady who didn't keep her opinions to herself. Mrs. Ackerley, her quiet companion, copped the lot."

Then why is she marrying you? Ian turned the bowl over in his hands as he speculated, but if Mrs. Ackerley wanted to make her bed with Lyndon Mather, she could lie in it. Of course, she might find the bed a little crowded. Mather kept a secret house for his mistress and several other women to cater to his needs, which he loved to boast about to Ian's brothers. *I'm as decadent as you lot,* he was trying to say. But in Ian's opinion, Mather understood pleasures of the flesh about as well as he understood Ming porcelain.

"Bet you're surprised a dedicated bachelor like myself is for the chop, eh?" Mather went on. "If you're wondering whether I'm giving up my bit of the other, the answer is no. You are welcome to come 'round and join in anytime, you know. I've extended the invitation to you, and your brothers as well."

Ian had met Mather's ladies, vacant-eyed women willing to put up with Mather's proclivities for the money he gave them.

Mather reached for a cigar. "I say, we're at Covent Garden Opera tonight. Come meet my fiancée. I'd like your opinion. Everyone knows you have as exquisite taste in females as you do in porcelain." He chuckled.

Ian didn't answer. He had to rescue the bowl from this philistine. "One thousand guineas."

"You're a hard man, Mackenzie."

"One thousand guineas, and I'll see you at the opera."

"Oh, very well, though you're ruining me."

He'd ruined himself. "Your widow has a fortune. You'll recover."

Mather laughed, his handsome face lighting. Ian had seen women of every age blush or flutter fans when Mather smiled. Mather was the master of the double life.

"True, and she's lovely to boot. I'm a lucky man."

Mather rang for his butler and Ian's valet, Curry. Curry produced a wooden box lined with straw, into which Ian carefully placed the dragon bowl.

Ian hated to cover up such beauty. He touched it one last time, his gaze fixed on it until Curry broke his concentration by placing the lid on the box.

He looked up to find that Mather had ordered the butler to pour brandy. Ian accepted a glass and sat down in front of the bankbook Curry had placed on Mather's desk for him.

Ian set aside the brandy and dipped his pen in the ink. He bent down to write and caught sight of the droplet of black ink hanging on the nib in a perfect, round sphere.

He stared at the droplet, something inside him singing at the perfection of the ball of ink, the glistening viscosity that held it suspended from the nib. The sphere was perfect, shining, a wonder.

He wished he could savor its perfection forever, but he knew that in a second it would fall from the pen and be lost. If his brother Mac could paint something this exquisite, this beautiful, Ian would treasure it.

He had no idea how long he'd sat there studying the droplet of ink until he heard Mather say, "Damnation, he really is mad, isn't he?"

The droplet fell down, down, down to splash on the page, gone to its death in a splatter of black ink.

"I'll write it out for you, then, m'lord?"

Ian looked into the homely face of his manservant, a young Cockney who'd spent his boyhood pickpocketing his way across London.

Ian nodded and relinquished the pen. Curry turned the bankbook toward him and wrote the draft in careful capitals. He dipped the pen again and handed it back to Ian, holding the nib down so Ian wouldn't see the ink.

Ian signed his name painstakingly, feeling the weight of Mather's stare.

"Does he do that often?" Mather asked as Ian rose, leaving Curry to blot the paper.

Curry's cheekbones stained red. "No 'arm done, sir."

Ian lifted his glass and swiftly drank down the brandy, then took up the box. "I will see you at the opera."

He didn't shake hands on his way out. Mather frowned, but gave Ian a nod. Lord Ian Mackenzie, brother to the Duke of Kilmorgan, socially outranked him, and Mather was acutely aware of social rank.

Once in his carriage, Ian set the box beside him. He could feel the bowl inside, round and perfect, filling a niche in himself.

"I know it ain't me place to say," Curry said from the opposite seat as the carriage jerked forward into the rainy streets. "But the man's a right bastard. Not fit for you to wipe your boots on. Why even have truck with him?"

Ian caressed the box. "I wanted this piece."

"You do have a way of getting what you want, no mistake, m'lord. Are we really meeting him at the opera?"

"I'll sit in Hart's box." Ian flicked his gaze over Curry's baby-innocent face and focused safely on the carriage's velvet wall. "Find out everything you can about a Mrs. Ackerley, a widow now betrothed to Sir Lyndon Mather. Tell me about it tonight."

"Oh, aye? Why are we so interested in the right bastard's fiancée?"

Ian ran his fingertips lightly over the box again. "I want to know if she's exquisite porcelain or a fake."

Curry winked. "Right ye are, guv. I'll see what I can dig up."

⁓

Lyndon Mather was all that was handsome and charming, and heads turned when Beth Ackerley walked by on his arm at Covent Garden Opera House.

Mather had a pure profile, a slim, athletic body, and a

head of golden hair that ladies longed to run their fingers through. His manners were impeccable, and he charmed everyone he met. He had a substantial income, a lavish house on Park Lane, and he was received by the highest of the high. An excellent choice for a lady of unexpected fortune looking for a second husband.

Even a lady of unexpected fortune tires of being alone, Beth thought as she entered Mather's luxurious box behind his elderly aunt and companion. She'd known Mather for several years, his aunt and her employer being fast friends. He wasn't the most exciting of gentlemen, but Beth didn't want exciting. *No drama,* she promised herself. She'd had enough drama to last a lifetime.

Now Beth wanted comfort; she'd learned how to run a houseful of servants, and she'd perhaps have the chance to have the children she'd always longed for. Her first marriage nine years ago had produced none, but then, poor Thomas had died barely a year after they'd taken their vows. He'd been so ill, he hadn't even been able to say good-bye.

The opera had begun by the time they settled into Sir Lyndon's box. The young woman onstage had a beautiful soprano voice and an ample body with which to project it. Beth was soon lost in the rapture of the music. Mather left the box ten minutes after they'd entered, as he usually did. He liked to spend his nights at the theatre seeing everyone of importance and being seen with them. Beth didn't mind. She'd grown used to sitting with elderly matrons and preferred it to exchanging inanities with glittering society ladies. *Oh, darling did you hear? Lady Marmaduke had three inches of lace on her dress instead of two. Can you imagine anything more vulgar? And her pleats were limp, my darling, absolutely limp.* Such important information.

Beth fanned herself and enjoyed the music while Mather's aunt and her companion tried to make sense of the plot of *La Traviata*. Beth reflected that they thought nothing of an outing to the theatre, but to a girl growing up in the East End, it was anything but ordinary. Beth loved music, and imbibed it any way she could, though she thought herself only a mediocre musician. No matter, she could listen to others play and enjoy it just fine. Mather liked to go to the theatre, to the opera, to musicales, so Beth's new life would have much music in it.

Her enjoyment was interrupted by Mather's noisy return to the box. "My dear," he said in a loud voice, "I've brought you my *very* close friend Lord Ian Mackenzie. Give him your hand, darling. His brother is the Duke of Kilmorgan, you know."

Beth looked past Mather at the tall man who'd entered the box behind him, and her entire world stopped.

Lord Ian was a big man, his body solid muscle, the hand that reached to hers huge in a kid leather glove. His shoulders were wide, his chest broad, and the dim light touched his dark hair with red. His face was as hard as his body, but his eyes set Ian Mackenzie apart from every other person Beth had ever met.

She at first thought his eyes were light brown, but when Mather almost shoved him down into the chair at Beth's side, she saw that they were golden. Not hazel, but amber like brandy, flecked with gold as though the sun danced on them.

"This is my Mrs. Ackerley," Mather was saying. "What do you think, eh? I told you she was the best-looking woman in London."

Lord Ian ran a quick glance over Beth's face, then fixed his gaze at a point somewhere beyond the box. He still held her hand, his grip firm, the pressure of his fingers just shy of painful.

He didn't agree or disagree with Mather, *a bit rudely,* Beth thought. Even if Lord Ian didn't clutch his breast and declare Beth the most beautiful woman since Elaine of Camelot, he ought to at least give some polite answer.

Instead he sat in stony silence. He still held Beth's hand, and his thumb traced the pattern of stitching on the back of her glove. Over and over the thumb moved, hot, quick patterns, the pressure pulsing heat through her limbs.

"If he told you I was the most beautiful woman in London, I fear you were much deceived," Beth said rapidly. "I apologize if he misled you."

Lord Ian's gaze flicked over her, a small frown on his face, as though he had no idea what she was talking about.

"Don't crush the poor woman, Mackenzie," Mather said jovially. "She's fragile, like one of your Ming bowls."

"Oh, do you have an interest in porcelain, my lord?" Beth grasped at something to say. "Sir Lyndon has shown me his collection."

"Mackenzie is one of the foremost authorities," Mather said with a trace of envy.

"Are you?" Beth asked.

Lord Ian flicked another glance over her. "Yes."

He sat no closer to her than Mather did, but Beth's awareness of him screamed at her. She could feel his hard knee against her skirts, the firm pressure of his thumb on her hand, the weight of his *not*-stare.

A woman wouldn't be comfortable with this man, she thought with a shiver. *There would be drama aplenty.* She sensed that in the restlessness of his body, the large, warm hand that gripped her own, the eyes that wouldn't quite meet hers. Should she pity the woman those eyes finally rested on? Or envy her?

Beth's tongue tripped along. "Sir Lyndon has lovely things. When I touch a piece that an emperor held hundreds of years ago, I feel . . . I'm not sure. *Close* to him, I think. Quite privileged."

Sparks of gold flashed as Ian looked at her a bare instant. "You must come view my collection." He had a slight Scots accent, his voice low and gravel-rough.

"Love to, old chap," Mather said. "I'll see when we are free."

Mather lifted his opera glasses to study the large-bosomed soprano, and Lord Ian's gaze moved to him. The disgust and intense dislike in Lord Ian's unguarded expression startled Beth. Before she could speak, Lord Ian leaned to her. The heat of his body touched her like a sharp wave, bringing with it the scent of shaving soap and male spice.

She'd forgotten how heady was the scent of a man. Mather always covered himself with cologne.

"Read it out of his sight."

Lord Ian's breath grazed Beth's ear, warming things inside her that hadn't been touched in nine long years. His fingers slid beneath the opening of her glove above her elbow, and she felt the folded edge of paper scrape her bare arm. She stared at Lord Ian's golden eyes so near hers, watching his pupils widen before he flicked his gaze away again.

He sat up, his face smooth and expressionless. Mather turned to Ian with a comment about the singer, noticing nothing.

Lord Ian abruptly rose. The warm pressure left Beth's hand, and she realized he'd been holding it the entire time.

"Going already, old chap?" Mather asked in surprise.

"My brother is waiting."

Mather's eyes gleamed. "The duke?"

"My brother Cameron and his son."

"Oh." Mather looked disappointed, but he stood and renewed the promise to bring Beth to see Ian's collection.

Without saying good night, Ian moved past the empty chairs and out of the box. Beth's gaze wouldn't leave Lord Ian's back until the blank door closed behind him. She was very aware of the folded paper pressing the inside of her arm and the trickle of sweat forming under it.

Mather sat down next to Beth and blew out his breath. "There, my dear, goes an eccentric."

Beth curled her fingers in her gray taffeta skirt, her hand cold without Lord Ian's around it. "An eccentric?"

"Mad as a hatter. Poor chap lived in a private asylum most of his life, and he runs free now only because his brother the duke let him out again. But don't worry." Mather took Beth's hand. "You won't have to see him without me present. The entire family is scandalous. Never speak to any of them without me, my dear, all right?"

Beth murmured something noncommittal. She had at least heard of the Mackenzie family, the hereditary Dukes of Kilmorgan, because old Mrs. Barrington had adored

gossip about the aristocracy. The Mackenzies had featured
in many of the scandal sheets that Beth read out to Mrs.
Barrington on rainy nights.

Lord Ian hadn't seemed entirely mad to her, although he
certainly was like no man she'd ever met. Mather's hand in
hers felt limp and cool, while the hard pressure of Lord Ian's
had heated her in a way she hadn't felt in a long time. Beth
missed the intimacy she'd felt with Thomas, the long, warm
nights in bed with him. She knew she'd share a bed with
Mather, but the thought had never stirred her blood. She reasoned that what she'd had with Thomas was special and magical, and she couldn't expect to feel it with any other man. So
why had her breath quickened when Lord Ian's lilting whisper
had touched her ear; why had her heart beat faster when he'd
moved his thumb over the back of her hand?

No. Lord Ian was drama, Mather, safety. She would
choose safety. She had to.

Mather managed to stay still for five minutes, then rose
again. "Must pay my respects to Lord and Lady Beresford.
You don't mind, do you, m'dear?"

"Of course not," Beth said automatically.

"You are a treasure, my darling. I always told dear Mrs.
Barrington how sweet and polite you were." Mather kissed
Beth's hand, then left the box.

The soprano began an aria, the notes filling every space of
the opera house. Behind her, Mather's aunt and her companion
put their heads together behind fans, whispering, whispering.

Beth worked her fingers under the edge of her long glove
and pulled out the piece of paper. She put her back squarely
to the elderly ladies and quietly unfolded the note.

Mrs. Ackerley, it began in a careful, neat hand.

> *I make bold to warn you of the true character of Sir Lyn-*
> *don Mather, with whom my brother the Duke of Kilmor-*
> *gan is well acquainted. I wish to tell you that Mather*
> *keeps a house just off the Strand near Temple Bar, where*
> *he has women meet him, several at a time. He calls the*
> *women his "sweeties" and begs them to use him as their*

*slave. They are not regular courtesans but women who
need the money enough to put up with him. I have listed
five of the women he regularly meets, should you wish to
have them questioned, or I can arrange for you to speak
to the duke.*

*I remain,
Yours faithfully,
Ian Mackenzie*

The soprano flung open her arms, building the last note
of the aria to a wild crescendo, until it was lost in a burst of
applause.

Beth stared at the letter, the noise in the opera house
smothering. The words on the page didn't change, remaining painfully black against stark white.

Her breath poured back into her lungs, sharp and hot. She
glanced quickly at Mather's aunt, but the old lady and her
companion were applauding and shouting, "Brava! Brava!"

Beth rose, shoving the paper back into her glove. The
small box with its cushioned chairs and tea tables seemed to
tilt as she groped her way to the door.

Mather's aunt glanced at her in surprise. "Are you all
right, my dear?"

"I just need some air. It's close in here."

Mather's aunt began to fumble among her things. "Do
you need smelling salts? Alice, do help me."

"No, no." Beth opened the door and hurried out as
Mather's aunt began to chastise her companion. "I shall be
quite all right."

The gallery outside was deserted, thank heavens. The
soprano was a popular one, and most of the attendees were
fixed to their chairs, avidly watching her.

Beth hurried along the gallery, hearing the singer start up
again. Her vision blurred, and the paper in her glove burned
her arm.

What did Lord Ian mean by writing her such a letter? He
was an eccentric, Mather had said—was that the explanation?

But if the accusations in the letter were the ravings of a madman, why would Lord Ian offer to arrange for Beth to meet with his brother? The Duke of Kilmorgan was one of the wealthiest and most powerful men in Britain—he was the Duke of Kilmorgan in the peerage of Scotland, which went back to 1300-something, and his father had been made Duke of Kilmorgan in the peerage of England by Queen Victoria herself.

Why should such a lofty man care about nobodies like Beth Ackerley and Lyndon Mather? Surely both she and Mather were far beneath a duke's notice.

No, the letter was too bizarre. It had to be a lie, an invention.

And yet . . . Beth thought of times she'd caught Mather looking at her as though he'd done something clever. Growing up in the East End, having the father she'd had, had given Beth the ability to spot a confidence trickster at ten paces. Had the signs been there with Sir Lyndon Mather, and she'd simply chosen to ignore them?

But, no, it couldn't be true. She'd come to know Mather well when she'd been companion to elderly Mrs. Barrington. She and Mrs. Barrington had ridden with Mather in his carriage, visited him and his aunt at his Park Lane house, had him escort them to musicales. He'd never behaved toward Beth with anything but politeness due a rich old lady's companion, and after Mrs. Barrington's death, he'd proposed to Beth.

After I inherited Mrs. Barrington's fortune, a cynical voice reminded her.

What did Lord Ian mean by *sweeties*? *He begs them to use him as their slave.*

Beth's whalebone corset was too tight, cutting off the breath she sorely needed. Black spots swam before her eyes, and she put her hand out to steady herself.

A strong grip closed around her elbow. "Careful," a Scottish voice grated in her ear. "Come with me."

The scintillating, seductive saga of the
Mackenzie clan continues...

FROM NEW YORK TIMES BESTSELLING AUTHOR

Jennifer Ashley

The Wicked Deeds of Daniel Mackenzie

Daniel Mackenzie lives up to his family's reputation for wealth,
looks, and talent. When he meets Violet Bastien—one of the
most famous spiritual mediums in England—he immediately
knows two things: that Miss Bastien is a fraud, and that he's
wildly attracted to her...

"I love the Mackenzies—every one of them."
—Sarah Maclean, *New York Times* bestselling author

"Ashley writes the kind of heroes I crave."
—Elizabeth Hoyt, *New York Times* bestselling author

jennifersromances.com
facebook.com/jenniferashleyallysonjamesashleygardner
facebook.com/LoveAlwaysBooks
penguin.com

M1480T0414

Properly improper—and daring to love…

FROM NEW YORK TIMES BESTSELLING AUTHOR

JENNIFER ASHLEY

The Seduction of Elliot McBride

Juliana St. John was raised to be very proper. After a long engagement, her wedding day dawns—only for Juliana to find herself jilted at the altar.

Fleeing the mocking crowd, she stumbles upon Elliot McBride, the tall, passionate Scot who was her first love. His teasing manner gives her an idea, and she asks Elliot to save her from an uncertain future by marrying her…

After escaping brutal imprisonment, Elliot has returned to Scotland a vastly wealthy yet tormented man. Now Juliana has her hands full restoring his half-ruined manor in the Scottish Highlands, trying to repair Elliot's broken heart—and maybe finding a second chance at love along the way.

"Ashley writes the kinds of heroes I crave."
—Elizabeth Hoyt, *New York Times* bestselling author

jennifersromances.com
facebook.com/LoveAlwaysBooks
penguin.com

An imperfect pair . . .
perfectly matched.

FROM THE *USA TODAY* BESTSELLING AUTHOR

JENNIFER ASHLEY

The Duke's Perfect Wife

Lady Eleanor Ramsay is the only one who knows the truth about Hart Mackenzie. Once his fiancée, she is the sole woman to whom he could ever pour out his heart.

Hart has it all—a dukedom, wealth, power, influence, whatever he desires—and every woman wants him. But Hart has sacrificed much to keep his brothers safe, first from their brutal father, and then from the world. He's also suffered loss—his wife, his infant son, and the woman he loved with all his heart though he realized it too late.

Now, Eleanor has reappeared on Hart's doorstep, with scandalous nude photographs of Hart taken long ago. Intrigued by the challenge in her blue eyes—and aroused by her charming, no-nonsense determination—Hart wonders if his young love has come to ruin him . . . or save him.

penguin.com

882°

FROM *NEW YORK TIMES* BESTSELLING AUTHOR
JENNIFER ASHLEY

The Mackenzies Series

THE MADNESS OF LORD IAN MACKENZIE

LADY ISABELLA'S SCANDALOUS MARRIAGE

THE MANY SINS OF LORD CAMERON

THE DUKE'S PERFECT WIFE

THE SEDUCTION OF ELLIOT MCBRIDE

THE WICKED DEEDS OF DANIEL MACKENZIE

Praise for the Mackenzies series

"The hero we all dream of."
—Elizabeth Hoyt, *New York Times* bestselling author

"I adore this novel; it's heartrending,
funny, honest, and true."
—Eloisa James, *New York Times* bestselling author

"A sexy, passion-filled romance that will
keep you reading until dawn."
—Julianne MacLean, *USA Today* bestselling author

jennifersromances.com
facebook.com/LoveAlwaysBooks
penguin.com

M1318AS0513